RETURN

Dreaming and the Psychospiritual Journey

Carol D Warner LCSW

This publication contains the opinions and ideas of its author. It is intended to provide helpful and informative material on the subjects addressed in the publication. The author and publisher specifically disclaim all responsibility for any liability, loss or risk, personal or otherwise, which is incurred as a consequence, directly or indirectly, of the use and application of any of the contents of this book.

WORKBOOK PRESS LLC
187 E Warm Springs Rd
Suite B285 Las Vegas NV 89119 USA

Website: https://workbookpress.com/
Hotline: 1-888-818-4856
Email: admin@workbookpress.com

Ordering Information:
Quantity sales. Special discounts are available on quantity purchases by corporations, associations, and others. For details, contact the publisher at the address above.

Library of Congress Control Number:

ISBN-13: 978-1-963718-27-0   Paperback Version
        978-1-963718-28-7   Digital Version

REV. DATE: 11/04/2024

DEDICATION

This book is dedicated to God, without whose direction, endless patience, nurturing, protection and guidance it would not have been possible. Dreams are in many ways the star of this book, for they are a vehicle for divine wisdom.

This book is also dedicated to all those worldwide who have suffered the unimaginable horrors of pedophilia, sex abuse, sexual trafficking, ritual abuse, and mind control with its attendant tortures and enslavement. Their blood, sweat and tears could fill oceans.

Though this book is about many subjects, both positive and negative, it is my desire to educate about God and the power of dreams, prayer and hope. As well, it is my desire to shed light on the dark underworld which has always existed (as in Ezekiel 8) and which has grown in recent years to unprecedented power.

CONTENTS

SECTION I
GROWING UP: UNSEEN FORCES AND FORMATIVE EXPERIENCES

SECTION II
DIMENSIONS OF THE INNER JOURNEY

SECTION III
DREAMS IN RECOVERY

SECTION IV
A DEEPER LOOK

SECTION V
MIND CONTROL AND SURVEILLANCE ISSUES

SECTION VI
SPIRITUALITY AND DREAMS

The Lord is my shepherd; I shall not want.
He maketh me to lie down in green pastures: he leadeth me beside the still waters.
He restoreth my soul: he leadeth me in the paths of righteousness for his name's sake.
Yea, though I walk through the valley of the shadow of death, I will fear no
evil: for thou art with me; thy rod and thy staff they comfort me.
Thou preparest a table before me in the presence of mine enemies:
thou anointest my head with oil; my cup runneth over.
Surely goodness and mercy shall follow me all the days of my life:
and I will dwell in the house of the Lord for ever.

—Psalm 23 (KJV)

INTRODUCTION

For many years, I have worked as a psychotherapist/healer. I have been in private practice since 1988, having worked in various agency settings before that. I am very appreciative and grateful for the wonderful opportunity given me to share with others the intimate details of their lives and to help ease their personal burdens. I deeply feel it is my privilege to be a part of the healing process; I am honored to be trusted with so much.

In this book, I write about some of the more difficult as well as some of the more extraordinary aspects of my work, my clients' stories, and my own personal journey. I tell my clients' stories and mine throughout the book: certain experiences in my life intersected in unforeseen ways.

To set the stage and to give understanding into my perspective, in the first chapters I share some formative early experiences which formed a template for how I perceived the world. I have had many unusual and powerful experiences, some of which have helped me to see more deeply into my clients' suffering. After sharing personal background which relates to the story I am telling in this book, I begin to explore the world of dreams and the inner journey.

One major focus of this book is on the work associated with the healing of trauma, particularly abuse of different kinds. Perhaps as you read this work you will find aspects of yourself in the people and concerns I describe. Many great writers have written about the universality of the human condition: each of us shares in the pain and suffering of life. No matter how lucky or privileged we are, we cannot escape it. The events of September 11, 2001, and the endless wars we have waged since then have brought the fragility of life back into sharp focus.

Maybe you have suffered depression or the trauma of sexual, physical, or emotional abuse: few of us escape all of these. Perhaps you have suffered trauma in some of its other guises: neglect, betrayal or abandonment, war, racism, addictions, illnesses, sudden accidents, or deaths. Someone close to you may be struggling with these issues, and you might seek further understanding of what he or she is dealing with. The experiences and lessons of those in this book may apply to you in some unforeseen way.

You will find a lot of hope in the stories included in this book. It is my hope that the stories of those who are healing and finding their souls in the process will be informative, engaging, and eye-opening. In these pages, I also describe some healing miracles, including three instances of complete and miraculous healings of disabling or fatal conditions. All these miracles happened through the power of faith.

We humans continually avoid looking inside, attempting to "fill" ourselves with that which is outside us and that which distracts or entertains us. In this, we share a commonality with the people described in this book. The difference may be that they decided to stop running for whatever reasons and to look inside. Perhaps their stories will inspire you. This book may help you to better understand the journey of someone close to you. It may help you find tools for your own personal journey, or it may give you ideas on how to support or help someone else. This book has been geared for a general audience, with some information that may be particularly helpful for therapists or for those who are in, or are considering being involved in, therapy. It is also geared to help with an understanding of the enslavement created by mind control in our modern age.

Carl Jung, the famous Swiss psychiatrist who brought spirituality into the realm of psychotherapy, believed that the hero's journey in the time to come would no longer be in the outer world. In his visionary thinking, he saw that the great hero journeys of the future would be exploring the inner world of the psyche. Perhaps only in traversing this inner journey will we begin to find the peace that will always elude us in our quests to fill ourselves from outside.

Throughout this book, I also discuss the abundant help we may receive through our dreaming. In many ways, dreams are the star of this book, for they shed immense light and give help in a variety of situations. I give many examples of dreams as tools for greater understanding in the healing process. Dreams never fail to tell us what we need to know; they guide us in our journeys and warn us when we need to be warned. In these pages, in addition to sharing a number of dreams that helped save my life and others that restored me to health after a disabling illness, I share many healing dreams of clients and of others. I discuss in detail the unique and often underestimated role of dreams in many types of recovery.

I address the issue of amnesia, memory, and false memory in trauma treatment, including regarding dreamwork. I also discuss careful and ethical guidelines for negotiating some of the difficult issues that have arisen in the aftermath of the false memory controversy of the 1990s. This material brings the reader a better sense of what went wrong and the steps one can take as a therapist or client to ensure safety in doing trauma work. There are safe, ethical ways to do the work and navigate the tricky waters of memory.

Names and other identifying information of the clients discussed herein have been changed to protect their identities. Susan's story, told over two chapters, is a consolidation of elements from a number of similar stories.

A series of life events got in between me and my initial writing of this book: I had let it go. I recently came back to this manuscript with a fresh eye and with many new experiences and skills. Over many years, I've developed expertise in the treatment of dissociative disorders (including what used to be called multiple personality disorder and is now called dissociative identity disorder). What I've learned and experienced in working with these disorders has challenged me clinically and personally in ways I could not have anticipated. Some of those clinical and personal experiences are described within these pages.

I came back to writing this book out of necessity. I was in a horrible, desperate situation and was advised that sharing certain information in a public venue was the only way I could ever be safe from the black ops programs which had been illegally initiated against me. The chapters in Section V were not originally intended to be part of this book. Through a process that I explain in detail later, I was subjugated to a grim decade of extreme surveillance, repeated break-ins to my homes and offices, intense intimidation, and multiple murder attempts. I am not a criminal or a terrorist, nor have I been accused of any crime beyond the occasional traffic ticket. There was no due process nor was there any attempt to explore any concerns with me. The persecution I experienced related to certain clients with whom I was working and what I learned in the course of working with them.

I am a therapist, bound by professional ethics to preserve client confidentiality. It was never my intention to disclose client secrets, yet I was pursued as if I were a criminal, with the intention to end my life. It is a miracle many times over that I am alive to tell this story. Ironically, I was advised that in order to establish safety for myself, I had to get my story out into the public. It can be truthfully said that I initially published this book in 2017 to save my life. It did. The attacks and stalking stopped with the first publication of this book and have not returned.

Most fortunately, I received excellent reviews for this book, a coveted Amazon "good read" designation, and numerous offers from publishers to republish my book. I am beyond grateful.

The chapters leading up to Section V give personal and clinical background that will help the reader understand the material in this part more easily. In Section V, I discuss the history of the development of some forms of mind control in this country. I review some of the literature on the subject and give the reader an overview that is woefully inadequate to the subject, since most of it is under deep cover. Nonetheless, I attempt to explore some of the general parameters. This overview includes deliberate use of various methods, including trauma, repeated rape, torture, and electronic means, to deliberately create multiple personalities that are then trained and locked behind amnesic barriers. With even a superficial understanding of how children and adults can be programmed and mind controlled to have parts hidden behind amnesic barriers, to be released for a specific assignment with a signal or code, the reader will begin to understand profound implications for the understanding of memory, amnesia and current events.

Edward Snowden began a very important dialogue with the people of the world about the massive scope of NSA spying over virtually everything we do. Many other whistleblowers have followed suit. Through sharing my experiences and what I have learned, I aim to help the reader gain a deeper understanding of how the encroaching surveillance apparatus can be used—and in fact has been used—to target innocent people in very dark ways as the government /corporate/military complex approaches its desired total control over the populace. We have been caught sleeping, numb to the mind control apparatus installed in every aspect of our lives. It is not benign, as we would like to think. It is my hope that this book will help the reader understand a bit more the scope of the problem. It presents some very grim issues, most especially the New World Order agenda and everything that goes with it.

This updated version of Return, the 5th printing, includes a section on the newest and deadliest iteration of agendas using mind control. I will explore the mass mind control surrounding Covid-19, globally planned and coordinated to achieve the bringing in of the New World Order, also known as the Great Reset.

Although I will be covering some very dark and tragic material, I am hoping that the story of my faith and how God has steered me safely through every danger, against all the odds, will inspire the reader. At every step, God was with me, reassuring me I would not be harmed and that not a hair on my head would be touched. He has lived up to his promise in every incident, inspiring great awe and gratitude in me, and no doubt great frustration in my persecutors. I take the reader through my early experiences in my walk with God and explore the deepening of my spirituality and faith. Had it not been for the recent experiences, my relationship with Jesus would not be nearly so deep and strong as it is now. For that I am immensely grateful.

I end this book on a positive, uplifting note. In the final section, the issue of spirituality in client- centered therapy is taken up in some detail, with many examples of spiritual healing dreams. Some are rather remarkable. I deal with the issue of dreams and spirituality from the dreaming experience of both the client and the therapist.

Above all, in this book it is my aim to convey the hope and faith that underlines the healing process and our humanity. Sometimes the process is gritty and horrific, but the human spirit, paired with God, has a tremendous ability to survive the unimaginable and to heal. I have been extremely blessed to have experienced or witnessed more varieties of healing than I could have ever imagined, both in my personal and professional life. Some of those miracles are described in these pages.

Section I

Growing Up: Unseen Forces and Formative Experiences

CHAPTER 1

BEGINNINGS, EDUCATION AND
FORMATIVE SPIRITUAL EXPERIENCES

I was born in Alexandria, Virginia, in 1952, just outside of Washington, DC. I lived with my father, my mother, and my maternal grandmother. My brother came along eighteen months later.

My birth was traumatic. My mother began hemorrhaging and was declared clinically dead while I was in the birth canal. A birth dream, which I will share later, indicated a lifelong unconscious pattern began as a result of this near-death experience for us both. Perhaps I was ambivalent about sticking around once I arrived, because I was a sudden infant death syndrome (SIDS) baby. In that time before baby monitors, it was not uncommon for me to stop breathing and turn blue.

Because of the SIDS, I slept with my grandmother in her room at night; she bore the frightening responsibility of making sure she would awaken to help me when I stopped breathing. She later told me that whenever she became aware I had stopped breathing and was turning blue, she would hang me upside down by my ankle and give me a slap or two on the back to get me started breathing. I speculate that my deep bond with her began and grew in those early days as I regularly faced my own demise.

I grew up in an upper middle-class neighborhood in Arlington, Virginia. In many ways, my childhood was fairly unexceptional. I was an introvert (an INFP for those who are familiar with the Meyers-Briggs test) and was often reading. I also loved to play outdoors and wander down through the creek bed behind my house to the Potomac River. My favorite activities included riding my bike and when winter graced us, sledding down the incredible sled run we had behind our house.

In other ways, my childhood was exceptional. In school, I always tested in the top percentiles. Despite this, I was not a particularly outstanding student, though I did well enough, with mostly As. I was not always interested in what we were studying and was often somewhat bored. I loved to read: my dad cultivated this early love by taking my brother and me to the library every Saturday to get new armfuls of books. I would read every one and eagerly looked forward to the next armful.

I remember going to the school library in second grade. After the librarian read us a story, we were set free to select some books. Everyone descended on the Dr. Seuss section to try to grab one or more of those very popular books. Not wanting to battle that craziness for a Dr. Seuss book and in a bit of a defiant spirit of "I don't need these Seuss books anyway," I went to the main part of the library and found the biggest and most interesting book I could find. This book turned out to be *Little Women*, a book of around 450 pages. I was determined to read the book. I did, and I loved it. Amazingly, I could comprehend this interesting story. From then on I devoured all the adult books I could find and never went back to books for my age range. From there, I focused especially on biographies of (mostly) women of accomplishment, those who were firsts in their fields. I was fascinated by the stories of their successes, often against the odds. At age seven, I was reading at an eighth-grade level. In third grade, I read extra science texts and read every science book I could find in the library.

There were a few other ways I stood out in my quiet way. I am including these not to brag but rather for how they may inform. At the end of a French language pilot program for early-elementary-age children in Arlington, I got the highest score in this highly educated county, which had an average IQ of 116, sixteen points above the national average. I don't remember paying much attention to the program. Much later, when I was scheduled to take the Miller Analogies Test (MAT) for graduate school entrance, I was bedridden with a severe case of mononucleosis and hepatitis. Since the next test was not coming up in time for me to apply to graduate school at Smith College, I dragged myself out of bed to go to Marymount College (where they administered the test), feeling horrible. When I called for my score a month or so later, they told me I'd received the highest score on the test they had ever seen. I was shocked! My concentration during the test had been very poor because of my illness, and I had been sure I would not do well.

Perhaps the score most indicative of the path my life has taken was a test my high school psychology teacher, Mr. William Lee, administered. He was a tremendous inspiration to me and helped influence my choice of careers. The test assessed one's self-actualization potential (although when Mr. Lee administered the test, he did not tell us what it was measuring). Self-actualization is the drive to achieve one's fullest potential and to find fulfillment in doing so. It can also be about service to others and relates to an inner moral integrity.

Afterward, Mr. Lee told me he had been administering the test to his classes for many years. In all that time, his own score for self-actualization had been the highest he had seen—until he gave the test to me. He told me with some surprise that my score was by far the highest he had ever seen and that it was much higher than his.

EARLY TRAVELS AND EDUCATION

My life has been full of extraordinary events, both good and bad. I will share a few of them in this chapter and also throughout the book for the insight they will lend about me and how I have been led into working with many people who have also met with extraordinary challenges for which the traditional therapeutic world often has no answers.

I took time off from college and ended up living in a small Mexican village named Tepoztlán. It was a powerful experience and gave me the desire to travel. While in college, I worked part-time as a nurse's aide and saved up money. After working at a Watergate restaurant the summer after college, I had saved enough money to travel. I was planning to travel around Europe for a while, but when I found I could afford an around-the-world ticket, I was very excited and jumped at the chance. No one I knew had the time, funds, or inclination for this journey, so I decided to go on alone rather than miss out on this wonder opportunity.

I traveled around the world for a year after college. It was a powerful experience about which I will write more later. I became very interested in the traditions and religions of the peoples whose lands I was visiting. I was fascinated by all religions, whether Russian Orthodox or Burmese Buddhist or Japanese Taoist. During the course of these travels, I met many people with generous hearts who helped make my experience immensely rich; I made friends with people of different cultures from Iran, India, the Philippines, and the then Soviet Union, which had just opened to tourism.

A year after getting home, my interest in religion and spirituality led me to apply to a Master's Program at the University of Virginia's in Religious Studies, where I was to learn about a range of subjects, including dreamwork, Christianity, Buddhism and Jung.

For several years after this graduate program, I worked in the newly emerging field of inpatient addictions treatment. There I was inspired to see how having a spiritual program and working the 12 steps were considered an essential part of a full recovery. I then went on to get a master's degree in clinical social work from Smith College in Northampton, Massachusetts. Because of this dual religious and clinical background, I move between those two seemingly separate worlds with more ease than most clinicians. In the next part of this chapter, I detail early formative experiences that helped form my understanding of the world.

FORMATIVE SPIRITUAL EXPERIENCES AND DREAMS

Soon after my mother's brother Joe died in a tragic plane crash in Brazil when I was seven, I saw his spirit hovering over my cousin and me as we sat in the bathtub at my paternal grandmother's house. It did not seem at all extraordinary or unusual to me to see him. I was glad to see he was okay. Since I thought everyone could see spirits, I didn't mention it to anyone.

Also, at the age of seven, I knew at a deep level that my life's walk would be with God. Though I had no idea what this would mean or how it would look, it was a calling that grew deeper as time passed, despite my occasional attempts to ignore it. I had no idea at the time how many trials I would need to successfully pass through. My life has been unusual, with many major challenges and extraordinary experiences. Throughout this book, there will be many examples of how spirituality has informed my life and my work.

These experiences have enriched me tremendously; in a number of cases, they have helped me and even literally saved my life. I learned quickly to pay attention to my dreams, for often God spoke directly to me through them. My training and experiences have taught me that nowhere does the human and divine spirit express itself more fully and consistently than in our dreams, our nightly voyages into the unknown regions of ourselves.

As an introduction to the material on spirituality and dreams throughout this book, this chapter features a more in-depth discussion of the origins of my interest in spirituality and dreams. In the next chapter, I will share a number of humorous spiritual experiences, some dreams and some not. Throughout this book, there are many sad and traumatic stories; it is good to be able to share some funny stories as well.

EARLY SPIRITUAL HISTORY

By the age of twelve, I had turned away from the Methodist faith I had been raised in, disillusioned by what I had seen of organized religion and by a conception of an externalized God that made no sense to me. Like many others, I could not relate to a picture of an externalized male God in the sky who tended to judge humans more than love them. I spent much time outdoors as a teen, and it was in nature that I found the peace of God. It was a gentle awakening that lasted years.

At the age of nineteen, I lived for six months in a small Mexican village that was known to be one of several powerful energy spots in Mexico. What this meant exactly, I am not sure. What I do know is that I experienced a profound opening into my own spirituality and a living, breathing sense of the spiritual presence in all things. It was as if, for those extraordinary six months, I had entered into what Mircea Eliade called "sacred time," in which everyday living, normally perceived as profane and secular, was imbued with the presence of the spiritual. It was an incredible experience and entirely changed my perception of the nature of reality in a positive way.

I realized deeply that spirit is everywhere—both within us and without us—and that it is in no way separate from us. I could see why I could not relate, even at a young age, to the idea of an external male God somewhere up in the sky, for now I knew that God was everywhere and most certainly to be found within. The idea of God having a male gender did not feel congruent with my experience, for the spirit I perceived contained both the masculine and the feminine. There was extraordinary beauty and harmony in this spirit, and I was quite awed. Such was my initial spiritual awakening, and from that point on I was changed.

When I returned to this country, I felt called into deeper work with spirit. It was all baffling—I knew I would only later understand. Eventually, I found my way back to college at New College in Sarasota, Florida, where I majored in English and fell in love with the Romantic poets. I wrote my thesis on the role of the imagination and Jesus in the poetry and visions of William Blake. I found a very inexpensive place to live in the country, a cottage on a number of acres of land. Throughout my first six months of living there, I had many profound spiritual experiences, on an almost daily basis. I did not even try to communicate what I was experiencing with my college friends at the time, for trying to put these experiences into words has always seemed beyond my ability. I do know I had a constant sense that we are separated from the "real" world of the divine by only a thin veil; during that time the veil was lifted repeatedly, and I felt I was experiencing the two worlds simultaneously. That period was a very beautiful gift of grace that has stayed with me.

MENNONITE FRIENDS

While living in Sarasota, Florida finishing college, I met an older man from the local Mennonite community. He was very kind and an evangelical. He asked me about my beliefs. He talked to me about coming to a local church to see what I thought. I was very hesitant at first but open and curious. He introduced me to a number of people in his Mennonite community. I spent a fair amount of time with one family in particular. They were very kind to me, treating me as if I were one of their own—even though I was clearly from a very different world. I had fled from living at the college because of the dominant drug-sex-and-alcohol culture. In the Mennonites, I found a wonderful alternative in their focus on simple, honest living dedicated to God. I am so grateful to them for their many kindnesses to me and for the opportunity to see how they lived. It was impressive to me to see their purity of purpose, for while they were human, they were visibly trying to live honest, good lives. I preferred to do business with local Mennonite merchants for they were, in my experience, scrupulously honest.

I had been baptized as an infant, and with my Mennonite friend's encouragement, I decided I wanted to be re-baptized as an adult and to consciously dedicate my life to Christ. They wanted to baptize me as a member of the Mennonite church. Despite my gratitude toward them for their friendship and nurturing, I did not want to be a member of any particular denomination or church. We talked about it, and in deference to my wishes, they agreed to baptize me in the Gulf of Mexico by full immersion. I was thrilled with the idea and grateful for their flexibility. I know I was a challenge to them.

When we arrived at the beach, it was a relatively cool day in Sarasota, with a number of puffy clouds. Two men and a woman accompanied me. The men explained how we would walk into the water: they would catch and hold me as I leaned backward into the water; then lower me into the water until I was fully immersed. We walked out into the Gulf of Mexico surf. As I leaned backward into their arms, I looked up and could see cumulus clouds covering the sun. As they lifted me back up out of the water, just a few seconds later, the sun was shining brightly, free of the clouds that had been there just a few moments before. I saw this as a beautiful affirmation of my new birth. It was just a start, however. I was mostly unschooled in Christianity.

Traveling around the World

After college, I spent a year traveling around the world. I suppose I was on a quest of some kind, though I did not fully know it at the time. I learned a great deal during that year. Because of my earlier experience in Mexico and my profound spiritual experiences since my return, I was very curious about religion and spirituality. I developed during my travels a strong interest in religions and faiths of different cultures. Everywhere I went, I recognized many similar truths taught in different forms.

I learned about different belief systems and how God was understood differently in various cultures and times. Whether I was staying and working on a kibbutz by the Sea of Galilee, being lovingly sheltered and fed on two separate occasions by two different families in Southern Iran when I could find no place to stay, visiting a temple at Kathmandu or a mosque in Turkey or church in Russia or Buddhist temple in Burma, studying mindfulness at a vipassana meditation retreat in Southern India, or staying with a family in a primitive tribe while trekking in the jungles of Northern Thailand, I found people everywhere who were loving and trying to express their spiritual nature as they understood it.

My footing in Jesus was still young and immature, and I was trying to understand the universal aspiration towards the Divine. I was fascinated by the many systems which had been developed, and was yet naive towards the differences. It had been a powerful experience staying by the Sea of Galilee for a month; and I was eager to learn more.

MY MATERNAL GRANDMOTHER'S STORIES ABOUT DREAMS AND SPIRITUALITY

Upon my return from my yearlong journey, I lived with my family while I decided what to do next. It was August of 1975, and it was to be a very eventful year.

My maternal grandmother, who had always lived with us and whom I felt closest to, always told fascinating stories. Her husband of many years died before I was born. She often told the story about how she and her husband, my grandfather, had made a pact that whichever of them went first would try to figure out a way to communicate with the remaining spouse from the other side.

My grandfather died in his mid-fifties. Ten years before he died, he was on his deathbed dying of pneumonia. This was in an era before antibiotics. My mother took notes at his bedside as he prayed to God to have ten more years so he could put together enough financial resources for my grandmother to have sufficient income for the rest of her life. My mom had the impression her father was dreaming; he talked about being in a trial, pleading his case.

Then she heard a deep voice that she believed belonged to God, saying her father's prayer request was granted. My grandfather miraculously healed completely. He took full advantage of the time granted him to buy some houses in Northern Virginia. He set my grandmother up so that, after he died, she could rent them out for a steady income or sell them to support her for the rest of her life. He died ten years later to the day! God had granted his wish, and then his time was up.

After my grandfather died, he began communicating with my grandmother through dreams. She told me she could feel his presence in these dreams and had no doubt it was he. My grandmother said these dreams were different from ordinary dreams because there was something about his eyes that made her feel as if this dream version of him was actually his spirit. My grandmother often told the story of how each time she came to a decision point on what to do with one of the houses, he would appear in a dream and give her advice on what to do. She always followed this dream advice and said it was always sound advice that benefited her. Her mother was the seventh daughter of a seventh daughter and was said to have very strong spiritual gifts.

A SAD TURN OF EVENTS

My grandmother had a major stroke within a month of my return from my around-the-world trip. The prognosis was terminal. She would never again be able to speak. While in the hospital, she pulled out all her tubes every time they put them in. It was clear she wanted to go home to die and wanted no tubes or machines to keep her alive. We respected her wishes. She was paralyzed and bedridden and needed around-the-clock nursing care.

Three eight hour nursing shifts were set up. I volunteered to take the third shift, sleeping on the floor by her bed in her room so I could look after her during the night. I believed she would be more comfortable sleeping if she knew that I, rather than a stranger, was in the room with her.

BEGINNING OF MY INNER DREAM JOURNEY

I made a decision to begin recording my dreams the first night I slept in my grandmother's room, in an attempt to use this dark time to come to a deeper understanding of human consciousness. I had read that one could learn a lot about one's psychological and spiritual nature through dreams. Now that I had done much journeying and exploring in the outer world, I was intrigued by the opportunity to begin to discover my inner world. I did not know what to expect, knowing only that I was looking forward to the journey, wherever it brought me.

We had no idea how long my grandmother would live. It was horribly sad to see her helpless and no doubt feeling very trapped inside this failing body. Many times I thought I could feel her immense frustration at being so imprisoned, with no ability to speak to make her thoughts and wishes known. I was very upset at how terribly unfair and unjust the situation was for her. She was a good and loving woman, who had done nothing I could see or ascertain that would merit such suffering. The combination of this situation and the impact it had on me and the search on which I was already embarked laid the foundation for the series of dreams that emerged over the next six months. Nothing could have prepared me for it. Though I'd had many spiritual experiences, my belief system was undeveloped. I had few ideas about death and the afterlife.

Spiritual Teachings in My Dreams

My first dream literally turned my world of beliefs upside down. It forced me to reexamine my beliefs about life and death and what happens after death. It is a long, very personal and very powerful story, one which I may someday be comfortable sharing with the general public. From this dream, I embarked on a course of research.

Then followed a series of instructional dreams, each of which built on the previous ones. It was as if my dreaming was a spiritual night school that presented a series of teachings about the nature of physical existence, life after death, soul purpose, and the meaning of suffering for soul growth. There were a number of teachings, always thought-provoking on subjects on which I had not previously thought deeply.

Through my dreaming life, a portal was opened for me into another world and the universal laws that applied there. The laws that governed existence in this world were not applicable in that world. I learned a great deal about God's tender mercies and the inescapable plan by which each soul develops and eventually returns home again to its true self in God. Because of my grandmother's suffering and impending death, these dreams came at a time when I was hungry to learn about spiritual realities and about what we experience as life and death.

I was extremely saddened by her sufferings. I had no previous context in which to understand them. The dreams helped me get through this period.

Through my dreaming experiences in spiritual night school, my focus became the spiritual nature of reality. My past waking-life spiritual experiences of previous years were consistent with the material presented to me over the months of my grandmother's illness. The teachings gave me great comfort and solace, assuring me that, even in the midst of this suffering, there was a higher plan. I was shown that my grandmother would continue on another, much happier plane of existence once she left this one. One dream even told me the day she would transition.

My grandmother died in her sleep early in the morning on the day foretold in my dream. I was in the room with her and woke to an eerie stillness. I knew from the stillness that she had passed. I got up and saw her lying there with her eyes open. I closed her eyes. I was deeply sad. She was my closest family member at the time. However, at that point, I was aware of feeling mostly relieved for her, knowing that her long suffering in this body had ended and that she was now free.

A FUNNY STORY AT A SAD TIME

After we had called the doctor for the death certificate, I went downstairs and showered. My grandmother was still lying in her bed, for the undertakers had not yet come to get her body. My room was directly under where her body lay.

I had a daily meditation practice then as now, and for some unknown reason, I decided to meditate naked (the only time I have ever done this). After a while, I sensed something and opened my eyes, only to see her spirit coming through the ceiling and floating above me.

I couldn't make up what happened next. She scolded me, "Girl, what are you doing there without any clothes on? Get yourself dressed!" It was her voice, and what she said was exactly the way she would have said it. Some might call this a bereavement-induced hallucination. Yet, I could see her vividly, and her voice was as clear to me as when she had been alive. It is said that when people pass, their spirits can be confused for a while, not knowing they are dead. I believe this was the case in this instance.

AN EARLY DREAM THAT SAVED MY LIFE

As mentioned, I began recording my dreams after my year of travel around the world. I was twenty-two. After six months or so, I began working as an editorial assistant at an editing firm in upper Georgetown. I lived in Arlington, Virginia, almost six miles from the Memorial Bridge, which crosses into Georgetown. Since I didn't have a car, I commuted to work on my bike. My route on the way home was along the C&O Canal, a place of peace and beauty during rush hour.

A dream came that had a very urgent message for me. I saw the section of the C&O Canal path where I rode home on my commute. There was a very dark cloud over that section. A voice in the dream, which I likened to the voice of God, told me not to ride to work, for my life would be in great danger if I did.

I considered the possible consequences of ignoring the dream. Could it possibly be true? Why would I have a dream like this if it weren't true? I decided it would be wisest to heed the dream warning, despite the inconvenience to me. Instead of using my bike, I got a ride part way and then walked the rest of the way, avoiding the canal and planning to continue to do so for an indefinite period.

Three nights later, I had another dream. In that dream, I saw that same area of the C&O Canal again. This time, the very dark cloud hanging over the area was gone. It was very sunny. In the dream, I "heard" it was now safe for me to ride my bike to work again.

That morning, like every morning back then, I read the Washington Post before my bike ride to work. To my surprise, I saw an article about a woman who had been murdered on the C&O Canal the day before. She had been killed in the very section of the canal I'd seen in my dreams, the section I rode daily. The murderer had been caught shortly after killing the woman. As it turned out, the killer had been wanted by the police for a while. He was a serial killer who had been on the loose for some time, having killed a number of women.

I now understood the reason for my dream warning me against riding my bike. The woman was killed right where I would have been riding my bike had I not been warned off by the dream. It was a lesson I would never forget.

The impact of this dream on me in my lifetime has been very powerful. I heeded the dream warning, and I was alive because of it. I was learning that sometimes you just have to listen, even if you do not understand. This brilliant set of dreams impressed on me the higher knowledge that can come through dreams and the imperative of paying attention to dream messages. I have turned to my dreams over and over throughout the subsequent years. Later in this book, I will relate more stories about how dreams have helped me and my clients in amazing and sometimes miraculous ways.

STUDYING DREAMS

The experiences I had through this dream series, through spiritual experiences throughout my young life, and through exposure to spirituality and religious beliefs from all over the world during my travels led me to pursue graduate studies in religious studies at one of the top programs in the country, at the University of Virginia. While there, I had the great good fortune to meet and work with the psychology professor who ran the Sleep and Dream Research Laboratory. Bob Van de Castle, Ph.D. was internationally known for his work with dreams. He taught me a great deal about dreams and their clinical, personal, and spiritual applications. Bob became a lifelong friend and mentor (he died at age eighty-five in early 2014) and had enormous influence on the development of my thinking about dreams. Bob Van de Castle's book, *Our Dreaming Mind*, is the text on dreams used in many undergraduate and graduate programs; it covers many aspects of the dreaming experience. He introduced me to the then-new International Association for the Study of Dreams, which he and I both were very involved with over the years.

In the years since, I have studied dreams from both psychological and spiritual perspectives, recorded and worked with my dreams, and helped many others to understand their dreams. I went on to get my clinical social work degree from Smith College in Northampton, Massachusetts, so that I could combine spirituality and dreamwork with clinical work in private practice. I have gone through two long-term Jungian analyses of my own, and in both the dream was a major tool of the work.

I have continued to read, study, and develop in the area of religious studies and spirituality, even as I studied and continued to develop my clinical skills. As an adult, I have a daily prayer-and-meditation practice. In addition, I continue to record and work with my dreams on a regular basis. I believe I am a deeper person, with more complexity, empathy, and understanding, because of my partnership with dreams. Dreams are an extraordinary transformational tool, and their wisdom guides us in every area of our lives. From my experiences, I bring with me into the clinical hour a deep appreciation about God and the spiritual nature of our existence. I have had many experiences of the invisible realm, whether they were spiritual in nature or even a result of the surveillance I have experienced over the years. All experiences have helped give me breadth of understanding.

My personal search, studies, and clinical experience have helped me to understand the powerful need many people have to explore the spiritual dimensions of their lives. Many people in crisis turn to spirituality to help support and guide them and from that point continue to develop their spirituality. I do not impose any spiritual belief system on my clients. If my clients wish to explore their spirituality in the context of their psychotherapy, I help them to be open to and explore their own inner experiences.

Each person must arrive at his or her own truth and at his or her own understanding of his or her experiences, whether spiritual or otherwise. Many people, as I have discussed and will discuss further, reject the idea of God that they were brought up with. This does not necessarily mean, as they often assume, that they are rejecting God; rather, it is often a particular conception or traumatic experience of God they are rejecting. For example, people entering 12-step programs commonly have trouble with the word God becaus of their trauma history, and they are encouraged to come up with an idea of a "higher power" that is more powerful than self and that is also forgiving and loving.

CHAPTER 2

DAD'S JOURNEY AND ITS IMPACT ON ME

My father's life and career have had a tremendous impact on my development and adult life. My father, John Stanley Warner, grew up in Washington, DC, during the Depression. He was the son of an auto shop owner who wanted his son, my dad, to follow in his footsteps, becoming a mechanic and taking over his auto shop. Dad, a brilliant young man with high ambitions, had other plans. He worked in a bank while he went through law school. This was during the early years of World War II. Dad wanted to enlist but decided it would be best to finish law school first. He joined the Army Air Corps the day after he finished law school. He became a copilot and flew thirty-five missions in a B-17 over Europe with the 390th Squadron. According to Dad's pilot log, his first mission was on D-day. It is hard to imagine what that must have been like for him and all the men taking part in that momentous chapter of World War II.

On one of his missions, Dad was forced to make an emergency landing in occupied France. The strong French Resistance watched out for downed Allied airmen and helped move them to safety. When Dad returned to his officers' barracks in Framlingham, England, he was shocked to see all the bedding had been rolled up: with that visual, he realized with horror he was the only officer who had survived. All his fellow officers were dead. This experience had a tremendous impact on him. The relentless bombing of Germany and the many horrors he saw and experienced in the war were very traumatic. Post-traumatic stress disorder (PTSD) had not yet been named as a diagnosis, but he experienced the symptoms. Like so many veterans of that era, he dealt with the trauma internally and with alcohol: he did not talk about his World War II experiences for many years.

When my parents retired and moved to Tucson in 1983, Dad became one of the four founders of the 390th Memorial Museum, which is situated on the grounds of the Pima Air and Space Museum in Tucson. This museum, which he continued to nurture (by volunteering and serving on the board of directors) over the next twenty-three years until his death, honors the heroism of these men from the "greatest generation" who so deserve to be recognized. Unlike many museums, the 390th focuses on personal stories of these men. There are now few remaining veterans who can attend the reunion in Tucson. Thirty-three attended in 2013 and only fifteen in 2014. There was no reunion in 2022.

I am honored to serve on the board of this very special gem of a museum. The crowning jewel of the museum is the gleaming B-17 in the center, the "I'll Be Around," the name of my dad's plane. B-17s are beautiful planes visually; they served as the bombing workhorses of the war. In fact, the B-17 was built specifically for World War II, the first air war. It was the Allies' superior air power that won World War II; the B-17s won the air war in Europe, supported by other planes. Production of B-17s ceased at the end of the war.

During the war, and perhaps because of the help given to him during his emergency landing in France, Dad became very interested in the French Resistance. In his war diary, he expresses concern for the welfare of the five thousand or so Office of Strategic Services (OSS, the precursor to the CIA) agents who were in Southern France supporting the French Resistance.

When Dad returned from Europe after his thirty-five missions, he was still in the Army Air Corps (soon to be called the US Air Force). Likely because of his interest in OSS assistance to the French Resistance, he was assigned to the OSS, where he served until his discharge. Dad stayed in the reserves and achieved the rank of US Air Force Major General. He was a very well respected man and consistently held a light of integrity in his endeavors.

Upon his discharge from active duty in the air force, Dad was hired by the OSS. As a young, talented attorney, he was asked to help write the charter for the new agency that was being formed out of the OSS, the CIA, or Central Intelligence Agency. Additionally, he authored the far-reaching and impactful National Security Act of 1947, which, among many things, established the CIA and also created the Air Force as a separate entity out of the Army Air Corps.

The National Security Act also created a legal basis for the massive surveillance state we have today, which has gone far beyond anything Dad ever could have imagined in his worst nightmares. At the time it was written, the biggest perceived threat to world peace was communists. Dad thought he was helping to save the world from communism. He did not foresee the criminal overreach the National Security Act would enable, and he was later horrified to learn of the many dark criminal programs the CIA implemented. He came to see these creations as mis-creations. This must have been extremely difficult to shoulder. I will speak more on this after I speak about some jobs he was proud of.

INTERESTING ASSIGNMENTS

Sometime in the 1990s, after declassification of the operation, Dad told me of one of his early assignments that was related to a CIA operation to help the Dalai Lama escape from Tibet into India in 1959. At this time Communist China had invaded Tibet. Beginning in 1950, these invaders were involved in a genocidal attempt to violently "assimilate" Tibet. The Tibetan religion in particular was being severely suppressed. The Chinese imposed martial law on Tibet and declared the Tibetan governing body defunct. The Dalai Lama, high priest of Tibetan Buddhism, was thus ousted from his position, replaced by the Chinese Panchen Lama. The Dalai Lama did not recognize the authority of the Panchen Lama.

With CIA assistance, the Dalai Lama's escape into India was successful. The grueling fifteen-day escape over extremely harsh, mountainous Himalayan terrain occurred mainly by night to avoid Chinese security, beginning on March 17, 1959. An entourage of twenty Tibetan men, including six of the Dalai Lama's cabinet ministers, accompanied the Dalai Lama into India *(http://news.bbc.co.uk/onthisday/hi/dates/stories/march/31/ newsid_2788000/2788343.stm)*. The Dalai Lama was initially feared dead in the harsh crackdown by the Chinese ,but was later followed in exile by over eighty thousand Tibetans. The Tibetan government in exile was thus established in Dharamsala, India.

This rescue operation put the CIA in a good light. They had been training guerrillas in Tibet for many years at that point in an attempt to destabilize the Communist Chinese for their own reasons. US governing bodies at the time saw the successful rescue of the Dalai Lama and the establishment of the Tibetan government in exile in India as a positive development. (The Dalai Lama later criticized the United States for its self-serving motives. There are many historical facets to the CIA in Tibet; these are not relevant for the brief overview here.)

The President and members of Congress at the time were briefed on the successful operation and wanted to meet this nineteen-year-old religious leader who was the subject of so much effort and controversy. (The operation was classified at the time and was not declassified until the 1990s.) Dad's job, as CIA Congressional Liaison, was to escort the young Dalai Lama to meet the President and members of Congress. Dad spent three days with the young Dalai Lama, escorting him around Washington, DC, leaders.

I later asked Dad what he thought of this young man: in his characteristic way, using few words, Dad pondered and said, "He was a very thoughtful young man." Coming from Dad, this assessment was a high compliment.

THE U-2 INCIDENT

Some might remember the U-2 incident of 1960, at the time a huge international incident with major repercussions for years for US-Soviet relations. In this incident, a CIA U-2 spy plane was shot down over Soviet airspace by a surface-to-air missile. The pilot, Francis Gary Powers, was arrested and the airplane remains confiscated. The Soviets discovered photographs taken of Soviet military bases.

Although the United States attempted to cover up the spy mission by saying the plane was a weather-research aircraft, Nikita Khrushchev, premier of the Soviet Union at the time, had intelligence to the contrary. The timing could not have been worse for the United States, as a Paris Peace Summit was scheduled to occur in several weeks. Faced with innuendos the CIA had been acting on its own and with criticism that he had lost control, Dwight D. Eisenhower, president at the time, admitted in a speech to the aerial espionage program, saying he had directly approved it.

The interception of the plane and the photographs marked a deterioration in relations between the Soviet Union and the United States, deepening the Cold War. Khrushchev left the Paris Peace Summit after only one day. The warming relationship between Eisenhower and Khrushchev was now severely compromised, and Eisenhower's previous invitation to visit the Soviet Union was rescinded. Eisenhower is said to have believed the visit would have been a major step forward in US–Soviet Union relations. Instead, the détente collapsed and was followed by years more of the Cold War.

Powers was sentenced to three years of imprisonment and seven years of hard labor. He had with him a coin that contained an injectable poison should he choose to commit suicide. After two years, he was released under a prisoner-exchange program, the story of which is told in the 2015 movie *Bridge of Spies*.

My dad was the first person to debrief Powers once he was released. This was a very significant assignment and one that gave him pride for the trust and responsibility given him. Although I know nothing of that debriefing, I am sure it was a very important event in my father's life.

DARKER REALITIES

Dad was CIA Congressional Liaison for a while, and eventually became General Counsel. When some of the sickening CIA abuses came to light in the 1970s, Dad was General Counsel, in the devastatingly difficult position of defending CIA abuses he had known nothing about in congressional hearings. The Church Committee was formed during this time to investigate the intelligence abuses. The subsequent hearings and scandal were front-page news internationally for several years. Dad had to expand his legal department, which had consisted of nine lawyers before the lawsuits, to forty-five lawyers to handle the dramatically increased workload. I will return to this period and its impact on me after sharing how Dad's career influenced my early life before the 1970s.

GROWING UP IN SPY CENTRAL

Growing up in "spy central," as I call it, was often unnerving. From an early age, I was aware of the surveillance we were constantly under. Daily, a man in a county government car sat in his car in the same spot on our street—a spot from which one could get the best view of our house and any comings and goings. I asked my neighbor if he or his family knew this man who always parked in front of their house, and he said they did not. My mom said she was often aware of the surveillance and told me that when she went to night school in Washington, DC, people tracked her. Perhaps this was a part of the cost of my father being very high up in the intelligence world. I naively thought for a while that they were protecting me.

I was fortunate in that many children of CIA employees were used against their wills in illegal and immoral mind control experiments and fared far worse than I. The main focus in my case seemed to be on surveillance of my father.

However, by the time I was twenty-two, I'd had a number of experiences that gave me objective indicators of the intrusive scope of the surveillance on me as well. When I was nineteen and moved to the small and beautiful Mexican town Tepoztlán, I lived innocently there, learning the language and culture, and spending time with residents of the town. A Mexican official, telling me he thought I needed to know, warned me of a very large file he had seen that had been compiled on me in the nearby city of Cuernavaca. I have no idea what that was about. It was chilling.

When I returned to college, I moved into a cottage in the Sarasota, Florida countryside. One day when I returned from work, it was clear someone had been rummaging through my place. My neighbors up and down the street reported to me that FBI agents had interviewed them about me, asking about the possibility of me being an international heroin dealer. To this day, I have never even seen heroin. I don't know if the drug story was a cover for their investigation and illegal break-in. I was puzzled and knew only that I was innocent of wrongdoing and they had no right to break into my house.

Rumor had it at the college I attended that the CIA had something to do with me and a former CIA director's (Schlesinger) daughter both being at New College at the same time. New College offered high-quality academics but combined that with no rules and a great deal of drugs and alcohol; the rumor was we had been sent there to get lost in the drugs and sexual freedom. It was true that I'd found out about New College from a CIA guidance counselor who had given my dad a New College catalog for me to review. I believed New College's small class sizes, many opportunities for independent learning and designing tutorials in whatever subject, and individualized evaluations rather than grades were perfect for me.

By the time I reached New College, I was a serious student, having gotten my rebellion out of my system by ninth grade. I did not want to get lost in the seemingly endless partying, sex and drugs. I eventually moved off campus into a little English cottage in the Florida countryside on several acres of land, which I rented for a very affordable one hundred dollars a month. It was a perfect place to study and relax, away from it all. If I wanted to hang out, I could go to campus and visit my friends.

Another unnerving spy experience occurred during my around-the-world trip after college. I had learned as a teenager in the 1960s not to tell people what agency my dad worked for; I would say only that he was a government attorney. While traveling in the Middle East (which one could safely do in the mid-1970s), two men in Beirut, Lebanon, pretended to be friendly but turned out to be spies. As we sat over coffee in a relatively safe public setting, one of them slipped up and mentioned how my dad worked for the CIA. We all looked at each other, all realizing at the same moment that they had blown their own cover. Somewhat shocked, I extricated myself from the situation, thankful for the man's blunder.

Because of these many episodes, when I returned from my year's trip, I requested my records from both the CIA and the FBI, under the Freedom of Information Act (FOIA). I wanted to see the scope of the surveillance on me and the reasons for it. I eventually received very heavily redacted pages from both the CIA and the FBI. The only visible word in the FBI file was Weathermen. The Weathermen were a violent group that operated in the 1960s and 1970s. I was indeed opposed to the Vietnam War, which we learned many years later, in Robert McNamara's testimony to Congress, was started when the US government made up the Gulf of Tonkin event. It was a lie, a false flag used to start the long war that caused the loss of so many lives and deeply divided a country. (The reader may wish to research false flags in history in order to get a fuller appreciation of the extent of usage of this military strategy.) However, I was equally opposed to violent protests and had nothing to do with the Weathermen or any political group and was not involved in illegal activities.

My mom told me once that Dad lamented that, although he was a top CIA employee (and won an award for being one of the fifty top people in the first fifty years of the CIA), he was not an insider. I am immensely grateful that he was not, for that could have had far greater consequences than the ones I have paid, and describe later in this volume. As the years have gone by, my dad's connection to the CIA has taken an enormous toll on me. The CIA and FBI have intruded themselves into my life many times, and not for good.

UNDER A DEATH THREAT

Before making my decision to do the year's trip, I had pondered my safety. Would I be safe as a young woman traveling around the world, always in new and unfamiliar places? As I pondered, I "heard" very clearly a reassurance in that kind of booming voice one might associate with God, "You will be protected." I knew God was telling me to go and that I would be safe. The reassurance felt powerfully real. I made the decision to go and embarked on my around-the-world journey feeling safe and protected.

As previously mentioned, there were many wonderful times and people during the year. When the inevitable threats and challenges came, I always had an escape route. Sometimes as a result of the challenges, I met amazing people I would not have otherwise met, people who befriended me and looked after me and who even shared their homes with me. Staying in these homes in places like Iran and Poland and India and making friends in places like Communist Russia and the Philippines gave me a wonderful, warm insight into lives and cultures so different from my own. During this time, I grew to trust God ever more strongly as the promise to keep me safe was fulfilled day by day.

When I returned from my trip, it was August 1975. I was living at home while I decided what to do next, likely graduate school. After I took my dad to work at the CIA each day, I spent my time looking for work and hiking along the many trails that led down to the Potomac River. I had grown up hiking these trails and knew them like the back of my hand. This was at the beginning of the Church Committee Senate Intelligence Hearings, of which I knew very little. As General Counsel, my father was heavily involved.

One day I had just climbed up the cliff from the river and was starting to follow the creek back to my neighborhood when I heard five shots rapidly fired in a row. Having no firearms training or awareness, I had no idea whether the shots I'd heard were from a shotgun or BB gun. I had no way of knowing whether these shots had been aimed at me, and I couldn't take any chances. I was in a clearing, and in an instant, I had to decide how to find safety. There was a tree behind me, but if I hid behind it and if this person was trying to kill me, I would be a sitting duck should he or she pursue me. That option was of course unacceptable. The other choice was to risk crossing the stream and a fifty-yard clearing to the cover of a wooded area. This choice would put me on my path home. I chose the latter. Quickly, careful to not panic, I made it across the clearing. I was immensely relieved to make it safely to the cover the woods provided and from there to make my way back home.

Once home, I called the police, hoping they would investigate what happened. A kind policeman came to our home and met with me. I told him what I knew. Because I had grown up hiking this trail, I was able to tell him exactly how to find my location when the shots had been fired.

After about an hour, the police officer returned. All the color was drained from his face: he was white as a sheet. He said that he'd easily found the exact spot I'd described. Next, he said there was no way I should be alive. He slowly opened his right-hand palm up to show me five shotgun casings. The policeman said all five shots must have missed me by only a fraction of an inch. He said the shooter appeared to be an expert marksman; the shooter missing me by such a fraction five times in a row seemed immensely fortunate for me.

At the time, I was very naive as to how the world worked. Since I had just been told I had escaped a certain death, the only way I knew to understand it was to believe I was very lucky to have a guardian angel to protect me. I also thought it ironic that I had just traveled the world without serious incident and now, practically in my backyard, I had almost been killed with those five shots.

Many years later I grew to understand the shots were a warning from the CIA to my father. This event happened in the fall of 1975, in the midst of the Church Committee Senate Intelligence hearings. The CIA was, by threatening my life, forcing him to comply with whatever it was they had asked of him. If he were to betray them, his beloved daughter would be dead. Given that, as CIA General Counsel, he was the point of the spear defending the CIA in the Church Senate Intelligence Committee investigations and since he well knew the nature of the pack of wolves who surrounded him, he had to have taken the warning seriously. His involvement in these hearings was to last several years.

AN UNEXPECTED EDUCATION

Dad confided in me a great deal during that time. I would drive him to work so I could use of the car during the day, and sometimes also pick him up to bring him home. During these times, he shared his concerns about his work. His words implanted themselves in my brain and have stayed with me to this very day. Dad was a quiet man who used his words sparingly: you knew to listen carefully to every word, as his words were so very carefully chosen. He told me what he could and said the CIA had done a number of "very bad things" (his words). He explained it was his job to represent and defend the CIA in the hearings dealing with the abuses delineated in the lawsuits. I heard the term black ops for the first time when he explained to me that the mind control operations the CIA had performed had been black ops, which meant the operations had been done in the shadows, had been kept hidden from everyone, and had been highly illegal.

I did not understand at the time how horrified Dad was by what he had found out the CIA had been doing. One day as I drove him to work, I asked him if he had known about the mind control experiments. He patiently explained that because of the need-to-know principle that compartmentalizes CIA operations, he had not "needed to know" the information until the cases had come to him for litigation. He'd learned what had been going on for the first time after the lawsuits had been filed. He was very unhappy about what he'd learned. I think he probably felt very betrayed.

Dad spoke of Director Richard Helms as "evil," something I had never heard him say about anyone. Helms had ordered the destruction of the records of the programs under question so that the Church Committee would never know the depth and extent of them. The ignorance of the scope of the problem, which the burning of records ensured, would enable the programs to continue. Only about ten thousand pages survived out of about sixty thousand. As chilling as those surviving pages are, we can only imagine what records were destroyed and what programs have continued unseen and in the shadows, perhaps under different names.

One of the things I remember clearly was Dad repeatedly telling me that, by the terms of the CIA charter that he'd written, domestic operations were forbidden to the CIA. This point and the numerous violations of this aspect of the charter were very important to him. The abuses that were being investigated in this particular lawsuit had, to my knowledge, all been done domestically.

As we know now, the CIA had probably never abided by its own charter. Dad explained the distinctions of the charters of the FBI and the CIA by saying the FBI was by law assigned to domestic matters and the CIA to foreign. Many of the allegations discussed in the hearings were illegal domestic surveillance and mind control experimentation programs.

Dad told me often that he and Director Bill Colby were in accord as they dealt with the lawsuit. First of all, they were both lawyers. Both wanted all subpoenaed records to be turned over, as the law required. They could do nothing about the records that Helms had already destroyed, but they could work to ensure the CIA would abide by the law with the records that had escaped destruction. They worked very closely together. Dad had a lot of respect for Colby, perhaps more than for anyone else I ever heard him discuss.

I didn't learn until many years later how horrified Colby and Dad had been by some of the programs. Colby knew of and was deeply offended by the mind control programs that had used children sexually as slaves and programmed them through rape, drugs, torture, hypnosis, and even bizarre satanic rituals. Colby was later filmed talking about this on the Discovery Channel documentary *Conspiracy of Silence*. The film was about the Franklin scandal, a child-sex-slave ring out of the Midwest that supplied young boys to serve the Bush Sr. White House as sex slaves. The show was blocked from airing at the last moment. It can still be found on the Internet. *Conspiracy of Silence* is not about conspiracy theory; it is a conspiracy fact. It discusses the active dark underbelly of CIA mind control and child sex slavery. Though I had no interest in pursuing these subjects, I was to encounter them head-on much later in my life. That story will emerge in the pages of this book.

As a twenty-two-year-old, I knew a great deal more than the average American about CIA mind control abuses, mainly that they were very real and of great concern. Because I knew that Helms had destroyed the bulk of the records, I knew early in my life that the abuses discussed in the newspapers were but the tip of the iceberg. Dad and I agreed that those programs for which the records were burned and that therefore never came to the light of day would thus be enabled to continue. I was grateful for what my dad told me and believed him when he said he had not known of these mind control programs before having to deal with the lawsuits.

IN THE MIDST OF A PACK OF WOLVES

Once Dad learned about these very dark, immoral, and illegal CIA operations, he faced a horrible choice: to hold on to the light the best he could in the midst of deep darkness or to turn toward the darkness. He chose the light. Despite being fired, likely for his integrity, Dad later won a CIA award for being one of the top fifty employees in the first fifty years of the CIA. In a letter from Porter Goss, the director during the fifty-year anniversary of the CIA's founding, Dad was commemorated for his integrity—a rare quality in an often dirty field based on deception and lies. He and Colby had done what they could, but Dad and Colby were both fired from the CIA.

As I researched and sought permissions for the quotes used in this book, Joel van der Reijden, researcher par excellence and founder of the Institute for the Study of Globalization and Covert Politics, sent me a document released in September 2014 under the Freedom of Information Act. This CIA Oral History Program document, entitled "An Interview with Former General Counsel John Warner," can found in Appendix A.

The discussion in my father's interview dovetails with my memory of what Dad told me at the time. Dad was deliberately kept naive to the nature and depth of the MKUltra program. He had been an outsider from the beginning and, because of the CIA's need-to-know principle, was told only what they wanted him to know. Because of my lifelong mistrust of the agency, I had often wondered about my father's motivations. In this interview, he explains the nature of the beast and his relationship to it:

> [In many cases of high-profile flaps], OGC [Office of General Counsel] didn't have the full, unadulterated story... Because the operators, in part, partook of Helm's [then director] view of things. Don't get the lawyers in it. That's part of the operational thinking ... About the Olson case ... the fellow that jumped out of the window [allegedly because he was unwittingly administered hallucinogens by the Agency] ... we didn't know it was part of a program that did this and did that ... Again, we weren't told the whole story of the program.

That "program that did this and did that" was MKUltra, a program with many sub-projects and implications that will come up many times in the course of this book. There is quite a controversy about the Olson case and what really happened, but that is not a subject for this book. For now, my focus in bringing it up is to show the lack of information my dad as General Counsel had about this extremely controversial and wide-ranging classified agency program MKUltra.

In the year after being fired, Dad grieved his many losses deeply. He told me he felt betrayed in so many ways by the very agency he had helped to create with good intentions. He had known of the OSS agents in the field in France and how they were helping the French Resistance. He wanted to support them in their heroism, and he wanted to help build a world safe from the horrors of war and militant communism. How could things have turned so dark and so evil? He and Colby had been given access to deep, dark secrets that would change forever how he saw the world and the agency. Because he stood up for what was right to the best of his ability Dad lost his job at an agency he could now barely recognize. I remember him telling me that although the director of the CIA position was political and subject to the president's choices, the General Counsel position had never been politically based. His predecessor Lawrence Houston had served as OGC from 1947 to 1973, through many presidencies. Dad was deeply disappointed at this betrayal.

Though I was not thinking about it, the death threat would by implication continue to hang over my head until my father died in 2006. Dad wanted very much to write a book about his CIA days, and post-retirement he often talked about it. I loved to encourage him to write it, as the idea of writing it seemed to come from a place deep inside him. I believe the programs he had become aware of ate away at him, as they seemed to with Colby. Then, something else happened that made him rethink the situation.

BILL COLBY'S DEATH

Bill Colby died mysteriously in April 1996 while kayaking near his home in Southern Maryland. Kayaking was one of his favorite activities. Colby, in his passion to bring the abusive programs to light, had already bravely stepped forward and was featured speaking about some of them in the Discovery Channel documentary *Conspiracy of Silence*. Colby was appalled at the widespread use of child sex slaves and the horrific mind control and bizarre rituals. He was determined to shed light on the abuses that he no doubt knew had never stopped.

I later asked my father what he thought happened to Colby, as the circumstances of Colby's death while kayaking were mysterious and out of character for him. It was then my dad told me Colby had been scheduled to testify before Congress. My dad thought Colby was very likely assassinated to prevent him from testifying. To this day, I don't know what Colby was going to testify about, but the point is he may have been murdered to stop the testimony.

From the time of Colby's death forward, Dad closed the door on his book idea and refused to discuss it ever again. I tried to bring it up with him several times after that, but it was very clear he had made up his mind. I doubt he would have cared too much if he were killed, as by then he was an old man in his late seventies. However, I suspect Colby's murder must have underscored the death threat that had previously been made on me, a death threat that, based on Colby's death, likely had no expiration date. If he wrote the book, he would be risking my life—and that was an unacceptable risk, one he did not take. The book idea was shelved forever. It is a very odd twist of fate that brought those programs to my awareness much later on.

IMPACT

These early experiences proved to be very formative for me, in a number of ways. I went on to pursue my graduate clinical studies at Smith College School for Social Work and eventually ended up in private practice in Falls Church, Virginia. In that practice, I encountered clients and had experiences that related back to what I had learned in those early days about CIA abuses and mind control. Colin Ross's book *Bluebird: Deliberate Creation of Multiple Personality by Psychiatrists* gives us some insight into the workings of Project Monarch and MKUltra and the heinous abuse inflicted on unwitting subjects. Bluebird reads as if the programs ended in the 1970s. Nothing could be further from the truth.

But I am getting ahead of myself here; all I knew entering the psychotherapeutic field was that there were terrible mind control abuses that had not come to light because Helms had destroyed most of the records. Therefore, I knew they likely had continued. I did not know details. It had not crossed my mind I would be working with victims of these programs.

The ongoing experience of being under surveillance, whether in the United States or out, made me much more sensitive to invisible energies everywhere than I would have been otherwise. Most people know now, more than forty-five years later, that we are all under surveillance all the time. I have been much more aware of this than most throughout my lifetime. My experiences with surveillance have continued on and off until this day. On a positive note, these experiences indirectly helped further my spiritual development, as they forced me to attune to other levels of experience than those we can see or hear.

CHAPTER 3

DREAM LEVITY FROM BEYOND THE GRAVE

In a previous chapter, I said I would share some humorous family dreams and spiritual experiences to add some levity to the many serious subjects discussed in this book. But first, I need to share the sad background information that leads into the experiences.

Beginning in April 2006, three family members very close to me died in close succession. My father was the first to go. Then within a month my aunt, my mother's twin, was hospitalized and died. Within two more months, my mother had a paralyzing stroke that killed her before the end of the year. I was living in Northern Virginia.

My father was eighty-eight at the time of his death; my mom (May Belle) and her twin (Lillie) were eighty-four. This was a very difficult time for me. Since 2002, I had been traveling back and forth from Northern Virginia to Arizona, where my parents lived, and in 2006 I started also going to Woodstock, Virginia, where my aunt and uncle lived. At the end, all three were hospitalized for some time; all three suffered greatly. This was perhaps the hardest part of the stress related to care-taking. The grief of dealing with so many deaths all at once was a bit overwhelming. I had been close to all three. The experiences that I will describe to you today greatly helped me in my grieving process and brought many smiles as well as general lightening. (There were many other experiences not included in this book; there is not time or space to convey all of them.)

It is important context for what follows for me to share a bit about their belief systems regarding death and the afterlife. There is a strong history on both sides of my family of spiritual gifts. I grew up hearing many stories of unusual experiences. Starting in my teens, we had many discussions about dreams, prayer, the afterlife, the possibility of reincarnation, and the meaning of death.

The only child of my mother's twin, Lillie, was killed in Vietnam just before he was scheduled to come home. Lillie went into a deep grieving from which she and her husband never fully recovered. In an attempt to understand what had happened, Lillie began reading everything she could about God, dreaming, prayer, healing, Jesus, the afterlife, spiritual experiences and much more.

She would come to the house with large grocery bags full of these books, which my mother, grandmother, and I devoured. I spoke earlier of the beyond-death pact made between my maternal grandmother and my grandfather and how he helped her greatly for more than thirty years after his death with financial advice in dream communications. My mother was more skeptical of these subjects than Lillie or me; nonetheless, these subjects were frequent topics of conversation until the time of their deaths. Lillie's husband was very interested in all these topics; my dad, less so, though as the years went on he had more experiences of his own.

No sooner had I returned to Northern Virginia after my father's death than Lillie entered the hospital. Her large intestine had burst, spilling out its contents into her stomach cavity, causing her to have severe sepsis. She would never recover but was in the hospital for six miserable weeks. I lived ninety minutes away from her home, and would go to pick up her eighty-seven-year-old husband, Sid, and then drive thirty more minutes to the hospital. Later I would take him back home and return to my own home, at least four hours of driving each time I went.

Sidney was not doing well—Lillie and he had always assumed he would go first. I was dealing with a very precarious situation in which she would likely not recover and in which he was deteriorating under the stress of his wife of sixty-plus years dying. Sid could be a very charming man, but he had always been emotionally unstable and prone to binge drinking. He had been totally dependent on Lillie and had no idea how to pay a bill or balance a checkbook. Dealing with his unstable state was challenging.

These trips took up entire days at a time when I was exhausted, spent, and hardly ready for so soon on the heels of my father's death. I also was still maintaining a private practice in Northern Virginia. I loved Lillie, and I went as often as I could, also supporting my mom, who was now completely devastated at the imminent loss of her twin, who had been with her, as she said, since they "were in the womb together."

When my aunt died, Sid was suicidal. I did my best to support him. Since dreams in the afterlife had been a frequent topic of discussion between him and Lillie, he looked to his dreams for contact with her, for proof she was okay. For months after her death, he was puzzled and dismayed that he had not had any dreams about her. He had expected she would communicate with him right away.

Sid spoke on the telephone with my mom every day. They gave each other comfort dealing with the sudden loss of their respective spouses. Sid and I talked on the phone regularly also, something we had never done before. He went to Lillie's grave every day and asked her to communicate with him.

"Don't Be Chintzy, Sid"

One day, about five months after Lillie's death, Sid called me and said he had sent me something in the mail (the first time ever). He said Lillie had finally visited and communicated with him in a dream. From his point of view, it was about time!

On the other hand, he was more than a little dismayed she had appeared to him only to ask him to send me something. There had been no personal message for him beyond this. It definitely wasn't the personal, loving communication he had been waiting for. (Before she'd been hospitalized, Lillie had told my mom she had been extremely upset with Sid for many months for some very hurtful and ugly things he had said to her. He could be a brutally cruel man with his words. I think she was probably not interested in sending a loving message to him this soon after her passing.)

Sidney told me about the dream in a phone call. In the dream, Lillie appeared to him, her husband of more than sixty years, and said emphatically, "Sidney, I want you to send Carol a check for all the traveling back and forth she did during my illness." And then, with great emphasis on the last word, she said, "And, Sid, don't be chintzy!" End of dream.

After relating the dream, Sidney told me, "Carol, I am a cheap man; that is my nature." I had to chuckle at his phrasing, for truer words had never been spoken. He continued, "But I wanted to do what Lillie asked, so I have sent you a check."

Sid did not disclose the amount. I thought maybe he would send $100 or $200. For him, that would have been very generous. When I received the check, I was shocked to see it was for $1000. And that was when gas was under $2.50 a gallon! Clearly Sid had been sufficiently moved by the dream to take this unusual action, however disappointed he was that Lillie had not had a more personal message for him. I suspect he was afraid he would not see her again unless he did what she said.

MY MOTHER'S DEPARTURE

Lillie died on June 28, two months after my dad's death on April 29, 2006. When my dad died, my mother said she was determined to survive his death and not be one of those spouses who died shortly after their spouse. However, I think the death of her twin right on top of the death of her husband was too much for her. As she had said, she and Lillie "were in the womb together."

My mother had a stroke on August 1, 2006, and was paralyzed. She never recovered. I went back and forth from Virginia to Arizona often, spending about half my time in Arizona. Both my brother and I were involved in making decisions about my mom's care; it was an extraordinarily difficult situation all around.

My mother went from hospital to rehab to home to back to the hospital and then home again. We installed caretakers round the clock in her home, where she wished to spend the rest of her days. Sadly, she was in extreme discomfort. It was excruciating to be helpless to relieve her suffering.

One day in December 2006, when I had just returned to Virginia, the in-home nurses called and told me to fly to Tucson immediately, as my mother was dying. I flew right out, adjusting my work schedule yet another time. My brother chose not to come.

Once I talked with the caretakers and spent some time with Mom, I somehow gained the impression she was holding on to life for me. I sensed she might be worried I would not be able to handle so much death at one time. In case this impression was true, I made sure to tell her that first evening back in Tucson that if she wanted to go, I would understand. She was suffering badly with no quality of life. My concern was for her suffering, not my grief I told her not to worry about me, that I would be okay. She died within hours. I think she must have been very relieved to go. The date was December 14, 2006.

UNEXPECTED HUMOR FROM BEYOND

I returned to Virginia after the holidays, sad and exhausted. At the beginning of 2006, all three relatives had been healthy and fully functioning—now they were all gone. I had spent my last reserves helping take care of them, dealing with the multiple crises that had begun in 2002. My back was out of whack, and my adrenals and kidneys were shot. I was exhausted and in pain. Soon after my return I went to my chiropractor for a series of visits to help rebalance me.

No sooner had I sat down in the waiting room of this office I had been to so many times than I heard a loud crash. A picture had fallen off the wall in front of me. It had landed on the floor, breaking the glass. Immediately I "saw" my mother and father together, chuckling at their humorous attempt at sending me a message. I talked about this impression with the receptionist as she swept up the glass. An interesting discussion ensued with another patient about examples of psychokinetic phenomena. I didn't think to look at the picture that had fallen before the receptionist took it.

After a while, I was taken into one of the nine treatment rooms, each of which had a variety of different pictures on the walls. The chiropractor soon came in and began working on me. All of a sudden there was another crash, and—you may have already guessed—another picture fell off the wall onto the floor. Neither of us was near the picture.

I started laughing at this second fallen picture, saying to my parents in spirit, "Okay, okay, I get the message: you're healthy and in very good spirits." I told the chiropractor about the other picture that had fallen twenty minutes before. I told him of my impression that, since this had happened in a doctor's office, it was my parents telling me it was now time to take care of myself. The chiropractor thought I was likely right.

After Dr. Sievers was done working on me, I went over to this second fallen picture and looked at it. It was a print emphasizing the need for preventive self-care. I was amused and was also glad to know my parents were playfully looking after me. Knowing the receptionist would never believe it when I told her a second picture had fallen (with the first fallen picture incident, she had told me nothing had ever fallen off the walls there before), I brought the framed print out to her.

When I showed her the print, she looked puzzled and asked me, "Why are you carrying around that print from the waiting room?" I told her that this was another print and that it had fallen in the treatment room. She laughed, grabbed the other print, and showed me both prints were the same. Out of sixty or more prints on the walls through the office suite, I had never noticed a duplicate! How coincidental was this that two identical pictures had fallen, in the only two rooms I had entered, with the same message emphasizing self-care? I had an image in my mind of my parents mischievously enjoying all of this.

An assistant in the chiropractor's office wryly said, "We're going to have to start charging you for this." I laughed. I figured this was the end of it.

ANOTHER FALLEN PICTURE

But it didn't stop there. The adjustments the chiropractor was making did not hold well. Because of my stress and tension level, my back would go out of alignment soon after I left the office. At the end of my visit just after the one when the pictures had fallen, I went to the receptionist to pay my bill. She said that while I had been in the treatment room having my adjustments, a picture had fallen in her office. She figured since it had fallen in a different room than I was in at the time that it was probably not related to me. I chuckled and said, "After what we've experienced already, I'm not so sure about that. Would you mind showing me this third fallen picture?"

She went to get it: it was a poster advertising the services of a female massage therapist whom I knew to be excellent, offering to do in-home massages. She used to work for the chiropractor but had left a year or more before. Unbeknownst to me, she was now working privately, and the chiropractor allowed her to use his office for advertising.

The idea of an in-home massage sounded like manna from heaven to me—the reason my adjustments weren't holding was my muscles were very tense, and I intuitively knew this was exactly what I needed. I wouldn't have been up to going elsewhere for massages, but the idea of getting a massage in my own home, where I wouldn't have to leave and deal with the stress of the infamous Washington, DC, traffic, seemed ideal. The solution was perfect; I got a series of ten massages—just what I needed. Had the print not fallen, I would have never known the massage therapist was now in business, and in the state I was in, I hadn't even thought of getting a massage.

FALLING BUGLES

At eighty-seven, Sid was alone for the first time in his life. He was healthy, very alert, and fully functioning; however, he had never done house cleaning, bills, finances, taxes, or anything to support the household apart from outdoor work and repairs. His wife had spoiled him. He was very grief stricken and often despondent. I tried to support him in every way I could, calling him regularly. As mentioned previously, their only child had been killed many years before in Vietnam. Sid was very much alone in the world.

One day on the phone Sid told me a story. He had a bugle from his army days that had been displayed for many years on top of a hutch in the corner of his bedroom. The bugle was carefully placed in the middle of the top of the hutch, not near the edge.

Sid told me that while sitting in the living room, he had heard a loud thump-thump-thump. He'd gone into the bedroom to see what had made the noise. The bugle was now on the floor in the middle of the room. He said that because of the trajectory it could only have gotten there with applied force. Sid had been an engineer and understood these things.

My uncle had known immediately that his wife was trying to communicate with him, and he'd said, "Lillie, darling, I know it's you. I'm so happy to hear from you." The event was a very happy confirmation to him that she was okay.

I went to see Sid a few months later for Easter, and he took me into the room where the bugle had fallen. Indeed, from the wide hutch top where the bugle was placed, there seemed zero possibility of the bugle falling by itself, much less falling at that trajectory. Sid was meticulous in his placement of objects through the house and was still very sharp.

A few days after my Easter visit, I received a letter from Sid telling me of a dream he had just had. The dream took the form of a dialogue between my aunt Lillie and my mom (May Belle). Sid wrote it down in its entirety upon awakening and sent me a copy of exactly what he had written.

The setting of the dream was heaven, with my mom and aunt watching me visit Sid on Easter and commenting upon various things. The humor in the dream is exactly what I would expect from my mom and aunt now reunified in the next world. The easy, humorous exchange between these twins who had been very close for eighty-four years—and the use of the word stuff—is exactly how they would have spoken.

May Belle: Look, it's only 12:35, and she's pulling into your driveway, the darling child.
Lillie (pouting): She never drove that far to see me.
MB (exasperated): She knows that Sidney needs her, and at that time you did not, for God's sake!
Lillie: I guess you're right. Of course, you are.
MB: What are they doing now?
Lillie: Sid is taking Carol into the other room to show her where we pushed the bugle off the hutch and onto the floor!
MB: That was fun! I just loved the way he started talking to you, saying, "Lillie darling, I know you did that, and I am so happy to hear from you," and all that stuff.
Lillie: That wasn't "stuff"; that was my darling talking to me!
MB: Look at them sitting there talking. Who would have guessed it? Isn't my little girl a darling?
Lillie: I remember when Sidney didn't talk very much at all, and now you can't shut him up. I like that; I really do.
MB: Let's, in a couple of days, knock that bugle off the hutch again. Want to? Sid would like that!
Lillie: Yes, let's do it in a couple of days at 3:00 a.m. when he is sound asleep. That will give him something to remember!
MB: Yeah!

I found this dream exchange hilarious. The fact that my mother and Lillie said they had knocked the bugle to the floor together was intriguing. My uncle hadn't imagined that my mom would be involved and was surprised by her participation.

A week or so later, I called my uncle, interested in what might have happened. He told me that two days after he'd had the dream, he had been awakened from a sound sleep in the middle of the night by a loud thump-thump-thump. Sid said he'd known immediately that the bugle had "fallen." Moreover, he'd known it was 3:00 a.m. He had looked at the clock, and it was indeed exactly 3:00 a.m.

Sid said he'd then spoken to my aunt and mom, amused, and gone over to investigate the bugle. This time, instead of falling forward off the hutch, it had fallen backward. It had fallen at an odd angle, so that it had hit first one wall and then another (the hutch was in a corner) before falling to the floor. Had my mother and aunt made good on their dream promise? Sid was sure they had.

The bugle incidents plus Sid's dream made me think further about the falling-picture incidents in my chiropractor's office. In all the incidents, at least two people had been involved, my mother being involved in all of them—was it easier to make objects move from the other side if there were two people involved?

I am aware this is anecdotal material and not science. To me, however, and also to my uncle, there were great gifts in these events. They were reassuring and humorous. They gave hope and light in the midst of an otherwise dark situation. They hinted at the promise of an abundant and joyful life in the next world. I can say for myself that the sum of these events and other events helped me to come out of this difficult time with greater strength and a much stronger faith.

CHAPTER 4

DAD AND THE AFTERLIFE

DAD'S FIRST GREETING FROM BEYOND

Before he died in 2006, Dad, Mom, and I had talked a number of times about life after death. He knew I saw loved ones after they had "died." In his later years, he could sometimes see spirits of loved ones who had passed. These were spontaneous experiences that happened to us; we did not seek them out. As he faced his own mortality, Dad grew more open to the idea of an afterlife. He knew of my grandmother's story of how dreams could be a vehicle to send messages from the next world. From the very beginning, he was a strong communicator. He would have a big role to play in times to come, and he came in like he knew it. The top-achieving major general in him never left!

Dad died two weeks before Mother's Day in 2006. I stayed on in Arizona through Mother's Day to support my mother, who was bereft, having been married to him for sixty years.

I woke up on Mother's Day morning from an awe-inspiring dream.

In the dream, I saw a beautiful horizon view of an ocean. The sun was either rising or setting; it wasn't clear. All of a sudden, a beautiful, enormous red rose appeared; it was huge, extending vertically from the ground into the sky. Somehow I knew that this rose (red roses were my mother's favorite) was for my mother.

Then, off to the right, at an angle, another beautiful red rose appeared. I was given to understand it was for me. Lastly, another large rose on the left appeared but just as suddenly disappeared, and I knew it was for my brother, who wouldn't attach much meaning to a rose.

I was thrilled with the beautiful dream and was very happy to have a Mother's Day present for my mother from my dad. My dad knew, of course, that red roses were my mother's favorite flower.

There was no doubt in my mind that Dad had somehow sent this beautiful dream painting. What a great gift this was, and with such exquisite imagery! My mom hadn't heard from him yet and was very happy for the message.

A STRONG WARNING FROM DAD

When my mother lay dying a few months after his passing, my dad's image and voice came through strongly one night. He kept me up for hours, earnestly telling me my co-executor was planning to steal my share of the trust. I knew that dad, as an estate attorney, had locked the trust up as tight as he could, with the help of a local attorney and accountant. Since Dad had been an estate lawyer, knowing the ins and outs of the law, I was naive enough to think that things were solid and that there was no risk to me. Because of this, at first I did not take his warnings seriously.

Dad would not accept my complacency and kept talking. It was hours past midnight, and I was tired and wanted to sleep. However, it became clear Dad would not let me get any sleep that night until he was satisfied with my response to his adamant warnings. He was very upset about what he described as my brother's plans to steal from me. There was even some cursing involved! My casual attitude toward his warnings upset him even further. Finally, around three in the morning, he bellowed out, in utter frustration at my hardheadedness, "This is not insignificant!"

I was taken aback. His bellowed-out adamancy told me I needed to listen. Weary, and now with a sudden change of attitude, I was listening. I told him I would take his words seriously and that I would be very careful. My parents had shared the estate documents with us long before their death, and the trust had seemed crystal clear. Although I couldn't understand how the trust document could be twisted to deprive me of my share, I told Dad I would keep my eyes wide open. My brother was wealthy—I was not—and it had never occurred to me that he would try to steal from me. I didn't want a penny more than was rightfully mine, and I had thought he was the same.

The next day my brother went alone, enshrouded in a dark cloud of mystery, to visit the attorney and the accountant. From that visit forward, everything changed. Overnight, the attorney and accountant, who had previously been friendly and helpful, displayed a very negative, even hostile attitude toward me, not unlike my brother's ongoing hostility toward me. It was clear they had formed a bias against me dating from my brother's visit to them.

I was now very concerned. I considered everything my dad had said and wrote the attorney, accountant, and my brother an email saying their changed attitudes toward me following their meeting with my brother had the "appearance of impropriety." I was careful in my words not to accuse them of wrongdoing. I warned them I would be watching very carefully and insisted that any future meetings or communications be held with all four of us, instead of excluding me. Naturally, I received no response to this warning e-mail.

THE "FINAL" TRUST DOCUMENT

Months later, the trust attorney sent me the final document. He, the trust accountant, and my brother had all agreed to it and had signed it. I could see and hear that my dad and my mother were right there with me when I opened the document.

On the surface, everything looked okay. However, I perceived my not-so-dead and quite alert parents sitting behind me looking on, insisting I crunch the numbers. I was going to do it anyway, but it was important to strongly register their strong emphasis. (It was an ironic twist of fate that they were there in spirit helping ensure their estate was delivered according to their wishes!) I was naive in my belief the attorney and accountant would not actually go so far as to perpetrate fraud, especially since I had warned them I was watching them carefully. They could have lost their licenses!

Despite my warning, however, all three of them had signed a fraudulent document. When I crunched the numbers, I was shocked to see the document had been twisted to give my brother almost everything, hardly the fifty-fifty deal the trust had stipulated (after other funds were paid out), in accordance with my parents' express wishes.

I called the trio of them out on the deception, saying that the numbers were wrong and that I would not sign a fraudulent document. There was nothing they could do; they had been caught with their hands in the cookie jar. For obvious reasons the attorney was quite attentive to me after that until the estate was divided correctly. Obviously, he risked disbarment had I chosen to pursue legal redress.

However, I had just lost both my parents and my closest aunt, my remaining uncle was sick with grief over the loss of his wife and was suicidal. I had also just lost my brother to this huge betrayal.

I was exhausted and depleted in every way. I had no energy left over for filing legal complaints against the attorney and accountant, nor for pursuing a discussion with my brother, who had said he never wanted to speak with me again. In the wake of this attempted theft, I was left to ponder how much my brother had offered them to get them both to risk their careers by breaking the law and violating my father's wishes.

The very real help my father gave me in the handling of the estate saved me from losing my share. I felt my father's anger at my brother's betrayal.

That was the last of the significant estate dealings. The corrected document was signed and executed according to the terms of the trust.

The night of the final signing, I had the following dream, set at my parents' home in Arizona, in the kitchen The kitchen table is full with many types of food. My father has prepared a delicious feast for us. I am surprised by the variety and quality of foods he has prepared [in reality he was not much of a cook]. I had no idea he had such culinary skills.

Everyone is busily talking and enjoying his food. My mom and his four children [two by his first wife] are there. The trust lawyer and accountant are there too, standing around us.

Dad is standing near the food preparation area. I go over to him to congratulate him on the excellent meal he has prepared. Then I see he is drunk and staggering. I'm very surprised about this since he was happily sober the last thirty years of his life.

I exclaim, "You're drunk." He passes out, falling onto the ground.

I woke up with the thought that this elaborate and abundant meal my father had carefully prepared for all of us represented his estate, which he had passed on through the agency of his carefully chosen helpers, the attorney and accountant.

My dad had been sober for thirty years at the time of his death. I understood my dad's drunkenness in this dream as a metaphor for his very real distress that his son would try to rob me of my rightful inheritance, thus betraying my father's express wishes. I also think my father must have been quite upset that the attorney and accountant he had so carefully chosen and trusted would betray his clear intention for the trust distribution.

My waking action as a result of this dream was to pray for my father's peace of mind. I was immensely grateful for his and my mom's help even as they transitioned into their new lives in the next world. I wanted them, now that the business transactions had finally been completed to their satisfaction, to not have to worry about me. Perhaps as much as I had needed their help, Dad now needed mine? He had skillfully helped me bring the matter to a successful resolution, and now he could rest. I was learning never to underestimate Dad's abilities in that next world to create bridges with this world and offer real help. In the years to come, he would help me in many ways, including most ironically helping me develop a personal relationship with Jesus.

In the next section, I transition into a focus on the inner journey. It consists of two overview chapters. The first will be a look at the spiritual nature of the problems clients may bring into session. In the second, I will discuss an ancient myth that gives us metaphorical insight into the nature of the psychotherapeutic journey itself.

SECTION II

DIMENSIONS OF THE INNER JOURNEY

CHAPTER 5

BECOMING AWARE OF THE PROBLEM

In this chapter, I will introduce the reader to some basic ideas and concepts about the inner journey, concepts that are woven throughout the rest of this book. I will share stories that illustrate these ideas and basic psychological dynamics.

One of the earliest stories we have of the journey is the story of Gautama Buddha's life. Many readers may be familiar with the story. He was an early student of the human mind and its relationship to pain and suffering. He lived 2,500 years ago and was born into privilege as a prince. He was deliberately sheltered from pain and suffering in his upbringing. He was not allowed out into the world to see the suffering around him and was brought up in a world of sensual pleasures and indulgences. He was well loved by his family. When he decided to go out on his own and see the world, he was shocked and deeply saddened when he encountered all kinds of human misery and suffering for the first time. The prince Gautama took it upon himself as his personal mission to understand the roots of human suffering and discover how to stop the endless rounds of pain that living in the human body entails. Pain and suffering, as he observed, are part of the human condition. He was determined to discover how to liberate the self from the conditions that keep one in the repeated rounds of rebirth into the human body and hence in repeated rounds of pain and suffering. (Regardless of whether one believes in reincarnation, we are all seeking, as the Buddha did, ways to escape the cycles of pain and suffering in our human condition.)

We are also similar in that we tend to find ways to escape from our pain and misery that turn out to be destructive, either to ourselves or to others. Some ways include alcohol and drug addictions, sex and love addictions, food addictions, workaholism, and addictions to spending money, to status, and to being busy. We may also seek relief from our pain by trying to please others at our own expense or by trying to assert power over others. We allow ourselves many forms of distractions.

The Buddha discovered that if we are to escape from this endless suffering, it is important to look within at our own grasping, desirous nature and to detach from those patterns that create pain. This gradually slows down the vicious cycle. If we continue in our addictions, of whatever nature, and in our distractions, we are certain to continue falling into the same traps. Perhaps we find relief in these outlets for a time, but eventually they will disappoint us and turn on us. Then we will cling even harder to these things, perhaps spending more, holding on harder to a loved one who is not available, or working more hours to try to escape the pain of an unpleasant home life. We all find our own ways to escape reality. Each method of escape will inevitably cause more pain.

As a psychotherapist, it is my job to help those who come to me to create new life patterns. It is my task to help them come to terms with the past and with the difficult present. It is important that I help my clients to identify and feel their pain, so that they may be freed from the compulsion to escape from it.

When a young child is put in a situation where he or she suffers great trauma, he or she does not have the internal resources to cope with the trauma. To help the child survive the moment, the psyche automatically uses defensive maneuvers. Sometimes the defenses include splitting off from one's true feelings (which can seem overwhelming and unbearable in the moment) and going somewhere else mentally and emotionally. This "disappearing" is termed dissociation.

Dissociation is a defense mechanism, spontaneously created by the overwhelmed mind, that enables the child to survive the incomprehensibly awful by placing the trauma behind an amnesic barrier. Research has indicated that dissociation is most likely to happen when there is repeated trauma before the age of nine. Dissociation is a survival tool that becomes dysfunctional for the adult who cannot connect with his or her own emotions and who cannot remember the past.

When old feelings of pain, rejection, or abandonment arise in the adult, the response is often unconscious. The unconscious responds as if the old trauma were being repeated, with an intensity of response similar to that which might be expected with the original trauma. This process is automatic, almost like having a light go on when turning on the switch. One could say that this response is programmed into the hard drive of the brain computer.

A very large part of the healing journey is to become aware of these internal processes and responses, so that one has the choice in the present of how to react to a given circumstance or feeling without dissociating. The task is to learn how to react to rejections, hurts, and traumas in new ways.

Our world is achingly full of trauma and misery. Not one of us has gotten through life without wounds and scars. With these wounds and scars come responses that do not always serve us well and sometimes even serve us quite poorly. We all carry a great deal of trauma and pain inside of us. We fear our pain. We have learned over time to avoid ourselves and our deep inner feelings. We universally seek distractions to keep from feeling our pain. In this, we are all similar, though the form and nature of our avoidance may be quite different.

Our materialistic culture reinforces at every turn the many escape routes available to us. A consumer culture manipulates us with the promise of happiness and a much better life if only we have the latest car, the biggest house, the trendiest designer clothes, the best spouse, the best job, or the finest collection of material goods in the neighborhood. We distract ourselves with food, with alcohol and drugs, with media and entertainment, with power, with sex and pornography, and now increasingly with video games.

The Buddha warned, so many years ago, that our desiring natures guarantee we stay in the cycle of pain, preventing us from finding our way out of our suffering. Our desiring natures lead us on many distracting paths, all of which take us away from our centers, from our souls.

If we are to find our way in the midst of this crazy but often extraordinarily compelling world, we must go back within to find out what is truly important and what we value in our lives as priorities. When a client comes to the office suffering from depression, I understand that on one level this depression is a spiritual call, a call back to the inner self that Carl Jung, a Swiss psychiatrist who was initially a student of Freud, called simply the Self.

This Self is simultaneously the center of the psyche responsible for creating order and the totality of the psyche, including both the conscious and unconscious minds. It connects with the universal by way of the collective unconscious. A direct encounter with the Self can be experienced as a connection with one's higher power, or with God. Healing from depression entails work with both the conscious and unconscious minds and often involves both emotional and spiritual healing.

By the time someone comes into a therapist's office for depression or some other problem, that person is most likely ready to begin facing the issues of his or her past. Sometimes the person has been triggered by the strains of recent events or crises. Other times, in a seeming paradox, when a person reaches a certain level of strength and stability in his or her personality and life, his or her unresolved emotional history begins to bubble to the surface. In doing so, it brings with it the pain and sorrow that have been pushed aside at a time when the person did not know how to handle these feelings.

The body and mind at some level retain a memory of all we experience, though the memory may be stored out of the range of consciousness. Current life events can trigger traumatic childhood memories, causing them to surface. For example, if a woman was sexually abused as a child, the birth of her own child could be a trigger.

Addictions of all types, to food, alcohol, drugs, sex, relationships, TV, pornography, video games, codependency, shopping, work, power, and so on, may be an attempt to transport ourselves into a realm where we can "disappear" and where we do not experience our negative feelings. Perhaps some of the neurochemical changes that occur with these activities will be found to be the same as those that occur in nondestructive means of self-transcendence. As long as we look to someone else or something outside us to "fill us," define us, or give us meaning, we are condemning ourselves to dissatisfaction and perhaps disaster.

Spiritual traditions the world over teach that the only enduring meaning is in the life of one's soul, in loving, and in serving others. These traditions teach that all else is temporary and will not endure, no matter how great the apparent security in our lives. Our children will grow up and move away; we may lose our jobs or retire; our bodies, as well as those of our friends and family, may grow ill and will grow old; our spouses and friends may disappoint us; our marriages may break up, or our spouses may die. We may lose the money we gain, or we may not gain it as we hoped. We may be victims of racism or hate crimes; we may be victims of physical, emotional, or sexual abuse. So many difficulties can and do happen along the way—but always the human spirit seeks to transcend these difficulties and to find reasons to endure. Our pain can be overwhelming at times; we repeatedly seek to avoid it and get caught in a vicious cycle of avoidance of self.

When we fall into despair, it may seem there is no light at the end of the tunnel. We may feel there is no way out of our situation. Our addictions seem to offer us a quick fix for upset feelings, relieving us of the burden of feeling them. Perhaps this seems to work at first, and it may even seem to work for quite a while. Sooner or later, though, after we have hidden enough of our feelings from ourselves, the poisons will begin seeping back up into our consciousness. These suppressed feelings may appear as dreams or as intrusive thoughts and feelings, or they may show up in our bodies through various ailments and infirmities. No amount of alcohol, chocolate, drugs, sex, shopping, gambling or focusing on others' problems will be able to help us to process the pain in our hearts. We may increase the quantities we use of our "drug" of choice, but ultimately the system will collapse when the roots of the problem are not addressed.

LEARNING TO SUPPRESS THE SELF

Michelle had been suffering with severe depression for over three years. She suffered from significant sleep disruption, one of the symptoms of depression. Michelle had not had a restful or full night's sleep during those three years and was on the verge of complete exhaustion. She was fortunate to have a strong enough physical constitution that her body had not collapsed into severe illness. Michelle had suffered the death of her father, the parent closest to her, at puberty and, as the oldest sibling, had felt responsible for making sure her younger brother was okay. The surviving parent had been thrown into a deep depression. As often happens with sudden parental death, Michelle had felt doubly abandoned, both by her father and her now emotionally unavailable mother. She further developed a pattern already started of suppressing her own feelings and needs and began colluding with her mother's focus on the younger son. Michelle learned very quickly to deny her own feelings and needs and to become a caretaker. Within a very short period, two other relatives died, one of them very close to Michelle.

How does a child handle such overwhelming losses? This scenario would be devastating enough in a nurturing atmosphere, one where there was some acknowledging and sharing of feelings. Michelle had to find her way in a home where the deceased was not discussed. The message she received was to not display (and therefore, by deduction, not to feel) her normal grief feelings. She was deeply sad, and the pretense was almost more than she could bear. The only available solution seemed to be to go along with the script that she was the strong one and could take care of herself and that the brother was the one who
needed the attention. At some point, taking care of others (both her mother's expectations and her brother's

"needs") became the fix for the uncomfortable feelings, and the reward was her mother's approval. The deep and powerful lesson for Michelle was that her own needs could not, and would not, be met and that it was just as well to forget them. Her only chance of finding approval was in suppressing herself.

It is not a matter of placing blame; Michelle's family was surviving in the best way they knew how. However, with her suppression of her needs and feelings, a lifetime pattern was set of denying her own needs and sad feelings, no matter how serious. Michelle was a sensitive listener and helpful friend to others in need. When, as an adult, the external stresses mounted to a critical level, the dam that had been holding back her feelings began to break, and she found herself overwhelmed by depression. It takes enormous psychic energy to suppress or repress feelings. The stronger the trauma or feelings that are suppressed or dissociated, the more psychic energy it takes to keep those feelings from emerging into consciousness. This drains energy that otherwise would be available to the person on physical, emotional, and spiritual levels.

Metaphorically speaking, if a dam is built to hold back water (suppression of psychic energy and feelings), then water (energy) builds up behind the dam (in the unconscious). This water is not then available for general use in the entire psychic system. As the pressure builds up behind the dam, whatever structural weaknesses (individual constitutional weaknesses, such as biological predisposition to heart disease, depression, etc.) are inherent in the dam's construction will be severely stressed. If pressure behind the dam mounts sufficiently, the integrity of the dam is threatened. Perhaps leaks will spring (early symptoms of illness of a physical or emotional nature). Left unattended, the problem can mount in intensity, and the mounting pressure can flood over the dam or even demolish it. This may be the eruption of serious and even life-threatening physical or mental illnesses.

For Michelle, the unresolved grief and abandonment issues accumulated inside her over her lifetime, until she became overwhelmed with a crushing depression. The weight of the grief and sadness she had stored over a lifetime, unprocessed and denied, was intense.

Working through these feelings requires a complete reorientation to one's emotional self. An antidepressant or other appropriate medication can be useful to help the overwhelmed individual to stabilize sufficiently so that he or she can begin to do the necessary emotional work in processing and sifting through these feelings. However, medication is no substitute for doing the psychotherapeutic work. It can be arduous and grueling work. Many find it too difficult. When people stick with the process and come out on the other side, their reward is great. Energy is freed up for relationships, for achievement, for pursuit of goals, for joy, and for pleasure.

The beginning stage of psychotherapeutic work focuses on stabilization, including stabilizing the client's mood, developing the therapeutic relationship, learning and implementing self-care regimens, setting boundaries, and resolving major crises. Depending on the person and his or her circumstances, this can take significant time. The next stage of work involves a deeper look at personal history, including examining patterns of abuse and trauma, grieving losses, and working on processing the trauma. New, more-constructive patterns can be developed as old patterns are shed.

For Michelle, unraveling the old, destructive patterns; grieving the losses she had faced; and creating new patterns in her life was a labor of love that took years of work. Progress often seemed slow and painful, yet the positive results were much more apparent to her friends than they were to her. It never came naturally to her to put her own needs first and take good care of herself, but it did get easier as time went on. She gathered her internal resources and went on to business school to fulfill a lifelong dream.

DEPRESSION AS A CALL TO REORIENTATION TO THE SELF

For many people, depression or other illnesses that require therapeutic intervention come as a call to a higher level of functioning and to a higher level of fulfillment and personal achievement. The person afflicted with this terrible illness must turn within to find out what has gone wrong, how to correct it, and how to get started on a new path to wholeness. Sometimes major life changes are made; sometimes they are mandated by the illness.

Joan began therapy in her early forties, stating that she was very unhappy but did not know why. Her teenage son (her only child) was going away to college the next year. We explored her history, including her relationship with her husband and their patterns of communicating, as well as the patterns of communicating she had learned in her family of origin.

Joan had grown up in an emotionally abusive family and had internalized many of the negative messages she had been given about herself. She'd learned to suppress her natural instinct to fight back and stand up for herself. Her self-esteem had long since eroded away. She'd married a man who liked very much to be in charge and who had had affairs during their courtship and early marriage. She kept her feelings about her childhood and early marriage buried deep inside and for many years focused on her career and raising her son. Yet, as her son was now more independent and her career felt habitual, she was bewildered by her deep sadness.

As Joan began to explore her feelings, she found enormous amounts of sadness and rage that she had buried during her childhood and that had remained unprocessed in the cellars of her psyche. Much emotion about her husband's early affairs had also been buried. Consequently, a great rift of distance and anger had grown up between them.

Now, many years later, her husband seemed bewildered by her curt and angry responses to him. Joan was at midlife, facing the second half of her life. Her depression, as overwhelming as it was, could be seen as a call to a greater healing. It was her psyche's way of signaling distress so she could find help in understanding the considerable emotion she had buried. It would not be easy to sort through, and she would need to feel the feelings she had always avoided. Her depression was too overwhelming to be treated by psychotherapy alone. She benefited from an antidepressant, which stabilized her sufficiently to give her the ego strength to do the therapeutic work.

To go back to the dam metaphor, when the dam breaks, the water behind it floods the countryside and can endanger anything in its path, depending on the amount and the force of the water. When depression is this severe, the therapeutic task is first to stabilize the client's mood and build self-care skills. Joan's therapy at this stage was non-analytic, being mainly supportive and problem solving in nature.

As therapy continued, we put a great deal of focus on her present-day relationship with her husband and on helping her learn to communicate her feelings and needs to him. She became aware of how much anger and sadness she had stored up, both from her childhood and from her early marriage, and learned to see how it had an impact on her current mood and on her perceived inability to communicate. As she faced the abusive patterns from her past and grieved her past losses, she was able to build skills to resolve the dysfunctional patterns in her present life. By the time she left therapy, a great deal of healing had occurred, and she was prepared to face the second half of her life in a fuller, more functional way. I received a note from her some years after she had terminated therapy. She seemed happier than she had ever been and was pleased with the changes she had made in her life. Her marital relationship was improved, and she noted that her husband was more helpful than he had previously been. She had learned to ask for what she needed.

Depression can be a wake-up call into our individuation process. A depression, properly worked through, is a healing on many levels that can propel one into a much higher level of functioning than before the depression. Spiritual healing is, I have found, an often necessary part of the healing from depression. One of the better-known varieties of this is the midlife crisis, which can take on different forms, including overt depression. At its heart it is a pull inward, to reevaluate one's values, to take stock of what one's life has been until now, and to search for a deeper meaning, one more connected to the resources inherent in the higher self and God. This search for deeper meaning is not limited to the midlife period, however. I often see it with people from their early twenties on. In later chapters, I will deal more extensively with the spiritual aspects of recovery.

CHAPTER 6

THE DEMETER-PERSEPHONE MYTH: A METAPHOR FOR FINDING MEANING THROUGH CONNECTION WITH THE INNER SELF

In this chapter, I will look at the ancient myth of Demeter and Persephone as a metaphor for the inner psychological journey that characterizes healing from depression or trauma. Symptoms of depression, anxiety, PTSD, and other mental illnesses are often a call to go down into the depths of the unconscious to recover one's buried history and feelings, to heal trauma and pain, and to free the energy and the wisdom trapped therein.

After a discussion of the myth, I will focus on Persephone and how her journey can serve as a metaphor of the process we go through as we do the inner work needed for personal transformation. The archetypal journey described in the myth serves as a template of the process of the journey stories throughout this book.

In the myth, Persephone spent a long time in the underworld before she returned aboveground to the world abloom in springtime, a process that I view as parallel to the time spent in the underworld of the unconscious during a depressive episode or while working through abuse and trauma, before the healing and reemergence into a more integrated state. I will also discuss the Persephone archetype as symbolic of the process of dreaming and dream working.

The myth of Demeter and Persephone was associated with the Eleusinian Mysteries, an initiation rite that was celebrated for over two thousand years, about the same amount of time that Christianity has thus far survived. The Eleusinian Mysteries were famous throughout Greece and, eventually, throughout the whole of the Roman Empire. At the core of this rite was the myth of Demeter and Persephone, a myth that apparently was reenacted during a secret initiatory ceremony. Some have speculated that a function of this initiatory rite appears to have been to bring the individual to an awareness of the whole self. This self, as defined by Carl Jung, is the whole self, including both our conscious and unconscious minds.

Carl Jung defined the unconscious as having two aspects. The first is the personal unconscious, which contains the totality of all we have experienced during our lives and which is not in our present awareness. The second aspect is the collective unconscious, that part of our unconscious that is not personal to us and that is universal to all humankind. The collective unconscious includes our instincts and our human tendency to form images of our instincts and patterns of behavior. These images, seen in dreams and myths, are called archetypes. The archetypes are "the unconscious images of the instincts themselves" (Jung 1959, 44). We discover our own archetypes through dreams, in which our psyches show us, through imagery, the patterns underlying our behaviors and thoughts. It is also through the collective unconscious that we experience our connection to God.

THE DEMETER-PERSEPHONE MYTH

Some believe the familiar version of the Demeter-Persephone myth may not be the version that was used throughout much of the two-thousand-year time span during which the Eleusinian Mysteries were held. (The mystery religions can be very dark in their interpretation and re-enactment of the myths. In this chapter I am speaking only of the myth itself and not how it may have been used in occult mystery schools.) Greek scholars have discovered that the Greek myths that have been handed down to us from the classical Hellenic period and that have long been considered as the Greek myths are rather late developments in the very long history of the myths (Spretnak 1978, 21). Pre-Hellenic society was matriarchal for many thousands of years. Goddess worship was very firmly rooted in Greece, as in most parts of the world. Goddesses were seen as the source of life, wisdom, and growth, as well as both creative and destructive forces.

People of those times saw pre-Hellenic goddesses as very involved in everyday aspects and energies of life. The goddesses were seen as compassionate and powerful. However, when conquering invaders from a northern, heavily patriarchal culture came into Greece over a period of many years, the nature of the gods and goddesses changed dramatically. The goddesses were recreated in patriarchal society as much more negative in character. For example, the snake and dragon—once symbols of the mother archetype in its natural cycle of death, rebirth, and regeneration—became symbols of malevolent and evil forces under patriarchal consciousness. Additionally, the nurturing, fertile, and related aspects of the goddesses were changed into darker, more-negative traits. These new versions of the goddesses are the ones that have been handed down to us. These negative archetypes of feminine consciousness demonstrate a feminine principle that has become devalued and even reviled.

Nurturing and cooperation have been replaced by competition and domination. Goddesses without power become shadows of their former selves and become vengeful. In the new consciousness, the conscious ego became valued over the subconscious; dreams, feelings, and the inner world were relegated to a lesser importance, thus reflecting sociocultural views of women and the feminine principle in the new patriarchal consciousness.

I will briefly discuss several versions of the myth and then address the Persephone archetype and how it may inform the journey to one's inner self. Throughout this book, the archetype of Persephone's journey will be seen as a pattern by which we can move into our psyches, work through our personal histories, and bring spiritual meaning into our lives. It is also a model for the work that many of the people described in this book have done in the unconscious underworld.

In an abridged version of the Demeter-Persephone myth as we know it today, Demeter and her daughter Persephone were living happily in an Eden-like earth paradise. Their happiness was destroyed when Hades, lord of the underworld, with the consent of Zeus, abducted and raped Persephone. Demeter, the goddess of fertility, searched all over for her daughter but could not find her. In her sorrow, she caused all crops to fail, and as a result, the people of her land came close to famine. Eventually Zeus, who had refused to aid Demeter in her search, felt obliged to help her because of the widespread famine. He persuaded Hades to return his captured bride. Unfortunately, Persephone had carelessly eaten the seeds of a pomegranate (which was food for the dead) while in the underworld. Because of this, she would have to return for one-third of each year to the underworld (which created winter for the world). Demeter and Persephone had a joyful reunion. Spring returned to the desolate land.

The rape and abduction of Persephone can be understood metaphorically as the violent suppression and repression of the feminine principle in the new patriarchal culture. In this new culture, the masculine principles of power, acquisition, domination, and expansion are encouraged without being related to the feminine principles of compassion and empathy, feeling, paying attention to the voice within, connectedness with the natural rhythms of the earth, and valuing the wisdom of the heart. Without a balancing of the masculine and feminine principles, the masculine principle alone becomes disconnected, cruel, uncaring, greedy, and selfish. This is not to say that the prior matriarchal culture was a balanced utopia, as some have implied. It may be that, in an overall historical perspective, the masculine energies had to come to dominance to balance out excesses of the feminine energies in the matriarchal culture. The task before us in our current time is to balance both masculine and feminine energies, respectful of both.

PERSEPHONE IN AN EARLIER TIME

Charlotte Spretnak offers a possible pre-patriarchal version of the myth, depicting a fundamentally different experience (Spretnak 1978, 109–118). The myth begins with Demeter, the goddess of fertility, who had given the gift of wheat to mortals, showing humans how to plant, cultivate, harvest, and grind the wheat. There was no winter, only an eternal growing season. Persephone, Demeter's daughter, lived happily with Demeter, much as in the newer version of the myth, walking and dancing through the open fields. Persephone grew saddened at the sight of the spirits of the dead who hovered around their earthly homes, confused and in pain, not seeming to realize they were dead. Demeter was needed to help feed the living, but Persephone said she wanted to help guide the dead in the underworld. Demeter was saddened and begged Persephone to reconsider, but Persephone was determined to go.

Persephone took with her poppies, wheat, and a torch to light her way. She descended for a long time, until she arrived at an enormous cavern where many thousands of spirits roamed aimlessly. She told them she would be their guide and taught and led them in this underworld.

Demeter was disconsolate. She roamed the earth, hoping to see her daughter emerge. The fields remained barren, as in her sorrow she withheld her powers of fertility from the earth. She waited for her daughter for many long months. One day, she saw a ring of purple crocus come up through the soil, surrounding her. The crocus whispered that Persephone was returning. As Persephone came out from the underworld, new energy stirred everywhere. Flowers and buds sprouted forth, painting the landscape with their colors. Demeter and Persephone rejoiced at their reunion, dancing for joy. Demeter's great happiness was seen everywhere as the miracle of new life in spring. Each year, Persephone would go back underground to guide the newly dead, and each spring she would return to her mother, bringing new life.

COMPARING THE TWO VERSIONS OF THE MYTH

Both versions of the myth are similar in that they end with life returning out of death. However, in the older version, Persephone voluntarily enters the underworld to help guide the souls of the dead. She performs this sacrifice actively and compassionately, as a service springing from her heart's desire. In the later myth, she is abducted, raped, and forcibly taken to the underworld, where she is held captive.

We may learn a great deal if we look at the two versions of the myth as representative of how society relates to the feminine principle (present in both men and women) at various times. Through the feminine, receptive mode, we pay attention to our feelings and instincts, listen to our deeper selves, and listen to God speaking through our hearts. Caring, compassion, and cooperation are valued. There is a sense of relatedness to the earth and to all of creation. When feelings and values of the heart are respected, there is less of a tendency to cut off from traumatic experience and the attendant painful feelings. The work of individuation—that is, fostering the growth of our true selves—is respected. We pay attention to our unconscious (Persephone's voluntary descent) through our dreams and through our inner and creative work as part of a natural cycle, not as something forced upon us. Life and death are seen as natural parts of a cyclic process.

In the patriarchal culture, the masculine principle dominates and oppresses both male and female. We became cut off from our inner selves, disregarding and devaluing our feelings and instincts, forcibly denying and distancing ourselves from them (symbolized by the rape and abduction of Persephone). Males have to live up to impossible standards of masculinity. Dan Kindlon and Michael Thompson write convincingly in their book *Raising Cain: Protecting the Emotional Life of Boys* (2000) about how boys are severely handicapped by the destructive emotional training they receive: Kindlon and Thompson argue that because of the messages boys are given from early on (messages such as "Boys don't cry"), boys are emotionally shut down for life by age six to seven.

Women's emotional upbringing often leaves them undeveloped and stunted as well. The denial of the feminine is the denial of the value of the relatedness to the inner self and its values. As women, when we learn to suppress and disregard our feelings, we also discard our compassion for ourselves and for others. We have been taught to devalue the wisdom of the heart and of the inner self in our strivings to succeed in the outer world.

We saw how, in the later version the myth, Hades, lord of the underworld, abducts and rapes Persephone. This represents how the metaphor of Persephone's journey has been changed into a violent suppression of the feminine principle, hidden away from us in our unconscious minds. When a culture does not value the feminine, the feminine principle is kept underground and out of consciousness. Male and female alike, we are out of touch with our true selves, with our spiritual and emotional essences. God lost his or her place of witness in the human heart and became projected as a male authority figure outside of self.

PERSEPHONE'S JOURNEY AS AN ARCHETYPAL MODEL FOR THE RELATIONSHIP WITH OUR INNER SELF

Many of us attempt to connect with that magical feeling of spirit through our addictions. For example, the alcoholic finds magic in the spirit of the bottle. However, over time, these "spirits" no longer work as they once did and begin to destroy the alcoholic. If the alcoholic finally gets sober, he or she is forced by his or her disease to find true spirit, for without connecting with his or her higher power, there will be no sustained recovery. The 12-step program has as its core a reliance on a higher power. Like Persephone, the alcoholic is thrust by his or her disease into the underworld, where he or she must find healing if he or she is to come out of it alive.

The journey of personal transformation parallels Persephone's journey. Those parts of us, some dissociated or cut off because they bear the horrors of pain and trauma and some that represent our dormant potential, lie in our unconscious minds, unknown to our conscious minds. Like the confused souls of the dead in the earlier Persephone myth who did not know they were dead, those parts of us murmur to us and haunt us, through dreams, through symptoms, through anxiety and depression, through calls to action.

The path to renewed health and life is through the descent into the underworld, into the inner journey. If we do not voluntarily take that path (and many of us do not), it will be thrust upon us, through illness, depression, midlife crises, and so on. Taking this journey, we will encounter what lies in the unconscious mind. Her journey shows us the way into a new relationship with our deepest inner selves and with God. It brings the unconscious to the attention of the conscious ego and helps us begin processing the material.

When Persephone reemerges from the underworld to return to Demeter, she brings with her new life. Similarly when we emerge from our personal underworlds, we bring with us the contents of our unconscious minds, which now fertilize our conscious minds. This process can also be likened to the process of the dreamer dreaming the dream, remembering it, and working with the material. The dreamer then integrates the material into his or her conscious life, thus enriching and bringing new life to the self's experience of the world.

This process can also be seen as a metaphor for the psychotherapeutic journey, beginning with depression, anxiety, flashbacks, or some other disruption of functioning; delving into one's history and personal unconscious; and coming through with new understanding that enriches the person's life and functioning. If one is lucky, there are experiences of spiritual awareness as one encounters the collective unconscious.

INNER BALANCE

The metaphor of the Demeter-Persephone myth is the story of the journey to a balanced relationship with our inner voice and to spirit. The act of Persephone voluntarily undertaking her journey into the underworld can be seen as a metaphor for how, through our receptiveness to our inner worlds, we place ourselves in proper relation to the divine through attunement within—through prayer, meditation, dreamwork art, therapy, dance, and other disciplines.

When our lives are out of balance, we become like the abducted Persephone, forced into the underworld against her will. We will be led to undergo the journey to transformation and meaning through our experience of the pain and symptoms of illness, nightmares, addictions, depression, and suffering.

Carl Jung was very interested in this myth. In his understanding of the myth, he got only so far as to say that Persephone was a Self-symbol for women and an anima projection for men (a projection of a man's inner self). He wrote that he thought his explanation of Persephone was inadequate because the Eleusinian Mysteries had equal appeal to both sexes and because he felt that any adequate explanation would have to be the same for both sexes (Kerényi 1967,xxxi–xxxii).

I believe a more accurate explanation of the myth involves looking at Persephone's journey as an archetypal model of our journey and relationship to the inner world and to the divine within. C.S. Lewis once said, "In our relationship to God, we are all female" (*That Hideous Strength*, 316). I believe what he meant by that is in order for us to hear God, we must take a receptive (feminine) stance. In doing so, we value and listen to our inner voice.

The two mythological versions of Persephone are archetypal models of different ways of relating to God and our inner selves. The earlier Persephone, in a culture where the inner voice is valued, voluntarily takes a receptive stance toward her higher self, to the Divine within. As Jesus said: "The Kingdom of God is within you." In the later myth, it is only after a forced abduction (symbolic of how our culture devalues and denies the inner voice) and through the accompanying pain and suffering that she is reborn.

Many of our modern Christian religious teachings seem far away from the basic tenet of Christ's teaching that the kingdom of heaven is within. For "whoever believes in me", as the Scripture has said, "out of his heart shall flow rivers of living water" (John 7:38-9. ESV). The Christianity of patriarchal, organized religion has often taken Christ as an inner experience of the heart and soul and turned it into an experience that is to be found through an outer male authority. How far away this must be from what was intended! Persephone reminds us that the divine son within is born of the transformational spiritual journey.

This transformational process of finding and living out the purpose encoded within us is the process of individuation. The result of Persephone's journey is the connection with the divine within. Now more than ever, we are forced to look within. Dysfunction, addictions, violence, unimaginable cruelty, war, terrorism, pandemic threats, pandemics and the threat of total global annihilation are constantly in the news. These horrors force us to turn inward, to learn about and to change ourselves. We are finding that no matter how hard we try, we cannot change anyone else. We can change only ourselves. As is said, "Peace begins with me." No longer do we have the options of escaping ourselves, for the stakes are much higher than they have ever been.

DREAMS AS THE BEST TOOL FOR CONNECTING WITH ARCHETYPAL WISDOM

Jung valued the dream as the main way we have of connecting with the archetypes, with the wisdom in the collective unconscious. He spoke also of another means, the process of active imagination. This is an elaboration of imagery or an idea that brings out the meanings inherent in the unconscious material. There are many other means of connecting with archetypal material, like through meditation and prayer, vision quests, and creative or expressive work. The dream, however, is guiding tool we have to help us heal our trauma and grief and to adjust our attitudes as well as to experience the numinosity of our higher selves, the archetypes of the collective unconscious, and the new myths and our evolving images. The dream is the carrier of the sacred energy on which we can most depend for our therapeutic and sacred work.

As we connect with our deepest selves through the process of dreamwork, Persephone's journey is a template that helps guide us through the underworld of the unconscious and brings transforming energy to the light of our conscious minds. She brings us wisdom from deep within ourselves, connecting us on an inner plane to the rest of creation. In our nightly descent, energies are brought to us that enrich and expand our consciousness. Those who track and work with their dreams are, like Persephone, voluntarily undergoing the descent into the unconscious to heal the split in their nature, so that they may find new meaning and learn new ways to survive and so that they may find what is "dead" in themselves and emerge renewed. Each time we work with a dream we descend and emerge anew. As James Hillman, a famous Jungian analyst, said, "Dreaming is a process which educates the dreamer into death."

Persephone's journey can be seen as a template, or archetypal model, of the psychological and spiritual healing process. Later chapters will also show that true psychological healing also involves a spiritual healing. Once the underground journey to healing has begun, the individual encounters the self, the highest part of the human being in which lies purpose and meaning. Eventually one may come to a sense of oneness with the higher spiritual dimension that connects us all.

In the next chapter, I will introduce the role of dreams in recovery. I will demonstrate how dreams can be key in recovery from trauma and addictions. Later, I will discuss dreams and spirituality in the context of therapy in some detail. Though you may not have experienced the level of trauma as the people described within these pages, you may find that you identify with the search for meaning, the journey to the Self, or to Christ.

SECTION III

DREAMS IN RECOVERY

CHAPTER 7

DREAMS HELP CONNECT US TO OURSELVES

Dreams are a connecting link to our past, present, and future. They give us a clear picture of our current state, give us clues as to how we got here, and provide us with a guide to our individuation from here on into the future.

Dreams can take us to unexpected places in our search for understanding problems that beset us. I have learned over the years dreams guide both client and therapist. They provide a valuable roadmap into the areas of the client's psyche that need attention and care. These areas are often inaccessible by guesswork alone, even by the most-skilled clinicians. Dreams can help point the way for exploration, if only we can stay open to what they may be trying to tell us. They also provide strength and sustenance for the hard times ahead.

Bernie Siegel, in his two ground-breaking works of some years ago *Love, Medicine* and *Miracles* and *Peace, Love* and *Healing*, eloquently describes how psychological and spiritual development can reverse the physical disease process, including cancers that are considered fatal. He, among many others, including Louise Hayes, Joan Borysenko, Arnold Mindell, Larry Dossey, Caroline Myss, Patricia Garfield, and Marc Barasch, look at illness and recovery holistically, taking into account the emotional, physical, and spiritual state of the individual in assessing both the illness and the steps needed for recovery. Dr. Siegel speaks often in his books about his use of dreams as diagnostic tools of physical illness. I personally owe my miracle healing from a long-term chronic illness to information presented to me in my dreams on how to heal.

In my almost forty years with the International Association for the Study of Dreams, I have heard many such stories of lifesaving or healing information presented in dreams. One such story is of a woman who had a dream that she had a cancerous tumor in a certain area of her body. She went to the doctor, who did a preliminary test and found nothing unusual. The woman was not to be dissuaded, however, having a strong feeling about the dream. She insisted on further testing, which revealed a fast-growing, potentially lethal tumor. The early warning enabled her to catch it in time to save her life.

Carl Jung was a pioneer in incorporating dreams and spirituality in the psychotherapeutic process. He took what Freud had learned and expanded upon it greatly, looking at dreams from a much broader perspective. Where Freud tended to look at dream symbols as disguising some unacceptable, often sexual meaning, Jung tended to look at dream symbols as being the best possible way to symbolize a given feeling, issue, or concept. Where Freud often saw these dream symbols as related to sexuality, Jung saw them as multidimensional, relating to the life of the body and emotions, as well as to the life of the spirit.

Much exciting work has been done in recent years in understanding the mysteries of the human psyche through working with dreams and through welcoming the life of the spirit into the psychotherapeutic hour. I will speak to some of the various areas in which dreams and spirituality can inform the therapy hour as this book progresses.

With so much work being done in these areas, it is sad that clinicians are rarely trained to include either dreams or spirituality in the therapy hour. Modern 12-step addiction recovery movements have found that drawing on the help of one's "higher power" is essential to recovery. Within these 12-step meetings, one's relationship with one's "higher power" is regularly addressed. It was very exciting for me, as a young clinician working in inpatient addictions units, to see how seamlessly one's spirituality could be woven into recovery. It definitely had a major impact on my development as a therapist.

Yet, in individual therapy, clinicians are all too often reluctant to speak about spiritual dimensions of recovery, perhaps in part because of lack of knowledge. Increasingly, there are degree programs in transpersonal psychology and Christian counseling, graduate courses in religion and spirituality for clinicians, and so on, as clinicians show more interest in these areas.

Although Freud's seminal work *The Interpretation of Dreams* was the foundation of the modern field of psychology, it is my experience that few clinicians know what to do when a client presents them with a dream. Yet these dreams take us to the core of the issues underlying a current problem and, through their nightly meanderings, point the way to recovery. One of the purposes of this book is to show many of the possibilities and empowerments of dreamwork.

Often recovery includes the process of making a connection with the higher self, the archetypal Self to which Jung so often referred. Courses that teach clinicians how to understand and work with dreams have been rare, though thankfully an increasing number of schools are adding such courses to their curriculums. (For more information on graduate schools that support dream studies, go to *www. asdreams.org* and click on "Education.")

BIRTH TRAUMA AND DREAMS

When I was working at a first-class twenty-eight day inpatient addictions treatment unit in Arlington, Virginia, the other counselors and I often went with patients to AA meetings. Because I was working with addicts and because my father was newly sober, I often went to Al-Anon meetings as well. After one particular meeting, a group of us went to a local restaurant for coffee. One man, a psychologist, was doing work on birth trauma and was very involved with a particular technique called rebirthing. As he explained it, our birth trauma forms the psychological lens through which we experience the world. He talked of Leonard Orr and his theory that this early trauma can be released by a type of breath work.

The conversation was intriguing. Although I was not particularly interested in studying the subject further, on the way home, I pondered the idea of birth providing an initial imprint that forms how we experience the world. I wondered about my own birth.

That night I had a dream that I was underwater in a large swimming pool. At one point, I struggled and gasped for air. Then suddenly I realized I could breathe through another means. I then emerged in the deep end. I looked around for someone to help me. The lifeguards were busy tending to an emergency elsewhere and were unable to attend to me.

When I awoke from the dream, I pondered the conversation of the night before. I wondered if it were possible that this was a birth dream. Although I was by now in my mid-twenties, I had never heard my birth story.

I called my mother and asked her to tell me about my birth. What she told me was very interesting in light of the dream. She said that when she was in labor, she began massively hemorrhaging. She was a petite woman, 5'1" and small boned. I was a fairly large baby. She bled out and was pronounced clinically dead. I was still in the birth canal at that time. The doctors worked long and hard to bring her back, and they were successful.

Her story was very interesting. With this input, the dream made perfect sense now as a birth dream. The time I was gasping in the dream may have represented when my mother was pronounced clinically dead and I was in the birth canal (underwater in the pool). She was revived, and I could breathe again, through the umbilical cord (from an unknown source). When I was then born, the doctors were busy attending to my mother. It must have been traumatic for me as an infant to experience this birth and then to have no one to attend to me. My initial experience of the world was thus abandonment.

Both my mother and I were in individual psychotherapy at the time. We talked about the dream and her experiences. We determined the dream suggested we both had unresolved unconscious issues relating to how each of us had experienced near death because of the other. Though we worked on resolving the unconscious resentment, this dynamic stayed with us to varying degrees throughout our lives.

I must have torn her apart inside. There had always been deep discomfort between me and my mother. Perhaps this was one root cause? It was interesting to contemplate.

I believe my mother's lifelong antipathy toward me, which I was dealing with in my own therapy, had something to do with my birth and the impact on her., and also my strong bond with her mother, my grandmother. We both tried working through our feelings—I believe I was far more successful at this than she. Despite periods of our getting along fairly well, behind my back she slandered me viciously to all my family members, nuclear and extended.

Once she was gone, I learned a long list of highly slanderous things she had said about me over the years to her twin sister. I was horrified. Everything I'd ever thought about her had to be reevaluated in light of this information. Do I believe it was all because of the birth experience? Absolutely not. Nor do I think it was unrelated.

My mother had not been eager to look after me as an infant when I had sudden infant death syndrome, and my grandmother stepped in and took me into her room at night. My grandmother and I bonded strongly. Then my mother became extremely jealous of my relationship with my grandmother, a jealousy which would continue until my grandmother died. And so it went. The birth trauma was the lens through which future experience was perceived. She had experienced me as a killer, and the lens with which she saw me was very negative. She became very jealous of my relationship with my father and tried to destroy that. She could not. With her vicious lies, she managed to alienate my brother from me, when we had been very close. Until my uncle told me the lies my mother had spread, I never knew what they were. I only knew their toxic impact on those in my nuclear and extended family..

A BIRTH-TRAUMA SERIES

The following dream series is one that helped unlock the underlying mysteries of a debilitating depression in Sheryl, a young woman in her early twenties. This particular series provided a link to understanding and working through some severe early trauma Sheryl had no idea she had experienced. Working with these dreams was also a key factor in freeing up her writer's block.

Sheryl was a very creative, talented young woman who came into my office suffering from a crippling depression. She had gone through a previous depression where she had become completely unable to function, and she did not want to fall back into that disabled state. She was a writer and complained that she was completely blocked in her writing. My experience in working with highly creative people has been that there is a high correlation between creativity and the ability to process the contents of the unconscious, whether they are presented in dreams, fantasies, or other artistic processes. (A fascinating book called *Writer's Dreaming* by Naomi Epel contains interviews with a number of very talented writers, including Amy Tan and Stephen King, and describes the impact and use of their dreams in their creative processes.) When a block occurs in accessing or processing the contents of the unconscious, creative productivity is also blocked. Sheryl stated that she usually had good dream recall. I encouraged her to keep a record of her dreams.

During the initial period of therapy, we worked on helping her to stabilize her mood. She tried to go without an antidepressant but found that her hopelessness and sadness were deep and unrelenting. She soon became willing to try medication. It took a while, but she responded well to the meds. Slowly she began feeling better. She struggled hard to understand her depression. Why did she get so depressed? No circumstances in her present life seemed to explain the depths of her depression.

Over time, Sheryl brought in a series of very dramatic dreams. The dreams a client brings in during treatment help identify the underlying issues and conflicts. In most of Sheryl's dreams, water was a prominent feature. Themes of life-and-death issues were frequent. I have condensed the following dream report to reflect the major issues involved in the first major dream she brought in, and I have put key phrases in italics:

> I'm in a dark room, watching the television news of the shuttle launch. *Suddenly I'm at the launch.* Then I'm in the shuttle. *The mission is to find the edge of the universe.* Everyone is happy. Looking down from space, it resembles a lake with a sandy beach. We look at the edges from the ship, as if to find something.

> Suddenly we meet with a space station way out in space. The culture that built it is lost, with only two survivors that we can see. They are under control of some power. *Their heads throb visibly with the throb of the noise in the room. They explain that the brain cells are being contracted, and it is very painful to them. We are in danger of falling under this power.* One crew member falls under its effects. We are in a room, a sort of bridge between the shuttle and the space station. [She inserted a drawing of this room, which was a long, narrow passageway.] *We must jump over a hole to get into the space station.* (italics mine)

When Sheryl presented me with this dramatic dream, my intuition told me it might relate to birth issues. Her inflections as she told me the dream, the way she related it, and the drawing that she showed me all seemed to be suggestive of this possibility. I decided to investigate the issue but not to press it if the evidence did not come together. After all, it was her dream, and her associations to it would lead us to its meaning.

As I mentioned, birth trauma can have a significant impact on one's subsequent development. The traumatic imprint can carry through one's lifetime.

Many of the symbols in Sheryl's dream come more sharply into focus when viewed from the perspective of the dream possibly discussing her birth. The darkened room could represent the womb. The dream opened with Sheryl watching the reporting of a shuttle launch on the TV. News reporting in waking life is a replay of recent noteworthy events. As such, news reporting in the dream could be a metaphor for the playback of something noteworthy that had happened to Sheryl. The shuttle launch could be the beginning of the birth process, her own "launching" process. It is also worth noting that the dream shifted from the perspective of Sheryl watching the news to Sheryl actually being at the launch site and then in the shuttle itself, with the mission of the shuttle being to find the edge of the universe. She drew a picture of the lake with the sandy beach, and it looked a great deal like an intact placenta.

Many details of this dream were confusing. The two survivors who were under the control of some power, whose heads were visibly throbbing, were quite mysterious. What could it mean that their brain cells were being contracted? What might it mean that the crew was in danger of falling under some "power"? The long, narrow room that was the bridge between the shuttle and the space station could be the birth canal. Sheryl's drawing suggested this. Sheryl stated that the throbbing of the heads, which corresponded with the throbbing in the room, seemed to be in the rhythm of a heartbeat.

We discussed the possibility that the dream could refer to some traumatic aspects of Sheryl's birth. Although Sheryl did not know the details of her birth, this possibility resonated with her. Had this not been the case, I would not have pursued this further. I suggested that Sheryl speak with her mother about the details of her birth, to see if she could find out any information to help us to understand this dream or to let us know we were on the wrong track.

The results of Sheryl's conversation with her mother were fascinating to us both. Apparently, her mother had had some very large tumors in her uterus while carrying Sheryl and had almost miscarried twice during her pregnancy. She'd spent the last third of her pregnancy in bed. Sheryl had been positioned in the uterus with her head between two tumors. Additionally, Sheryl had had to be pulled out with forceps.

In the dream, the aliens had headaches and felt that their brain cells were being contracted. At the point in the dream where the dreamer said, "We are in danger of falling under this power," it seems that, if this dream was about Sheryl's birth, that this stage of the birth must have felt very painful, very dangerous, and life threatening to the fetus. The power that endangered her might well have been the power of death. When Sheryl was finally born, she had only one functioning lung and had to be placed in an incubator. The correspondences between the dream and the very traumatic birth process that Sheryl's mother had described were striking and could not be explained away by mere coincidence. Could this dream have come to Sheryl as a way of helping her to understand and process this severe trauma that she had undergone, so that she might be able to work through some of the feelings and understand how they might shape her current perception of her experiences?

Another dream two nights later began in a similar fashion:

I went to a beach which changed into a small lake with sandy shores [just like the space dream]. *The undertow was very strong, and you had to be careful. If you rode the waves just right they could lift you high into the air and it felt like flying, but if you miscalculated you could drown.* Legend had it that the people who used to live here had a god/chief who was hungry for people, and he pulled them under the water. That chief was still angry, and killed the people swimming in the lake.

People came to do a documentary on the tribe from which the chief came, and on the Legend.

While on my way, I go with my mother to have her audition for "Knots Landing," with a carnival owner. I saw the red and yellow lights of the ride nearest me, and heard a throbbing back beat to the music in the fair. Then I saw Carol [therapist] and she said this music and the lights from the fair were why I had the space dream. Then Carol left.

I went to meet with the documentary people. I go swimming briefly, and the waves take me up. I see a rainbow while near the rock. As I get near the shore, I hear the chief or "god" of the people, and he tells me whom he wants to kill. I try to reason with him. He's black, very handsome, and very tall and strong. He tells me he has no choice but to pull people under the water. Then I'm afraid he'll take me too, so I stay away from the water, but I feel a pain in my head and fear he could kill me even though I'm away from the water. As afraid as I am, I'm very attracted to him. He can read my mind, and he could kill me, but I am drawn to him. (italics mine)

And then, the same night, she had this dream:

I see images of mothers of all races killing their children to protect them from something bad.

Blood from the dead at the lake rolls down a waterfall in India. I'm standing in a pool of water and blood, and trying to get out, but am not scared. *The way to get out is the direction the water and blood are going.* (italics mine)

Sheryl knows the doctor who delivered her, as he is a family friend. She said he is very similar in appearance to the chief. She said the pain in her head could come from when the forceps were used.

I asked Sheryl to do an active-imagination exercise to understand more about the role of the chief in the dream. Active imagination is a technique that originated with Carl Jung, in which a person dialogues, either out loud or in writing, with a character from a dream or an aspect of one's psyche (for example, the inner child). This exercise taps into subconscious currents of thought and emotion and in the amplification may bring up material from the unconscious. The following quote is from this exercise:

Sheryl (to chief): Why is death so prominent here?
Chief: Because I am death.
Sheryl: Past, present or future?
Chief: Death is ever present.
Sheryl: Are you my death or my fear of death? Or are you my hope, past, present or future for
      death?
Chief: I am the peacefulness of rest in your desires both in the past and future. I am the reality
      of violence in a death of your own making. I am the peace you want, but you cannot have
      me. There is a different way to peace. The peace you seek will enable you to go forward.
      The rest you will get from me will take you beyond time—it is not for you now.

Sheryl's dream suggests that, with her birth, she experienced her first encounter with the struggle between her instinctual fight for life and her yearning for the peacefulness of death, of oblivion. This archetypal struggle is one that Freud postulated as being always present throughout one's lifetime: the struggle between Eros, the instinct to live, and Thanatos, the death instinct. This struggle between life and death has been a key aspect of Sheryl's depressions and has appeared in different forms.

We had already talked about the possibility that the first dream was a birth dream, and now my character in the dream linked the two dreams. Subsequent dreams will be corrective if there is a wrong understanding; in this case, both the corroboration from her mother and the second dream indicated we were on the right track. The last dream, with mothers and their babies, and Sheryl standing in the pool of water and blood whose flow would take her where she needed to go, also reinforced the birth theme. As previously mentioned, the birth experience provides a framework, or perspective through which subsequent experience is felt and perceived. Thus, for Sheryl, whose entrance into this world was experienced in such apocalyptic terms, the world was not experienced as a gentle, nurturing place. Sheryl was a wanted and loved child; however, her mother's illness and subsequent multiple hospitalizations caused Sheryl to experience feelings of abandonment and internalized self-hatred over significant periods of time. In later years, when her depressions first began emerging, they came with all the overwhelming effects of those early experiences,

As we processed these dreams and Sheryl worked through the feelings that came with them, her mood markedly improved. She noted numerous links between the dream themes and those waking themes in her present life that contributed to her depression. The dreams and the dialogues that she'd had with her mother on the subject of her birth and early childhood gave her insights into her depressed moods. They helped her to detach from the complex of feelings and begin to work her way out of it. Also, as I mentioned, she had been experiencing a very painful writer's block. Working with her dreams helped Sheryl reconnect with the creative workings of her unconscious, and she began writing again.

SHERYL'S RETURN YEARS LATER

Some years after terminating therapy, Sheryl came back to see me after a series of stressors in her life had contributed to her feeling once more that her life and her mood were unmanageable. She was again depressed and preoccupied with death—not as overt suicidality but as an intense yearning for peace, a yearning that was not particular whether peace was found in a positive or a negative manner. This struck me as being the same issue addressed in her dialogue with the chief from one of the dreams from several years before. When I read back to her the dialogue with the chief she had done previously, she was stunned at the strong parallels between what she was now experiencing, what she had experienced before, and the birth issue.

The same issues recur throughout our lives. We may work through them successfully at one period of our lives only to find they come back later, to be resolved at a deeper level. Our core issues stay with us throughout our lives, and we work through them at different levels. In this instance, Sheryl worked through her depression with a deeper understanding of the impact of that early traumatic experience. She understood how that yearning for oblivion had begun in those early experiences and had become a default position for her when she was stressed and under pressure.

My experience has been that people who were placed in incubators as infants in the era when it was thought unhealthy to touch these babies can suffer severe depressions and abandonment anxieties. The birth experience may be traumatic enough, yet to be isolated and not held or loved for weeks on end seems to have profound reverberations that can last through a lifetime. The sense of aloneness, panic, fear, and deprivation must be overwhelming for the tender and impressionable infant psyche.

One man who had been isolated in an incubator for six weeks as an infant felt powerless as an adult to contain the enormous flood of hopeless and powerless feelings that overwhelmed him in situations in which he felt even marginally rejected or abandoned. His had been a difficult life and very difficult birth. The intensity of the feelings flooding him in these situations may be related to those early experiences of hopelessness and abandonment. Babies do not have the neurological and brain development to be able to process highly traumatic experiences. René Spitz's famous studies on failure-to-thrive babies who did not develop when human love was not given to them support the hypothesis that early neglect and lack of nurture can have a profound effect on the young infant. The infants he studied failed to develop emotionally, intellectually, and physically and seemed profoundly depressed.

CHAPTER 8

RECOVERY DREAMS

This chapter gives a broad overview of ways dreams can assist in the recovery process. I will begin by looking at some of the more commonly seen recovery dreams, such as the recovering alcoholic's dream of drinking or the ex-smoker's dream of smoking a cigarette. I will also look at how dreams can provide clues to unconscious triggers for self-destructive behaviors, such as eating binges in someone with an eating disorder. I will briefly discuss here the role of dreams in understanding abuse memories and will examine this role in much more detail later.

Over the past fifty years of working with my own dreams and forty-five years working with the dreams of clients, I have become fascinated with and enormously respectful of the many different functions of dreams in the healing process. I work daily with people who are recovering, or beginning to recover, from all kinds of problems, including addictions to drugs, alcohol, food, sex, or love; emotional, sexual, physical, or spiritual abuse and their long-term emotional consequences; and mental disorders such as depression, bipolar disorder, and dissociative disorders that have both psychological and biochemical roots.

Symptoms the client brings to the therapist's office are most often the tip of the iceberg of the problem. I introduced in the previous chapter how dreams provide a bridge to the unconscious mind, which, when explored, can lead to an understanding of the problem. In trauma recovery, one of the major functions of dreams is revealing the feelings associated with the trauma that might have been numbed out, or dissociated, in self-protection. That dream understanding can help the client to understand the impact of the trauma by linking it simultaneously to the past event and to the present symptom or behavior.

I digress briefly here to comment on the controversy about repressed memories in the 1990s and on the dangers inherent in working in the vague, shadowy areas of the unconscious that produce both memory and fantasy. I respect the issues presented on both sides of the controversy and have learned much from the debate. One cannot deduce from a dream alone whether a given action presented in the dream actually happened. A great deal of caution and discernment is necessary in working with these very difficult issues. Many more factors must be taken into account and sorted through very carefully. These factors will be explored in detail as the narrative goes on.

ADDICTION RECOVERY DREAMS

Some of the most dramatic addiction recovery dreams occur in the early stages of recovery, when there is physical withdrawal as well as psychological distress. Recovering alcoholics are very well familiar with the drinking dream in which they are still drinking. The dreams are startlingly real. They may wake up terrified, convinced they were drinking. The next day they may exhibit many of the physical and psychological symptoms that they exhibited when they were drinking, the dry drunk syndrome.

Before Todd went into residential treatment for his alcohol and cocaine addictions, he had a dream in which he was using meth and heroin. While he had abused alcohol and cocaine, he had never tried meth or heroin. Todd said he knew when he awoke that the dream was a warning; meth and heroin were the next step for him if he continued in his patterns. He believed he might not survive if he ventured into those drugs. This dream served as a wake-up call to him, and he is now happily clean and sober a number of years later.

The following is another early stage recovery dream:

I'm at a social gathering, with a drink in my hand. I know I shouldn't be drinking, but I tell myself that it's okay this time. I have several more. As I wake up, I realize what I have done, and feel trapped, afraid, back in the cycle of my alcoholism.

Drinking dreams are very common for alcoholics in their first year of recovery. The dreams tend to occur when the recovering alcoholic is under significant stress or experiencing physical withdrawal or when blood sugar levels are out of balance. (Blood sugar imbalances can mimic withdrawal symptoms. These imbalances are an unfortunate effect of the large quantities of sweets and coffee that alcoholics often consume in early recovery, and they perpetuate the cravings for alcohol. A balanced diet, with sufficient protein, is highly recommended for recovering alcoholics.)

Drinking and using dreams can be warnings about relapse risk. Nora, a recovering alcoholic who had recently celebrated seven years of sobriety, had been under a great deal of stress over the previous eight months. The stress had picked up during recent weeks. During one particularly stressful week, she had a drinking dream every night. Each night, the dream was essentially the same: she found herself drinking. The only variable was that she was drinking different alcoholic beverages on different nights. Nora was not struggling in real life with the desire to drink, as is common with the occurrence of drinking dreams in earlier recovery. Instead, she was feeling, as she'd felt when she was drinking, that her life was unmanageable. She was feeling the same out-of-control feelings that she had during her drinking days. Nora saw her dreams as a dramatic warning about her stress level. She believed they pointed her to the need for positive change and more self-nurturing.

Smokers who are quitting, or who have quit, often have smoking dreams. One ex-smoker had this particularly seductive dream over the years since she'd stopped smoking, with minor variations:

I am in a situation in which I suddenly realize that I am smoking a cigarette. I begin to feel alarm about this, because I know that I can't smoke just one without being hooked back into the addiction. Then I realize, much to my delight, that for a while now, I have been able to smoke an occasional cigarette whenever I choose, and that I have not become addicted again. I go for days or weeks or months without smoking if I choose, without difficulty, and then I can smoke again when I want to, without complications.

This dream was an addict's wish come true—in the dream, she is no longer addicted and can indulge once more without fear of consequences! The feeling of pleasure and delight is in stark contrast to the fear and alarm in the beginning of the dream. The dreamer dreamt this dream when under stress and when it is tempting to fall back on old coping tools, including denial of self-destructive behavior. The dreamer's denial in the dream is significant: it points to her tendency to deny her self-destructive patterns.

Using dreams that occur later in recovery may occur when the dreamer is under stress and when they may be at risk for using again. In this case, the dream may serve as a warning to the dreamer. Other meanings of these dreams can be determined by exploring the current waking situation of the dreamer, including emotional patterns similar to those in the dream.

A twenty-two-year-old alcoholic woman who had been in recovery began drinking again. She was trying to convince herself that she could control her drinking and manage the unmanageability of her addiction. She began to have more and more problems when she drank, but she was not willing to look at them. She brought the following dream to therapy and pronounced it "bizarre."

> I am in an open bathroom where people can see me. I have to go to the bathroom, and discover, to my horror, I have a penis! I try to hide it as I urinate. I am stunned, and have no idea how this happened. I'm mortified and want to make it go away, but I can't make it go away. I hide it as best as I can.

When I asked the dreamer what she thought it meant, she said emphatically, "I have no idea." When I asked her what she would title it, she said, "Nightmarish Discovery." As we worked with the dream, I asked her what aspect of her life was like a horrifying secret that embarrassed her and that she couldn't make go away. Her eyes grew wide in a classic "aha "moment, and she blurted out, with obvious chagrin, "My alcoholism." We both laughed. The dream used a dramatic symbol to get her attention. It took a while longer, but, happily, she did go through residential treatment and then continued to improve.

DREAMS AND EATING DISORDER RECOVERY

Rose was twenty-one and suffered from an eating disorder. She stated she had stopped purging but continued to binge. Her history of depression included suicide attempts at twelve and fifteen. Her bulimia had been so severe, with two to three purges daily, that she'd had to have all her fillings replaced. Rose felt that her slim mother's hyper-attentiveness to Rose's weight was at the core of the issue. She also believed her mother's severely controlling behavior greatly contributed to her depression.

In our initial visit, Rose told me that at age fifteen she had been fondled by an older man but that she did not think this had had much impact. To her great surprise, she sobbed as she recounted the details of the event. Rose wanted to maintain her emotional composure during this initial therapy session and was dismayed she could not. This often happens in an initial session, for emotions often build up to such intensity they can no longer be held back once treatment is initiated. As the session drew to a close, I explained that dreams can be valuable as a recovery tool, as they can supplement our conscious awareness with information on what may be going on below the surface of our consciousness.

Rose came in the following week with an explicit and powerful dream in which she discovered that a good friend of her father had sexually abused her as a child. In the dream, her mother had been aware of the sexual abuse but had done nothing to help her. The father's friend denied in the dream that the abuse meant anything. Rose had cried uncontrollably while in the dream. She was stunned both by the dream and by her uncontrollable crying. The man who had abused her in the dream was the man whom she remembered fondling her.

The initial dream in therapy often outlines the major issues of the treatment to follow and the course treatment will take. Given the combination of Rose's reaction in the initial session and this initial dream, it seemed sexual abuse might be a key factor underlying both the eating disorder and the depression. It also seemed that working through her feelings both about the abuse and about being unprotected by her parents (regardless of whether they, in fact, had any idea that the abuse had occurred) would be a crucial part of our work together. This indeed proved to be the case. During the course of treatment, Rose identified other instances of sexual abuse. The abuse was ongoing over a period of several years with one person in particular. Rose felt ashamed of telling me about those instances because she believed she had been a "willing" participant.

TRIGGERS UNDERLYING AN EATING DISORDER

One of the aspects that characterized Rose's binges was that she had little or no idea of what triggered them. She simply felt the impulse and acted on it. I asked her to do several things to help her to understand the connection between emotional triggers that might set off the impulses and the actual impulses themselves. One was to keep a dream journal so we could track what was going on at a subconscious level. The second was to spend five minutes writing in a journal about what she was feeling when she felt an urge to binge. Then, if she still wished to binge, that was her choice. The idea here was to help give her some delay time between impulse and bingeing, so that she could begin to understand what emotional triggers led to her binges.

Rose's dreams were full of images of sexually abused children, of being trapped somewhere with bad guys, of being pregnant and not wanting to be, and of dead, decaying naked women. As we looked at her episodes of bingeing, it became clear that there was a connection between these distressful dreams and her bingeing. As upsetting feelings began coming to the surface, they felt very threatening. Rose began to understand she had unconsciously used bingeing over the years to "swallow" these feelings and keep them down.

Rose also found through keeping a journal that her binges were triggered when she felt sexually attracted to someone or when someone was attracted to her and asked her out. Because of the early sexual abuse, sexuality and all of her feelings associated with it had become very threatening to her. The extra fifty pounds she carried served as a protection to her, to shield her from the issue of sexuality. Rose is a very beautiful woman, however, and even with the extra weight she found so repulsive, men found her desirable. However, since she felt bad about the way she looked, she used her weight as an excuse to not go out often in public.

Sexually abused women often pad themselves with extra pounds for protection. They often feel, consciously or unconsciously, as Rose did, that if they are obese, no one will be sexually attracted to them and they won't risk abuse. In the unconscious mind, there is no sense of time having passed; the danger and the unpredictability that the abused child felt stays alive in the adult unconscious. Therefore, even when the adult is in no danger of sexual abuse in the present, the undercurrent of feelings in the unconscious, until worked through and resolved, signals danger with an eruption of anxiety when sexuality is involved. This anxiety may operate constantly, or it may break through at a certain stage of the adult life, rendering formerly pleasurable sexual activity now frightening and terrifying.

Most triggers for Rose's binges related to sexuality and to control issues relating to her mother. It was very helpful that she kept a dream journal, for as we worked through the dreams, we received information about the emotions that were triggers for the binges.

Sometimes Rose woke up wanting to binge. In those cases, her dreams of the night before provided a very helpful link between what she was processing subconsciously and the desire to binge. Our later work went into more depth around her feelings about the sexual abuse. To stabilize the bulimia, Rose had to gain an awareness that these feelings served as triggers.

ENCOURAGEMENT THROUGH DREAMS

Jean had been in therapy for several years for severe depression. She had issues of neglect and abandonment from growing up in an alcoholic family and had trauma resulting from childhood sexual abuse. She'd suffered from alcoholism as a young adult and now had an eating disorder and a spending addiction. She worked hard in treatment. However, it was very hard for her to dare hope she could be free from the weight of her childhood emotional baggage. Although her life was beginning to change in some very positive ways, she had deep inner doubts that she would be able to succeed in attaining her goals. She sabotaged herself out of fear of change.

At this crossroads, she introduced a recent dream by saying it had made her feel incredibly free and happy. It made a significant emotional impact on her. The dream went as follows:

I am outdoors, in an open area. Several men are out there also. I watch them with amazement as they start running, and take off flying, with no machinery. It seems so easy for them.

One of the men comes up to me, and begins to instruct me on how to fly. He tells me, "Just run down the hill, and flap your arms." He shows me how to do this. I start running down the hill, and much to my amazement, I begin flying. I feel full of joy and wonderment. The feeling of being able to fly is so powerful!

After I come down, I decide to try again. This time, however, I look down at my body with its excess weight, and I am very afraid that I won't be able to fly, that my pounds will weigh me down and keep me from being able to take off. However, despite my fears, I am able to fly again, just as before. The feeling is so incredibly joyful, and I feel unbelievably free!

After I return to the ground, a fit young woman comes up to me. She asks me if she too can fly. I tell her yes, I am sure of it; that if I can fly, then anyone can.

In addition to feeling ecstatic about the experience of flying, Jean felt an increased sense of confidence about her ability to perform. The sense of being able to fly was so powerful and seemed so real that it left her actually wondering if it were possible. (This is a common experience with flying dreams, for often the sensations of being able to fly are so vivid and so powerful, the dreamer, once awakened, wonders if it were real or if it were a dream.) She believed the dream encouraged her to make a sustained effort by letting her know she would be successful.

A dream such as this, because it is a product of the dreamer's own psyche, offers encouragement and motivation that can be far more powerful than that which any therapist or spouse or friend can offer. It comes from deep inside, from a place where the dreamer's deepest darkest fears and secrets are known, and seems to say, "Your fears are only fears; try, and you will be surprised at what you can do." The power of the feeling of flying, which here seems to represent success, stays with dreamers as a gift to give them strength and courage when they feel their steps are faltering.

In the next two chapters, I go into more depth about some of the relevant considerations when looking at dreams and memory issues in recovery from trauma. Dissociation is a natural reaction by a young brain to severe and repeated trauma. As a result, where there is a traumatic childhood history, memory of those traumas is often hidden behind an amnesic barrier to protect the young self from being overwhelmed. Careful, client-centered dreamwork as described in the next two chapters can be an extremely important tool in trauma recovery.

CHAPTER 9

DREAMS, MEMORY AND TRAUMA RECOVERY, PART 1

Mary was one of four sisters. Her three sisters had always had memories of incest with their father. There was a multigenerational family history of alcoholism, incest, and suicide. Mary had no memories of having been sexually abused but came into therapy with severe depression and many questions about the possibility she too might have been sexually abused. After all, all her sisters had been abused. If she had been abused also, she wanted to remember.

Mary had severe amnesia for a large portion of her childhood. Severe childhood amnesia is very unusual and is a clinical warning flag, indicating that there might be significant trauma. However, it was extremely important not to jump to any conclusions. It would take time and careful work to sort out the pieces of her history, and it was entirely possible that we would never know what lay in those missing years. She had suffered with severe, disabling depression that had rendered her bedridden through long periods of her adult life. In the recent year, she'd spent hours or days weeping without having any idea why she was so sad.

In this chapter, I will discuss some basic concepts when dealing with a possible history of trauma. I will use Mary's story to exemplify various aspects. Throughout the chapter, a grounded and neutral approach is urged as a means to avoid the pitfalls of an earlier period out of which the false memory controversy arose. This grounded and neutral approach applies to dreamwork as well. (Some of the information in Mary's case dates itself, arising out of the context of the times in which we were working.) I will describe the stages of trauma treatment and the tasks that are done in each stage. I will also discuss some related dreams. Later in this book, I will describe other dreams illustrative of the various stages of psychotherapeutic work.

STAGE-ORIENTED TRAUMA TREATMENT

Current trauma treatment guidelines wisely urge against a focus on having memories of the abuse and instead refocus the client on managing his or her everyday life. As the client grows stronger and becomes stabilized, memory will come on its own (Courtois, 1999). Mary's dream wisdom guided her to go slowly.

The first stage of treatment may take up at least half of treatment for trauma survivors and is about creating safety and stabilization. The emphasis is on building the therapeutic relationship and trust between client and therapist, developing solid problem-solving and boundary-setting skills, developing a healthy support system outside the therapist, helping to stabilize functioning in all spheres, teaching emotional modulation skills, and establishing a safety plan. This first stage is critical for laying the groundwork for the later trauma work, which can be very destabilizing. Trauma work is discouraged in stage one. Building skills for grounding and self-care are encouraged instead.

Because childhood sexual abuse is a horrendous betrayal of trust between the child and the adult in a position of authority, the victim's ability to trust becomes severely damaged. The first stage of work is the building of a trusting relationship between the client and the therapist. This is especially true of childhood-abuse victims. The first stage is a time in which the client is constantly monitoring whether he or she feels heard and responded to with empathy and fairness. Most of all, the client is testing out the waters to see if this is a relationship where he or she can feel safe. Abuse victims have extraordinarily fine-tuned antennas when it comes to perception of trust and safety issues. The more damaging the abuse, the longer the establishment of basic trust will take.

Even when the client wishes to explore sexual-abuse issues, the first stage of treatment is for stabilization. Delving into trauma is destabilizing at this point. I learned this particular lesson the hard way, very early in my career, before I found a supervisor and learned specific trauma-treatment skills. I was working with a woman who had early major trauma and wanted to explore her abuse. We explored the abuse in the early stages of therapy. When she would arrive home after therapy, she would be overwhelmed by depression. It was too much too soon, and we did not get very far—but I learned an extremely valuable lesson about the value of pacing and boundaries in the process.

THE NEED TO RESPECT DEFENSES

When a child is repeatedly traumatized, defenses develop automatically to protect him or her against the overwhelming flood of feelings. When repeated trauma occurs, the child dissociates, separating himself or herself from what is happening. The body experiences the trauma, but the psyche keeps itself from emotionally experiencing the pain by disconnecting.

The child dissociates also from what he or she can perceive as even more horrible than the pain: the pleasure of what is occurring. Our bodies are designed to feel pleasurable feelings when sexually stimulated. However, when the child instinctively knows the abuse is a heinous act, the physical pleasure causes horror and shame. It makes the child confused; the child may believe if the act caused pleasure, he or she must have wanted the sexual activity. Abusers often will use the sexual pleasure the child experiences to bully the child into thinking he or she wanted and/or asked for the abuse.

As I have mentioned, I have learned to respect the timing of the psyche in presenting material to the conscious mind. It is important not to aggressively pursue memory, for the protective barrier that defends against remembering is often needed to preserve functioning. Dissociated events and feelings can be overwhelming.

There has been much debate about the reliability of hypnosis. Many states do not now allow material discovered under hypnosis as admissible evidence in court, because people are highly suggestible under hypnosis and may produce fantasy information that the hypnosis reinforces them into believing.

REMEMBERING NOT A MEASURE OF PROGRESS

Mary had been seeing me twice weekly for over a year. Our focus was on mood stabilization and on learning and applying boundary-setting and problem-solving skills. One day, she angrily confronted me about how she had not yet had memories and suggested that maybe therapy was not progressing as rapidly as it should. She was in a support group for sexual abuse survivors, and having memories seemed to have become somewhat the equivalent of getting a good grade in class. This was before the false memory controversy, when sexual abuse recovery groups were focused on the idea of having memories. Those group members who thought they might have been abused but who did not have memories were wrongly being told by other group members that having memories was a quantifier of progress.

This false belief subjects the client to pressure to produce memories, which is unhealthy for many reasons. This pressure to produce, whether it is self-pressure, pressure from support group peers, or, worse, pressure from the therapist, sets up the very conditions that can be fertile ground for confabulating memory or for competitively measuring therapeutic progress against another.

Mary questioned my approach. I told her I took her concerns very seriously. Further, I explained that the work that we had been doing was to help stabilize her severe depression and to build a mental and emotional foundation for the work ahead. This preparation would strengthen her ego (her conscious ability to cope with frightening material while still functioning in the world around her), so that if memories did emerge, they would not overwhelm her. Our focus was on her healing, not on memories. The stabilization and boundary-setting work had been very important and was a necessary preparation for whatever was to come.

Mary asked about whether I would try hypnosis on her to retrieve memories, and I explained that I did not believe in aggressively going after memories. Dissociated memories emerge in the natural course of the therapeutic process, in their own way and time. I explained how hypnosis can be unreliable in accessing memory, as cases had been reported in which hypnosis has served to convince the hypnotic subject that something had occurred that had, in fact, never occurred. Where there is traumatic amnesia, it is preferable to respect the slow process of the psyche's natural timing.

DREAMING AND PACING

Since Mary wanted to remember her forgotten childhood, I suggested that she ask her higher self, through her dreams, to guide her as to what she needed to know. I explained dreamwork is one of the best and safest ways to explore memory. The psyche has wisdom and timing all its own and presents material when the client is ready to look at it and not before. This technique of dream incubation has been used since ancient times and has been revived in the growing dream study movement of the past thirty years. Gayle Delaney, in *Living Your Dreams and Breakthrough Dreaming*, and Patricia Garfield, in *Creative Dreaming*, are two popular authors who have written about the dream incubation process. These books have been out for a while and are highly recommended. In short, dream incubation is the act of requesting a dream from one's higher mind. There is a section explaining more about dream incubation in a few pages.

My respect for the timing with which the psyche presents material through dreams has been born out of many years of experience in working through dreams. The wisdom of the higher self guides the timing in which material is made available to the conscious mind in the dream. If a client is unprepared to deal with sexual-abuse material, this will emerge in some way in the dream material.

When I suggested to Mary that she try dream incubation, I was suggesting that she check in with her higher self and see for herself what would emerge. She was happy with the suggestion, as she felt empowered to take action. She asked me for more details on how to incubate, which I gladly gave her. This strategy gave her a bit more control over her therapy process and lessened her perceived dependency on me as the one who, she felt, was keeping her from having memories. Before I proceed with what happened with Mary and her dream-incubation process, I want to say a few words about memory issues to help explain why dreaming might be so valuable in recovery from trauma.

MEMORY AND THE BRAIN

Theoretically, much of what has happened to us in our lifetimes is retained in memory, in various forms. Research on memory demonstrates that there is essentially complete childhood amnesia before the age of two or three and that memory is sparse in the first five to seven years of one's life. Modern brain research has discovered that many different brain structures carry different kinds of memory— auditory, emotional, visual, and olfactory memories as well as memory of activities. According to Bessel van der Kolk, the right side of the brain carries implicit memories, or those memories that are stored without words as emotional responses, and sensorimotor sensations related to experience. He says that, before the age of three, memories are stored on a sensory-motor level and on a visual-pictorial level. In addition, when people are traumatized, they tend to regress to a preverbal level of development in storing, processing, and being able to remember and express the trauma. Trauma interferes with declarative memory, in conscious recall of the traumatic experience. It does not interfere with implicit memory, or memory that is stored in sensory-motor and visual-pictorial means.

In one study done by Van der Kolk of mostly confirmed abuse victims who had at one point forgotten the abuse, most of these victims remembered their abuse first through visual, kinesthetic, and emotional means. Auditory and olfactory aspects were next. Only a small percentage, 6 percent, remembered their abuse for the first time with a verbal narrative. Van der Kolk states that post-traumatic stress disorder is a re-experiencing of the sensory aspects of the trauma and that traumatized people are mostly unable initially to reconstruct memory verbally. Talk therapy addresses the frontal and prefrontal parts of the brain. However, traumatic memory is stored in the brain stem and in the limbic system, an entirely different area of the brain. It is stored there as emotional charges and as isolated pieces of sensory-motor and visual-pictorial information.

In a clinical setting, memory fragments tend to emerge as flashbacks, bodily sensations, nightmares and dreams, and visual imagery, smells, or auditory impressions. If, on a neurophysiological level, trauma interferes with conscious, verbal recall of a traumatic experience but does not interfere with sensory- motor and visual-pictorial memory, then it makes perfect sense that dissociated memory emerges in the clinical setting through bodily sensations, imagery, and dreams.

Research on dreams has indicated that dreaming originates in the pons area of the brain, which is in the brain stem, which is where van der Kolk says traumatic memory is stored. If what van der Kolk says about where and how trauma memory is stored is true, then on a psychophysiological level-dreams might provide one of the key means of access to the sensory-motor and visual-pictorial aspects of stored traumatic memory. Clearly more research needs to be done, but what we do know now points out with more clarity than ever that dreams can be a key means of accessing traumatic memory. We know better than to take dreams literally, and I will speak more to this later, yet the information they give us may be more valuable than is generally assumed, especially by those who debunk the information that comes through dreaming.

DREAMS AND AMNESIA

Joe went out riding his motorcycle late one night. The next thing he knew, he woke up in a hospital, unable to move. From then on, he was a quadriplegic. Apparently, he had taken an exit ramp too soon and had somehow hit the car in front of him. No one had really seen what had happened. He had no memory of the event. Routine drug and alcohol screening done shortly after the accident showed he had not been under the influence.

Joe's traumatic amnesia for this horrendous accident is explained in Van der Kolk's model of neurophysiological processing of trauma, in which an extreme trauma overwhelms the area of the brain responsible for conscious, declarative memory and creates narrative amnesia. However, with Van der Kolk's model, we would suspect that memory is not lost altogether but is stored in a sensory-motor and visual-pictorial manner in the brainstem and limbic system, where it is inaccessible to ordinary consciousness.

For many years, the accident and its cause puzzled Joe and his family. He was known to be a careful motorcyclist; it would have been very uncharacteristic of him to take an exit ramp as early as he had.

Some time, after the accident, Joe began having a recurrent nightmare that took him back to the night of the accident. In the nightmare, he was riding along on the highway on his motorcycle when a car full of teenagers forced him off the road. He saw no faces, as it was quite dark. Each time Joe had the nightmare, it repeated itself exactly.

Joe believes strongly his nightmare is an accurate representation of what actually happened. To him, this would make sense of an accident whose occurrence otherwise made no sense whatsoever. He has no proof and likely will never have any corroboration. However, a man once said something to Joe's brother that made it sound very much as if he knew something more about the accident. Maybe someday that man will come forward and explain his mysterious statement; maybe that day will never come.

Victims of trauma who have amnesia for significant portions of their childhood often find that one of the ways they can begin to put the pieces back together is through dreams that present with issues from the past. These dreams may not represent memory literally, as with the man in the motorcycle accident, but may contain valuable information nonetheless. (In a later chapter I will examine some of the complex issues around sorting out the various elements of dream content.) These dreams can provide extremely useful departure points for exploration of the issues that they bring to light.

DREAM INCUBATION

Dream incubation is a request to the higher self, (the Self in the Jungian sense of the word), or to God for information on a particular subject. The subject can be a request to solve a problem, a request for information, or even a request for healing (as in the dream incubation I did to heal from my fifteen- year debilitating illness). The ancient Greeks had elaborate rituals whereby a person requesting healing would fast and pray for a prescribed period of days and go to a healing temple to incubate a healing dream.

Modern dreamworkers have modified the ancient procedures and have experimented with dream incubation rituals that bring the ancient religious ritual into the modern, psychological arena. As we know, we utilize only a very small portion of our brains in our daily lives. Dream incubation is one method at our disposal to tap into some of the dormant mental power we all have.

It is critical, I believe, that dreamers approach dream incubation with sincerity, respect, and as full an awareness as possible of all the issues. Dreamers must be prepared for the possibility that the answer they receive may not be what they expect. It is critical that dreamers state in their intentions that they are seeking healing and a truthful response, not the truth as they think it is or fear it is.

If a dreamer is convinced that she experienced sexual abuse as a child and asks for a dream about how her father abused her, her psyche will not be compliant and will not produce such a dream if this sexual abuse did not happen. The dream that would result from such a loaded question would be bound to surprise the dreamer. A leading incubation question is not advised.

Instead, a therapist might help the client to look at the symptoms and reasons that led her to think she was sexually abused and help her to formulate a neutral incubation question based on her need to understand what factors contributed to the formation of the symptoms. Such a question might be, "What do I need to know at this time to further my healing?"

A neutral incubation question should reflect that the dreamer does not know what happened and is seeking to understand. Written exercises are especially helpful as a pre-sleep tool for preparing for the actual incubation. For example, the dreamer should write down the focused incubation question. Then, the dreamer should journal what he or she thinks and knows already about the topic. All sides of a given incubation topic should be thoroughly explored, including hopes and fears, to maintain as much neutrality as possible.

The psyche will not give information the dreamer is not ready to handle. The response to dream incubation is inevitably, in my experience, not necessarily what the dreamer wants to know but always what the dreamer needs to know.

All dreams, even fragments, from a given incubation night, relate to the incubation question. Two of the most common statements that I hear from people who have attempted dream incubation are "I dreamed, but the dreams didn't have anything to do with the incubation question" or "I had some dreams, but they were unimportant, so I didn't write them down." It takes work to understand the symbols in any dream. The dreams that seem so unimportant or unrelated to the incubation topic generally prove to be very significant.

When I help someone to incubate a dream, I tell them to make sure to write down any dreams, fragments, or thoughts occurring during the night, regardless of whether they seem related to the subject at hand. There will be plenty of time later to sort out the material that comes up. If nothing comes up on a given night, I encourage the dreamer to continue with the incubation on subsequent nights. Results are not always obtained on the first try; it is important to continue incubating on subsequent nights until a dream is remembered.

Since Mary was insistent, she was ready to explore memories of her childhood, I spoke with her about dream incubation. I knew her dreaming mind with all its wisdom would present her with what she needed to work with for her healing. I knew we could work safely with the dreamwork. I also knew trauma work could be dangerous at this stage. We talked about how to prepare and how to do the actual incubation itself.

All three of Mary's sisters had ongoing memories of being sexually abused by their father. They had never had amnesia for their abuse. This suggested a high likelihood that Mary had also been abused by her father, but it was also important to acknowledge the possibility that she was for some reason spared the fate of her sisters. Mary's family history on both the maternal and the paternal sides was rampant with alcoholism, suicide, depression, and incest. I knew that her dreams would tell her what she needed to know, though not necessarily what she wanted to know.

The results of Mary's dream incubation, and from a series of follow-up incubations, were quite interesting. No dreams emerged about sexual abuse. Instead, what came out in her dreams over a period of more than a month was the consistent message that she had a pervasive unconscious terror of looking at the traumatic material in her past. The dreams were fear dreams—fear of her falling apart, of her not being able to function, of her losing all that she valued. Over and over, the same messages emerged. At an unconscious level, the dreams made eminently clear that she feared she would completely fall apart or go crazy if she were to have a memory of sexual abuse.

Until this point in the therapy, Mary had greeted my discussions on the unconscious mind with a very skeptical stance. She had a very pragmatic view about the mind and its workings, which made it very difficult for her to understand how she could have amnesia for most of her childhood. But now, with these dreams that had emerged out of her incubations, she could connect in a more sustained way with her feelings. Mary slowly came to accept that this terror of knowing might truly be part of her psychological makeup. She began to understand defense mechanisms and why and how they develop. They are designed to protect the person from being overwhelmed. This acceptance was not won easily, and she struggled with negotiating this new frontier.

SECOND STAGE—REMEMBERING, MOURNING, INTEGRATING, RESOLVING

In the second stage, after stabilization, information may come through in various ways. Memory work should be done gradually by piecing together information from a variety of sources. The experience can be compared to how one can begin to see the picture in a jigsaw puzzle when more pieces are put in place.

Four of Nancy's siblings had always had memories of being sexually abused. Nancy did not have memories of being abused but came into therapy with strong suspicions she had been. She had a memory of what she identified as possibly the bottom of a round birdcage. The memory of that object carried an emotional charge she could not explain, nor could she place the object. Later in our work, after she experienced a graphic memory of her father abusing her in her sister's bedroom, she shared her memory with her sister. Her sister said she had had a birdcage hanging from the ceiling of that room. Nancy had no memory of this. It is possible she focused on the bottom of the birdcage while the abuse was happening to dissociate from the horror of what was happening. Focusing on an object in the room, or even on a ceiling tile, is very common as a means to dissociate from abuse. One of Nancy's siblings said she had always known their father had abused Nancy.

In mid-treatment, Nancy had a violent rape dream. In the dream, her father brutally raped her on the front lawn of her childhood home. She was struck by the brutality and the vividness of the dream. She had awakened terrified, unable to return to sleep, wondering if this was an actual memory. She also wondered if her dreaming mind had completely fabricated this awful thing.

Nancy came to believe the dream was not an actual memory but rather a symbolic condensation of the brutality and the violence inherent in the sexual abuse she came to believe she'd suffered. At the time Nancy had the nightmare, she had gathered enough information from abused family members and her own memory fragments that she believed her father had most likely abused her. She did not believe this nightmare was an actual recreation of a specific event that had happened. However, because the front yard was a public place where any passersby would have been able to see what was occurring, she wondered if being abused in the front yard might be a metaphor for her wondering how she could have been abused when she had so many siblings who might have seen.

Nancy had wondered how the abuse could have occurred when her mother and her siblings were home much of the time. She thought the dream could reflect the awful feelings of powerlessness and confusion she might have felt as a child being abused in the family home—no one seemed to see what seemed so obvious to her, nor did they help her.

Most dreams of sexual abuse are not direct recreations of the abuse. Rather, research has shown that dreams tend to reveal trauma in symbolic form, rather than as an actual replay. I will go into some of this research in some detail in a later chapter.

Means of access of memories include current symptoms, body memories, dreams and nightmares, flashbacks that may include visual and aural memories as well as smells and sensations, gentle probing of the past, and information from family members and from school and medical records.

Recent research on memory, some of which has been discussed earlier and some of which is discussed later in this chapter, explains much about the piecing-together process of memory retrieval. Our memories are of different types and are stored in different areas of the brain. Traumatic memory is often not remembered in a linear and sequential fashion, as is non-traumatic memory. The nature of the storage and retrieval process of traumatic memory is much more like putting together the pieces of a mystery, rather than "remembering" a distinct story with a beginning and end. The more of the available cues we utilize in memory work, the fuller and more accurate picture we are liable to obtain.

DREAM HELP IN UNDERSTANDING DEFENSES

The subject of sexual abuse came up repeatedly in the dream writings of Charlotte, a high-ranking government employee with whom I had worked for about a year. It was very frightening to her to contemplate the possibility she had been sexually abused. Despite these risks, she wanted to know the truth and said she was ready to handle it. She wanted me to hypnotize her to help her retrieve memories. I encouraged her instead to keep doing her work, saying she would gain access to material from her past as she became strong enough to remember.

The following week, she brought in a dream.

> I'm in college, in a male optometry student's bedroom. He tells me he will charge me $1000 to check my eyes.

> Then I'm on a school bus. The ground shakes, and the earth splits. Somehow, I realize it's a movie, and drive away.

> My brother's fiancé was murdered 4 days earlier. Somehow, it is now before her death, and I know this will happen. I'm sitting with her, with the terrible knowledge she will be killed. My dilemma is whether I should tell her. I feel numb and dazed, and wake up sad.

The symbol of the male optometry student's charging her so much to check her eyes reveals how costly Charlotte feared looking into her past, checking her eye ("I"), would be. Charlotte feared the knowledge would be earthshaking and ground splitting. Part of her realized this was a fearful projection and that she would be okay. She realized that her brother's fiancée represented herself and her feeling that if she learned about her past, a part of her would die with the illusions of her childhood and everything would change.

Charlotte asked me as we worked with the dream, "Do I want to know?" This was her first significant recognition of strong unconscious counter forces to her conscious desire to know. She feared if she remembered sexual abuse that she would not be able to tolerate the memory and that she would go crazy. This unconscious fear of going crazy was in direct contrast to her conscious wish to know what happened. Our work with a third dream revealed her fear that a history of being sexually abused would repulse her husband, who then, unable to tolerate it, would leave her. Again, this was in contrast to her conscious attitude, for he was supportive and loyal. Charlotte consciously believed he would stick by her no matter what she discovered.

As treatment went on, her dreams returned repeatedly to the issue of sexual abuse. There were times when she got very tired of looking at it and wondered if she was making it up. There were times when she decided that she had not been abused, and made a conscious effort to forget about it. This ambivalence, going back and forth on what one believes happened, is completely normal for this process.

My stance was to remain neutral and to let her come to her own conclusions. Gradually, as she worked the material, she realized depth and consistency to the material; it fit together with her symptoms and waking life. Memories gradually came through in her waking life. She had frequently questioned whether she was on the wrong track and if her dreams, body symptoms, and memory fragments were misleading her.

There was no one piece that provided the answer; rather, it was the entirety of the process and the internal consistency of what came up in all areas of her life, including her dreaming life, that led her to the conclusions she eventually drew. Charlotte's dreams were extremely helpful in facilitating and informing the process, and her associations to them led her to many fruitful areas of exploration.

A FEAR DREAM REVEALING DISSOCIATION

Tara, a middle-aged woman, began therapy with me, having been in therapy for most of her adult life. Tara was very intelligent and had an engaging personality. She was obese and reported ongoing problems with drug abuse. She said she used drugs to "disappear." She was married, with two children. She remembered her grandfather had sexually abused her, but she also had much amnesia for childhood. She appeared scattered (dissociated), and because of her history of possible abuse, I suggested we do the Dissociative Experiences Scale (DES), an easily done questionnaire that gives a general idea of the degree of dissociation a person experiences. It is not a diagnostic tool but rather an indicator.

Dissociation can be understood on a spectrum, from everyday experiences all the way to dissociative identity disorder. Many of us may identify with everyday types of dissociation where we forget where we left our keys or wallet or where we are absorbed in thought while driving and don't remember driving those last two blocks. These experiences are on the low side of the dissociative spectrum; on the higher end are experiences such as losing periods of time in one's current life, not remembering doing things people say one has done, having periods of amnesia for childhood and the present, and having different, separate personalities.

Tara's score on the DES was thirty-nine. Anything over thirty indicates a high degree of dissociation and warrants a deeper look, including ruling in or ruling out dissociative identity disorder. Tara spoke of her inner personalities and how she had conversations with them all the time. We talked about the possibility of her having a dissociative disorder. The thought of it frightened her, even though she freely spoke of the others inside. She tried to put away thoughts of the others. She succeeded in doing so temporarily, and then came the kickback: she began having intense cravings to use drugs. She resisted and came in with the following dream:

I'm with a black woman who is 20 years older than me. We know each other in the dream. She seems to be wise. We are walking to my apartment. When we arrive, I can tell the apartment has been broken into, and bad people are in there. I know it is very dangerous, and I will be killed and shredded if I go in there.

My female friend and I have a silent agreement: she goes in to meet her death, and I escape. She sacrifices herself for me. It is okay, her death is not something I feel guilt over.

Tara was puzzled by this nightmare. When we discussed it, she said it had been prearranged that the woman would go in, thus sacrificing herself. Tara's fate was to escape. Tara said the apartment reminded her of the apartment where she had been abused as a child. She thought the danger in the dream was about her fear of remembering more of her abuse. Though she too had the conscious stance of wanting to remember, some recent flashbacks had caught her off guard, and she had grown afraid. Her strong drug cravings coincided with her desire to forget.

The dream helped Tara understand how her memory had been split off. The older woman, who was silent in the dream, is a part of her that knows everything that went on in that apartment. That part of Tara carries the memory that Tara does not consciously have. The older woman's sacrifice of her life in the dream represents the splitting-off of Tara's consciousness into another part that would silently carry the memory. The splitting-off of consciousness was a defensive maneuver that automatically occurred so Tara would not be overwhelmed by the trauma.

BOUNDARIES AND INCEST

A sexually abused child grows up without a sense of intact body and relationship boundaries that a child growing up in a more functional family would have. In an incestuous relationship, the child's body is used for the adult's pleasure. Where a child would normally develop a sense of individual identity and intactness—"This is my body, and that is yours"—the child instead is subjected to, at seemingly random times, the adult exercising his or her right to invade and use the child's body. All boundaries and rights the child may feel entitled to are stripped away by the violating sexual act.

The child may be intimidated by force, bribery, or threats into complying with the adult need. A common threat to the child is that if he or she tells, no one will believe it. Another one is for the abuser to threaten the life of one or both of the child's parents if the child tells. These threats can be powerfully effective.

Jason was sent to his grandmother's house for babysitting every afternoon while his parents were at work. He had excellent parents, and his mom trusted her mother to take good care of Jason. Many years later, when he was twelve, Jason became severely anorexic and had to go into residential treatment. He began remembering and talking about the sexual abuse and violence he had suffered at the hands of his maternal uncle, who had also lived in his grandmother's house.

Once he had stabilized, integrated back into his life, and had some time under his belt in outpatient therapy, Jason was able to talk about how his uncle had repeatedly threatened to kill his parents if he ever told. To emphasize this point, one day when he was not pleased with Jason, the uncle started walking down the street, saying he had a gun in his pocket and that he was going to Jason's parents' house to kill them. This made a terrifying impression on the then-very-young boy: it must have taken everything he had inside to stay mum. He had behavioral problems for years while he kept the horrible secret. Jason's parents always wondered how they could not have known; little did they know how very loyal he was to them, believing that only if he kept the secret perfectly would they live. Being very intelligent, Jason was able to avoid showing them any signs they might recognize of sexual abuse.

Alternatively, the abuser may try to win the child with attention, affection, and gifts and may lie to the child that this is how adults and children "love" each other. The child learns, either by word or by action, that he or she has no right to say no.

The ramifications of this lesson are far-reaching for the sexually abused child who develops into adulthood. When a traumatic "lesson" is offered repeatedly, it burns itself into the impressionable developing young psyche. In this case, saying no becomes a non-option; resentful compliance with the wishes of others becomes the norm. This pattern continues into adulthood.

It is common for survivors of incest and other forms of sexual abuse to interact with others in relationships in adulthood in the same passive/helpless interactive pattern. The partner in one of these adulthood relationships may have no idea that the sexual-abuse survivor is feeling so intimidated by him or her. The partner may only see the agreeable side of the survivor, until one day the survivor explodes into anger and rage, accusing the partner of all kinds of selfishness, coercion, and intimidation. To the partner, this behavior will inevitably seem bewildering, out of proportion to a given situation, and completely out of the blue. Most likely the partner has been clueless about the resentment the sexual- abuse survivor has been storing up about decisions made, actions taken, and so on. The survivor has not yet learned how to step out of the learned helplessness and powerlessness into an empowered and self-assertive mode.

The initial stage of therapy with sexual-abuse survivors is to begin exploring these dysfunctional communication patterns. It is time to encourage the development of a sense of personal empowerment by learning to recognize one's needs, feelings, and reactions and then to express them in an emotionally modulated manner.

The survivor's needs in childhood were not taken into account. The childhood victim became acutely attuned to adult needs and learned to suppress his or her own before they could emerge far enough to be identified. Learning to identify these feelings and needs is also an essential part of the therapeutic process. I often ask, "How does this make you feel?" to trauma survivors, which is a common question for virtually any form of psychotherapy. Yet, very often with this population, especially in early stages of therapy, I can see genuine puzzlement on their faces. In dissociating from childhood trauma, they have dissociated from their feelings.

DREAMS INTRODUCING SPIRITUALITY

As Mary continued in treatment, she began to have dreams set in churches and with a number of spiritual elements. She had not had a strong religious or spiritual involvement until this point but now began her personal quest. She at one point dreamed of a marriage held in a church. As we worked with the dream, it seemed that this marriage was an integration of material from her unconscious and conscious minds, now that she was learning to negotiate between the two. Marriage dreams, which Carl Jung often discussed, signal a new unifying configuration in the psyche, as the dreamer learns to connect with the larger, unconscious self. Mary began a stronger involvement in her waking-life church. She also began meditating, exploring in a different way the relationship between her conscious, subconscious, and superconscious minds.

An important part of recovery for trauma victims often includes developing one's spirituality. This may or may not occur in a traditional church setting; many have been abused in church settings or have suffered religious abuse and may seek an alternative spiritual practice. What is essential is that the client is developing a trusting, stable relationship with God or one's higher power as he or she understands it. Prayer, journaling, dreamwork, meditation, artwork, women's circles, men's groups, spiritual retreats, and support groups are often an essential part of this reconnection process.

Dreams can lead the way in this developing spirituality: first by expressing the inner need for connection and then by showing the way or introducing spiritual feelings or figures. Often, numinous or spiritual dreams emerge that give the dreamer the sense of being loved and supported in the world of spirit.

The horror and the psychic and physical brutality of child sexual abuse is so traumatizing and so devastating to the child that he or she feels utterly bereft of any loving, protective, and supportive presence. This most certainly includes feeling deprived of protection and love from God (even if this is not something that the victim/survivor learns to identify for many years to come). It is often vital that this spiritual link, this sense of love and safety from a spiritual dimension, be established, so that the victim can tolerate the horror of remembering what happened in childhood. (I will speak in detail about dreams and spirituality in treatment in a later chapter.)

Just as the first stage of therapy for an incest or sexual abuse survivor is the establishment of trust and safety in the therapeutic relationship, an equally important part of recovery can be the establishment of trust and safety in the survivor's relationship with God. Twelve step recovery groups emphasize that working the steps is the key to recovery. A key element of working the steps is the active partnership and relationship with one's higher power, however one might conceive of it. The sense of deepening spiritual connection that often emerges through dreams may prompt trauma recovery victims to explore further their relationship with their faith during their waking hours. This can, in turn, provide a source of solace and strength during the painful recovery work and can imbue the present and the future with a sense of meaning and hope where the past seems desolate and senseless.

Mary gained a great deal of strength and solace from her growing sense of spiritual connectedness. She was growing stronger, and her core self was becoming more solid. Not long after this, she spontaneously experienced her first memory of sexual abuse. Other memories followed. Much of the memory retrieval came through spontaneous flashbacks, body memories, and dreams. We took our time in putting together the puzzle pieces, which came from a variety of different sources.

Even with our careful preparation, Mary's pain and grief at what she remembered was great. She became depressed, with lots of tears. Although she was initially quite opposed to medication, she found that she had to go on an antidepressant to remain functional in her daily life. Facing and grieving her past was harder than she could have ever anticipated.

The beauty of allowing the psyche to guide and inform the process of exploring abuse material, is that it has a timing and a pacing appropriate to the needs of the individual client. The pacing comes from within the client himself or herself and will not be hurried. The clinician, no matter how experienced and skilled, never knows what he or she is really dealing with when it comes to a client's amnesia for portions great or small of childhood.

Once Mary was stabilized, her dreams gently guided her to face her terror, before moving on to remember her forgotten childhood. She had been disinclined to believe me when I told her she needed to take her time. But since her own inner self also informed her, not just once, but a number of times, that she had a great deal of fear and terror inside that needed to be addressed, she gradually accepted this. Her dreams gave me a great deal of important information. It is, after all, the responsibility of the treating therapist to "determine if a given client has sufficient self-functioning to tolerate relatively quick progression to trauma-focused interventions, or whether she or he requires extended therapeutic attention to identity, boundary, and affect regulation before significant trauma work can be undertaken" (Briere 1996, 11).

Mary's psyche pointed her, through the dreamwork, to a new spirituality that respected the unseen presence within. Her new meditation practice helped her to attune to her higher self and to find comfort in the presence of God. Mary's developing faith in God gave her strength, support, and a resource to turn to for comfort when she did eventually begin remembering and when she began experiencing the anguished feelings from which she had dissociated at the time of the abuse.

I have condensed a great deal of material in the description of Mary's healing process. Her healing process was guided and informed by her dreams in a gradual, safe manner. As it was, Mary experienced a major depression as a result of coming face-to-face with her horrible childhood experiences. Often the depression is a necessary part of the confronting, grieving, and working-through process of childhood trauma and cannot be avoided. However, with ample preparatory work, and with emphasis on stabilization and building psychological and social coping tools, the depression and trauma work can be experienced in a context of safety and self-empowerment, as in Mary's case.

THIRD STAGE: CONSOLIDATING AND SEEKING CONNECTION AND PURPOSE

In this stage, many memories have been metabolized. The client has integrated his or her traumatic past into his or her life narrative and is looking for ways to become empowered. It is a time of seeking meaning and reconnection in the community. It may be a time of seeking and building new connections, relationships, and even work. Resilience is cultivated, as is a new identity of thriving rather than of being a victim. It is also a time for finding meaning and purpose.

Stella had been in therapy twice a week for a number of years to deal with her depression and her dissociative identity disorder. She had identified a total of fifty-six personalities, a number of them children. She worked hard in therapy. Her dreams were very useful to us, often giving us information. Though she, like many multiples, was leery and anxious about the idea of integration, a number of the personalities spontaneously merged with others as treatment proceeded. Stella's dreams sometimes had a number of cars on top of a roof, like on a rooftop parking garage. She believed that the number of cars, originally large, related to the number of alters (personalities) in her personality system. As she healed, the number of cars on the rooftop gradually decreased to six or seven. In a rather dramatic series of events, she spontaneously integrated the remaining known alters and became just one. It was a very happy day for her and for me. There were no more rooftop dreams.

The next chapter provides a more in-depth look at issues that come up during trauma treatment and general guidelines for understanding them. A client-centered approach is encouraged in sorting through difficult memory material.

Chapter 10

DREAMS, MEMORY, AND TRAUMA RECOVERY, PART 2

In this chapter, I will go into more detail about therapy with trauma clients and will further explore some delicate and complicated issues around dreams, memory, and trauma work. My aim is to provide a discussion, with illustrative examples, that will be of value both to clinicians and to anyone who is interested in learning more about dreams and sexual abuse. Persons in therapy may benefit from understanding some of the safety issues that come up in memory work and from knowing how to recognize questionable practices.

Many readers remember the highly publicized controversy in the 1990s about recovering memories, when it was reported some clinicians led their clients into "recovering" memories more fantasy than reality. In the wake of the recovered-memory controversy, guidelines and principles for treatment evolved that guide the clinician in a neutral, ethical stance in memory work. It was important that this happened. Poor psychotherapeutic practices such as the use of hypnosis to recover memories were brought to light during that time—these poor practices have been strongly discouraged with the newer guidelines. The treatment guideline focus is on the three stages of treatment and providing proper therapeutic support at each stage. I will discuss the now defunct False Memory Syndrome Foundation in more detail in Section V.

Michael Yapko, PhD, in his book *Suggestions of Abuse* and Dr. Elizabeth Loftus and Katherine Ketcham in their book, *The Myth of Repressed Memory: False Memories and Allegations of Sexual Abuse*, discuss a number of disconcerting examples where therapists have done harm through their "therapeutic" interventions. I will speak more about this in a later chapter.

Ongoing therapist education, consultation, and supervision are ways to ensure that the client is receiving the most balanced, quality treatment possible. There is no such thing as a therapist who does not make mistakes, and in this relatively new field of trauma-recovery work, we are all learning. Professional guidelines for responsible and ethical treatment have been developed. One of the best overall sourcebooks of responsible treatment guidelines is Christine Courtois's book *Recollections of Sexual Abuse: Therapeutic Principles and Guidelines.*

The therapy client is in a vulnerable position. Children who have been severely traumatized often grow up to be approval seekers, sometimes searching desperately for love at the hands of those who may in turn abuse them. This pattern of approval seeking will extend into the therapeutic relationship, as any relationship pattern of the client will eventually replicate itself, or attempt to replicate itself, within the therapeutic relationship. The balance of power within this therapeutic relationship is, almost by definition, unequal, with the therapist holding the greater balance of power. A skilled therapist will empower the client to trust his or her own inner feelings, intuitions, and thoughts, thereby correcting the pattern of learned helplessness that was instilled by traumatic early experiences.

Additionally, there is a mystery element to memory work that makes it compelling, much like the experience one has in reading an absorbing thriller or murder mystery. A skilled therapist will recognize this and keep this tendency to get caught up in the fascination accompanying the psychological work in check, for both therapist and client may be susceptible to getting caught up in their fantasies of what might have been. It is crucial to stay grounded in the present reality and to let unconscious material emerge in its own time. External confirmation should be sought wherever possible, in addition to the internal confirmation that may come up in the course of the treatment.

The client wants to "succeed" at therapy, and the therapist wants to help "heal" the client; either of these factors alone, and especially both of these working together, unrecognized, can lead to both client and therapist coming to premature conclusions. It is extremely important that the client feel completely free to bring in fantasy, dream, and unconscious material into the session, without fear of criticism or censure or of having it "explained away." Yet there must be a long sorting-out period, where the material is considered from the point of view that it might be a subjective reality or an objective reality or both.

When time and care are taken with recovery work, these questions naturally arise as part of the process. The client may go through periods of wanting to believe that what he or she has remembered is true, because it feels so overwhelmingly true and explains so much. The client will also go through periods of not wanting to believe what has come up because it is so horrible and he or she may have no conclusive "proof." The client may also be afraid it will destroy his or her family, or his or her relationship with his or her family. These stages may fluctuate and are natural. It is important for the therapist to make observations to the client on these patterns, rather than to become caught up in believing one side or the other.

CYCLES OF REMEMBERING AND CONSOLIDATION

Since remembering may be followed by denial and questioning, time and care must be taken to work through and integrate the material thoroughly before the client comes to a conclusion. It is extremely important to allow the client to go through these stages as many times as is necessary in order for the psychological healing to occur and for the various issues involved to be resolved.

Unfortunately, many people are not in a financial position where they can afford the luxury of the kind of long-term treatment that is necessary to thoroughly and competently treat the complex issues involved in sexual abuse. Many abuses and mistakes can be avoided in treatment by taking the necessary time to work thoroughly with the issues.

A woman who believed she might have been sexually abused as a child was struggling with conflicted feelings after visiting with her family. As an adult, she valued her relationship with her parents, despite its difficulties. She was afraid that if she found out she had been sexually abused as a child by her father, her relationship with her family would be destroyed. She had massive amnesia for childhood up until around age eleven.

At one point, she made a decision she had not been abused and said she no longer wished to deal with the possibility of abuse. It would have been unwise to try to talk her out of this, because she needed to be in charge of her own therapy. If this was a defensive maneuver, the material would continue to emerge.

This stage did not last long. In a creative writing exercise she spontaneously wrote a story about a little girl who was terrorized by a sexually abusive, alcoholic father. The story was, of course, not proof of anything. However, the strong emotional impact the story had on her forced her to reevaluate her denial and make room for a more neutral position.

A series of dreams around this time continued to have material suggestive she had been abused as a child. Where an erroneous or one-sided conscious stance is taken, the unconscious will find a way to bring into consciousness what needs to be addressed.

Tools such as dreamwork, exploring flashbacks and body symptoms and memories, memory work, and so on, can be extremely effective when used in a careful and competent manner. The material that comes through must be expressed fully, without judgment as to what it means. As treatment continues, there is a quest for objective knowledge to balance out what has come through subjectively. In the final stages of treatment, "the self and the inner voice of intuition are integrated with thoughtful analysis and objective knowledge" (Grand in Alpert 1996, 272).

Mary's memories emerged slowly and painfully. We worked carefully over several years, paying attention to what came through her inner knowing, as well as to the information she obtained from her siblings. Mary went through waves of denial and remembering, very slowly coming to her own conclusions that her father had sexually abused her as he had her three sisters.

Eventually, Mary felt ready to confront her father with what she had remembered. In an unusual instance of admission (perpetrators rarely admit what they have done), her elderly father acknowledged that he had abused her. He also apologized to her.

The admission and the apology did not make the horror of what Mary had undergone any easier for her to bear, yet she felt some satisfaction that he took responsibility for his behavior. Few victims of sexual abuse ever get even this much from their perpetrators.

Since memory work is a difficult, murky, and often uncertain process, no matter how much care and caution has been taken, questions as to the veracity of the recalled memory frequently linger in the client's mind. Just before her confrontation with her father, Mary now had a better understanding of the oceans of tears she had cried over the years. Her father's admission validated to her that her memory and her pain were real. Whatever doubts she'd had until this point were now gone, and she could move ahead in her healing process. If her father had denied wrongdoing, Mary could have been thrown into a tailspin of doubt.

Confirmation of memory can come from any one of a number of sources, including from the abuser, from a sibling who was aware of what had gone on and who might have been abused as well, from a relative who had awareness of what had gone on, or from medical records. Confirmation has occurred often enough in my practice that I have come to trust the process of memory reconstruction as well as to respect the potential for abuse of this process.

One woman, who had experienced memory work with several therapists, reported there was a very strong difference between exploring a memory that she later thought to be real and trying to "force" a memory. She reported that there was a forced and false quality when she felt led in memory work, rather than being allowed to go with her own imagery. For her, the distinction was clear. A client without experience in memory work, who starts with a clinician who tends to lead or suggest, may never have a chance to develop his or her own sense of what feels true and what does not and can be extremely vulnerable to suggestion.

CLIENT EMPOWERMENT

If a client states that any piece of work does not feel right or comfortable, this feeling must be respected. If the client wishes to stop, it is time to stop. A therapist cannot know the truth of a client's experience. We are not omnipotent or all-knowing. Our job, and our ethical imperative, is to help our clients explore their own truths, not what we think their truths are.

It is extremely important to give the client as much control and empowerment during trauma work as possible Trauma work can be extremely painful, and clients have a natural tendency to want to stop when the pain becomes too great. The client should always know that stopping is an option. If we have a tool to offer that the client does not wish to use, it is incumbent upon us to respect that decision.

EMOTIONS COMING THROUGH

Sometimes the powerful emotion that comes through, seemingly out of nowhere, can be a possible indicator of the veracity of the memory. The emotion that was blocked internally at the time of the original trauma may come to the surface during trauma work. In the actual traumatic situation, a display of emotion may have been prohibited for any one of a number of reasons, and/or the client may have found he or she could endure the situation only by stepping out of himself or herself, or dissociating.

In the safety of the therapeutic situation, the helplessness, terror, and pain of the original traumatic event can be experienced. The client's unconscious fear that he or she could not tolerate the pain has kept the emotions frozen these many years. The client has been hostage to these feelings and has used many methods of control to keep them from reemerging, to keep him or her from feeling the pain.

(During the height of the false memory controversy, taped regressions were aired on public television where clients were led and egged on into demonstrations and outpourings of intense affect. These emotions were then cited as proof of abuse. Such leading is a dangerous and unethical therapeutic technique. The lack of affect that accompanies leading is distinct from the affect that accompanies spontaneous recall. The client should make a decision on the veracity of memory based on a combination of factors, over time, as detailed in this narrative, not on emotion alone.)

Common defense mechanisms that are used to avoid those painful feelings include overeating, alcohol and drug problems, sexual promiscuity or sexual avoidance, controlling behaviors in interpersonal situations, and self-mutilation. These behaviors can be caused by factors other than sexual abuse and are in and of themselves not diagnostic of a history of sexual abuse.

By reintegrating previously dissociated traumatic experiences and feelings, the adult client can gradually gain a sense of his or her own ability to tolerate the reality of his or her past without needing to seek an escape. The child's psyche was too fragile and too vulnerable to experience the full emotional impact of what had happened to him or her. The adult, in the relative safety of the therapeutic room, may still be terrified of the overwhelming affect, but may gradually be able to face the trauma and experience the dissociated emotion.

MEMORY ISSUES

Lenore Terr, MD, wrote *Unchained Memories*, a book describing court cases she has worked on involving memory issues and sexual abuse. She is a well-known memory expert who has testified as an expert witness in numerous cases involving memory that has reemerged. In her book, she describes a case in which she felt that a child's tale of sexual abuse was false. She concluded that the child's accusations of sexual abuse against a doctor were less a lie than "an unconscious restitutive attempt" on the child's part to win her mother's full attention. There were many other contributing factors, but the mother in this case was already suspicious of the doctor. The mother interviewed the daughter on her own, without guidelines as to how to question without excessive leading. The child exhibited no symptoms specific to child sexual abuse, according to Dr. Terr. Additionally, she had little knowledge of those sexual details that she would have had very specific knowledge of had she witnessed these acts or had them performed on her.

Children who have been sexually abused have very specific and highly precocious knowledge about sexual activities that does not correspond to anything that they would know about at their early age. This knowledge often is acted out in sex play. One mother, whose two young boys had been sexually abused, reported regular explicit sexual play (reenactments of the abuse) that involved highly specific details and sexual knowledge far beyond that which one would expect in preschool boys.

Dr. Terr puts forth some guidelines in her book about differentiating between a false and a true memory. Whereas she is talking in the following about children, the same is true for adults who have recovered childhood memories.

> One way to determine whether someone's memory is false is to look for symptoms or signs that correspond to the remembrance. If a child is exposed to a shocking, frightening, painful, or over exciting event, he or she will exhibit psychological signs of having had the experience. The child will reenact aspects of the terrible episode, and may complain of physical sensations similar to those originally felt. The child will fear a repetition of the episode, and will often feel generally and unduly pessimistic about the future.

> If, on the other hand, a child is exposed only to a frightening rumor of the symptoms of another victim of trauma, the child may pick up a symptom or two, and even, perhaps, the whole "story"—but will not suffer a cluster of symptoms and signs … A horrifying tale alone does not cause the mind to malfunction. Even if the most adept of brainwashers inserts the tale, the child will exhibit no symptoms to go along with the "memory." (Terr 1994, 161–62)

When memory begins to reemerge into consciousness, whether in a flashback, body memory, memory work in therapy, or in a dream, the face of the abuser is often obscured, even though many other details of size, coloring, clothing, and so on, may be clear. Perhaps this protects the victim, who is being retraumatized by remembering the abuse, from being completely overwhelmed by seeing the identity of the parent or relative (for whom the victim may still feel much love) as the horrible betrayer. Sometimes persons in the process of recall have a very strong sense of the identity of the abuser even without the facial cues, by how the abuser "feels," smells, acts, looks, and so on, in the memory. This is yet another point where identity can be confused, and where false accusations can be made, if the work is not carefully done. I will describe a case to illustrate this point.

WHEN MEMORY REMAINS VAGUE: TOM

Tom came in for treatment because of problems around intimacy and closeness with his live-in male lover. He also suffered from sexual addiction. His mother had been severely alcoholic when he was growing up. She was often passed out, drunk, or otherwise dysfunctional. He and his siblings had to fend on their own most of the time. The father's job entailed a great deal of travel, and he was often gone for most of the workweek.

Tom remembered having to fix his own meals at a very young age and feeling very scared and abandoned in his chaotic family situation. After we had been working together for a while, and after his living situation and mood had stabilized somewhat, he began having a memory of being in the shower, as a young boy of about six or seven, with a man whose face he could not clearly see.

Over time, several memories emerged of Tom's having been sexually abused. One of these incidents began with an image in the shower and continued with Tom being forced to sodomize an older man. The face of the man did not emerge, which is often the case in remembrances of abuse. By putting various clues together, including the man's size, the location of the shower in Tom's home, and several sensory clues, Tom surmised that the man might have been his father. There were many other puzzle pieces to investigate, however, and many other questions about other people who had been around him.

Tom puzzled over memories of always sleeping at night with his hands folded over his genitals, as if in protection. He also remembered finding semen stains in the morning that, from their location on the bed coverings, did not seem to be his from a wet dream.

By the time Tom had the shower memory, he had already done a great deal of grieving about his childhood. He had many angry feelings toward both of his parents, as he felt that neither of them had been available to him, emotionally or physically, during his childhood. Tom had a number of specific and general symptoms that are often seen in survivors of childhood sexual abuse. These included flashbacks and body memories, involvement in inappropriate sexual relationships at a very young age, terror of intimacy and numerous control patterns to avoid intimacy, sexual addiction, major depression when beginning to process the sexual-abuse material, and large blocks of childhood amnesia. The material he remembered was consistent with his symptoms of trauma. Nothing that came up, whether in therapy sessions or outside of them, contradicted his emerging thoughts that he had been sexually abused. Tom began attending a group for survivors of childhood sexual abuse and did a great deal of reading and processing work on his own. After a while, the focus of his questioning changed from "Was I sexually abused?" to "Who sexually abused me?"

In one session, Tom relived the shower memory mentioned before, in its entirety. He expressed a great deal of grief and agony, in a very emotional abreaction. As is common with such sessions, where previously dissociated feelings are now experienced fully, he was overwhelmed by the intensity of the affect that now flooded through him. His sense of betrayal and violation was immense. Tom's feelings of vulnerability, helplessness, self-blame, and worthlessness were profound. He also felt enraged. A clear visual picture still did not emerge of the man who had abused him in the shower, but he still believed that the man who had abused him was most likely his father. He was sure that the abuser was an older person, that it was someone whom he'd perceived as being in authority, and that he'd felt very helpless and powerless to refuse to do what had been asked of him.

Tom discussed the issue of sexual abuse with several of his siblings. None of them had any memories of having been abused or remembered any circumstances that had led them to believe that one of their siblings had been abused. This kind of external investigation is important because helpful details can sometimes be gathered. Sometimes a sibling can give information for a given time period that can help the client to put some pieces together. In this case, nothing came up, which neither confirmed nor denied the possibility of Tom having been abused but did add to his uncertainty.

Tom did a great deal of work on his sexual abuse. He grieved the loss of his mother to alcoholism, the loss of his father to a job that kept him away from home, and the loss of the basic sense of security and trust he'd never had. He grieved over the sexual abuse and over the daily abandonment he'd experienced on many levels.

At one point in his work, Tom decided he wanted to bring his father into therapy with him, to discuss the many issues he had been processing, including the sexual-abuse issue. On the one hand, Tom wanted a relationship with his father, the relationship that he had never had. On the other hand, he was furious and felt enormously betrayed even in the possibility that his father had sexually abused him. He felt the need to discuss his feelings with his father. It took some negotiating, but Tom's father, who lived in another state, agreed to come into the area to meet with us.

There were many tricky issues to negotiate in setting up this meeting. It was very important for Tom and me to discuss his goals for the sessions, his fantasies of outcomes, and what he could realistically expect. An attack on his father clearly would not work or be desirable. An atmosphere would have to be created where his father could feel objectivity on my part. I warned Tom about the neutral stance I would have to take in order to facilitate the work. We discussed how this might be hard on him, especially since it was so critical that as much objectivity be put into the sessions as possible so that maximum results could be obtained. I had many reservations about this meeting, but he wanted to move forward with it.

At every step of the way in abuse work, the therapist must be very careful of his or her own (counter transferential) responses to the material. It is easy to empathize with a client's pain and trauma and to get caught up in "rescue" mode in which the therapist tries to make up for the original losses by being super therapist and rescuer.

Tom knew that part of him wanted me to be able to "fix" his pain. A previous therapist had spent time outside therapy with Tom as a "friend," and Tom had initially hoped I would do the same thing. We were able to discuss this when it came up and work through it, so that his frustration and anger at what I could not do did not build.

As the sessions with Tom and his father approached, I had a set of my own feelings to work through and keep in check, especially as the father was a possible abuse perpetrator. Since Tom's father lived out of the area and there was no other forum in which to do the work, I had some serious soul-searching to do regarding whether I felt I could manage and detach from my own feelings sufficiently in order to maintain objectivity. I decided I could, especially given the lack of evidence pointing to the abuser being the father.

We also discussed the likelihood that, regardless of what may have happened, Tom's dad would deny that he had perpetrated any sexual abuse against Tom. Even a survivor who has never lost his or her memories of being abused and by whom can be thrown into a tailspin and regression by the power of the denial system. We spent some time working on this issue and prepared our general agenda for the meetings. There were many things that Tom wanted to discuss. We would begin gently, discussing general situations and memories of childhood, and wait until the second meeting to discuss the possibility of sexual abuse by Tom's father.

It could not have been easy for Tom's father to come into this setting, where his son already had an established relationship with the therapist. I thought he was very brave to come to the sessions, as he would be at an emotional disadvantage. He stated he wanted to build a better relationship with his son. Because of the built-in limitations of the situation, we had to find a way to make it work. I immediately addressed this issue with Tom's father when he came in and reassured him that these meetings were designed to discover information and allow both to learn more about each other. I let him know that the tougher part would be the next meeting but that this first meeting would be about information sharing.

Fortunately, the first meeting came together well. Both Tom and his father seemed to learn a great deal about each other that first night. They also seemed to leave with a much greater appreciation of what the other had gone through. Tom was able to talk about his feelings of abandonment at his father's absences and his mother's alcoholism. Tom's father spoke of his deep regret that he'd had to travel so much in his job and how responsible he'd felt to provide well for his wife and five children, despite the hardships they all had been under. His marriage had been a miserable one, but he'd felt he needed to stay married until the children were old enough to fend more on their own. Perhaps for the first time in Tom's eyes, his father assumed more-human proportions as a flawed, unhappy man who had functioned as a single parent. His father acknowledged how deeply troubling it had been for Tom to grow up in this home and said he'd wished he could have done more to help the situation. The love between them was palpable in the room. This discussion helped build an understanding and a bond that had not been there before and prepared a foundation for the much more difficult discussion that was to follow the next day.

When Tom discussed the event in the shower the next day, his father remained attentive, engaged, and nonjudgmental. He did not get defensive, and he seemed guileless. It is doubtful anything could have prepared him for what Tom said to him. When Tom said that he thought that the man in the shower might be his father, his father listened carefully and waited until Tom was through before he responded. He said simply that he had never been involved in this manner with Tom. He asked appropriate questions, such as whether Tom was sure of the abuser's identity.

Tom admitted that he had never had a visual memory of the face of his abuser but that he had put together other pieces and guessed that it might have been his father who had abused him. They discussed this for a while. His father listened carefully to what Tom had to say before he said emphatically but not defensively that he had not abused his son. The father's lack of defensiveness, his seeming certainty, and his willingness to engage in an exploration of the details were all noteworthy. Tom conceded that he could very well be wrong about the identity of the abuser but not about the abuse. Tom's father was appropriately concerned about the abuse and admitted it could have easily happened with his many absences and the dysfunction in the family, but he was adamant that he was not involved.

Tom later said he believed his father. It was up to Tom to decide; he made the decision to believe his father and to move on. If more information came up later on, he would reconsider, but for now he would let it go as an issue between him and his father. He and his father have since developed a much-better relationship, though it is not as close as Tom would like.

The value of the dialogue between the two of them speaks for itself. In many cases, it might not work or even be advisable. In this case, I learned a very valuable lesson about the importance of proceeding extremely carefully and not taking anything for granted in recovering pieces of memory. The event Tom remembered may well have been accurate (though we will never know for sure); his sexual addiction and acting out certainly suggested a deeper problem.

The work is complicated: the most important thing is to stay open to discovering whatever the truth is. It is a human tendency to like certainty, and it is tempting to hold on to an idea once we have formulated it. However, it is important to stay open to discovering the next level of truth and not have to be right.

Supervision, both formal and peer, is a useful tool for sifting through difficult therapeutic challenges. Additionally, I personally find prayer work and meditation very helpful in this regard. It helps keep me honest and guided by the highest motivations, as well as open to any higher guidance that might lead me to consider other options.

The case I will discuss in the next chapter is one that challenged all my belief systems as a relatively young clinician. It is a type of case many clinicians and their clients have been forced to confront. The issues I have been discussing come into play, as well as other, more complicated issues. This type of case came up often during the height of the false memory controversy—and still does, in increasingly greater numbers—and polarized people on both sides of the issue. Looking at this example will shed light on the attempt to find a balanced and neutral perspective even in the midst of emergent bizarre and controversial material and will also introduce the reader to some of the many issues that arise with ritual abuse.

SECTION IV

A DEEPER LOOK

CHAPTER 11

A DIFFERENT ORDER OF MEMORIES

In this chapter and chapter 14, I will discuss the healing process of a very brave and determined woman, Susan. (Susan's story is a composite story utilizing material from a number of clients who presented with similar issues.) When I first began seeing this kind of material in the early 1990s, there was nothing in the literature or my training to prepare me for it. However, my training and instincts imbued in me cautious guidelines for clinical work. All I knew was to do the clinical work carefully, without trying to figure out where it was going.

The type of satanic abuse material that emerged was controversial during the false memory controversy. Over the years since, I have worked with many clients who have many memories of ritual abuse. All are dissociative, with much trauma and memory loss; most have dissociative identity disorder (DID, formerly called multiple personality disorder, or Unspecified Dissociative Disorder. Their stories are often eerily similar.

Experienced clinicians will recognize the types of material that emerged in this composite case story. Most of it is fairly typical of what is seen in dealing with emerging memories of the imagery, rituals, and experiences involved with ritual abuse (RA). Some will recognize the patterns also associated with cult mind control programming, of which RA is often an essential part. There are a number of books on treatment of trauma and dissociative disorders, on ritual abuse, and on mind control, some of which are mentioned in this book and included in the references list at the end.

My aim in writing this book is not to replicate the material so carefully produced by other authors. What I have to uniquely offer is an understanding of how to work with the many dreams that will inevitably come up in the course of working with ritual abuse material. I focus in some depth on the powerful role dreamwork can have in dealing with this kind of material when done in a client-centered manner.

Another unique piece I can offer to the puzzle is how my earlier conversations with my father about CIA abuses and programs informed what I encountered in the workplace more than thirty years later. These conversations and the knowledge imparted to me helped me be more tuned in to this possibility of mind control than other clinicians.

For the current discussion, I deliberately chose a story that ended mid-treatment, with all the ambiguity that naturally occurs while the material is being processed. I wanted the focus to be on careful, ethical clinical work in dealing with controversial and challenging material, rather than on the end result. This is in part to show a more general audience how this material can and does emerge without therapist leading and that it can be handled professionally and carefully.

The False Memory Foundation, created in the 1990s and disbanded in 2019, falsely gave the public the impression that there is no such thing as amnesia for sexual abuse and other forms of trauma.

Nothing could be further from the truth. As early as the early 1900s, there was a lot of interest in multiple personality disorder and an understanding that the traumas that created the disorder were known only to some of the personalities, with others not having access to material hidden behind amnesic barriers. Experiments in mind control were being done in the United States, Germany, England, and elsewhere, using hypnosis to create amnesic barriers behind which lay personalities willing to take actions that were against the moral and ethical code of the person being hypnotized. The hypnosis could also include suggestions that the hypnotized person executes the implanted command and afterward have absolutely no memory traces of either the hypnosis or the action(s). Amnesia and memory issues will be discussed in some detail in chapter 14 and in Section V.

In presenting this material, I advocate a stance that empowers the client in following his or her own truth and that keeps the therapist as a guide to the client's own material rather than as an authority. I will weave several threads into this discussion of issues that come up as the treatment progresses.

The overall therapeutic focus in trauma and memory work is on the client's healing and not on whether what emerges is true. *The measure used for treatment outcomes is the client's improved functioning,* not whether the client is certain of what happened to him or her as a child. Memory work can be very confusing. The dreams in this case gave a great deal of information, the processing of which helped Susan to get better. Whether the dream material represents actual occurrences is something only Susan could determine. Nonetheless, the material was in her unconscious and, for whatever reason, had to come out into the light of day to be digested and metabolized in order for Susan to improve.

What I aim to demonstrate through abundant examples is how dreams and dreamwork can be interwoven into the therapeutic process. Dreams are one of the most valuable, informative, and least understood parts of working with trauma.

Susan came in for her initial therapy appointment at a point in her life when her frequent panic attacks and migraines had become unbearable to her. She was very intelligent and successful in her chosen profession. She was thirty-eight years old and married with three children. Her marital relationship at the time she entered therapy was distant, with some verbal abuse directed toward her. She did not know how to address the verbal abuse. Her life, however, was stable, and although she had coped with her symptoms for many years, she now felt she could tolerate them no longer.

Susan described her history of panic attacks, which occurred sometimes as often as three to four times per day. She did not drink. Her panic attacks seemed related to specific situations, such as feeling suddenly trapped and unable to escape. This could be in bed or in a line. Her daily life was dominated by fear she would have a panic attack. Additionally, her migraines seemed to come out of nowhere and were disabling when she had them.

Susan said she derived no real enjoyment out of life. She reported her symptoms had begun shortly after her mother's sudden death when she was in middle school. Susan experienced the loss as a double loss because after her mother died, her father started drinking more heavily and became depressed and emotionally inaccessible. Tears or mourning were not allowed or tolerated; there was a very stoic attitude toward bearing one's emotions in silence. Susan felt that because of this sudden double trauma, which she had never been able to work through, that she kept everyone at a distance, including her children. Her abandonment anxiety was quite high.

After evaluating Susan, I told her I thought she suffered from depression. This surprised her because no one had previously mentioned this. She wore a very convincing facade that kept those in her life from guessing the depth of her anxiety and sadness. She agreed with me.

As treatment continued, her symptoms began to worsen. At times, she reported that she felt she was having a "nervous breakdown." For the first time, she had been seen for who she was inside rather than for the facade she presented. This allowed her to begin to connect with her true feelings. She stopped pretending to be happy and became aware of how deeply sad she was. People also began to comment on how sad she seemed. As is common when beginning to deal with severe trauma, her depression now threatened her ability to function.

I referred Susan to a psychiatrist who put her on an antidepressant and gave her Xanax to take when she felt a panic attack coming on. Her symptoms began improving by the end of a month. She now had increasingly more energy available to deal with the difficult issues coming up in her therapy. The antidepressant could not take the pain away, but it could stabilize her mood sufficiently so she could begin work on the issues.

The metaphor of a physical wound that has developed an infection aptly describes the festering of early traumatic experiences in the psyche. That wound must be cleaned out in order for it to heal, which can be a very painful experience. Once the wound is cleaned, it can heal, and the threat of infection compromising the entire system is taken away.

WHEN THERAPISTS HAVE DIFFICULTY ALLOWING THEIR CLIENTS' PAIN

A therapist must be able to tolerate great discomfort. Although it is rewarding to see a severely depressed patient get better, these rewards come slowly. Some therapists choose to stick with short-term work and techniques because they need to be able to fix their clients' pain. Such therapists can put subtle pressure on their clients to perform. Because trauma victims have been forced to comply and develop highly attuned antennae for what others want of them, the last thing such a client needs is to feel pressure to pretend to be feeling better because the therapist has an unconscious need to be the magician who can relieve the client's pain.

I once supervised a highly skilled short-term therapist who had learned an impressive range of short-term therapeutic techniques over the years. Unfortunately, she had little skill in allowing her clients the time and space to work through their pain in their own way and in their own time. It was as if she had a need not only to "fix" them (in her way, missing their signals) but also to bypass their pain. As we worked together and repeatedly met with this dynamic in supervision, it emerged she had been repeatedly sexually abused during her childhood.

She talked with me about her fear of facing her past. She feared, as do many abuse victims, that if she faced her past, she would be overcome by the feelings that emerged. Given her personal fears, it was little wonder she could not tolerate deep pain in her clients. Instead, in avoiding her own pain, she tried to "fix" their pain with tools she had learned. Instead of allowing her clients to feel, express, or otherwise process their feelings, her tendency was to immediately offer a tool to change the feeling, thus colluding with the clients' tendencies to avoid facing that which lay inside the self.

Over time, this therapist painfully learned she could not "fix" people's pain, especially if she were unconsciously invested in avoiding it because she could not allow herself to process her own depths. Sometimes the greatest gift she could give her clients was to be present to their pain. At other times, the appropriate use of these short-term tools helped to resolve traumatic memory and expedite a client's healing process.

THE THERAPIST AS "CONTAINER"

Clients need to know their therapists can be "containers" for them when they are experiencing these frightening emotions. Therapists have to be comfortable enough with others' pain to withstand the extremes of feeling that are produced by recall of horrendous episodes of trauma, betrayal, and abuse. In this way, a client can feel that it is safe to experience these feelings, because the therapist is there, providing the safety net and emotional container as the client goes through the experience. (It is axiomatic in depth psychology that unless we are able to allow ourselves to experience the depths of our human pain and agony, we will not be able to experience the heights of joy.) The feelings that can get stirred up in the therapist (countertransference) and the secondary, vicarious traumatization can have a profound effect and are discussed later in this book.

Through all the years I have been in private practice, I have had on the wall behind my chair a painting of a Native American female potter with long black hair. She is surrounded by beautiful pottery she has made. She is working on one particularly beautiful large pot with beautiful symbols and designs painted on it.

When I am explaining to new trauma clients the process of therapy, I talk about how the first stage for us will be in building the "container"—that is, we are building a foundation of trust and safety that will, like the pot, be strong and large enough to contain even the most powerful emotions and memories we will be working with in the times to come. To me, this visual helps explain to a client the importance of our building a strong, trusting alliance for the work ahead.

BEGINNING TO REMEMBER

After Susan was in therapy for six months, she and her brother, also in therapy with another therapist, began remembering some physical abuse from their childhood. Details were sparse, but it became apparent that there had been significant problems. Susan became more aware of the verbal abuse from her husband and of her pattern of allowing it by not challenging her. We worked in therapy on ways for Susan to tell her spouse she disliked it when she talked to her in this manner. Susan's wife responded well to Susan's assertiveness, and the verbal abuse tapered off significantly.

Susan became more aware of how much she disliked her job and how drained she felt at work and home by her children's needs. The panic attacks were now happening less often, and she had more time and energy available to focus on how she felt about what was going on in her life. After nine months in treatment, she remembered more instances of physical abuse from childhood.

Susan was a prodigious reader. Unbeknownst to me, she was reading about sexual abuse and wondering if her amnesia was related. Susan brought up her concerns about a possible history of sexual abuse. (In the beginning of treatment, I asked her if she had been sexually abused as a child. She thought not, remembering only some occasions of physical abuse, which we discussed.)

Now that Susan was bringing up this material, I encouraged her to approach this with an open mind. If she had been sexually abused, this material would come up in its own time. We went over her sexual history, which revealed two significant details: (1) although her sexual life seemed normal in most respects, she felt panicky when she felt pinned down or trapped, and (2) she did not recall any pain or bleeding during her first experience with sex. This second detail may or may not have been significant, as some women do not experience unusual pain or bleeding during their first sexual experience. On the other hand, the absence of a hymen during the first adult sexual experience can be a supporting sign of childhood abuse.

As she looked at her symptoms, including the depression, she realized they served to keep her apart from people. For example, all her available energy was directed at keeping control over her panic attacks when in public. Her symptoms did indeed serve the secondary purpose of keeping her safe from people, or from intimacy, for her symptoms never allowed her the freedom to get really close to anyone. She was close with one brother, the only person she really shared with.

Nine months after she began treatment, Susan reported her first dream:

> I'm in my childhood bed. Someone is doing oral sex on me. Perhaps it is my mother. I'm in middle school.

Susan also reported her brother had similar dreams and waking imagery. Susan's brother did not tell anyone about this for a very long time, because of the shame he felt about the imagery.

Susan had no memories of anything like this happening and did not know what to make of the dream. It was understandably very disorienting and upsetting to have a dream like this, seemingly out of nowhere. Her feelings, both during the dream and in the waking state, reflecting on the dream, were unpleasant. Within Susan's dream, she had a feeling of this being very wrong. This feeling was consistent with how she felt about the dream after she awoke. She experienced a great deal of shame as she thought about the dream.

Susan told me that she knew she had to tell me this dream, even though she did not want to, because she realized she had to be completely open about what came up if she wanted to get well. She also said she felt anger toward me because she knew she had to tell me these things and because a big part of her preferred to keep them to herself.

It was premature at this point to come to any conclusions about what the dream meant. The aftermath was very difficult for Susan. She was having a very difficult time. She anguished and slept poorly. Within a very short time, Susan reported another dream:

> I'm lying down, and it is nighttime. People are surrounding me. Everything feels wrong. I lie motionless and keep saying 'no, no, no.' All attention is focused on my genital area. There is an attempt to penetrate me with something. It hurts. Someone notices that I am bleeding, and gives me a cloth to stop it. I don't want to be there. I feel alone and afraid. The people around me are cold and dark and scary.

Susan thought that she was around thirteen years old in the dream. She stated that the object inserted into her vagina was not a penis, but she did not know what it could have been. Susan remembered nothing about her home life during this time. She could not even remember where she'd gone to school for at least one of these years or what some of her schoolteachers had looked like. She did not know what to make of this dream but was startled by its graphic nature. This dream was extremely puzzling to her.

Susan noted that these two very troubling dreams had emerged in October. I asked her if anything had happened in October that might account for depression she experienced annually during that month. She came up with nothing. (Often anniversary reactions to traumatic events recur around the time of year of the initial trauma—even years later—often without the person who experiences these reactions being aware of why he or she is so upset.)

When Susan returned for the next session, she said she had been doing a great deal of thinking about the dream over the past week. She could not explain why, but her intuition told her the dream related to a rape and an abortion. She had seemed to be the "subject" in the dream.

Susan talked with her father about the dream. Susan asked him if he might have witnessed a similar scene, but he said he could not think of anything. Susan expressed her general frustration at attempts to find out about events from her childhood from her father. Susan's mom had been an alcoholic, and her dad had been a heavy drinker. Oddly, Susan's father had told her at one point that he had no memories of the years he had spent with her mother. Susan could not fathom this, for her mother and her father had been married for almost twenty years and had raised four children. How could her father not remember anything about these years? She wondered if this could possibly be true and, if so, what could have caused this. Susan and I discussed the effects of alcohol in destroying memory as a possible cause of some of the memory loss. However, the memory loss was extreme, especially given that her father had held a responsible job for many years. Her father's massive amnesia was one more unanswered question in a rapidly expanding list.

Since she had begun having these dreams, Susan was now having frequent panic attacks and migraines again. She also had experienced some hypnagogic imagery as she was falling asleep that greatly disturbed and puzzled her. In this imagery, there were alternating images of her mother and of her older brother. Both looked, as Susan described it, evil and wicked. She could relate to having felt abandoned by both of them and to having felt not accepted or cared for by both of them—but she did not understand the connotations of evil. Maybe it meant she was very angry at them? She was being very careful to try to understand the symbols as metaphors rather than as literally true.

Because of Susan's increased panic attacks, high anxiety, and difficulty sleeping, we upped therapy from once to twice weekly. At this stage, things may seem worse—as if they will never get any better. The commitment to healing is a commitment to becoming conscious, a slow and painful process. Susan was a very strong person, dedicated to this process. Despite her fears, she had an intuitive trust of the psyche and its processes.

She wanted to be able to talk with her family members about the very confusing material surfacing in her mind. However, they discouraged her, saying she was on the wrong track. This is very common. A family member or loved one may look at the information and dismiss it out of hand as preposterous, especially when the face that the client had previously presented had seemed so "normal." Encountering the denial of loved ones can be very upsetting, even to the point of causing setbacks in recovery.

This juncture in reality testing with loved ones who may be in denial can serve as an important opening in the therapeutic dialogue to explore what is happening. The client's concerns need to be explored, not minimized. Information about treatment stages, especially in cases of possible childhood abuse, can be reiterated in a manner that respects the client's concerns. This kind of dialogue can strengthen the therapeutic relationship between the client and therapist.

Susan's previous apparent "normalcy" to the outside world had been maintained at excruciating cost. The panic attacks had kept her mentally and emotionally preoccupied. Yet, to her partner, children, and coworkers, she had been a well-adjusted woman. She had been expert at keeping the magnitude of her suffering from others. The symptoms had served to keep the lid on her unconscious material, and now that she was more stable, the lid was off. The material that had been previously suppressed had begun to emerge, and her symptoms reappeared.

Many books can help loved ones to understand the therapeutic process and to know what to expect and how to help. Laura Davis's *Allies in Healing* and Ken Graber's *Ghosts in the Bedroom: A Guide for Partners of Incest Survivors* have been out for a while and are good. Also effective, especially if the loved one is not in therapy, is to invite the loved one into a session to describe and educate about the healing process, why it is occurring, what to expect, and how to help.

Susan decided to stop discussing the details with her partner, who reacted poorly to her disclosures. This is unfortunately quite common. She decided to ask for support only when she thought her partner could offer it to her. She assessed her husband was better at giving more tangible forms of support than in understanding complicated emotions and psychological processes. She did not think bringing him into a session would help.

We began to observe the pattern that her anxiety attacks and headaches grew strongest as material was preparing to emerge from the unconsciousness and just afterward. When Susan was having frequent panic attacks, she would retreat into herself. This private reflection time allowed her to process the emerging images and feelings. These were excruciatingly painful yet also productive healing times for her.

Susan's next dream was also puzzling:

> I see myself as a 5 year old girl. I am crying inconsolably. There are some others around, including a man who is very mean and who calls himself the Doctor. He has blood on his hands. Something about my beloved cat, which has been killed?
>
> He tells me it is my fault, that I am bad, and have Satan within me. He performs some strange motions and says Satan's eye is in me and will be watching me always.

Susan was understandably shaken up by this dream. She remembered her precious cat but couldn't remember what had happened to it. She said she had the impression from the dream that the man had performed some kind of surgery on her to make her believe that she was wicked and that he'd put Satan's eye in her. She did not understand why he wanted her to believe she was responsible for the cat's death.

As this stage of treatment progressed, there were periods when Susan was more symptom-free than in years. This gave her strength and reassurance that she was on the right track and that one day she would be feeling much better. In depression and trauma recovery, these early periods of a client being relatively asymptomatic or of feeling much better overall tend to come and go. When the client moves out of these periods and back into depression or the previous symptoms, it can feel as though he or she has never felt any better and never will. It can be very helpful for the client to know that these are normal recovery symptoms and that periods of depression grow shorter as recovery proceeds. As with Persephone and the underground journey, the deep wisdom of the psyche leads the client back into a deeper layer of the material needing to be processed and metabolized.

In the next several chapters, I will discuss some related treatment and recovery issues. I will return to Susan's story in a later chapter. Those familiar with ritual abuse will have recognized common themes in the material given thus far in Susan's story. These include strong symptoms and flashbacks in October, incest, devils, a magical surgery to implant Satan's eye to always watch over the child, a pregnancy and abortion at age thirteen, and a beloved pet being murdered, with the child being blamed as evil. These themes and many more emerged throughout the 1990s all over the United States and in ever-increasing numbers since then.

CHAPTER 12

CHILDHOOD DEVELOPMENTAL ARRESTS AND PACING IN HEALING

In this chapter, I will delve further into the impact of trauma on the developing psyche. Though the material in this section of the book is heavily weighted on understanding severe trauma, the information may be informative for a more general audience in understanding the impact of trauma and how people heal. No one among us can get through life unscathed by trauma, and who does not struggle with various dysfunctional patterns in one's flight from oneself? The need for pacing in the healing process is addressed in this chapter through the concept of the therapeutic window. Dreams are discussed as safe vehicles to teach us about defenses we have built to shield us from the pain of our experiences.

In our culture, with its emphasis on instant gratification and the quick fix to feel good, little time and space is allowed for the natural healing rhythms of the psyche. The wearing of a "happy face" is valued over the expression of "negative" emotions such as sadness and grief. Sometimes, as discussed in an earlier chapter, depression is the appropriate response to stressors and trauma; it is a call from deep inside to attend to what needs to be healed and what needs to be grieved and mourned.

There can be no true healing from childhood trauma and/or neglect without depression and grief. Many undergoing this healing process have to face depths of agony, betrayal, and anguish that many of us could not fathom. Survivors learn as children that to survive and adapt, they must cut themselves off from these very painful feelings. Those who make it into therapy have found that these defensive mechanisms are no longer holding back the river of tears. They inevitably find that, against their very will they must face and feel the pain that is inside, for it will be silent no longer. It will be heard, seen, and felt.

The determination to face the demons in one's past is a mark of health and is a part of the striving to be whole. I like a definition of mental health attributed to Scott Peck: mental health is the "excruciating commitment to face reality, regardless of how painful."

The very real pain of the grief work of depression can be, and often is, inadvertently increased during this tortuous healing process by those around the client. Family and friends who do not understand tell the survivor that he or she was "better" before. They may say that this therapy is making the survivor worse and that maybe he or she just needs to "get over it," "lighten up," and focus on the present instead of dwelling on the past.

Imagine you are in the depths of grief while mourning the death of a loved one and those close to you tell you to think happy thoughts and just move on. In reaction to such a statement, you would likely feel extremely misunderstood and more alone and bereft than before. This is very much what it is like for trauma survivors working through their issues. The process of working through a trauma history is, in effect, grieving one's lost childhood: grieving for what happened and grieving for that which never happened. This grieving could not be done in childhood. Maybe your mother or father was alcoholic, or maybe your parents fought constantly. Maybe you were beaten or raped or emotionally abused, maybe all of these and more. There was no way at the time to address your feelings, because you had to find a way to keep moving forward, and that usually means finding a way to avoid your painful feelings.

The healing work is even more complicated if the survivor suffers from post-traumatic stress disorder (PTSD), which is characterized by recurrent intrusive recollections of the original trauma, nightmares, hyper-vigilance, an exaggerated startle response, and avoidance of persons, places, or situations that might bear a resemblance to the original trauma(s). The recurrent and intrusive memory is not something that can be switched off at will. Furthermore, it may appear as a phobic fear, body memory, or flooding of affect that may be difficult to pinpoint or explain. Sometimes PTSD appears as a delayed response to a trauma, which can make it even more puzzling to understand.

In order for the survivor to move on, grieving and healing work needs to be done. The survivor must perseverate on the issues until they are digested, understood, and healed. Time needs to be spent going over and over the issues—not to hold on to the past but to heal and finally let go of the past.

One woman with a very dysfunctional family background explained how this worked for her. In the early stages of her recovery, she found herself thinking about the same things and telling the same stories repeatedly, almost obsessively. She could not understand at the time why she did this, but she could not seem to stop herself. Later in recovery, she realized she had needed to go over and over the traumatic events in her mind so she could process and metabolize her experience. She knew she had needed to grieve what had and had not happened, so she could understand the impact these events had had on her and her development. She wanted to find a way to bring back what she had learned from her past into the present. In doing so, she learned to give herself the compassion and caring her parents had been unable to give. She also learned she could give herself the respect and nurturing she needed. This, in turn, enabled her to feel more "fuller" inside, with something within to give to her husband and child.

As mentioned previously, trauma victims learned very early on that the way to survive was to become numb to the painful and horrible things they experienced. Numbing out and dissociating can be an adaptive and creative coping strategy in an intolerable situation. When the child grows to adulthood and finds, at some stage, that something is very much missing in his or her life, he or she often feels a terror of being alone, because it is when one is alone that the terrible and painful feelings from the past tend to intrude, pushing their way into consciousness. As an adult, the dissociation no longer serves as a helpful coping mechanism. It serves to keep the trauma survivor from facing his or her feelings and from finding constructive means of coping.

At some point, adult survivors of childhood abuse will find themselves depressed or otherwise symptomatic. One common scenario in women sexually abused as children is that the woman finds herself increasingly agitated during her first pregnancy and may become inexplicably depressed after the birth of her first child. She may find herself terrified that the child will be abused and may not understand the source of this fear. For now, with the birth of her child, she has a continual reminder of her own childhood. The subconscious memories are stirred up as some of the pain that was dissociated in childhood comes to consciousness. Any number of different scenarios or crises can present themselves to lead the abuse survivor into treatment, including a new intimate relationship, a marriage, a divorce, the birth of a child, life stresses, or even, paradoxically, the achievement of a level of stability in the external aspects of one's life. Addictions or compulsive behaviors often present as major issues.

Susan had achieved a measure of stability in her relationship and in her career. Her three boys were no longer so young as to be completely dependent on her. These factors served to give her the solid base she would need for embarking upon the challenging work that lay ahead. She would likely not have been able to process the material that came up at an earlier stage of her life, because she would not have had the internal and external stability to do so. Whatever the case is, would it not be foolhardy to expect that Susan, or any other abuse survivor, could work through a childhood full of trauma with barely a sniffle and come out of treatment in ten weeks or twenty, fully restored? Yet this is what our fast-paced culture (and the insurance providers) so often expects of them.

These survivors internalize in childhood, from the lack of love given to them, that they did not deserve the time, love, and nurturing they truly needed. Now that they are adults, we may grow impatient with their pain and tell them they are taking too long in their recovery, that we know better than them in what they need, and that they need to speed up the process. In effect, we give them the same message they internalized as children. It is important not to re-victimize the healing survivor with our unthinking comments, our impatience with their pain, or our inability to tolerate their suffering.

The psyche teaches us what we need to know, in the amounts we can handle, when we can handle it, over the amount of time we need. This internal regulating system has a greater wisdom than any of us possesses in our conscious, rational minds and leads the individual through the dark journey in the service of healing and wholeness. There is no model in our society for patience and wisdom in the processing of our pain.

Diagnoses most commonly associated with abuse victims include addictions, eating disorders, major depression, bipolar disorder, borderline personality disorder, dissociative identity disorder (DID), dissociative disorder not otherwise specified (DDNOS), and of course post-traumatic stress disorder. The latter four diagnoses are always associated with trauma and/or abuse of some kind, whether emotional, verbal, physical, or sexual. The first four can have multiple determinants, including biochemical and genetic, and do not necessarily indicate a severe trauma history. Most trauma and abuse survivors have some degree of depression, in addition to whatever other diagnoses they carry.

AMNESIA FOR CHILDHOOD

According to Lenore Terr, MD, in her book *Unchained Memories: True Stories of Memories, Lost and Found*, dissociation usually requires repetition of trauma, and those who have learned to dissociate easily have learned to do so through experience of repeated traumatic situations. Terr goes on to describe some of the data and exceptions researchers have found, which dramatically demonstrate the power of the mind in most cases to remain intact under the impact of a severe single trauma.

> A few one-time-only traumatic events are so marked by extraordinarily dehumanizing sights and sounds that dissociation takes place in the very first moments, even though the child might not have had any practice. The large group of essays collected by Professor Arata Osada from schoolchildren who survived the bombing of Hiroshima shows that the vast majority of these young witnesses remembered the events of August 6, 1945 with the kind of clear, precise details that marks the memories of most victims of first-time childhood trauma. The children I interviewed following the Chowchilla school bus kidnapping retained this kind of clear, brilliantly lit memory of their experiences. But a few of the Hiroshima youngsters wrote about the sense of passing through the atomic bombing in a trance. This is the subjective sense of dissociation. Dissociation makes for fuzzy, unclear recollections or a series of holes in memory. Because the experience of Hiroshima was so dehumanizing and unbelievably horrible, immediate dissociation became possible for a few. (Terr 1994, 87)

There seems to be a window of time within which a child can most easily learn to dissociate. If there is no trauma before age nine to ten or so, it is less likely that, even with repeated trauma, a child will begin dissociating from his or her experiences. This is because the brain and central nervous system are still developing at a rapid rate in those first vulnerable years. Extreme torture victims may be an exception to this, for even without a prior history of abuse, they may learn to dissociate or go out of body to survive the torture.

THE DIFFICULTY OF WORKING THROUGH CHILDHOOD TRAUMA

The working through of childhood trauma is so difficult, in part, because the child who experienced the abuse was not psychologically mature and had to use whatever psychological means possible to endure the experience. It is difficult to understand the belief systems and defense systems formed in response to the trauma. Additionally, the adult survivor must go through a learning process of how to remain present when his or her tendency is to dissociate. Judith Herman clearly portrays the psychological dilemma the child faces with ongoing abuse, as compared with the position of the adult who experiences repeated trauma:

> Repeated trauma in adult life erodes the structure of the personality already formed, but repeated trauma in childhood forms and deforms the personality. The child trapped in an abusive environment is faced with formidable tasks of adaptation. She must find a way to preserve a sense of trust in people who are untrustworthy, safety in a situation that is unsafe, control in a situation that is terrifyingly unpredictable, power in a situation of helplessness. Unable to care for or protect herself, she must compensate for the failures of adult care and protection with the only means at her disposal, an immature system of psychological defenses.

> The pathological environment of childhood abuse forces the development of extraordinary capacities, both creative and destructive. (Herman 1992, 96)

Patricia was sexually abused and physically and emotionally tortured by her older brother over a period of many years. When she came into treatment, she stated she'd always had many memories of what she had experienced at her brother's hands. As we worked, she accessed more memories, some of which were very difficult to acknowledge but which were consistent with what she had always remembered.

Patricia's brother often hid and spied on her. At one point, when she was taking a bath, she became aware of someone's attention focused on her. She realized with horror he was watching her through a peephole in an adjacent closet. She fought him often with all the bravery she could muster, but he was bigger and stronger, and she was unable to fend him off. She never knew when he might be watching her, and she was constantly fearful.

Patricia dissociated much of the feelings associated with these incidents. She recalled a very formative experience that occurred while she was being bathed by her mother, at five years old. Her mother noticed that her genital area was reddened and asked how this had happened. Patricia said her brother had done this to her. Her mother's incomprehensibly awful response was to slap her, berate her, and humiliate her for making up such a horrible story about her brother. This horrible betrayal taught

Patricia her mother would not help protect her from her brother's torture and abuse. She had nowhere to turn for help. She internalized that she was a very bad little girl who was guilty of awful things. Patricia suffered from paranoia. The paranoia had two key elements: that people were watching her and that they knew she was guilty of committing horrible acts, for which she might be caught. For example, when in a severely stressed period, she believed that the FBI thought she had bombed Oklahoma City and that the authorities were after her. Part of her knew this was not true, but under stress her paranoia took over.

It is important to note that these two paranoid symptoms were symbolic of two of the most formative and critical experiences she had experienced. The first was she had internalized the feeling of constantly being watched. The second was she had internalized from the abuse and her mother's awful betrayal that something was horribly wrong with her and that if these horrible things were happening to her, then she must deserve them. Despite a number of years in therapy (with someone unskilled in treatment of sexual-abuse issues), Patricia had never put the pieces of her occasional paranoia together with the experiences of her childhood. She was not schizophrenic, though her paranoid episodes were psychotic regressions.

The paranoia emerged when she was under stress. The first episode occurred after her first adult sexual encounter, when the man with whom she was in love had to move for a job. Rather than face the difficult task of saying good-bye, he stood her up on their last night together and left without a word. It was a year before he spoke with her again. The guilt that was stirred in her at having sexual relations along with feelings of abandonment and that she had done something wrong combined to produce her first episode of paranoia, a dissociated trance state that combined the various elements of her experience.

The memories of the shame, fear, and terror Patricia had experienced as a child had been split off from her consciousness, only to reemerge intrusively in adulthood. Though she never forgot the sexual and physical abuse she experienced, she dissociated, repressed, and isolated the intolerable affect. Sometimes the dissociated memories came back in symbolic form.

When Patricia was not experiencing paranoia, she could talk about it. We could piece together how the development of paranoia might have occurred and what it might symbolically represent. Yet when she was experiencing the paranoia, it was very hard for her to consider that her paranoid conviction was anything but the absolute truth. During some of these episodes, I became a suspect as well, and she would wonder if I were not a part of the conspiracy. When we began to work directly with the sexual abuse as an issue, she tended to regress into deeper depression and paranoia. It would then typically take several weeks for her to find her way back, each time a little stronger than before. Yet during these periods, the paranoia could be quite severe and the depression disabling. (I have mentioned this regressive feature of abuse and trauma work in previous chapters.)

An objective look at the severity of the current symptoms and at the substantial paranoia and depression Patricia had experienced throughout her adult life produced a clear picture. The picture was of someone who developed a way of understanding the events in her world in the only way that her undeveloped and unformed psyche could understand them. Her worldview, akin in analogy to the software that was running on her mental computer, was shaped and carved out by the horrendous trauma she'd experienced in those early years. Further, the dynamics of this extensive worldview were rooted deeply in the psyche, in the unconscious, where they were not readily evident or accessible. Nonetheless, these dynamics constituted the infrastructure of the psyche and were not to be underestimated in the power they had over her individual personality.

The basic premise about the development of defense mechanisms is that they are created to enable the child to adapt. Defense mechanisms protect the child from being completely overwhelmed by a given experience or set of experiences. As mentioned, the work of recovery from trauma involves a great deal of looking at and experiencing what has been too frightening to face. Hence, by definition, recovery work involves dismantling some of the defense mechanisms so that the survivor can face those terrifying realities and work through the associated feelings and memories.

As Richard Kluft pointed out in a talk at the 1995 Eastern Regional Conference on Abuse, Trauma, and Dissociation, defense mechanisms have a profound "homeostatic value" (Kluft 1995)—that is, they have the function of regulating and maintaining the internal balance and equilibrium of the individual. These mechanisms deserve, as Kluft points out, our respect because they are very good at doing what they do. The work of healing involves cautiously and carefully looking at the defenses and why they were invoked and processing the experiences that have been defended against.

THE NATURAL TIMING OF THE PSYCHE: THE THERAPEUTIC WINDOW AND DREAMS

A skilled therapist is able to empathize with the client, respect his or her pace, and allow the client's psyche to present the issues as they need to be addressed. The psyche is a self-regulating homeostatic system, with the defense mechanisms being one of the means of regulation. In this respect, dreams are a guiding tool par excellence in working with trauma victims, for they come out of that deep self- regulating center of the psyche that Jung called the Self. They are remarkable tools for addressing the most relevant issues. The regulating center of the Self knows the capacity of the individual to tolerate new information and can assess how much a particular defense mechanism is needed at any given time. In Patricia's case, dreams provided some critical information for her, always giving her what she needed but never giving more than she could handle.

John Briere, an expert on child sexual abuse, discusses the "therapeutic window," which he views as the optimal range within which trauma recovery work is done (Briere 1996). The defining characteristic of this therapeutic window is that the client is neither so comfortable in therapy that he or she is not challenged, with little growth occurring, nor pushed so hard that his or her defenses are dismantled faster than he or she can handle. It takes skill for the therapist to work within this window and to recognize the signs that point out when the window has been undershot or overshot. The process of therapy involves a continual calibration process, adjusting and fine-tuning whenever indicated.

The child in a supportive and nurturing environment gradually learns to adapt to frustrations without becoming overwhelmed. The presence of discomfort is tolerated as the child learns from experience that he or she will not be overwhelmed by the presence of unpleasant emotions. A child who is developing these internal psychological structures is able to make positive use of a time-out for negative behaviors. The child can be sent to his or her room for inappropriate behavior and can calm down in due time, without the fear of psychological disintegration a more traumatized child will have.

When, on the other hand, a child experiences repeated trauma, the process of learning to process, manage, and integrate painful feelings is significantly disrupted. The basic sense of safety a child needs is not consistently present. The child may live in a constant state of anxiety and fear, never knowing when the next traumatic episode may occur. Since the child is physically and emotionally dependent on the caretaker, he or she develops defense mechanisms for lessening the pain and anxiety associated with the abuse. To preserve the necessary relationship, the child internalizes himself or herself as "bad" and sees the abuser as "good."

The relative narrowness of the conscious mind is like the tip of the iceberg, with the vastness of the unconscious mind analogous to the vastness of the iceberg that lies under the surface of the water. We may think we are operating out of our conscious minds, but often our behaviors emerge out of our larger unconscious minds, with their scripts, conditionings, feelings, wounds, and complexes. Part of the work of therapy is to understand why we may act in a certain self-destructive or self-defeating manner, which might not make sense at a conscious level.

Dreams are an ideal tool for providing information through the therapeutic window, linking present behaviors and feelings with unconscious motivators. Rose, whose eating disorder was discussed in Chapter 5, had stopped purging when she came in for treatment but was still bingeing. She reported that on days when she relapsed, she began planning her binge episode shortly after she woke up. She had no idea why, but she woke up with the desire to binge. As I mentioned previously, she was keeping track of her dreams. Her dream journal included not only dream material but also day residue, that is, the emotions and events from the previous day.

When we focused on her dreams the night before a binge, we often gained insight into what was going on at an unconscious level that stirred up her craving to binge. Usually there was some material from the day before, either in her experience or in her reflection, that would trigger the dreams. The material presented in her dreams often had to do with her reported childhood abuse or with control issues related to her mother.

One of the most important functions of her dreams was to link the current daily material with the deeper, older issues that were being triggered. When we processed a dream, we worked within the therapeutic window. The dreams were always the perfect pacing tool for the work, revealing what needed to be processed at a given time. Rose's dreams placed the daily issue in the context of the larger underlying issues and thus helped her to understand the impact of her childhood trauma on her current situation. Dreams present just the right amount of material to be challenging to the dreamer but not so much as to push the dreamer past his or her current psychological capacities.

Dream material tends to show the dreamer what defenses he or she is using, as well as how these defenses help shape the dreamer's perception of the world. If a dreamer has frequent dream themes of being helpless, passive, running away from danger, and so on, it is important to take a look at these themes to examine not only the lens through which the dreamer sees the world but also how the dreamer reacts to stimuli that he or she perceives as threatening. Dreams of the dreamer as a victim, reacting to events in his or her world rather than taking an active stance in his or her life, give important information about the dreamer's stance in waking reality events. The dreamer may not realize in waking life that he or she is reacting in these ways, for defense mechanisms are unconscious. However, dreams will often point out these mechanisms in a gentle, nonthreatening manner that may be much easier to digest than if someone, even a therapist, tells the dreamer of negative patterns.

CHAPTER 13

DREAMS AND TRAUMA: IS IT JUST A DREAM?

There are many styles of working with dreams, ranging from the traditional analytic perspective (for example, a Freudian approach) to the more modern client-centered style. In the former, historically the analyst has been viewed as the authority who knows what dream symbols mean and who can tell the dreamer what the dream means. The therapist in this model carries a great deal of power. In this tradition, there is much room for the therapist to project his or her own meaning and issues onto the client's dream, regardless of whether this meaning feels right for the dreamer. In this model, if a client disagrees with the analyst's perspective on the dream, the disagreement can be viewed as resistance, or the rising up of the client's defenses against understanding his or her true self or motivations.

There are many pitfalls in the use of this style of dreamwork in therapy, especially when working with trauma-related issues and when there is amnesia. There is potential within this traditional dream- analysis style for leading a suggestible client down a path more suited to the therapist's projections.

In his book *Suggestions of Abuse: True and False Memories of Childhood Sexual Trauma*, Michael Yapko critiques the use of dreamwork in therapy by presenting a scenario in which a therapist tells his client, who has no memories of abuse, that he has been sexually abused. (This is extremely leading and is neither ethical nor professional.) The therapist expresses certainty; the client is confused, vulnerable, and suggestible. Yapko presents the ensuing therapy process as follows:

> So, the suggestion is accepted to have dreams. The client has a dream featuring inappropriate sexuality, or abstract symbols interpreted as inappropriate sexuality, and the therapist now has "confirmation" of repressed memories of abuse, no matter how vague or ambiguous the dream …

> The client's dream (or series of dreams) is then taken as "evidence" of repressed memories of abuse. Dreams as evidence? But the client's confusion gives way to noncritical acceptance of confidently presented misinformation. The client has been masterfully manipulated into forming hard conclusions out of thin air, all at the therapist's direction …

> Dream interpretation involves making projections about someone else's projections. Who says a dream of falling down means this, while a dream of flying means that? This area is the astrology of psychotherapy. (Yapko 1994, 121–22)

What Yapko presents here is, at the same time, unethical therapy and unethical dreamwork. Although some psychoanalytic traditions allow for the analyst to tell the analysand what his or her dream means, this is to be discouraged. I will present research results in this chapter that strongly caution against jumping to conclusions about sexual abuse from dream content alone.

It is important not to throw the baby out with the proverbial bathwater. Just as not all therapy is bad therapy, not all dreamwork is bad dreamwork. Dreams, properly worked, are some of the best tools we have in working with trauma. Skilled dreamwork does not involve making definitive interpretations about someone else's dream images, any more than skilled therapy involves the therapist telling the client what his or her childhood experience was, what he or she is feeling, or what he or she should do.

DREAMS OF ABUSE: RESEARCH RESULTS

Dr. Elizabeth Loftus and Katherine Ketcham speak of dreamwork in their book, *The Myth of Repressed Memory: False Memories and Allegations of Sexual Abuse*. They make the important point that traumatic events are rarely recreated in a dream exactly as they occurred in waking life (Loftus and Ketcham 1995, 160). Dr. Deirdre Barrett, a well-known dream researcher at Harvard Medical School, conducted a survey of therapists who treat dissociative disorders, questioning these therapists about their clients' dreams. Dr. Barrett found in her survey that only a few dreams were "undisguised recreation of real episodes, especially for recent repressed events" (Barrett 1994, 167).

More commonly, the dreams contained distortions, as in this fascinating example of the combining of a traumatic event with dream symbolism: "One woman dreamed of being eight years old, pregnant, and very frightened—with her mother nearby but not available for help. This led to her first memory of a sexual assault at that age, the most vivid aspects of her recollection being the belief that her belly would swell up, confusion about how a baby would get out, and her inability to seek her mother's help" (Barrett 1994, 167). This dream contains a number of the client's emotional concerns at the time of the assault and creates a kind of emotional picture of her situation at the time of the assault, in condensed symbolic form. There is no actual recreation of an assault within the dream material, only a statement that the dream led to the memory of the assault. No details are given in the study of how the client remembered the assault or of the client-therapist dynamics.

The findings of another study, done by Belicki and Cuddy, were that, for sexual abuse survivors, "nightmares did not typically replay the actual, abusive event." According to this study, "what these nightmares seemed to portray was the emotional reality of the event, for example, that for many women the actual trauma did not feel like a sexual event but an act of profound violence" (Belicki and Cuddy in Barrett 1996).

SKILLED DREAMWORK, A VALUABLE TOOL

The great beauty of skilled dreamwork is that it helps the client to explore his or her own feelings, associations, and perceptions more clearly so that the client may come to know himself or herself better. Our defenses are down when we are dreaming, and our dreaming minds are able to present to us information we might not receive in our waking lives. We see this in both the Old and New Testaments of the Bible, where information is often given at night in dreams. The connection between God and humans appears to be more direct when dreaming.

Good dreamwork is extremely empowering, for the conclusions drawn from it are the dreamers' alone. The same can be said for good trauma treatment. Unfortunately, most therapists have little formal training either in treatment of trauma or in dreamwork skills. However, the lack of skills in some psychotherapists does not diminish the amazing power of dreams to teach and help us in our therapy work.

A great deal can be learned from dreams when it is the dreamer's associations to the material—not the therapist's associations—that are explored. Ownership of the dream belongs to the client—that is, the determination of the meaning of the dream should be left up to the dreamer. The therapist's ideas may be explored but must never be imposed upon the dreamer.

Also, as previously mentioned, the client needs to set the pace in therapy. A skilled psychotherapist should be able to tolerate the ambivalence of not knowing. This perhaps is a learned skill, much as is patience. There is no wisdom in "having all the answers," as the mysteries of the psyche and the capricious nature of memory can play tricks on anyone.

When a client presents a dream to me, no matter how many hundreds or thousands of dreams I have successfully worked with, I often have a feeling that I shall never be able to understand or to fathom this dream. Carl Jung wrote about this phenomenon, an initial feeling akin to awe before the great mystery of the dream. Despite this feeling, I have come to understand that the meaning will unfold, not because of what I know, but because of what the client might discover about the dream through his or her associations and dreamwork. In general, it is a critical therapist role to be the container for the tension of the ambivalence inherent in exploring a client's personal history. Exploration of these historical connections is a key part of the therapeutic work, but conclusions must rest with the client.

Discussion and controversy about the value of dreamwork have been going on for a long time and are not likely to be resolved anytime in the near future. As early as 1919, Freud spoke of the tendency for severe trauma to replay itself in dream life. He considered the tendency to remain fixated on trauma to be biologically based. He believed that after severe trauma, dreaming life repeatedly takes the patient back to the traumatic situation in nightmares.

The following quotation is as relevant today as when Carl Jung delivered it in 1931:

> The use of dream analysis in psychotherapy is still a much-debated question. Many practitioners find it indispensable in the treatment of neuroses, and consider that the dream is a function whose psychic importance is equal to that of the conscious mind itself. Others, on the contrary, dispute the value of dream-analysis and regard dreams as a negligible byproduct of the psyche. Obviously, if a person holds the view that the unconscious plays a decisive part in the etiology of neuroses, he will attribute a high practical importance to dreams as direct expressions of the unconscious. Equally obviously, if he denies the unconscious or at least thinks it etiologically insignificant, he will minimize the importance of dream analysis. (Jung 1974, 87)

The symptoms that bring clients into therapy develop in the unconscious mind. For me, the question is not "Are dreams valuable in therapy?" but rather "How can the therapist and client best approach the dream in therapy?"

Ann, an overweight client, complained of a terrible nightmare she had dreamed several nights before. She had some memories of molestation in childhood and of having been raped by a relative. Her first memories of childhood molestation by some cousins had come at a time when she had lost a great deal of weight. She experienced images and feelings about being very young and being sodomized.

When Ann began a medically supervised weight-loss program while in therapy, she began to experience strong anxiety. As she lost weight, her defensive wall of fat began to dissolve. As a result, Ann gradually remembered some memories of trauma that had led her to put on the weight. She re-experienced the pain the trauma had caused her. Ann was afraid of losing more weight, afraid she might remember what her bingeing had helped her to forget. Several weeks into the weight-loss program, she had the following nightmare:

I am with my father. I am my current age, and he is alive again. He reaches over to hug me. He is touching me in my private area and forcing me to touch his erect penis. Suddenly, I remember. I am furious, and I confront him. I tell him I remember now what he did to me as a child, that he abused me repeatedly, even as an infant. I have absolutely no doubt that this has happened. I confront him, telling him that I know that he did this to me. I am full of anger and rage.

Ann awoke from this dream sobbing. When she told it to me, she did not ask what I thought, nor did I say. She told me that, at a deep inner level, she had a strong conviction this really happened. Her father was dead, and there could be no corroboration.

This dream could be viewed as an anxiety dream, reflecting Ann's fear she might uncover more abuse in her history. However, what is uncharacteristic about this dream, as different from usual anxiety dreams, is that Ann possessed such absolute inner certainty, both in and out of the dream, that it revealed a truth to her about an actual series of events.

I discussed earlier in this chapter how nightmares are often symbolic recreations of the emotional reality of events, rather than direct recreations of the traumatic events themselves. In this case, Ann was certain about her dream memory that her father had repeatedly abused her, even though there was no direct recreation of those events. She experienced a deeply felt and horrifying emotional reality in the dream, which she believed represented an emotional reality from her past.

When a dreamer experiences a deep inner certainty about the truth of something he or she experienced within a dream, it may likely be true. Ann experienced intense emotions within the dream and came to her own conclusions. The sensation she felt of her father's erection in the hug served within the dream to bring back her memory of the earlier events. Ann did not believe the dream scene was an actual memory; however, she believed what she realized in the dream to be true.

Ann's parents were both alcoholics and very inattentive to Ann and her brother. Her younger brother has always had recall of a great deal of inappropriate sexualizing on their father's part toward Ann. Ann only learned about this from her brother after she told him this nightmare. Her brother told her that he clearly remembered a time when their father, while drunk, had masturbated in front of both of them. Ann had no recall of this incident.

Ann now at least had some corroboration of inappropriate sexualizing, which forced her again to ask herself if the dream reflected a history of sexual abuse. She believed it did. There were many other pieces, symptoms, and memory fragments that came up during therapy that provided further material to support her hypothesis of having been sexually abused by her alcoholic father. It takes many pieces of the jigsaw puzzle to begin to see the whole picture.

THE PARALLELS BETWEEN CLIENT-CENTERED DREAMWORK AND CLIENT-CENTERED THERAPY

Client-centered dreamwork focuses on the client's responses to, feelings about, and understanding of his or her dreams. The therapist is a guide and a helper but is careful not to impose a particular theoretical framework on the dreams or the dreamer. This style was popularized in such books as Gayle Delaney's *Living Your Dreams and Breakthrough Dreaming: How to Tap the Power of Your 24-Hour Mind* and Montague Ullman and Nan Zimmerman's classic book, *Working with Dreams: Self-Understanding, Problem-Solving,* and *Enriched Creativity through Dream Appreciation.*

In an early paper, predating the modern dreamwork movement, Carl Jung wrote about the necessity of throwing aside theoretical orientation when working with a client's dreams. He spoke to the need to not make premature judgments on hazy material. As with trauma work, both client and the therapist need to learn to live with ambivalence.

Jung, in a paper entitled *"The Significance of the Unconscious in Individual Education,"* addresses the general issue of how to bring unconscious contents of the mind into consciousness in the therapeutic setting. He states that the "best practical method, though also the most difficult, is the analysis and interpretation of dreams." He goes on to elaborate a general methodology, beginning by saying that understanding a dream is not unlike trying to decipher hieroglyphics:

> First, we assemble all the available material which the dreamer himself can give as regards the dream images. We next exclude any statements that depend upon particular theoretical assumptions, for those are generally quite arbitrary attempts at interpretation. We then inquire into the happenings of the previous day, as well as into the mood and the general plans and purposes of the dreamer in the days and weeks preceding the dream. A more or less intimate knowledge of his circumstances and character is of course a necessary prerequisite. Great care and attention must be given to this preparatory work if we want to get at the meaning of the dream. I have no faith in dream interpretations made on the spur of the moment and concocted out of some preconceived theory. One must be careful not to impose any theoretical assumptions on the dream; in fact, it is always best to proceed as if the dream had no meaning at all, so as to be on one's guard against any possible bias. Dream-analysis may yield entirely unforeseen results, and facts of an exceedingly disagreeable nature may sometimes come to light whose discussion would certainly have been avoided at all costs had we been able to anticipate them. We may also get results that are obscure and unintelligible at first, because our conscious standpoint has still not plumbed the secrets of the psyche. In such cases it is better to adopt a waiting attitude than to attempt a forced explanation. In this kind of work one has to put up with a great many question marks. (Jung 1954, 154–55)

Some of these points that Jung makes as essential to proper dream interpretation are certainly also applicable to therapy. He emphasizes that it is important to elicit as much information as possible from the client, in as unbiased a manner as possible, and without imposition of a theoretical framework. He also states that an essential part of the clinical work involves living with uncertainty and questions.

Johanna King, PhD, in her paper *"Theory to Practice: Dreams and the Treatment of Sexual Abuse,"* presented at an International Association for the Study of Dreams Conference, discusses the regrettable lack of training in dreamwork skills in graduate schools across the country. She points out that "clinicians well-trained in basic therapeutic skills could easily transfer these skills to dreamwork, given a moderate amount of input and opportunity" (King 1995, 3). Good dreamwork, like good trauma therapy, allows the client to draw his or her own conclusions and empowers the client to decide what understanding of the dream feels right to him or her.

A skilled trauma psychotherapist once asked me to supervise her in working with dreams in trauma treatment. During our first and only meeting, she brought several client dreams to me and asked how I would work with them. Since skilled dreamwork uses the same client-centered guidelines as working with traumatic material, asking the client questions without leading, many of the interventions and questions I suggested were the same as if we were working with other forms of material in therapy, such as flashbacks or physical symptoms.

Though there are many great tools for working with dreams, the basics of good therapy are, as King said, the basics of good dreamwork. The therapist was very upset with me and called me to tell me how disappointed she was with our meeting. There was nothing I could tell her; I had no magic to offer, just good, solid dream working skills.

Carl Jung, in the quotation above, discusses important points about effective dreamwork; he was a pioneer in the area of respecting the dreamer's perspective on the dream. By modern standards, he might have been in practice more authoritative in his dreamwork style than might today be advisable. Nonetheless, we owe a great deal to him.

Client-centered dreamwork leaves the final authority for the understanding of the dream with the dreamer, not with the therapist. My experience may tell me that a given dream image means something in particular. For example, if it is fixed in my mind that fire dreams usually have to do with anger and I insist to my client that her dream of fire has to do with her unrecognized anger, my projection may miss the point entirely. The dreamer might have been in a terrible fire; the fire in her dream may be about a sense of danger she feels about something she is experiencing in her present life, and my projection would miss the mark. The dreamers need to be the final authority as to the meaning of their dreams, no matter how right the therapist thinks he or she may be.

The symbolism our dreaming minds use is as highly individual as our individual life experiences. Dream imagery can be complex, imbued with the emotions and experience of the dreamer. It is through good interviewing techniques that a therapist can best help his or her client understand a dream. The therapist would be wise to explore the client's associations to the dream and to allow these associations to clarify the dream content. The day residue from the previous day should also be explored, including in particular whatever was on the client's mind at the time of going to bed.

Many dreamworkers, including myself, have been influenced by the pioneering dream leader Montague Ullman, who died in 2008. Ullman, in a book co-written with Nan Zimmerman, *Working with Dreams: Self-Understanding, Problem-Solving,* and *Enriched Creativity through Dream Appreciation*, discusses a model that he developed for group dreamwork. Although the model is for group dreamwork, many elements translate effectively into an individual dreamwork setting. Those who have been fortunate enough to train with Montague Ullman or to participate in his workshops cannot help but come away with the tremendous respect he gives to the dreamer as the person best equipped to understand the meaning of the dream.

The International Association for the Study of Dreams (IASD) is a fascinating multidisciplinary international organization dedicated to promoting the study and understanding of dreams. Anyone who is interested in dreams is welcome to join and attend the conferences, whether or not they work with dreams professionally. Many of the leading people in the field of dreams belong to this organization and participate in its conferences. Although CEUs are offered, many come to the conferences just to learn more about dreams. IASD is a marvelous resource for anyone interested in learning more about dreams. (See *www.asdreams.org).* In early conferences and in some of the articles in its journal, Dreaming, IASD explored the pioneering area of trauma and dreams, specifically sexual abuse and dreams.

ETHICS AND DREAMWORK

I became involved with the International Association for the Study of Dreams (IASD) in year two of its now forty year existence. Its broad membership base includes artists, researchers, anthropologists, psychotherapists, writers, musicians, dream-group leaders, pastors and clergy, and lay people interested in learning more about dreams. This broad membership base, with a focus on an educational mission, makes IASD conferences very interesting and full of life. The annual conferences have multiple tracks that cover many interest areas. Dreams speak to every area of our lives.

I became involved on the board of directors in 1985 and soon joined the Ethics Committee. Since we were such a diverse group with different skills and interests, some of us bound by professional ethics and training and some not, I was concerned about safety issues and dreamwork at our conferences and elsewhere. During the early years we experienced some incidents when best practices were not used; I was involved in helping to resolve them. These experiences helped me learn a great deal about the possible pitfalls of dreamwork and what safety precautions are needed.

By 1996, I was chair of the IASD Ethics Committee, tasked with creating a dreamwork ethics statement, a guideline for ethical dreamwork to ensure a confidential and safe environment for our conference attendees. We also knew we were entering an era when dreamwork would increasingly be done on the Internet, and we wanted to develop guidelines for safe and ethical sharing so we would be prepared for the Internet era.

Below is the IASD dreamwork ethics statement. The first two paragraphs are most relevant to understanding IASD's strong emphasis on the importance of dreamwork being client centered:

IASD DREAMWORK ETHICS STATEMENT

IASD celebrates the many benefits of dreamwork, yet recognizes that there are potential risks. IASD supports an approach to dreamwork and dream sharing that respects the dreamer's dignity and integrity, and which recognizes the dreamer as the decision-maker regarding the significance of the dream. Systems of dreamwork that assign authority or knowledge of the dream's meanings to someone other than the dreamer can be misleading, incorrect, and harmful. Ethical dreamwork helps the dreamer work with his/her own dream images, feelings, and associations, and guides the dreamer to more fully experience, appreciate, and understand the dream. Every dream may have multiple meanings, and different techniques may be reasonably employed to touch these multiple layers of significance.

A dreamer's decision to share or discontinue sharing a dream should always be respected and honored. The dreamer should be forewarned that unexpected issues or emotions may arise in the course of the dreamwork. Information and mutual agreement about the degree of privacy and confidentiality are essential ingredients in creating a safe atmosphere for dream sharing. Dreamwork outside a clinical setting is not a substitute for psychotherapy, or other professional treatment, and should not be used as such.

IASD recognizes and respects that there are many valid and time-honored dreamwork traditions. We invite and welcome the participation of dreamers from all cultures. There are social, cultural, and transpersonal aspects to dream experience. In this statement we do not mean to imply that the only valid approach to dreamwork focuses on the dreamer's personal life. Our purpose is to honor and respect the person of the dreamer as well as the dream itself, regardless of how the relationship between the two may be understood.

I am very proud to say IASD's dreamwork ethics statement has been adopted by dreamers and dream organizations as the gold standard for dreamwork ethics internationally.

To sum up: the dreamer must be in charge of his or her own dreamwork process, without being led. The dreamer's ownership and authority over his or her dreams is key. A conclusion about whether a client has been sexually abused should not be drawn based on a single dream but rather in the context of the entire therapeutic process, in which traumatic material is slowly pieced together. The meaning of a particular dream becomes clear through the dreamer's own associations to the dream material. Sometimes there are no answers at the time of the dream, which can be a frustrating experience for both the dreamer and the therapist. The meaning(s) of a dream may take time to emerge.

More Research on Trauma and Dreams

In the 1990s, some very important research was done on dreams and childhood sexual abuse. Unfortunately, since that time not much research has been done in this area, so I will focus on the existing research. That research points to the importance of recognizing that specific dream content is not predictive of a history of sexual abuse.

In their paper, "*Identifying a History of Sexual Trauma from Patterns of Dream and Sleep Disturbance*," which is included as a chapter in Deirdre Barrett's excellent book *Dreams and Trauma*, dream researchers Kathryn Belicki and Marion Cuddy make a number of important points that need to be taken into consideration in the assessment of dreams as related to sexual abuse. Belicki and Cuddy conducted their research among university students. They gave a depression inventory and several questionnaires to the students to determine those students who reported no history of abuse, those who reported a history of sexual abuse, those who reported a history of physical abuse, and those who reported a history of both physical and sexual abuse. Belicki and Cuddy reported that the "sexual abuse group reported more nightmares, more repetitive nightmares, more sleep terrors, and greater difficult falling asleep after a nightmare than did the no abuse group. On all measures they showed greater disturbance than the physical abuse" (in Barrett 1996).

Belicki and Cuddy went on to study the differences in nightmare content in students with trauma histories. Their interest was first in identifying nightmare content differences between dreamers in the four categories mentioned above. They wanted to ascertain whether a group of therapists who were aware of these research findings could predict a history of sexual abuse based on nightmares. The findings of this study in these two areas are quite important in identifying general themes but perhaps most importantly in making us aware that one cannot draw accurate conclusions about a sexual-abuse history based on nightmare content alone.

The students who reported a sexual-abuse history were found to have some significant differences in nightmare content compared to students in the other groups.

In terms of the specific findings, the women who reported having been sexually abused tended to have more sexual themes in their nightmares and sexual activity was more likely to be associated with such negative qualities as distrust, shame, guilt, jealousy, anger or violence. However, although sexuality was more frequent, most reports of nightmares had no sexual content. Only 15% reported a nightmare with a theme of explicit sexual abuse.

Another frequent theme was explicit violence. Although violence, or the threat of violence, was common in all women's nightmares, when explicit details were present, such as blood or dismemberment, the dreamer was likely to have been sexually abused. Sometimes the violence was a result of aggression on the part of humans, animals or supernatural characters; other times it was caused by such events as car accidents and natural disasters. While women reporting physical abuse often dream of themselves dying (typically without explicit details of violence), women reporting sexual or no abuse were more likely to dream of others dying.

Several types of dream characters and objects were more common in the dreams of the sexually abused. They were more likely to have a male stranger as a pivotal character in the dream. These characters were often faceless (or the face was invisible), or shadowy, or described as somehow evil. Sometimes the women described dreaming of an evil "presence" which might enter her room or body. Snakes and worms were slightly more frequent in the dreams of the sexually abused and references to parts of the body/anatomy (any part) were more frequent as was, not surprisingly, references to sexual anatomy. In terms of this last point, the higher scores for anatomy usually occurred because sexual trauma survivors were more likely to describe the physical appearance of dream characters. (Belicki and Cuddy in Barrett 1996)

A key finding of this research was, as mentioned earlier, that the nightmares of sexual-abuse survivors typically tend to portray the emotional reality of the abuse rather than replaying the actual event. A further factor, which the researchers did not discuss but which might have an impact on the dream material, is the confusion that results when seduction and affection were involved in the sexual abuse (leading the child victim to think, "this means I am special") versus sexual abuse in which the victim was overtly forced into the abuse.

The findings point out themes and content elements more common in the dreams of those who are sexually abused. However, the researchers found no dream themes or elements that point with certainty to a history of sexual abuse. In addition, since only 15 percent of the students in this study with a sexual-abuse history had dreams with explicit sexual abuse, we cannot draw accurate conclusions about a lack of sexual-abuse history from a lack of explicit sexual-abuse dreams.

The researchers went on, in the next part of their study, to "study whether therapists … could make use of a general description of these research findings to successfully identify people with a history of sexual abuse." The nightmares from the same four groups (women reporting a history of sexual abuse only, both sexual and physical abuse, physical abuse only, and no abuse) were used. The raters, who included clinical psychologists and undergraduate students, were given the research findings and asked to identify which nightmares came from which groups. The raters were not very accurate in their identification of persons with a history of sexual abuse. Although the psychologists did better than the students, their results were still only somewhat more accurate than chance.

These results are important to note as further caution to those of us who are clinicians to be careful about the conclusions we draw about our clients' dreams. We must be careful to allow our clients to work their own dreams. We are most effective as guides when we ask questions to stimulate the dreamers' own thinking and feeling processes. A dreamer's associations to his or her own material will almost always clarify the meaning of the dream. Therapists may be aware of general trends but must be very careful to respect the dreamer if he or she says that a particular idea or meaning does not click for him or her as being a correct way to understand a dream. As Belicki and Cuddy state, "Although nightmare content yields clues to a history of abuse, at present there is no simple formula that will confidently point to such a history."

Similarly, Deirdre Barrett, in her article "Dreams in Dissociative Disorders," states, "No characteristic of the dreams of dissociative disordered patients in this survey is so distinctive as to never be found in those of other dreamers" (Barrett 1994, 174). Dr. Barrett makes some very interesting points about the dreams of patients with dissociative disorders, based on a survey she did of forty-eight therapists, questioning them about their patients' dreams. In her summary of the results of the survey, Dr. Barrett notes the actual dream content of patients with dissociative disorders cannot be distinguished from that of non-dissociative dreamers, except in frequency of dream themes.

Dr. Barrett found that it is the patient's associations to his or her own dreams that distinguish the dissociative- disordered patients from a more normative population. It is here that careful dreamwork pays off richly, for in this associative process the patient can connect to his or her own personal material, including information about other personalities (in the case of dissociative identity disorder, formerly known as multiple personality disorder), and to memories of early trauma and forgotten recent experiences. Respectful, nonintrusive dreamwork can allow access to threatening material, at a pace (therapeutic window) at which the dreamer can continually monitor whether he or she wishes to proceed. Since it is the dreamer's own material, there is a built-in safety factor in that the images and connections do not come from outside the self but rather from within the self, even if they come from a deeply buried part of the self.

In her survey, Dr. Barrett found the majority of respondents reported some dream-related memory recovery. Dissociative-disordered patients tend to have both recent and early memory loss. The results of this survey indicated that both recent and early memory recovery via dreams were reported with similar frequencies. Some dreams were "undisguised recreation of real episodes, especially for recent repressed events," but more often, the dreams contained some distortions. Dr. Barrett cautions in her summary that "nothing in this survey suggests that dreams can be definitive in establishing the existence of a dissociative disorder, although the associations that arise in discussing them might" (Barrett, 194, 174). Her results strongly indicate that therapists should not infer abuse or trauma-related dissociative disorders based on type or frequency of dream or nightmare content alone. However, Dr. Barrett adds, "The situation in which dreams of dissociative disordered patients appear to be most helpful is once one knows the patient has dissociative phenomena and is trying to track down specific content of childhood traumas which played a role in initiating this defensive style and/or content of recent amnestic periods" (Barrett 1994, 174). She goes on to speak about how helpful dreamwork can be for patients with dissociative identity disorder. In these cases, dream content and dreamer associations to this content can be very beneficial in identifying various personalities and even in facilitating communication between them.

To sum up, the existing research on dreams and abuse makes it clear that it is not scientifically supportable to infer a history of sexual abuse or to make a diagnosis of a dissociative disorder (often associated with a history of sexual abuse) from dream content alone, though a higher frequency of certain types of dreams may point to a higher likelihood of sexual abuse history.

All the dream researchers I have just discussed emphasize that it is the dreamer's associations to the dream content that will lead the dreamer to the meaning of the dream. Insofar as is humanly possible, the therapist needs to strive to maintain a stance of neutrality and to empower the client to make his or her own observations and conclusions. In this manner, the dreamer can discover, or begin to discover, the richness of his or her own inner life and the incredible world of guidance and help that lies therein. From a clinical perspective, when dealing with trauma and memory issues in dreamwork, this safe and ethical client-centered approach prevents the risk of therapist leading.

Having taken a look at existing research on dreams and trauma and on the necessity for a careful, client-centered approach both in trauma therapy and in dreamwork, I return in the next chapter to Susan's story and some surprising elements that were to emerge.

CHAPTER 14

BACK TO SUSAN

My aim in this chapter, as I continue with Susan's story, is to continue to look at the therapeutic process. The material is very complicated and goes more deeply into controversial areas, most especially ritual abuse and her belief in reincarnation. As the story continues, I will demonstrate the importance of staying neutral and client centered and of being a process facilitator rather than an arbiter of truth, psychological or spiritual. Although the controversy over false memory has quieted down, the same issues continue to emerge in therapists' offices in ever-greater numbers. Ritual abuse may have been culturally swept under the rug in the 1990s with the false memory controversy, but the phenomenon continues, and treatment protocols and models have developed tremendously since that time. Recent events and disclosures have reopened awareness of the reality of ritual abuse accompanying much of the sex trafficking and drug dealing going on today.

Ritual abuse and satanic cults are a reality in every city and town of our country. It is not a matter of whether one believes they exist; law enforcement has long known they are in every community. Ted Gunderson, an ex-FBI chief, has had more to say, and in depth, than just about any other person in law enforcement. Videos of him speaking on this subject can be found on YouTube. He was particularly involved in the Franklin cover-up, which involved Satanism, pedophilia, and the White House. I mentioned this case earlier because of Bill Colby, ex-CIA director, who spoke on the banned (but still available on the Internet) documentary Conspiracy of Silence.

What is ritual abuse? In a 1989 report, the Ritual Abuse Task Force of the LA County Commission for Women provided the following definition:

> Ritual Abuse usually involves repeated abuse over an extended period of time. The physical abuse is severe, sometimes including torture and killing. The sexual abuse is usually painful, humiliating, intended as a means of gaining dominance over the victim. The psychological abuse is devastating and involves the use of ritual indoctrination and ritual/intimidation which conveys to the victim a profound terror of the cult members and of the evil spirits they believe cult members can command. Both during and after the abuse, it includes mind control techniques which convey to the victim a profound terror of the cult members … most victims are in a state of terror, mind control and dissociation. (*https://ritualabuse.us/ritualabuse/articles/report-of-the-ritual-abuse-task-force-los-angeles-county-commission-for-women*)

Skilled therapists continue to hear ritual-abuse victims' experiences and assess the deep wounding that ritual abuse causes. From the standpoint of therapeutic work, therapists and clients need to understand that these issues can be dealt with effectively when they emerge, no matter how challenging or controversial they are. Therapists and victims alike are in need of finding safe, non-leading, and therapeutically sound ways to understand and work with the material. The core nature of RA is spiritual abuse, which I will explore in the next chapter.

When we left off with Susan's story, Susan was looking at some early dreams that contained some sexual and physical trauma and some that involved satanic themes. Before she had these dreams, she had been doing reading on her own initiative. She wondered if her symptoms of depression, extensive childhood amnesia, frequent panic attacks and migraines, and fear of intimacy pointed to a history of childhood sexual abuse. There was no corroboration from family members. All of them, including her mother and siblings had extensive amnesia. The dreams brought up many disturbing questions for Susan, especially given the extensiveness of her amnesia for childhood. Her associations to her dreams included sad and angry feelings but little that she could relate to her waking life. She was experiencing much more discomfort in her waking life as these feelings came to the surface, which is entirely typical of sexual abuse survivors who have dissociated memories. Yet it was far too early to draw any conclusions or do anything other than to adopt a wait-and-see attitude.

Another dream surfaced in which Susan was very frightened and hiding in a closet. Susan thought the dream was significant but did not know how. All she knew was the dream was emotionally charged.

As we worked with the dream, it seemed resistant to the usual techniques, and we did not get very far. I then decided to use a technique with her that Carl Jung called active imagination. This technique, known by many other names, is also a well-known Gestalt psychology technique for working with dream symbols. In this technique, the dreamer is led to "enter" into a dream character or dream image and explore what it feels like to be this character or image. The dreamer is guided to explore how it feels to be this character or image as the dream events progress, to explore the spatial surroundings, and to explore any other associations that may come up.

Roger Woolger, a Jungian analyst, describes this technique of active imagination and differentiates it from the more directive and active position that a hypnotherapist may take.

> Jung developed a method which is neither as laissez-faire as the Freudian method nor quite as directive as hypnotherapy. His technique, which he called active imagination, is best described as an interaction with the unconscious. We learn to sit, as in meditation, and simply observe a fragment of a dream or hypnagogic image without any attempt to guide, control, or interfere with it. The aim is to allow the image to come to life of its own autonomous psychic energy, our ego letting go of all expectations, presuppositions, or interpretations. After a certain period of practice and initial coaching by the therapist, this inner image will start to move in some way and our observing ego learns to participate in the story very much as the dream ego in normal dreaming. This waking dream ego is encouraged to encounter the dream situation as directly as possible, not to retreat, and to fully allow any emotions such as fear, anger, sadness, longing, etc., to arise during the inner psychodrama. (Woolger 1987, 89–90)

This technique can be extremely helpful in exploring images from dreams that are resistant to other techniques. I could have easily interpreted Susan's dream to her as her fear of looking at her childhood, represented by her fearfully hiding in a closet. Although at some level this was undoubtedly true and Susan might have accepted my projection, this would have missed completely her own reasons for the production of this dream.

We used the active imagination technique with the image of Susan hiding in the closet. I asked her to describe to me anything that arose within her, without my suggesting or leading in any way. A chilling scene unfolded in which Susan was at her grandfather's house. She was terrified, hiding in the closet. Her grandfather eventually found her and molested and beat her. All the emotions one might expect to accompany such a traumatic event accompanied this exercise. She felt horrified, hurt, betrayed, enraged, and afraid for her life.

When the exercise was over, Susan told me that she remembered her alcoholic grandfather. He physically abused his wife. She did not consciously recall this event in the closet but stated she could see how it easily could have happened, because this man was frequently drunk and definitely violent and, during summers, she spent a fair amount of time at his house.

Here, for the first time in our work, something had appeared that she believed could plausibly contain material from her largely forgotten past. The powerful emotions she felt indicated to her that something real in her subconscious had been tapped.

Lenore Terr and others point out that where false memories are imagined, there is little accompanying emotion or sense of drama. However, since it is possible that false memories can have emotionality, the only absolute test for real versus false memories is corroboration. As it stood, we had nothing concrete to go on; there was no proof, and no corroboration was possible. Susan had long since lost touch with that side of the family, and she had no idea whom she might be able to speak with. Little more could be done now with this piece other than to suspend judgment and wait and see.

After this work with the dream, she had the following dream:

I'm in bed with my partner. The phone rings and a woman says it is time for me to die. I want to get out of bed, and hiss at my partner. My eyes flare like a devil with evil anger.

In the next scene a bad man in a mask abducts a five-year-old child, perhaps me. [Susan thinks the bad man may be her father.] I am very afraid of this man. The child may be used as payment for something.

Susan associated with this dream by saying that she had intense, "evil" anger in her and that she was afraid it could destroy her and maybe others. She experienced the anger as very real and extremely frightening. When she woke up from this dream, she remembered a previous dream in which there had been blood on the bed, and she had a strong impression that the scene was part of some kind of satanic ritual. She knew nothing about such rituals and did not know where that waking impression came from. She related the two dreams as now being tied together by this thread, a terrifying prospect. Susan expressed the very understandable fear she would not be able to handle this work.

In the second part of this dream, a "bad" man had something to do with trading a child as a payment for something. Susan's dream associations were that drugs were involved and that in the dream she was the payment for these drugs or other contraband. She could not explain on a rational level these associations to the dream. She could only say that these were things she "knew" about the dream.

It was understandably disconcerting to have a dream in which her father was portrayed as someone who trafficked her in trade for something. She was also upset at the imagery of the devil being within her. We discussed the possibility that the symbol of the devil within her might relate to her suppressed angry feelings about hurts and disappointments in her childhood and a feeling of "badness" she might have over her anger. Susan's association was that it could be related to ritual abuse.

The death threat in the dream was also puzzling. It came at a time in Susan's therapy when she was just beginning to access abuse material. Perhaps she was unconsciously afraid she might die if she remembered abuse. Perhaps she had suppressed anger at her wife and was afraid she might not be able to survive if she were to be honest with her wife about her feelings. Maybe their marriage would break up. There were many possibilities. She wondered about the death threat and whether it could be related somehow to the dream in which she had been told Satan's eye was in her, observing her to make sure she did not remember or share information about Satanism. Was she forbidden to remember what had happened? We tried to look at all possible explanations. There were no easy answers, but we followed her associations to the dream symbols. Her associations led increasingly to issues of satanic rituals.

At this time, I did not yet know about ritual abuse or about the increasing frequency with which the issue of ritual cult abuse was coming up in therapy sessions all over the country. Susan had decided earlier not to do any reading on ritual abuse, because she did not wish to skew what might emerge. She seriously doubted anything like this had happened but was now wondering. After all, much of her childhood was missing. Entire years of her childhood were gone.

(I later learned that the "Satan's eye", mentioned in the first Susan chapter, is often hypnotically implanted as a threat to keep the child from telling about the abuse. The suggestion is implanted that if the victim begins to remember, Satan will know because his eye is inside. From there, the child is programmed under the torture of the mind control in the rituals to commit suicide if he or she begins to remember. This is called suicide programming and is a phenomenon well known to clinicians who work with RA and to their RA clients.)

I respected Susan's position, reinforcing her trust in the process with my experience that the psyche shows us what we need to know about our past, in the proper time. Perhaps these satanic symbols were the best way her unconscious mind knew to express that which had been relegated to the shadow or unaccepted and unknown part of the personality. Perhaps the physical and verbal abuse that Susan and her brother remembered had forced her to split off her anger and hurt into a "bad me" part of her personality, expressed in the dream by her having the evil, wicked devil inside of her. As a child, she may have internalized that she must be bad or evil, for that was the only conceivable explanation for why these horrible things would happen to her.

After this surfacing of satanic elements, it was a number of months before there were more. During that time, I did not inquire about such material, nor did Susan mention it. Over time, I became aware of the considerable growing awareness in the therapeutic community and controversy in the media around "satanic" cults. The range of opinion at that time ran the gamut, from one side thinking that ritual abuse was a very real and serious phenomenon responsible for many horrible atrocities to the opposite opinion thinking that it did not exist and that blaming an organized cult was a way of avoiding looking at very painful personal material about one's family or parents. The material was grisly. Perhaps there was more than a small part of me that was grateful the subject had not come up again in Susan's therapy hours.

Susan's next dream occurred about one month later:

> I'm with some adults, my brother and a few other children. My parents are away. My uncle locks me and my brother and the other children in the cellar with us. I feel somewhat dizzy and disoriented, as if I am on drugs. We are forced to do things to each other's private parts. One person has their pants off, one is licking. A man in the room has a camera pointed at us.

Susan was puzzled and understandably distressed by the dream. Within the dream, she felt powerless to do anything except what she was told to do. She felt as if she might have been under the influence of a drug. She felt revulsion about what happened. She had the sense that what was done was for the sake of the camera. Susan had no memory of any event that would correspond to what she'd dreamed, nor did she have any associations that would clarify a symbolic meaning of the dream. However, she did state she had always had a powerful hatred of cellars and basements. No conclusion could be drawn from this dream, only questions.

Several days later, Susan brought in a dream that repeated some of the earlier material while adding some new material:

> It is dark, and I am outdoors with a group of people who are wearing black robes and who are in a circle. I am on a table in the center. My mouth is filled with something. It is awful, dirty, Satan-like. All I can think about is to get it out. I try not to swallow it. I want to throw it up, but it goes down my throat anyway. It stinks. It shouldn't be in me—I need to spit it out.

Susan could not think of any associations to the people in black robes and was disturbed they came up in a dream. Susan's waking association to what was in her mouth was that it was semen and that she was repulsed. She connected it within the dream to something satanic but had no memory of ever having been in a situation where she felt this way.

Susan thought she was a child in the dream, not an adult. The references in the dream to Satan are striking. At this point in therapy, Susan did not know whether she had been sexually abused. As we worked with this dream, Susan had a very vivid sense of what it felt like to be a young girl and to have this semen in her mouth and of how repulsive and disgusting it felt to her. Susan had been raised as a Catholic. It is possible that if a young Catholic girl had been sexually abused, she might associate the abuse with the devil and with evil. This could all be buried and mixed together in the subconscious mind.

I helped Susan do active imagination work with the dream. Before we did the work, I told her not to worry about whether the imagery that came up was truth or fiction but rather just to let it flow spontaneously. Before any sorting could be done, the imagery and feeling had to be allowed to emerge into consciousness. Afterward, there would be plenty of time to review and assess the information.

As Susan focused on the image of the girl, I asked her to describe her surroundings. She looked around and found herself in a motel room. I asked her to tell me if she saw anything else. She saw a man coming toward her. He then forced his penis into her mouth. She reported to me that this was a familiar situation for this girl; she had been in this situation before. She felt smothered, trapped, and abandoned.

As Susan got in touch with these feelings, she wept uncontrollably, which was very uncharacteristic for this usually emotionally controlled woman. She described how the man yanked her head back and forth while he shoved his penis down her throat. She tried to get it out but could not. She then felt something wet dripping down her mouth. She, as the young girl, wondered if he'd peed in her mouth. She found the substance wet and awful. As the scene continued, the man tried to penetrate her. She resisted, and he hit her. She felt completely powerless and very afraid of him.

Once it was over, the man left, and then she dressed and went to her father, who was waiting for her outside. When she as the adult woman observing the girl realized this, she felt desolate and abandoned. She knew her father had betrayed her and allowed this to happen to her. On the drive home, nothing was said about what had happened. There was a heavy silence between them.

When this was over, it took Susan a long time to bring herself back to the present. She was overwhelmed by the intensity of the emotions, wondering where they'd come from. Susan remembered no such event and was at a complete loss why she would have such an intense emotional experience if there had been no actual experience of abuse in her past. She identified the man as someone her father knew, a man whom she'd never liked and around whom she had been very uncomfortable. He had always felt very "dark" to her. This was the same man who had come up in her associations to the dream where her father was using her as cash payment for something. She thought this man had some kind of shady association with her father. She wondered now if that previous dream was related to this experience. She had suspicions that her father and this man were involved in some drug trading.

In the next session, Susan wondered why she did not "remember" these events. They'd felt so real to her in my office the previous week, and she had been sure they must have happened. Yet she still did not remember them in the same way she remembered day-to-day events. She wondered if she was crazy or if she'd imagined all of this. That there were no clear answers to be found frustrated her even more. Living with the ambiguity and the ambivalence of the unanswered questions was extremely difficult.

Susan gingerly discussed the material that was coming up with her father and brother. She made no accusations. Her father insisted nothing like this had happened and implied that something might be wrong with her for looking at this material. Susan felt pressure to keep the lid on, discontinue looking inside, and just try to be happy. She had always done this but no longer could.

Susan knew only too well the tremendous cost of sweeping under the rug all these feelings and images inflicted upon her. She had tried for years to look the other way, and her symptoms had only gotten worse. Now, regardless of what was the truth of her history, she was having periods in which she was doing significantly better and in which she had relief from her debilitating symptoms. She could no longer go without questioning the massive childhood amnesia she experienced or without questioning why others in her family had experienced similar amnesia for very large periods. Susan's panic attack symptoms had been significantly alleviated, and she assessed that even if she did not have answers to what was coming up, she was heading in the right direction with this work.

Susan's father was adamantly against Susan's therapy and repeated his belief that she was getting worse rather than better. Susan recalled her father's involvement in prostituting her in the dream and decided he would probably not be of much assistance to her in reconstructing her own personal history. Susan decided to stop sharing with her father and brother what she was going through with this work, because their reactions sent her into a tailspin. She had trouble enough trusting her own feelings and reactions; when she felt pressure from them, it was too confusing.

The following dream, reported about a month and a half later, brings out an interesting aspect of dissociation:

> Someone is beating me as he is pulling my clothes off. I cannot see his face, it is blacked out. The man beating me is out of control and starts to rape me. I can't take it! I can leave my body—now I am not there—I cannot feel the pain. He is finished now. I go back into my body, which hurts greatly.

In this and other dreams, Susan reported she had repeatedly been aware of the experience of leaving her body and watching the abuse from another perspective in the room, outside of her physical body.

The next dream, which followed a month later, is also illustrative of this sense of seeing from an out-of-body perspective:

> I'm in my bedroom. My father comes in and hits me with his belt buckle repeatedly. He is completely out of control. I am bleeding from my mouth. Now I'm out of my body, looking down at myself.

Despite her amnesia, Susan had always remembered that her father had been physically abusive toward her and her brother during her childhood. She tended to minimize the violence. The out-of-control nature of the abuse in this dream and the rape in the first dream forced her to take another look at what she remembered and to reassess it. Susan now found herself wondering even more strongly about the messages portrayed in the other dreams. Given what she knew about her father's alcoholism and his history of physically abusing his children, she found the dream where her father beat her with the belt buckle believable and consistent with her remembered experience. She did not know what to do about the rape dream, nor did she know who the man was who had raped her, as his face had been blacked out. Susan found it interesting that, despite these types of dreams, her symptoms were improving. Still, there was no external corroboration, and there were many questions. Her next dream was even stranger.

I am outdoors at night. Someone dressed up in a dark robe is leading others in dark robes in some kind of ritual. When she speaks, she sounds like my mother.

I am undressed and lying on what I know in the dream is an altar. I am unable to move. I feel drugged. My legs are spread apart. I know I have been here before. I can't bear it. The next thing I know I am watching myself from a perspective above myself. I watch as I am raped by a series of men.

Susan seemed to be in shock as she recounted the dream. She said she had been very hesitant to bring it into the session, but she knew it was important. She had begun experiencing severe pelvic pains around the time she had the dream and wondered if they were related. Trauma is stored in our bodies, and it is not uncommon for trauma victims to manifest bruises, welts, and pain as a form of body memory. For Susan, the pelvic pain seemed to corroborate the dream material. She wondered how something like this could have happened to her, but she believed it had.

DISSOCIATION, OUT-OF-BODY EXPERIENCE, AND THE SOUL

Here I digress briefly on the subject of being out of body, since it may offer an important piece of the puzzle for trauma victims trying to build connections with their spirituality.

The out-of-body perspective is commonly reported in memories of trauma and torture victims. In psychiatric literature, dissociation has been discussed as an intrapsychic phenomenon—that is, it occurs as a kind of splitting within the psyche so the unbearable feelings and memories are walled off in a separate part of the psyche, away from the conscious ego, which is available for thinking, feeling, and functioning.

Some writers might consider these out-of-body perspectives as a simple, perhaps imagined vantage point of consciousness. However, the subject may be more complex than this. There are a number of well- known modern writers (Monroe, Eadie, Atwater, Eben Alexander, and so on) who discuss out-of-body experiences, both as part of near-death experiences and otherwise.

Susan was religious and believed in the life of the soul apart from the body. She departed from traditional Catholic doctrine in her strong belief in reincarnation, believing she had lived a number of lives. She also believed she had memories of some of them. For her, a dream of being out of body was not baffling or puzzling. Even for someone with a more traditional religious orientation, with a belief there is a soul that leaves the body at the moment of death, there exists the possibility the soul might be capable of leaving the body at extraordinary moments.

In Susan's dreams, she witnessed herself leaving her body temporarily to escape pain. In her belief system, the soul enters the body at some time before birth, departs at death, and might leave the body at times in between. Might a person sometimes actually leave their body during unbearable trauma? Is some percentage of dissociation explained by actual out-of-body experience? It is wise not to conflate dissociation and out-of-body experiences overall, but I do wonder about possible overlap. For therapeutic purposes, I find it helpful to explore the client's beliefs about his or her experience rather than to impose my own.

Trauma survivors often report they remember their trauma from a vantage point out of their body, watching the abuse from above, from behind, or from somewhere else in the room other than in their body. I believe that addressing this phenomenon at the appropriate time (not in the midst of memory work) can be a rich opening to help clients explore their spirituality, something that can help immensely through the healing process. As I have mentioned before, abuse victims often lose their faith in a benevolent God, outside of them, who has failed to protect them. The experience of being out of body opens up the possibility that there is an eternal self apart from the physical body that may live on after death. If clients are questioned gently, and at an appropriate time, about what they think may mean, the door may open to a discussion about personal spirituality.

In a later chapter, I address how dreams can open up the dreamer's mind to spiritual aspects of reality. For now, I wish to emphasize that when the client can be helped to explore his or her own spiritual beliefs, the way is opened for exploration of healing spiritual resources for coping with the trauma. Because abuse can be so horrific, the abuse survivor has become terrified to look within, where so much pain and suffering lies.

The hope and the dawning realization that internal spiritual resources may be available can be immensely helpful, for the survivor can learn to rely on his or her own higher self as a guide. A prayer or meditation practice can be cultivated. Going to church or reading inspirational literature may be helpful. A journal or dream journal can be started. The voice of this inner self, in both its psychological and spiritual aspects, can guide and inform the healing process. As time passes and the client develops more trust in that inner voice, the guidance provided from the self becomes a more prominent feature of the healing process. Dreams are one of the best tools to provide access to that self.

PSYCHOLOGICAL NAVIGATION AND REINCARNATION

In this section, Susan's dreams and memory work took her into another area that can be difficult for both client and therapist to process in therapy if belief systems collide. As always, the best therapeutic rule is to go with what the client presents rather than impose one's own belief system.

Susan reported recurrent dreams throughout her adult life of being in Nazi Germany, in a concentration camp of some kind. The images and feelings of these dreams haunted her. They had come up again recently. She had often wondered about a possible past-life experience there, in that time.

A number of abuse survivors have related to me over the years that they remembered past-life experiences in Germany. At the very least, the symbolism of the devastation and utter disregard for human life of the Holocaust provides a perfect metaphor for the horrendous experiences of many of these abuse survivors. At some level in the psyche, these "remembered" experiences provide access to the feelings of horror and absolute betrayal involved in the survivors' abuse experiences.

Rabbi Yonassan Gershom's books *Beyond the Ashes: Cases of Reincarnation from the Holocaust* and *From Ashes to Healing* discuss many cases he has dealt with of those who believed they were victims of the Holocaust in their most-recent past lives. Roger Woolger in his book *Other Lives, Other Selves* repeatedly makes the point that from a psychological perspective it does not matter whether one believes in the reality of reincarnation in working through these memories. In his perspective, the fact is that these highly emotionally charged, traumatic experiences are stored in the unconscious and must be processed and worked through when they come up, as with any other memory. The integration, or metabolizing, of the traumatic and emotional components of these past-life contents can occur regardless of the belief system of the client or therapist. I agree completely with this. The processed emotions are thus integrated into the self-structure of the client. Whether the traumatic event is symbolic or real may never be determined; however, the trauma is worked through in the service of healthier functioning. It would be a therapeutic error for a therapist to not work with this material because it does not fit into his or her belief system or to prematurely dismiss it as "psychotic."

The dreams Susan believed were of a past life often involved being in a Nazi concentration camp, where she felt trapped and powerless over the fate about to befall her. She believed she had been involved in medical experiments. In her present life, we explored the various times and places where she experienced her panic attacks. A number occurred when she felt trapped in some way. There was an emotional link between the occurrence of her panic attacks and the feeling of being in Nazi Germany, powerless over her fate.

I asked Susan to try to identify any key words or key phrases that came up for her as the panic attacks began and then went into full force. As she focused on this, she realized that the key sentence that replayed itself during these attacks was "I have no control—there's no way out." I asked Susan to repeat this phrase over and over, with the emotion with which she felt it in those situations. This non-hypnotic technique, developed by Jungian analyst Roger Woolger, is useful for taking a person back to the earlier time in which the current situation has its roots, through association with the powerful emotions of the earlier experience. People often go back to childhood memories and relive some of the traumatic circumstances that caused the emotional blockage in the first place. Sometimes people go into what they consider to be past-life experiences.

What Woolger says in the following quotation applies equally to the emergence of traumatic memory that may come through in using active imagination with dream or other imagery.

> In guiding individual sessions it is necessary to take these experiences as completely real—as if they were literal experiences. Absolute respect for the psychic reality of the experience is necessary so that this "other life" can be reconstituted and relived in all its fullness. The stance of the therapeutic "as if" provides an attitude of unconditional concern and is the basis for the successful release and expression of the story in all its confusions, pain, or fragmentation. And whatever embroidering, distortion or unconscious reworking may have occurred, each client's story needs nevertheless to be heard totally without judgment or without interpretation, fully encouraged to be told as real. (Woolger 1987, 320)

As Susan repeated the phrase, she found herself as a child, reliving a grisly scene in Nazi Germany. In this situation, she experienced feelings of helplessness and of being completely trapped. She felt there was absolutely no way out of her predicament. There were scenes in which she was involved with horrendous medical experimentation on children. It seemed to her, as she reviewed what she experienced in this scene, that the key word was acquiescence. She gave consent in that scene only because she had no choice.

The parallel between this kind of submission and the submission a child would experience if being sexually abused is clear. Was this her mind's way of distancing from, or creating a metaphor for, the horrors of abuse? Alternatively, was it part of an emerging pattern that connected several lives? If the latter, then she now had an opportunity within this life to work through the trauma. It was not my role to determine. Susan, however, now believed the scenes in her recurrent dreams set in Nazi Germany made more sense to her. She also had another dream after this session that elaborated on the details she had experienced in the therapy hour.

At this juncture in treatment, Susan had been having panic attacks for over five years. They had recently eased. Now, after having gone through this experience of reliving that time in Germany, she was able to step back and look at how her symptoms connected with this past-life complex. She could now dissociate herself from the automatic reaction of feeling panic when she felt confined. She could separate her current self's options from her past self's experiences. As we worked with her panic attacks, I helped her to look closely at what she told herself as the attacks started and to counter it by telling herself that she now had options, that she could get out of the situation if she wished, and so on. This cognitive-behavioral technique alone had not worked previously, but now, with this new emotional understanding, it worked quite well. For almost one and a half months, she had absolutely no panic attacks, a huge step forward.

REEMERGENCE OF SATANIC MATERIAL

As so often happens with long-term trauma work, the survivor goes through alternating cycles of remembering and accessing unconscious material and of not accessing and instead assessing and integrating various kinds of emotional, physical, and cognitive material. These consolidation periods, which may feel more calmer, can feel like stagnation, yet these therapeutic plateaus can be positive periods of building and strengthening.

After a period of relative calm, both because of the complete absence of panic attacks and migraines and because of the consolidating work that was going on, Susan's panic attacks recurred. She began to have a number of memories of sexual abuse. She decided to review all her dreams to look at the themes and to note any patterns. When she reviewed them, she was stunned by the themes that stood out and the relatively high frequency with which they came. She found the following recurrent themes: physical and sexual abuse, incest, Satanism and satanic rituals, child sacrifices, kidnappings, drugs, and child pornography. She was always a child in these dreams or an observer into a time past. She was never an adult while involved in these activities.

Dreams of these subjects are rare in a general population. A well-known content analysis study of five hundred dreams of college women found the above-listed themes appeared with no frequency or such low frequency that the researchers did not even refer to them in any of the scoring categories (from a personal conversation with Robert Van de Castle, PhD, now deceased, about Susan's dreams in relation to his content analysis work, written up in Hall and Van de Castle 1966). Dr. Van de Castle strongly reinforced that Susan's many dreams with these repetitive and consistent themes were highly statistically significant and well outside of known norms.

Despite Susan's previous resolution to not go to her father with discussions of this material, she decided she needed to try again. She wanted to share some of the dreams and dream themes with him, while not yet mentioning the dreams in which he was involved. She wondered if he knew anything that might help her to understand why she was having these dreams, set in her childhood, about these gruesome subjects. Susan did not go into this conversation with accusations or with a confrontation. She had come to no conclusions. Rather, she went with many questions about what these dreams could possibly mean and whether they could reflect actual experiences she might have had. On the other hand, was there anything else in her experience that could account for the way her psyche had seized upon this symbolism?

Susan's father again said he remembered little about the time he and his wife had raised Susan and her brother. This adult amnesia is in itself quite striking and could be due to one or a combination of factors, including (1) the progressive deterioration of his memory from many years of alcoholic drinking; (2) complete suppression and repression of these years, owing to a variety of possible factors; and (3) a more conscious form of denial, or lying. Susan's father admitted he remembered one instance of physical abuse.

Susan's father told her she had gone too far. He further told Susan that I had led her into these wild and crazy ideas. Although there was no terminology for it at the time, he was raising the possibility of whether this was false memory syndrome. He was unable to hear that Susan had come to no conclusions but rather was coming to him for any possible assistance in understanding why these things might be consistently coming up out of her own unconscious.

As is typical when a client is faced with such blanket denial from a loved one, no matter how far along the client is in the recovery process, Susan became disoriented and went through a period of feeling she was losing her mind. For weeks she was upset, telling herself that maybe nothing at all had happened and that maybe her mind and emotions were playing cruel tricks on her. She talked about quitting therapy, thinking that if she stopped looking at what was coming up, it might go away and leave her alone. This is not uncommon. Susan decided to terminate. I respected her decision, even though I knew this would not solve the problem in the manner she was hoping. I told her the door would always be open should she change her mind.

Almost immediately, she experienced a number of powerful and disturbing nightmares that continued the imagery of the devil and satanic rituals. Within two weeks, she had changed her mind and returned to therapy. The feelings, dreams, and imagery were coming from within her—I was not the cause. No matter how much Susan wished she did not have to deal with this, it was not going away. She would have to find a way through it, not around it.

Susan was now taking time to meditate regularly. Over her adult life, she had done a good bit of meditation. When she entered therapy and made a commitment to taking better care of herself, she restarted her daily meditation practice. Susan found that many images appeared to her when she meditated. Meditation was a time in which she could relax and process in an unhurried fashion the events and feelings of her current life and earlier times. Sometimes the images that came to her were memories. Some she recognized. Others were images that made no particular sense to her, and she did not know whether they were symbolic material or memory material.

We worked in therapy with these images in a similar fashion as with dream imagery. Always, I encouraged her to enter the image and let whatever came through emerge; it would be impossible at the time of the reentering to decide if a given image or scene were literally true or a symbolic representation of something else. It would take time afterward to sort things out.

In April, while she was meditating, Susan saw an image of herself in a basement. The door ahead of her could open, but she definitely did not want to go in. She walked down the hall to another door, but she did not want to go in there either. She experienced fear and dread in both cases. Susan brought these images to me, feeling they were important somehow, but she did not know how to get anywhere with them. She was also afraid to look at them alone. It felt very unsafe to her. Later on in the month, Susan had the following dream:

> I am forced into a coffin, and the cover is closed. I am terrified. After a while it grows
> harder to breathe. No one comes to take me out.

As Susan explored the dream, she experienced both physical and emotional aspects of the experience. When she entered the imagery, she felt extremely confined, unable to move her arms to knock on the underside of the lid of the coffin. Then she went out of body and viewed the scene from outside the coffin. After a period, she reconnected into her body through powerful rage and fury. The entire room where we sat was charged with the intense affect she felt as she raged at being trapped and confined without the possibility of movement. It was as if she were discharging tremendous amounts of stored-up rage and tension.

Susan was overcome and bewildered by what she had just gone through. The scene itself made no sense to her. Why would a child be forced into a tightly fitting coffin and made to stay there? She was clearly not naive as to various types of child abuse, but this was inconceivable to her, as it would be for most of us.

The frightening material continued to emerge on its own, in some depth and detail. There was no external corroboration. The missing years were enormously puzzling, and the material that emerged had a striking internal consistency of its own. However, in reaching for clues for her past in the external world, Susan found mainly question marks and similar gaps in memory in her family members. Susan mentioned that when she'd had a gynecological exam as a young woman, the gynecologist had said she had a great deal of vaginal scarring. According to the gynecologist, this would not happen under ordinary circumstances. Susan wondered about one of the earlier dreams, wondering if she had been impregnated and then had a makeshift abortion. There were no definitive answers to these questions.

Susan continued in her search for healing and truth. I was consistently impressed by her bravery, her tenacity, and her determination to find out about her past in spite of the horrible feelings, images, and memories. There was little support around her in her pursuit of her healing. Most of her support system seemed to think her past was better left alone.

TURNING THE CORNER

As Susan relied more on her internal resources, she was able to function better in her daily life. Still, there were no definitive answers. Sometimes she was sure she had experienced ritual abuse; at other times, she was not so sure. In terms of treatment outcome, it did not seem to matter, for by the very process of exploring and working through the material, she got better and her symptoms improved.

As treatment progressed, Susan grew stronger and more confident. She was able to assert herself with her partner and family. She got out of a career that had been unsatisfying and began a new career. The panic attacks resolved. She was gradually able to go off the antidepressant and anti-anxiety medication. She changed her lifestyle, making sure she incorporated time to meditate and pray and to exercise in the outdoors every day.

Her spiritual life gave her comfort and a profound sense of nurturance. As she had worked through the negative material in her unconscious, she found beneath it a strong sense of connection to God and to Mary. This new and powerful connection gave her joy and great sustenance.

Though Susan had in recent times done her best to stay away from material on ritual abuse to keep contamination at a minimum, she was exposed to some information as time went on. She learned that many persons with dissociative identity disorder (DID), what used to be called multiple personality disorder, claim to have been victims of ritual cult abuse. I had been keeping my eyes open to the possibility of a dissociative disorder over the time we had worked together but had not thus far seen any evidence of DID. However, she definitely had dissociative amnesia, the inability to remember personal information; her amnesia was, by her reports, only for childhood.

On several occasions, Susan asked me if I thought she suffered from dissociative identity disorder, not because she saw any signs of it but because she had heard that people who had reported being victims of ritual cult abuse often have this disorder. We frankly discussed symptoms of DID, yet neither of us could identify symptoms beyond dissociative amnesia. Interview scales were later developed to help identify dissociative disorders, but this was before that time. We decided to keep our eyes open to this possibility yet not to put undue focus on a diagnosis. She definitely was amnesic for her childhood and therefore had dissociative amnesia, but loss of time in the present was not an issue for her.

Less than two years into treatment, Susan and her family decided to move north so her spouse could take a promotion with her company. We slowly concluded our work together. Susan's plan was to seek help after she was settled in her new home. When Susan terminated treatment, she believed she had been through horrible trauma as a child, almost certainly ritual abuse. We were in the mid-stage of trauma treatment; much work about her childhood trauma was yet ahead of her. It was likely she would go back and forth many times on whether she had been a victim of ritual abuse before she came to a conclusion about what had happened.

Susan felt much better than when she had entered treatment. She was free of the distressing symptoms that had brought her into therapy—the panic attacks, the depression, and physical symptoms. There were still areas where she felt she had work to do, for she was discontent still having large gaps in her memory for childhood.

However, with Susan's impending move, it was time to wrap up our work and not delve any more into the past. Rather, it was time to help her consolidate her gains and build on her strengths. Susan was fortunate in that she would not have to work right away. She would have time to get herself and her family adjusted in their new home before she had to make any major decisions about what to do. She was eager to move on with her life. Her aim was to establish a grounded and balanced life in her new environment. We terminated on a positive note, with the door open for contact in the future, if she so chose.

DANGEROUS THERAPY

I heard from Susan almost nine months later. She was in distress and wanted to have a telephone consultation. We set up a time to talk. On that phone call, she told me a very unsettling story about what had happened. After she had settled into her new home, she'd established contact with a therapist in the area. She had started going to this therapist without telling the therapist any of her thoughts and suspicions about ritual abuse in her past. She'd wanted to see if the material would emerge again with the new therapist. The same material did continue to emerge, and the new therapist soon identified ritual abuse as a major factor contributing to Susan's symptoms.

Susan was distraught over the work, however, and wanted a second opinion about the direction it was taking. She recounted that her therapist had told her emphatically that she suffered from multiple personality disorder. The new therapist's logic was that all victims of ritual cult abuse were multiple personalities; therefore, since Susan had suffered satanic cult abuse, she must be a multiple. Of course this is faulty logic.

Susan said her therapist had asked her to "give names" to various moods she felt, such as anger, sadness, and so on. These named mood states were then identified as separate personalities, thus filling out the diagnostic picture of multiple personality disorder. Absurd? Absolutely. Dangerous? Extremely. I was horrified as she told me her story. It grew worse.

Susan did not manifest other symptoms of dissociative identity disorder. She did not feel that these so-called "personalities" were separate and distinct, with histories, traits, and personalities all their own. They did not feel dissociated to her (or from her) in that way but rather felt as they always had, as moods. She felt this diagnosis was a forced fit, almost like trying to put a square peg into a round hole. However, she was in a very vulnerable position and had begun doubting herself. After all, her therapist seemed convinced that Susan was a multiple. (Further, and not at all incidentally, Susan related to me that her therapist had confided that she herself was a multiple. Susan told me she did not know whether the therapist was now still suffering from this disorder or whether she was a multiple who had successfully integrated her personalities.) Susan told me that since she had always trusted my opinion, she wanted to hear what I thought about her new diagnosis and treatment.

Susan's story got even more frightening and revealed a number of other therapeutic errors. She described regressions in which she was led to see things or people. She felt there was a forced quality to these regressions and that they did not naturally flow out of her own stream of consciousness. Rather, they came from the therapist. She would be in a scene, and the therapist would suggest or lead her in a certain direction. She would go along with it even though it did not feel right to her because the therapist was the authority and seemed to know what she was doing.

Susan told me that she had never felt this way when doing trauma work with me. She said that, with me, it had always felt as if the material that emerged was her own. She said memory work with the new therapist felt wrong. It felt like something not her own was being superimposed on her, something that never felt right. When she had worked with me, she'd experienced the work as authentic and true to her own unconscious material. Her work with this new therapist felt disturbingly not true to herself.

Susan related other aspects of this therapy that she found disturbing. Then, when she had finished relating her story, she asked me if, based on my knowledge of her and based on what she was telling me now, I thought she was a multiple. Moreover, what did I think about the regressions as she described them?

We went over the material carefully and reviewed her symptoms. There was no missing time in her current life and no reports from family or friends about inconsistencies in behavior or personality style. She definitely had dissociative amnesia for childhood. However, there appeared to be no more indication of dissociative identity disorder (DID) now than previously. Though it could not be ruled out entirely, it seemed to me a positive diagnosis could not be made for the disorder based on the evidence available at that time. A diagnosis of DID cannot be forced by giving names to moods, as the new therapist contended. At this time, another diagnosis, Dissociative identity disorder not otherwise specified (DIDNOS) was a DSM-IV variant on DID and was sometimes more challenging to diagnose. With DIDNOS, the different alters, or personalities, might operate under the surface only, never allowing themselves to be directly seen. This could not be ruled out at this point either, but neither could I rule it in.

We reviewed the regressions. Susan's overriding sense that the material that had emerged came from her therapist and not from her own psyche was indicative she was being suggestively led into seeing and experiencing "memories" that did not exist. She reiterated how, in our work, she had not once had this feeling of being led. She told me the difference was almost palpable.

We talked weekly for a brief while as Susan sorted out these issues. She terminated her other therapy, concluding it had been very harmful. She told me if she had never had the experience of working with a skilled therapist who allowed her to develop her own material and decide what it meant for herself, she did not know what might have happened. She thought that because our work together had given her self- confidence and a stronger sense of trusting her inner voice, that it had enabled her to move on before she could be more seriously harmed by this new therapist. Susan voiced a concern about what this therapist could do, or might have done, to someone more vulnerable and with fewer inner resources than herself. She was concerned this therapist could take someone more vulnerable than herself over the edge. This therapist had apparently told Susan that she had a malpractice case already pending against her. Susan and I discussed her reporting this therapist and her feelings about it. Susan never told me the therapist's name, and so I was not in a position to report her. I do not know the decision Susan ultimately made.

LIVING WITH AMBIGUITY

Susan got back on track and increasingly became involved in a dynamic, community-oriented church she had found. This involvement, plus a marked increase in her spiritual interests and time spent in prayer and meditation, provided a positive support system and outlet for her. She felt increasingly called into a spiritual life and seemed to have considerable gifts in this area. Her symptoms were greatly reduced.

Before long, she terminated phone therapy with me, feeling ready to go on by herself. She was feeling very positive about her present life and was full of hope for the future. She told me, in a rather abrupt shift from what I had been hearing, she no longer believed she had been a victim of ritual abuse. She could not explain the material that had come up, but she was not now feeling the need to explore it. The anguish and the symptoms had faded, and she now experienced herself as a person free to create a new life for herself.

Such back-and-forths in beliefs regarding personal history are, as I have mentioned, common for trauma victims. These switches can be difficult to understand. Whether the ritual abuse happened or whether it was a metaphor for something else was not up to me to determine. It was her material, and it was and is up to her to take it, work it, and digest it as best she can. I do not know whether she has once or several times more changed her mind about the ritual abuse as a historical reality in her life or whether she still believes it did not happen.

The issue of historical authenticity was not the therapeutic focus. The treatment focus was on Susan's healing and moving on with her life in a positive manner. When last we spoke, she was doing well. It was important to Susan's recovery that she worked with the material as it emerged, and metabolized and integrated the feelings associated with it into her consciousness. She healed through this process, and her many symptoms were resolved.

The field of trauma and abuse treatment is a relatively new one and continues to evolve, especially in the wake of the false memory controversy. Modern brain research has informed the work. Professional standards for treatment of trauma highlight the need for careful, neutral consideration of client material.

I have received ongoing training and supervision and have learned a great deal about trauma treatment and dissociative disorders since my work with Susan. I took many years of postgraduate training in treating dissociative disorders from the International Society for the Study of Trauma and Dissociation (ISSTD). My supervisor and ISSTD teacher for many years was Joan Turkus, MD, past president of ISSTD and well known for her work with dissociative disorders.

The story of Susan's treatment illustrates many common themes presented by many of those with dissociative disorders. These themes include incest and sexual abuse, pregnancies and abortions, feeling drugged, dark cult rituals that include animal and child sacrifice, being filmed in child pornography, "surgeries" that implanted an "eye" in the child to always watch him or her or a "bomb" that would go off if the child ever decided to tell what had happened, suicidal programming if the person remembered what had happened, unspeakable cruelty, and being prostituted out from a very young age. A list of forms of torture endured in ritual abuse is included in the next chapter.

Despite what I have learned in the many years since, I would not have substantially changed the treatment. I was careful not to pressure Susan one way or the other and allowed her room to make up her own mind. Today, I would be even more scrupulously careful. However, I think this example still stands as a good one for demonstrating how dreams can be used in treatment for working through unconscious material.

Ultimately, the measure for treatment outcome has to be client satisfaction with symptom reduction and overall improvement of quality of life. On both these counts, Susan felt significantly better at the end of treatment than at the beginning. Her relationship with her family was stronger, and they had found healthier ways of communicating with each other. She felt more confidence in her social abilities and was able to live a normal life, without the intense fear that had previously governed her every move outside of the home. Additionally, she had a strong and well-grounded spiritual life that offered her a great deal of support and inspiration, both in her church community and in her prayer, meditation, dream, and journaling work. Susan now had many tools for handling and processing painful issues as they came up. She had also found a renewed sense of meaning and purpose in her life, which nourished her tremendously.

Susan's dreams taught her to trust her inner self. They helped her to get in touch with her feelings and her spirit. Through this process of trusting, she found a new sense of peace with herself and a vigorous, vital connection with her higher self and with the God of her understanding. It is vital for trauma survivors to have the sense their material comes from within them, rather than from the leading of a therapist. Susan had been terrified of what lay within her at the beginning of treatment, but at the end she had a level of trust she'd never experienced previously.

As a note on the issue of treatment and authenticity of cult abuse material, I quote Colin A. Ross, MD, from his book *Satanic Ritual Abuse: Principles of Treatment.*

> Most debate and discussion about satanic cults, both inside and outside the dissociative disorders field, focus on whether or not they are real. This misdirection of attention sidesteps process and structural issues and traps the field in a fruitless fixation on content. Content is fundamentally important in a court of law but not in a psychotherapy office, and usually cannot be verified or disproven conclusively within the boundaries of a well-conducted therapy. Part of the problem is that the boundaries between the media, the psychotherapy office, and the courts are permeable, and therapists and survivors lose sight of the fact that different criteria apply in each sphere and cannot necessarily be transposed from one sphere to another.

> "Believing the client" may appear to be a good guiding principle for therapy, but it directly conflicts with the legal principle of "innocent until proven guilty" when a survivor sues a perpetrator. Principles of belief, conviction, support, and affirmation that may be helpful within the therapy framework may be destructive to both therapist and client if they foster groundless suits, media exposure, alienation of relatives, and countersuits. (Ross 1996, 151–52)

Ross's guidelines are good general guidelines insofar as the focus does need to be on stabilization, healing, and recovery. The International Society for the Study of Trauma and Dissociation provides excellent year long postgraduate seminars in treating dissociative disorders but does not address mind control. Section V of this book goes more deeply into the history of mind control and how it became interwoven with ritual abuse.

Susan's treatment was complex. There was an ongoing need for us both to live with great ambiguity. It was a struggle to live with uncertainty, when at times for both of us there was a tendency to want to take a position one way or the other. Ultimately, the most important aspect of the treatment was whether Susan improved, and she did. The most important thing for the therapist to remember is to stay client centered. This means working with the material the client presents, allowing the client to develop it and to work it at his or her pace, no matter how uncomfortable it may feel for the therapist. The therapist remains a guide and a helper, but the client needs to feel empowered to make the decisions regarding authenticity of the material.

MEMORY MAY REMAIN VAGUE

Remember Tom, the man who thought he remembered sexual abuse in his childhood and who had a mental picture of being in the shower with a man who he thought might be his father? Tom was in therapy for seven years and terminated when he moved to another city. He transformed during these years from a fearful, withdrawn, depressed, and dysfunctional man into an empowered and well-respected leader, both in his workplace and in the service organizations in which he volunteered. Sexual abuse was a theme we dealt with many times over his years in therapy. He had many symptoms that might have related to sexual abuse and many vague memories of abuse of varying kinds from when he was younger. None of these was ever corroborated.

When we processed the abuse work in his termination month, Tom commented that he was not sure of what had or had not happened. Nonetheless, he said, he realized his healing proceeded as he worked through the feelings that came up around the "memories" and was not contingent on his certainty regarding the memories' authenticity. He was aware he may never know what happened and had made his peace with that. Though his memories were not as extreme as Susan's, the treatment principle was the same: to allow the client to make up his or her own mind regarding the authenticity of the material. (Note again here the parallel between good therapy and good dreamwork, in which it is the client who is the final authority on his or her own material.) Most important is the treatment focus on symptom reduction and improvement in the quality and satisfaction in the client's life.

SECTION V

MIND CONTROL AND SURVEILLANCE ISSUES

CHAPTER 15

RITUAL ABUSE AND MIND CONTROL: THE USE OF SPIRITUAL ABUSE TO ENSLAVE

RITUAL ABUSE AND MIND CONTROL

One of the most difficult and most controversial subjects in the psychotherapeutic field is the subject of ritual abuse. In more than twenty-five years of working with dissociative disorders and ritual abuse, I have found, as have many writers, that the bizarre content of the dreams and memories of the ritually abused have many similarities. The difference I have found with other ritual abuse cases I have worked with—as opposed to Susan's position when last we spoke—is that the more thoroughly and deeply a person works through his or her memories, traumas, dissociated parts and dreams, the more strongly the person comes to believe he or she was ritually abused. This includes people who came to me with significant recovery already. The healthier and closer to wholeness one becomes, the more they understand the dark rituals and horrific abuse that split them apart in the first place. Some people may falsely believe they are victims of RA, but with careful, non-leading therapy, this will be uncovered in time.

Another aspect that commonly occurs with ritual abuse is mind control. This is far more difficult to comprehend and work with. I will speak in more detail about this in later chapters. Programming uses the ritual abuse to create dissociation in the victim's mind, causing the victim to split off parts of his or her personality as a way of dealing with the horror. Those sophisticated in mind control programming then assign these dissociated pieces, or "alters," to specific tasks outside of the awareness of the main personality or personalities. An example in popular culture of this is Richard Shaw in *The Manchurian Candidate*. Shaw has various alters, including some which may be triggered by a code or preassigned word or phone call to take on a specific task, unbeknownst to the rest of the personality." As Section V progresses, I will explore a brief history of mind control in the United States and discuss in more detail how it is frequently combined with ritual abuse to create mind-controlled slaves.

Ted Gunderson, an ex–FBI chief, spoke extensively about the widespread problem of Satanism and mind control in the United States today. He may have died of arsenic poisoning, but his persuasive and informative videos are readily found with an Internet search. Gunderson's bravery in exposing the dark underbelly of satanism and mind control inside this country cannot be underestimated. He paid with his life, but he succeeded in getting the word out to those who would hear.

Russ Dizdar (deceased 2021), worked with many ritually abused persons in his role as pastor. He agreed with Colin Ross's 1990s estimate of at least ten million ritually abused and mind controlled subjects in this country. This sounds like an absurd number, but it is from those who have been doing the work for their entire lifetimes and who have an understanding of the magnitude of the problem. His book, *The Black Awakening*, goes into great detail of the purpose and methodology of satanic mind control.

Dizdar was also a police chaplain who worked extensively with the police in detecting local cults and helping free victims of ritual abuse from the mind control that has been put upon them, often from birth. In ritual-abuse mind control programming, the alters that are deliberately created by severe abuse which can serve various purposes, such as spy, assassin, sexual slave, and many more. Satanic rituals are conducted throughout the year in hidden locations. Dizdar estimated that by the age of 13, the average satanic RA/MC victim has been subjected to approximately 500 rituals. These serve to keep the victim confused, enslaved and dissociated.

Not all ritual-abuse survivors are mind controlled, but in modern history, in the line of ritual abuse/mind control (RA/MC) developed in Hitler's Germany and by Dr. Joseph Mengele in the brutal concentration camp experiments, the two are often linked. A suspected history of ritual abuse is often paired with Joseph Mengele, for the extreme dissociation caused by the horrors of these rituals is a prerequisite for trauma-based mind control programming. This may sound absurd at this point to the reader, of whom I ask patience, as in subsequent chapters these ideas are explored more fully. There are also other types of cults which use ritual abuse for their own ends, more than a few of which are active in my hometown of Tucson, Arizona.

In order to give the reader a taste of what is involved in the horrific creation of deliberately created multiples, I include below an excerpt from Ellen Lacter's chapter *"Ritual Abuse in the Twenty-First Century: Psychological, Forensic, Social and Political Considerations"* from *Guidelines to Differential Diagnosis* between *Schizophrenia and Ritual Abuse/Mind Control Traumatic Stress*. Lacter is a psychologist who has expertise in ritual-abuse treatment. The following excerpt lists forms of torture used in ritual abuse. These forms of abuse may be used to cause dissociation so those split-off parts can be programmed to serve the cult or mind control programmer. You will recognize some of the horrific things that emerged in Susan's psychotherapeutic process on this list.

Susan described more than a third of these forms of torture at some point in her treatment, even though I may not have listed them in this narrative. Many of my clients and others who have written about their experiences believe they have been subjected to many of the below. Some have described experiencing all of them.

KINDS OF TORTURE ENDURED IN RITUAL ABUSE AND TRAUMA-BASED MIND CONTROL

Knowledge of the methods of torture used within ritual abuse and trauma-based mind control provides a basis for recognition of related trauma disorders. Individuals subjected to these forms of torture may experience intense fear, phobic reactions, or physiological symptoms in response to associated stimuli. In some cases, the individual, or particular dissociated identities, experience a preoccupation with, or attraction to, related stimuli.

Victims may be able to describe the torture they have endured, or they may fear doing so. In many cases of ritual abuse and mind control trauma, the abuse remains dissociated when the individual first seeks treatment. Typically, the initial presenting problems are symptoms of anxiety, depression, or trauma derived from childhood sexual abuse, usually by a family member, who is eventually understood as a participant in the abuser group.

The following is a partial list of these forms of torture:

1. Sexual abuse and torture.

2. Confinement in boxes, cages, coffins, etc., or burial (often with an opening or air-tube for oxygen).

3. Restraint; with ropes, chains, cuffs, etc.

4. Near-drowning.

5. Extremes of heat and cold, including submersion in ice water, burning chemicals, and being held over fire.

6. Skinning for sacrifice or for torture. Pain-inducing drugs, chemicals, and/or adhesive tape can create an illusion of being skinned without permanent injury or scars.

7. Spinning.

8. Blinding or flashing light.

9. Electric shock.

10. Forced ingestion of offensive body fluids and matter, such as blood, urine, feces, flesh, etc.

11. Being hung upside down or in painful positions.

12. Hunger and thirst.

13. Sleep deprivation.

14. Compression with weights and devices.

15. Sensory deprivation.

16. Changes in atmospheric pressure (for example, using rapid pressure changes in a hyperbaric chamber to produce the "bends" and intense ear pain).

17. Drugs to create illusion, confusion, and amnesia, often given by injection or intravenously.

18. Oral or intravenous delivery of toxic chemicals to create pain or illness, including chemotherapy agents.

19. Limbs pulled or dislocated.

20. Application of snakes, spiders, maggots, rats, and other animals to induce fear and disgust.

21. Near-death experiences; such as by drowning or suffocation with immediate resuscitation.

22. Forced to perform or witness abuse, torture and sacrifice of people and animals, usually with knives.

23. Forced participation in child pornography and prostitution.

24. Raped to become pregnant; the fetus is then aborted for ritual use, or the baby is taken for sacrifice or enslavement.

25. Spiritual abuse to cause victims to feel possessed, harassed, and controlled internally by spirits or demons

26. Desecration of Judeo-Christian beliefs and forms of worship; e.g., dedication to Satan or other deities.

27. Abuse and illusion to convince victims that God is evil, such as convincing a child that God has raped her.

28. Surgery to torture, experiment, or cause the perception of physical or spiritual

bombs or "implants."

29. Harm or threats of harm to family, friends, loved ones, pets, and other victims, to force compliance.Use of illusion and virtual reality to confuse and create non-credible disclosure. (Lacter, 2008, pp. 89-91)

SPIRITUAL ABUSE IN GENERAL

It is sad but true that spiritual abuse is at least as common as other kinds of abuse, including physical, emotional, and sexual abuse. It can be devastating, for it takes away the hope which comes from spirit. Spiritual abuse is discussed far less often than other kinds of abuse. Perhaps this is in part because of the lack clinicians have in dealing with spiritual material because it is deemed outside of their field. One key goal of spiritual abuse is to prevent the individual from accessing the Divine.

Religious or spiritual abuse can include emotional, physical, or sexual trauma, with the added factor of the inappropriate use of religious or spiritual authority. Rigid or harsh indoctrination or the use of fear to control behavior may be used. Young people who have been traumatized or alienated by harsh, unloving, and unforgiving "religious" experiences in their homes, churches, or communities often grow up to equate "God" with the God of their childhood. Religious or spiritual abuse is more likely to occur when, instead of people being encouraged to find the "living God within" as Jesus taught, they are taught to look outside themselves, to the church, to priests, to ministers, and to group leaders for spiritual guidance and intercession. The sexual-abuse scandal in the Catholic Church is a prime example of spiritual abuse. The spiritual authority that priests carry gives children the message the abuse is condoned and teaches them God will not help them. The lies they may be told can demolish their conceptions of a benevolent God.

SPIRITUAL ABUSE AND MIND CONTROL

When spiritual abuse is deliberately induced, such as with ritual abuse and mind control, it can be devastating. Over time, I, like many clinicians, have worked with many clients who believe they have experienced ritual abuse. Susan's story, in which the possibility of ritual abuse (RA) came up repeatedly through her dreams, flashbacks, and other experiences, is typical for the types of abuse that occur with RA. Susan's story is atypical in that most RA victims usually do have some form of dissociative identity disorder. Susan did have dissociative amnesia and, but dissociative identity disorder was not evident as of the time she terminated psychotherapy.

Many ritual abuse victims are seen in therapists' offices across the country and throughout the world. As stated, many report themes similar to Susan's—of satanic rituals, animal and child sacrifice, physical and sexual abuse, child pornography, bestiality, sexual slavery, drugs, being placed in coffins with snakes or spiders, and other gruesome experiences. Often, they are greeted with disbelief because of the horrific and unimaginable nature of what they have experienced.

A number of clients came to me already having been diagnosed as DID or other dissociative disorder. Some of those with DID have no dreams or memory of ritual abuse of any kind; others did. Some came in already having done years of healing work, believing not only that they had been abused in rituals but also that the ritual abuse had been a part of mind control in which they were indoctrinated by drugs, torture, rape, sophisticated electronic means, hypnosis, and other means. Some stated they had been involved against their wills from birth or early childhood in programs such as Project Monarch and MKUltra.

Working with these mind controlled clients brought me full circle to those early days when I had those discussions with my father in the mid-1970s about CIA mind control abuses. How could it be possible that—although professionally I went as far away as possible from my father's career choices of military, law, and intelligence and into my fields of psychology and religion—yet I ended up right in the middle of the same mess, dealing with the victims of those programs under scrutiny that some naively think stopped decades ago?

The scope of this book does not include delving deeply into multiplicity, ritual abuse, or governmental mind control. Many people have risked their lives to get out important information on these topics. References listed at the back of this book go much more deeply into these subjects, but I will do my best to give a brief historical and clinical overview.

My clinical experiences have continuously included people, sometimes operating at very high levels in our society, who believe they have experienced all of the above. Some believe they are currently being accessed/handled, which includes rape, torture, drugs, dark rituals, forced sexual perversions, and near-death experiences. It is almost too awful to believe. Because of my experiences, I will discuss some aspects of RA and mind control in this chapter and in the next.

Alison Miller's book *Healing the Unimaginable: Treating Ritual Abuse and Mind Control* is an excellent resource, as is her newest volume, *Becoming Yourself: Overcoming Mind Control and Ritual Abuse*, written for those who have experienced ritual abuse and are trying to recover.

In *Healing the Unimaginable*, Miller says, "One of the worst features of ritual abuse is spiritual abuse. It consists of: (1) simulation of religious figures in perverted ways; (2) forced teaching of occult beliefs; (3) forced perpetration, especially real or simulated sacrifice of animals, babies, and/or adults, followed by teaching the child that s/he is evil" (Miller 2011, 57).

The horrific spiritual abuse suffered by ritual-abuse victims is shocking and exceedingly hard to digest. By means of awful rituals, personalities split off from the main self because the abuse and trauma are too awful to bear. The mind controller then shapes these personalities into whatever he or she wants them to be. Miller gives examples of how the child is made to feel he or she is evil, and that no one will help them. The child's faith in God is deliberately destroyed through trauma, making them believe they must turn to Satan.

> The inescapable nature of the abuse takes away any belief that the child might have that a benevolent deity will come to a victim's rescue. Later, survivors (and their therapists), depending on their belief system, have to face the reality of divine non-intervention, at least in any tangible sense.

> This is often made explicit by the abusers. For example, a child being abused in a Satanist group is told to pray to God to come and save them. The child prays, and God does not appear. Then the child is told to pray to Satan, and a man in a Satan costume comes and tells the abusers to stop hurting the child. The child naturally assumes Satan is the benevolent deity.

> The indoctrination goes one step further when God is blamed for the abuse. For example, one client shared with me that someone who was said to be God, and was dressed up in a white robe, physically and sexually abused her painfully at a young age, "creating" alters by telling them to split off. Another child was made very angry by the perpetrator group torturing her, then showing her a bearded man tied to a cross, who they said was Jesus. They told her that what was happening to her was all his fault. They gave her a weapon and told her to hurt or kill "Jesus."

These abusive groups explain divine non-intervention by making the children they abuse believe that God has chosen not to help them because they, the children, are evil to the core. One child was taken into the presence of "Jesus," tied to a cross. When she went to rescue him, he spat in her face. He said that he would rather die than be saved by her because she was so evil. (Miller 2011, 66–67)

Spiritually traumatized children are more easily controlled when they believe they are evil and no one will help them. The brutal spiritual indoctrination often includes the children being forced to perpetrate on others or on animals, further reinforcing their belief they are evil and will never get out of the cult:

One of the most heartbreaking parts of ritual abuse is the spiritual abuse that results from forced perpetration. Occult groups of various kinds force children (and adults) to participate in torture, rape, animal sacrifice, and real and simulated murders. To those who must take part, the murders are very real, even if the victim is not actually killed. And in some cases the murder is real (Miller 2011, 67).

These children are then told they are evil and rejected by God forever. God is presented to them as angry, judgmental, and unforgiving. Rejection and abandonment are extremely powerful experiences, and these children are then told that, because of their evil, they are now bound forever to Satan and that God will never accept them. This is an extremely powerful dynamic, causing great shame in the ritual-abuse victim.

Cisco Wheeler and Fritz Springmeier, in their volume *The Illuminati Formula:Used to Create an Undetectable Total Mind Controlled Slave*, describe a common RA ritual used to program a child to hate God.

A hypnotic drug will be given to the victim when they are about 6 years of age. This will relax the person and allow the programmers to take the child into the deepest trance, so that the programming will be sure to enter into the very fiber of the child's being. After several hours of being in a deep trance, as the drug begins to wear off, the child will be strapped very secure into a tight-fitting coffin. A man with long white hair, and a long robe, with sandals, staff and a white robe will present himself before the child, and announce that he is "God the great I AM". Then "God" will look in a big book and announce he cannot find the person's name so he will have to send the person to hell for being bad. The coffin will then be lowered into a deep pit, like a mine shaft, and the victim will be told that when they can no longer hear God's voice that they will be a cat and not human. God can't find them in the book because they have no soul, and are a cat. Deeper and deeper the child is lowered. They are told this is the penalty for having tried to pray to God.

The programmers make sure that the slave is implicated in many gross sins, such as the murder of innocent children, in order to ensure that the person is sure that God hates them. Then the victim is told that God is a consuming wrath who hates them. The injustice of God creating a world of suffering is also taught to the slave. All this is to ensure that the victim hates God. That hatred toward God will express itself in the victim's system's willingness to do any sin, without conscience. (Springmeier and Wheeler, 1996, Chapter 10)

Spiritual abuse is so devastating because it takes away faith and hope in something good that is better than ourselves both in people and in God. A therapist need not be an expert in religious and spiritual issues to be able to help many clients with their spiritual trauma and the many conceptual distortions that come with it. As with other aspects of therapy, it is important to help clients explore their trauma and beliefs and correct their cognitive distortions. However, when it comes to ritual abuse and spiritual distortions deeply layered into the structure of the personality, almost all clinicians need more training.

My initial aim in writing this book was to include only an overview of ritual-abuse treatment issues and then move on to the final section. However, while preparing this book for publication, a series of events occurred that forced me to reconsider. These chapters discuss, from historical, clinical, and personal perspectives, issues related to mind control on unwilling victims, as well as tell my story.

CHAPTER 16

DARK HISTORICAL REALITIES

Certain covert operations have been incompatible with American principles and ideology and, when exposed, have resulted in damaging this nation's ability to exercise moral and ethical leadership.

—US Senate Select Committee on Intelligence

The individual is handicapped by coming face-to-face with a conspiracy so monstrous he cannot believe it exists.

—J. Edgar Hoover

The term "conspiracy theory" was invented and put into public discourse by the CIA in 1964 in order to discredit the many skeptics who challenged the Warren Commission's conclusion that President John F. Kennedy was assassinated by a lone gunman named Lee Harvey Oswald, who himself was assassinated while in police custody before he could be questioned. The CIA used its friends in the media to launch a campaign to make suspicion of the Warren Commission report a target of ridicule and hostility. This campaign was "one of the most successful propaganda initiatives of all time." So writes political science professor Lance deHaven-Smith, who in his peer-reviewed book, *Conspiracy Theory in America*, published by the University of Texas Press, tells the story of how the CIA succeeded in creating in the public mind reflexive, automatic stigmatization of those who challenge government explanations.

—Paul Craig Roberts

We are grateful to *The Washington Post, The New York Times, Time Magazine* and other great publications whose directors have attended our meetings and respected their promises of discretion for almost forty years. It would have been impossible for us to develop our plan for the world if we had been subject to the bright lights of publicity during those years. But, the work is now much more sophisticated and prepared to march towards a world government. The supranational sovereignty of an intellectual elite and world bankers is surely preferable to the national autodetermination practiced in past centuries.

—David Rockefeller, founder of the Trilateral Commission,
in an address to a meeting of the Trilateral Commission in June 1991

Use monetary and sex bribery to obtain control of people already occupying positions in high places in the various levels of all governments and other fields of endeavor. Once an influential person had fallen for the lies, deceits, and temptations of the Illuminati, they were to be held in bondage by application of political and other forms of blackmail, threats of financial ruin, public exposure, and physical harm, and even death to themselves and their loved ones.

—Adam Weishaupt, Illuminati Founder

Until the American people understand that behind everything going on today are powerful occult forces intent on creating a world government, until you understand that, nothing makes sense.

—-Stan Monteith, *Blood Sacrifice*, Vol 1

For we wrestle not against flesh and blood, but against principalities, against powers, against the rulers of the darkness of this world, against spiritual wickedness in high places.

—Ephesians 6:12, KJV

Much of this chapter was written in response to events that happened as I was proofing and rewriting parts of this book before the initial publication. I had no plans to go into this historical material on mind control and dissociative identity disorder but events that transpired completely changed those plans. Hopefully the reader will forgive my extensive use of quotes in this research chapter. I am not an expert in these matters.

THERAPIST TARGETING

The unexpected happened, and I am extremely fortunate to have escaped what was planned for me—again. I was not going to write about this and the many illegal and unconstitutional activities perpetrated against me beginning 2008, but circumstances have forced me to revise my decision. Unfortunately, as this near-fatal incident (which I will describe later) dramatically proved to me there is no safety in keeping the knowledge I have gained to myself. I was told by wise counsel, someone who had worked at the head of state level, that my only safety lay in publishing the information.

It became radically clear the powers that be did not want the information in this book out. Pedophilia, child sex trafficking, mind control and Satanism were barely a blip on the national radar in 2007 when this began. I uncovered a plot to murder me unfolding slowly right in front of my eyes. As crazy as it may sound, it is not uncommon for potential whistleblowers to be dealt with by murder, often made to look like an accident, in the United States today. An alarming statistic is that during Obama's Presidency, more whistleblowers were prosecuted than by all other Presidents combined. *(https://washingtonsblog.com/obama-has-prosecuted-more-whistleblowers-than-all-other-presidents-combined).* This alarming statistic underscores the hostile climate to those who wish to bring forth wrongdoings. This trend has continued under the Biden administration. At this point, I will back up a bit and provide background about what happened over recent years which got me here.

Sometime after I started training and working more intensively with dissociative identity disorder, I began to be aware I was under intense surveillance. The first round of it began when I was working with Estelle, a very high-up mind controlled and programmed multiple, someone who had been a *presidential model*—that is, a woman bred and trained from birth to be an elite sex slave to presidents and other heads of state. A presidential model is ostensibly to provide safe sex for presidents and heads of state. The charade is that slave users are told these are prostitutes, as if the slaves are volunteering and not coerced for the job, often from very early childhood.

There are various motivations for the provisions of sex slaves. Everything is videotaped and saved, to be used for blackmail purposes. Some alters are trained to give sexual gratification in whatever way the target wants, no matter how perverse, other alters are trained spies with photographic memories, yet other alters are couriers relaying messages between important players, and so on. The spiritual, emotional, sexual, and mental depravity to which these unwilling slaves are subjected is beyond the ability of most of us to comprehend.

Marilyn Monroe is said to be the first famous Presidential Model, the first one allowed to be seen in the public eye. Cathy O'Brien and Brice Taylor have both written autobiographies about their experiences, which in many ways were heartbreakingly similar to Estelle's. Estelle, who was a client of mine, was brilliant and was beautiful in her younger years; she was used as a highly trained sex slave, spy, courier, breeder, and much more. She "served" a number of presidents. She, like many others, identified herself as having been part of Project Monarch, Project Bluebird, and Project MKUltra since birth. From birth, she had been subject to RA, having been tortured and traumatized in every vile way imaginable and repeatedly raped. She was prized as being of the highest Illuminati bloodline on both sides of her genealogy. In her operational years, she was much sought after as a sex slave, having been used as a sex slave since she was a child. Unfortunately pedophilia is extremely common in this world, it is an agenda they are pursuing. (Estelle had a lot of good therapy in her life. Her psychiatrist, who had worked with mind control and other presidential models, assured me that not only were her stories sadly true but that she had even testified before the Senate about the atrocities committed on her.)

Sounds unbelievable? Of course. However, these were the programs that came to light when my father was CIA general counsel. He could not tell me details at the time; all I knew was he had been horrified. Estelle, like a number of other recovering high-level mind control victims, including Brice Taylor in her book *Thanks for the Memories*, stated Joseph Mengele had been her handler for many years, until his death sometime in the 1980s. At that point, another man, who had been trained by Mengele and whose cover was as a taxi driver (very convenient for driving her to assignations), became her handler. "Handling" included brutal torture and regular rape to keep her dissociated and sick. I will return to Estelle and my own story in the next chapter, but for the rest of this chapter I will share a brief (and no doubt quite incomplete) historical overview of mind control in Germany, Britain, and the United States.

THE THIRD REICH NOW THE FOURTH REICH

Someone who has studied the subject for many years informed me that there are different major cult groups, each of which has their own system of ritual abuse and mind control and each of which thinks it is poised to take over the world. The one I will be writing about here, one which has impinged on my life in many ways, beginning with my father's career, is as described here. The Nazis planned for the Fourth Reich, a total global takeover, while they were still building the Third Reich. It is important to understand that although the German Army surrendered, the Nazis never did. In his article *"The Secret Treaty of Fort Hunt,"* Carl Oglesby tells the story of Reinhard Gehlen's Nazi spy organization, which formed the basis of our modern Central Intelligence Agency and National Security Council.

The unconditional surrender that the Germans made to the Allied Command at the little red schoolhouse in Reims was the surrender only of the German Armed Services. It was NOT the surrender of the hard SS core of the Nazi Party. The SS did not surrender, unconditionally or otherwise, and thus, Naziism itself did not surrender. The SS chose, rather, to seek other means of continuing the war while the right wing of the United States Military Establishment, through fears and secret passions and a naivete of its own, chose to facilitate that choice. The history that we have lived through since then stands witness to the consequences. *(https://archive.org/details/the-secret-treaty-of-fort-hunt/page/n11/mode/2up)*

Once they knew they were losing the war, the Nazis sent allegiant Nazis all over the world to create what was to be the Fourth Reich. The Fourth Reich was to be different from the Third in that it would be characterized by takeovers from within, not overt takeovers. It would take hold from within politics and governments, financial institutions, the medical field, educational institutions, and churches. This underground system would be so well established by the time it fully emerged that the populace would be unaware and unable to resist once it overtly manifested. Hitler's term for what they were planning was the New Order. Sound familiar? This is the same New World Order we hear so much about, from George Bush Sr. to Henry Kissinger to Bill Clinton to Obama to Pope Francis. In this New Order, US sovereignty is to be surrendered to the greater order. Horrifying?

The Nazis migrated and established themselves in every major country of the world even before the end of the war. They were helped by the Vatican, the United States, Russia and many other countries. (Interestingly, the monarch butterfly, chosen as a name for the CIA mind control programming of individuals in Project Monarch, is unique for having its habitat worldwide.)

We brought top Nazis into this country with Project Paperclip and other means (explanation to follow). At the end of World War II, we were led to believe the Soviet Union was the new threat. We overestimated the Soviet threat, likely due to Nazi disinformation as they saw the Soviet Union as their mortal enemy; we saw them as more advanced than us in a number of areas, including psychic research. As a result there was competition between major countries, including the United States, Britain, and the Soviet Union, to bring in Nazi scientists, doctors, and others. What we did was bring in people still allegiant to the Nazi cause.

We know the goals of world domination and extermination of Jews that characterized the Nazis. We know the Holocaust was one of the darkest and most gruesome events in recent history. The part most people know nothing or little about is the dark inner occult glue that held the Nazis together. History books mostly do not mention the inner core of Nazism was their drive to invoke and be overcome (possessed) by dark demonic energies, which were to help them achieve their nefarious goals. This was their belief system, and they used dark rituals to this end. Hitler himself believed he was a channel for Lucifer (Ravenscroft; Rosio; Sklar).

Himmler, head of the feared SS, was steeped in the occult. He built his Wewelsburg castle to be the center of the (occult) world. Dark occult ritual ceremonies were to be held there to overtake and possess the participants with demon spirit energies (Rosio; Sklar). Those dark energies were also invoked to possess world leaders. You don't believe it? When looking at these times and people, it is important to look at what they believed, not what you believe. They believed that through their satanic rituals they were bringing in the supermen, the Aryan god-men who would take over and rule the world.

There are now a number of volumes and videos about Nazi occult beliefs, some of which are listed in the references list at the end of this book. The History Channel did an excellent four-part series entitled *The Occult History of the Third Reich*. Another excellent series is *Blood Sacrifice (vol. 1, Cleansing the Soil for the Aryan Antichrist and Blood Sacrifice* (Cutting Edge Films, 2013), and *vol. 2, Thy Kingdom Come—Hitler's Complete Conquest of the German Christian Churches* (Cutting Edge Films, 2017). In this, as with many volumes on the subject, the central place of Satan in Nazi inner circles begins to become clear. Richard Bey, in volume 1 of *Blood Sacrifice*, asserts, "To adequately understand Hitler, you have to understand black magic witchcraft. You have to understand what it teaches, and what its goals are, and you have to understand the spirits from the abyss, starting in 1899 when Hitler was born and culminating in 1945; their plan for Germany, their plan for the world and their plan for Hitler. Once you understand all that, you'll begin to understand Adolf Hitler and his role in world history" (Richard Bay in *Blood Sacrifice*, vol. 1, video).

In the same video, Stan Monteith (recently deceased) comments on how the occult practices have continued and grown in the underworld until the present day: "Until the American people understand that behind everything going on today are powerful occult forces intent on creating a world government, until you understand that, nothing makes sense."

THE FOURTH REICH'S PLANS

The underground path of creating the Fourth Reich includes cadres of satanically abused "soldiers" or "chosen ones" who are programmed to be loyal in hidden and deliberately created personalities. They are represented in all walks of life, from the highest to the lowest. The ultimate goal of this Satan's army is to take over the world. Dizdar's aforementioned book, *Black Awakening,* goes into great detail about this. It is no secret Hitler planned for his supermen to rule the world for a thousand years; he often talked about his plans. What is much less known is how he planned to do it if he lost World War II.

Mengele's mind control experiments during the Holocaust worked on perfecting the technology of trauma-based, deliberately created multiple personality disorder. How much we were doing here in the United States at that time is largely unknown, though an informed anonymous source said a great deal was going on in the United States. George Estabrooks in his book *Hypnosis* describes how he created a mind-controlled robot by hypnosis and splitting the mind in the World War II era.

By the end of the war, the Germans knew how to create the perfect assassin, spy, sex slave, courier, and psychic killer, all in one divided person. Each personality could be called out with a code or lock, and once it accomplished its task, it would go back inside, with the host person having no idea what he or she had done. The technology was also perfected such that the created personalities would, as instructed, go against the host personality's morals and ethics. The perfect Manchurian candidate, like the perfect Nazi, has no morals or ethics. The candidate is stripped of his or her humanity. The front personality retains all its values and morals and has no awareness of parts inside that murder or prostitute or spy or whatever they are programmed to do. Even under interrogation, these dark personalities remain under the lock and key of the programmers.

THE GREENBAUM SPEECH

In 1992, at a rapidly growing and extremely popular annual conference held in Alexandria, Virginia, I attended a session that was to have a huge impact on my understanding of the connection between those CIA programs that my father had had to defend, the Nazis, and many of the ritually abused clients with whom I was working.

This lecture was given by D. Corydon Hammond and was originally entitled *"Hypnosis in MPD: Ritual Abuse."* It is usually known as the *Greenbaum Speech* and can be found on the Internet by that name. The talk was delivered at the Fourth Annual Eastern Regional Conference on Abuse and Multiple Personality, Thursday, June 25, 1992, at the Radisson Plaza Hotel, Mark Center, Alexandria, Virginia. This talk for clinicians explained how Hammond had found similar mind control programming in ritual abuse (RA) victims all over the country and in other countries. No longer was the programming mainly being done in Germany; not only were German immigrants all over the world subjecting their families to RA and mind control, but other groups globally were doing this as well. With Operation Paperclip importing Nazis into the United States (often into high positions), RA in the United States exploded.

When you start to find the same highly esoteric information in different states and different countries, from Florida to California, you start to get an idea that there's something going on that is very large, very well coordinated, with a great deal of communication and systematicness to what's happening. So I have gone from someone kind of neutral and not knowing what to think about it all to someone who clearly believes ritual abuse is real and that the people who say it isn't are either naive like people who didn't want to believe the Holocaust or—they're dirty …

Certainly, what some patients have said is all of this spook stuff, horror stuff, possession and everything else that's been popularized in the last twenty years in Hollywood is in order to soften up the public so that when a Satanic World Order takes over, everyone will have been desensitized to so many of these things, plus to continually cue lots of people out there. Is that true?

Well, I can't definitely tell you that it is. What I can say is I now believe that ritual- abuse programming is widespread, is systematic, is very organized from highly esoteric information which is published nowhere, has not been on any book or talk show, that we have found all around this country and at least one foreign country. (Hammond 1992)

Hammond gave information in the talk about how to work with various levels of programming. He said much of the programming is CIA related, with programming often done on military bases.

My client Estelle, whom I will talk more about later, was a deliberately created multiple personality, of the type talked about in Colin Ross's book *Project Bluebird: Deliberate Creation of Multiple Personality* by CIA Psychiatrists. The type of programming she had been forced to endure since her birth was the kind Corydon Hammond discussed. As I mentioned, she was tortured and traumatized and raped from the time she was born. She was involved in various CIA mind control programs from birth, and against her will, including Projects Monarch, MKUltra, and Bluebird. She was subjected to frequent satanic rituals, unimaginable torture, and depravity to split her mind so her alters could carry out various assignments.

Mengele was well known as a brutal, sadistic man who did horrific medical experiments in the Nazi concentration camps. What is not so well known is that many of these experiments were mind control experiments in the camps. This of extreme significance. It was there he developed and used brutal torture techniques that are described in the recent December 2014 Senate Intelligence Committee's report on CIA interrogation techniques. These and other mind control techniques split the subject's mind off into different personalities that can be used for different purposes, such as sex slave, assassin, spy, and so on. He was often brought into the United States to program US citizens. He was brutal and cruel. Estelle said he was her handler from her birth in 1947 until his death somewhere in the 1980's. There are a number of recovering high-level mind-controlled slaves who also report Mengele was their handler/programmer.

These techniques have been developed into more sophisticated forms since the 1940s, with increased use of electronics and drugs for mind control programming. The programs are widely used today worldwide and in the United States on innocent children as well as Illuminati bloodlines, the military, special forces (for creation of the super-soldier), people in every walk of life, and prisoners. This is done in order to create a secret army of mind-controlled slaves, Manchurian candidates on steroids. Sounds incredible and impossible? I would think so too.

Unfortunately, these are the very real programs that so horrified my father when he found out about them when assigned to defend them in the 1970s. He was forced to defend the CIA to Congress, under threat of my being killed (an incident I described early in this book). How could this happen in the United States? Aren't we supposed to be the "good guys"?

WHY THE NAZIS WERE TRUSTED AND PUT IN TOP POSITIONS OF POWER IN THE UNITED STATES

The CIA, under the guise of Project Paperclip, imported top Nazi scientists, doctors, and others at the top of their fields and put them in charge of key projects throughout the US government, hospitals, and other institutions. In 1945, President Truman authorized Project Paperclip.

Truman's order expressly excluded anyone found "to have been a member of the Nazi Party, and more than a nominal participant in its activities, or an active supporter of Nazi militarism." However, those restrictions would have rendered ineligible most of the leading scientists the JIOA had identified for recruitment, among them rocket scientists Wernher von Braun, Kurt H. Debus and Arthur Rudolph, and the physician Hubertus Strughold, each earlier classified as a "menace to the security of the Allied Forces."

To circumvent President Truman's anti-Nazi order and the Allied Potsdam and Yalta agreements, the JIOA worked independently to create false employment and political biographies for the scientists. The JIOA also expunged from the public record the scientists' Nazi Party memberships and régime affiliations. Once "bleached" of their Nazism, the scientists were granted security clearances by the U.S. government to work in the United States. Paperclip, the project's operational name, derived from the paperclips used to attach the scientists' new political personae to their "US Government Scientist" JIOA personnel files. (Wikipedia, "Project Paperclip"; 2016; italics mine)

THE NAZIS AND THE FOURTH REICH

Thus, the Paperclip program of importing top Nazis was born in secrecy and deception even to our president at the time. Just who was pulling the strings? We imported those with continued allegiance to the Nazi cause, which planned for global takeover from within various countries worldwide. The war ending did not mean to them the end of their plan. As mentioned, it is very important to understand the Nazis planned ahead to survive past World War II. Their goal was to create the Fourth Reich, a system of global domination. It would be achieved not overtly as with the Third Reich but covertly by gaining hidden inside control of banking and the financial world, of governments and the military, of hospitals and universities, of the churches, the media and education from pre-school through graduate school, and by mass mind control of the people.

Jim Marrs' excellent and very well researched book *The Rise of the Fourth Reich: The Secret Societies That Threaten to Take Over America (2008)* goes into great detail, following a financial trail to the Nazis and beyond. Many wealthy Americans and corporations, including such notables as Prescott Bush of the George Bush lineage, who made his fortune with Nazi investments; Chase; Standard Oil; Henry Ford, who provided trucks for the Nazi troops; and Charles Lindbergh, supported Hitler and helped him build up his armies *(Trading with the Enemy: An Exposé of the Nazi-American Money Plot 1933–1949.)* Another book, *The American Axis: Henry Ford, Charles Lindbergh,* and the *Rise of the Third Reich* by Max Wallace, gives many details of which the general American public may not be aware. Further, by Charles Higham gives additional perspective into major US corporations continuing to work with Nazi Germany throughout the war.

These books are but a very small sampling of the books and other information available about a continued US-Nazi connection throughout the war. I am not a historian and, with the exception of this brief overview, find it best to let the reader do his or her own research. I am mentioning the above mainly to demonstrate all was not as it seemed nor is it now as it seems. The Nazi-US corporate connection continued throughout the war until today. If we think the connection would stop at the end of the war simply because the Germans lost, it might reflect naïveté about the nature of the relationship to begin with and a lack of education about the very real connections. We have only to look at our modern society to hear the voices of government and media in collusion to begin to understand what began so many years ago; the takeover of our sovereignty and the mass mind control of our citizens. As we see through many current events, including Covid and the mandates, Jan. 6 and the Durham report on the weaponizing of the FBI and DOJ against U.S. citizens, the agenda for New World Order/Great Reset control is in full swing.

A significant part of those means of takeover would be covert, through infiltrating governments, businesses, hospitals, schools and other institutions by seeding them with those loyal to the cause. The takeover would also be through various systems of mind control. We know Dr. Joseph Mengele did gruesome, systematic experiments in the concentration camps. We have heard about the medical experiments but have gotten little information about the mind control experiments. He worked on how to split minds through torture and trauma and from there to create different personalities with the split-off pieces, or deliberately created multiple personality disorder. He was then purportedly hired by the CIA to do mind control on American citizens, against their will.

MIND CONTROL IN THE UNITED STATES

The history of mind control in the United States before and during World War II is also a dark chapter, though much less understood, as much of it continues to be secret. There are different cults vying for power and world domination, a large part of which is to be accomplished through the covert world of mind control.

George Estabrooks, PhD, known for his experiments with hypnotism and the deliberate creation of multiple personalities, gives us a peek into that world. In his paper *"Hypnosis Comes of Age,"* published in Science Digest, April 1971, Estabrooks says there was a fascination with multiple personalities in the United States in the early 1900s.

Clinical hypnotists throughout the world jumped on the multiple personality bandwagon as a fascinating frontier. By the 1920's, not only had they learned to apply post-hypnotic suggestion to deal with this weird problem, but also had learned how to split certain complex individuals into multiple personalities like Jekyll-Hydes.

The potential for military intelligence has been a nightmare. Neither we nor Germany were the only countries investigating this issue and learning how to split minds to create multiple personalities for military and intelligence purposes. North Korea and China also deeply investigated mind control. Chemical and electronic research into how to covertly control minds was also done.

Estabrooks, no doubt a sociopath in his own right, went public with some of his work, which gives us a deeper insight into some of the work being done in the United States on mind control that paralleled what was going on in Nazi Germany. Some researchers say the British, Germans and US were working on developing mind control techniques long before World War II. It is likely a great deal more research and experimentation on mind control was done in the United States before we brought Nazi scientists and doctors to the United States after World War II, when the US and Nazi doctors combined their techniques. Some suggest this collaboration predated the war and even continued covertly during the war, as the goals of the Nazis, the globalists, and the covert US shadow government of creating a one- world government by deception were similar. Jim Marrs' book *The Rise of the Fourth Reich* details many instances of such collaboration.

One of the biggest dilemmas in mind control was how to program a person to act against his or her moral and ethical beliefs. It was found this could be circumvented by creating alters (alternate personalities) hypnotically and keeping them locked behind an amnesic barrier. Estabrooks is perhaps the most famous of the early mind control researchers in the U.S. He wrote of the problem of wartime communication in which codes can be broken, spies may be bought, and human judgment can be questionable. In *"Hypnosis Comes of Age,"* he says the "hypnotic courier" provides a solution to this problem, stating that he was involved in creating these human couriers during World War II. He gives an example of an army captain who was ordered to Washington to pick up a mechanical equipment report and return. This was the cover story and also the only story the army captain knew. It was the story he gave to his wife and friends. When the captain arrived, Estabrooks put him under deep hypnosis:

> Then I gave him—orally—a vital message to be delivered directly on his arrival in Japan to a certain colonel—let's say his name was Brown—of military intelligence. Outside of myself, Colonel Brown was the only person who could hypnotize Captain Smith. This is "locking."

> I performed it by saying to the hypnotized Captain: "Until further orders from me, only Colonel Brown and I can hypnotize you. We will use a signal phrase the moon is clear. Whenever you hear this phrase from Brown or myself you will pass instantly into deep hypnosis." When Captain Smith re-awakened, he had no conscious memory or what happened in trance. All that he was aware of was that he must head for Tokyo to pick up a division report.

> On arrival there, Smith reported to Brown, who hypnotized him with the signal phrase. Under hypnosis, Smith delivered my message and received one to bring back. Awakened, he was given the division report and returned home by jet. There I hypnotized him once more with the signal phrase, and he spieled off Brown's answer that had been dutifully tucked away in his unconscious mind. (Estabrooks 1971, 44–50)

Estabrooks believed anything goes in war and wrote how all is justifiable to prevent defeat. That is the unethical mindset that is taking over the world of clandestine affairs.

Did we know at the time the other Germans exported all over the world would build their secret armies of supermen, a.k.a. satanic soldiers or "chosen ones," wherever they lived? Armies of mind controlled soldiers were created and their capabilities greatly enhanced. It appears a shadow side of our government aligned with them in the globalist goal of world takeover. How many of our leaders in every field are controlled Manchurian Candidates. Are there bigger players pulling the strings? When we hired Gehlen's German network of Nazi spies with their own agendas to work for the United States after the war, did we have any idea what they would be doing? The code of loyalty the Nazis took was to forever be loyal to Nazism.

Dr. Ewen Cameron, a psychiatrist, began working on mind control in the 1930s. By 1945, OSS Chief Allen Dulles sent Dr. Cameron to Nuremberg to study Deputy Führer Rudolph Hess, Hitler's occultist close friend. In 1950, Dr. Cameron and Naval Commander Dr. Wrenshall Oliver founded the World Psychiatric Association, which provided a legitimate and reputable safe haven to harbor Nazi and SS psychiatrists. Dr. Cameron is notorious for his unethical, tortuous mind control experiments at McGill University in Canada. The CIA gave him money in cash and through front groups to keep the CIA name off the horrendous experiments. Shockingly, though also revealing the extent to which psychiatric medical professionals were implicated in horrific breaches of medical ethics, he was president of the Canadian Psychiatric Association, American (1952–1953) and World Psychiatric Associations, the American Psychopathological Association, and the Society of Biological Psychiatry during the 1950s.

Many mind control multiples look just like you and me and are considered sleepers. Those with deliberately created multiple personalities who will not reveal their "chosen one" trained side until summoned. It is likely the United States wanted the advantage of any technologies available, including mind control, apparently without ethical constraints. Sociopathy is unfortunately endemic in all the governments involved.

Most people in the United States do not know the fascist Fourth Reich has been built both in our own land and across the world. Nelson Rockefeller's family had prewar and wartime dealing with the Nazis and strove to protect both his family and the Nazis. In creating Israel out of Palestine, the Latin American vote bloc was needed to partition Palestine. Rockefeller wanted to be able to move Nazi fugitives and money after the war and made a deal to deliver the Latin American votes if the Jews would keep silent about the flow of Nazi money and fugitives to South America. This deal would rule out Zionist Nazi-hunting units, testimony at Nuremberg about the bankers who kept and moved Nazi money, and leaks to the press about Nazis in South America or Nazis working for CIA director Dulles. With the conclusion of this deal with the devil, the subject of the Nazis was to be permanently closed. The choice was simple, Rockefeller explained: "You can have vengeance, or you can have a country but you cannot have both" (Marrs 2009; Loftus and Aarons 1997).

HITLER AND THE NAZI DEMONIC OCCULT

How did Hitler amass so much power so quickly, and what kind of power was it that created the Holocaust and that would prompt Hitler, when he knew he was losing the war, to order that all of Germany's infrastructure be destroyed? (Albert Speer, in his book *Inside the Third Reich*, discusses how at different times he pleaded with Hitler to not destroy Paris and not destroy Germany.) The globalist business and banking ties that supported Hitler's Germany and helped bring them to power are a known quantity. What is much less known, and much less understood, is the dark occult core of Nazism.

Hitler himself said, "Anyone who interprets National Socialism merely as a political movement knows almost nothing about it. It is more than religion; *it is the determination to create a new man.*"

We know Hitler was obsessed with building his army of supermen. What made them supermen? Firstly, they were chosen as pure-blood Aryans who, as part of the Lebensborn breeding project and birthing centers, were bred with female Aryan breeders and Aryan men in Lebensborn centers. Because of their "pure blood," they were bred to be part of what would be the Third Reich's army.

What is not as commonly known is these children were consecrated to Satan from conception onward. If you study occult rituals, you will find it is common to ritualize children born into ritual cults by summoning demons to take over and possess the body. Dizdar, a prodigious researcher, asserted in many of his podcasts that both mother and father in the bloodline programs were demonized and that, with the act of conception, they believed the new child was demonized (possessed) also. This demonization is reinforced throughout life in dark rituals.

The satanic rituals so often done in Germany beginning in the 1920s were at the core of Nazism and the new pagan religion they were trying to promulgate. As stated, Nazism was not just a political movement and should not be understood as such: it was at its core a very dark spiritual practice. They truly believed that through possession, they received their power from Satan and Lucifer. Through blood sacrifices and perverted sexual rituals, portals to the demonic powers would be opened, and these demons would be sent to influence and possess leaders. Trevor Ravenscroft, author of *Spear of Destiny*, says the inner core of the Thule Society were all Satanists who practiced black magic: "The inner core within the Thule Group were all Satanists who practiced Black Magic. That is to say, they were solely concerned with raising their consciousness by means of rituals to an awareness of evil and non-human intelligences in the Universe and with achieving a means of communication with the Intelligences. And the Master-Adept of this circle was Dietrich Eckart" (Ravenscroft, 1982). The Thule Society, with Satan at its heart, "served as political assassins, murdering those who stood in the way of their ascent to power, engaging in ritual murder and vile perversions, including human mutilations and sacrifices to Satan" (Rosio, 1992,144).

Dietrich Eckart was a high-ranking, dedicated Satanist who believed it was his destiny to "prepare the vessel of the Anti-Christ" whom Lucifer would inspire to conquer the world. He studied with Aleister Crowley, one of the most influential and darkest of black magic practitioners in modern times. When Eckart was on his deathbed in 1923, he supposedly said, "Follow Hitler! He will dance, but it is I who have called the tune! I have initiated him into the 'Secret Doctrine,' opened his centres of vision and given him the means to communicate with the Powers. Do not mourn for me: for I shall have influenced history more than any other German" (Ravenscroft, 1982).

The Secret Doctrine, mentioned in the above quote, was a volume channeled by Helena Blavatsky. It was purportedly written by what they call "ascended masters" who would guide humanity's evolution. Hitler kept a copy of this book by his bedside, believing he had been called into the service of Lucifer and the ascended masters.

Ravenscroft, Rosio, and others wrote of Hitler's interests in the occult. It is said that Hitler openly sought to be possessed by Lucifer, that through Hitler the powers of darkness would rise and take over the earth. Bob Rosio, in his book *Hitler and the New Age,* describes Hitler's Luciferic initiation, the means by which Eckart initiated Hitler into the service of Satan (Rosio, 49). Through the dark initiation, "a monstrous sexual perversion was at the core of Hitler's whole existence." It is said that, as a result of the initiation, Hitler was only able to experience pleasure by causing pain to another (Rosio, 1992, 144).

For those not acquainted with occult rituals, both ancient and modern: The purpose of the ritual is the invocation of dark demonic spirits. Once these demons are summoned, those in the ritual invite the demons to possess all the participants. Others are named in the rituals for the demons to possess. Oftentimes in these rituals, demons are sent to world leaders to possess them. They may be sent to other enemies to destroy them. They are sent to the churches to water down their doctrine to nothing. Each participant in the ritual is said to be possessed by these demons which are invoked. All of this may sound like absolute madness. It is indeed madness and an unimaginable psychopathy. Hitler's invoked possession was reinforced by ongoing satanic rituals in which he and other inner circle Nazis participated.

OCCULT SEX RITUALS THROUGHOUT HISTORY

Dark occult rituals go back as far as Babylonian times and the time of Nimrod building his Tower of Babel. Sexual rituals, both consenting and not consenting, have been featured in dark occult rituals throughout history. In the book of Ezekiel, God shows Ezekiel corrupt rulers worshipping dark forces in secret; entire families are caught up in apostasy and perversions. God shows Ezekiel almost everyone is corrupted in this darkness.

In his book *Lucifer's Lodge: Satanic Ritual Abuse in the Catholic Church*, William Kennedy says:

It is no real secret that "sex-magic" rites, including the practice of sexual aberrations, have formed part of certain occult sciences from the very beginning. The practices of the priests of Babylon, Egypt, Greece, Rome, and India all involved sex rituals, with temple prostitution as an integral part of their tradition, as did those of the priesthoods of numerous other cultures ... Throughout the Old Testament, the priests of Israel are shown struggling desperately to keep the public, the monarchy, and even their fellow priests pure of the religious taint of the heathen gods of their neighbors...

Wise King Solomon is famous for having dabbled in the magical arts, but he is equally well-known for his exceptionally large harem of foreign women. It perhaps goes without saying that the sex practices of these ancient cults rarely stayed within the bounds considered acceptable by modern standards. Homosexuality, bestiality, incest, and group orgies were common, and there was certainly no age restriction on the participants, nor any requirement that the participants be consenting. Rape was common, and the murder of the victim before, during, or after the sex rite was common as well. Infanticide or abortion was not an uncommon end for the unhappy fruits of these unions. In other instances, the children were raised with privileges, as the divine offspring of the god to whom the ceremony had been dedicated. (Kennedy, 2006. 2–3)

HIMMLER'S USE OF OCCULT ENERGIES TO CONQUER AND MESMERIZE

Himmler, number two to Hitler, was fascinated by all aspects of the occult. He created an occult corps that included the SS, the Ahnenerbe (the occult bureau of the Nazi party), and the Karotechnia. He had a huge budget, which he used to send people around the globe to seek the darkest occult practices, demonically charged seats of occult power, sites of human sacrifices and demonic presence, and portals to the demonic. Asia and Tibet were of particular importance to him for their occult teachings. Himmler's goal was to create a worldwide dark occult grid and open ancient dark portals to facilitate the development of the New World Order. It is hard for us to imagine the extent and funding of his dark quest, with untold resources at his disposal. Through Himmler's efforts, many Tibetan Buddhist priests were imported into Germany, with the goal of harnessing their psychic powers to aid Germany in its militia and spiritual takeover goals. Rosio stated Germany purportedly spent more money on this psychic exploration than the United States did when developing the atomic bomb (Rosio, 1992, 145).

One begins to get a sense of how deeply the Nazi inner culture derived its energies from its occult focus. The Nazis utilized various of the darkest rituals used over history in their pursuit of global dominion. Himmler wanted to replace Christianity with his dark satanic religion as the means to take over the world.

With the Lebensborn breeding program, which was designed to breed the perfect Aryan supermen from pure-blood SS (highly occult) and unwed mothers, Hitler hoped to build his army to lead and control the world. Further, as many as four hundred thousand Aryan children were kidnapped from their parents in German-occupied countries. These children were given to the satanic SS, which was then in charge of their education and upbringing. Pedophilia is a key feature of their upbringing. Hitler once said,

My program for educating youth is hard. Weakness must be hammered away. In my castles of the Teutonic Order a youth will grow up before which the world will tremble. I want a brutal, domineering, fearless, cruel youth. Youth must be all that. It must bear pain. There must be nothing weak and gentle about it. The free, splendid beast of prey must once again flash from its eyes ... That is how I will eradicate thousands of years of human domestication ... That is how I will create the New Order (Hitler 1933).

How does one create such hardened, cruel men? In Nazi times, youth were put into mandatory indoctrination groups from an early age until adulthood. According to Rosio, these schools trained German youth into Nazi occult beliefs. The youth were bound by oath to both Hitler and Satan and taught they would be the future Nazi world ruling class (Rosio, 1992, 91).

Himmler's infamous Hall of the Dead in Wewelsburg castle is also called the Hall of Satan. He built the castle with the aim of it being the center of the world, where the darkest demonic energies would be summoned and released in horrific ceremonies. Sex rituals and human sacrifices were at the core of the occult rituals with the goal of invoking demons to possess the participants and then send them out out to compromise and take over world leaders. These rituals have been practiced in different ways since the beginning of time—they were not new with the Nazis.

Why are sadistic rituals such an essential component in dark occultism? Kennedy goes on, "But what is the ultimate purpose behind the perpetuation of these Satanic traditions by the various secret societies that practice them? Evidence points to a concerted effort for world domination: the 'New World Order' plot of modern conspiracy theories, an agenda that is right in line with the traditional idea of Satan as Prince of This World'" (Kennedy, 2006, 3).

Himmler's goal was to create a new religion, to exterminate Christianity, and to incorporate satanic rituals into the New Order. Infiltration of churches and use of their established structure to create a "new" religion in line with the Nazis' satanic/Luciferian beliefs was a means to an end. In Nazi Germany, the swastika was placed within the symbol of the cross in churches as a way of using the existing church structure to promote the new religion.

Further, Himmler, as chief of police, was responsible for establishing concentration camps and for devising dark methods for the Holocaust. It is impossible to understand this level of depravity and death without being able to understand the satanic roots.

It is clear to this writer, as it is to many others, that the satanic rituals and mind control programming—which Mengele used in the camps, which he and other welcomed Nazis imported into the United States, and which combined with our own dark scientific mind control implementation and occult rituals—are at the heart of much of what therapists in the United States and around the world encounter today in their clients in record numbers.

It is said the US music industry and Hollywood are dominated by MKUltra victims. (This article from *Vigilant Citizen* explores Miley Cyrus' Sex Kitten Programming, a type of programming widely used in Hollywood and in the music industry. (*https://vigilantcitizen.com/musicbusiness/miley-cyrus-releases-new-video-hospital-mind-control*)

There are different groups in power globally who use these dark methods and who compete with each other for world control. For example, the dark energies seeking world domination may use Islamic extremists to do their evil work. Those who open themselves to dark energies will receive these dark energies and work within their own cultural/religious context. That is a subject for another writer to explore in more detail. For the purposes of this book, I am focusing on those groups that have been affiliated with at least one part of the CIA (such as the Gehlen Org) and that had extensive collaboration with the Nazis. Some still use trauma-based programming, including RA; others may use electronics and sound.

WHICH GROUP IS WHICH?

Worth mentioning, to add more to the layers of deception and confusion about who is who and who did what is John Loftus, who, *in America's Nazi Secret: An Insider's History*, claims that after World War II the State Department established a group called the Office of Policy Coordination (OPC). This group, together with British intelligence, recruited and managed Nazi networks after the war (Loftus 2010, 33) and sent war criminals and fascists undercover into the Soviet Union. They also facilitated the paperless entrance of many Nazis into the United States through Canada. Loftus calls the OPC the second CIA, which aims to be hostile to the other CIA. Loftus says the OPC ignored statutes and wrote letters to INS to allow the Nazis across the US border from Canada without visas.

Loftus claims that while the original CIA was hunting Nazis, the OPC was busy recruiting them; the two organizations' interests were inimical to each other. In his book, Loftus States: "A series of attempts were made between 1951 and 1959 to merge OPC with CIA, but the unit continued to maintain its own independent files, agent networks, and operations. This anomaly of a separate independent agency with CIA was the direct order of Allen Dulles, former head of OPC" (Loftus 2010, 33).

This arrangement formed a shadow CIA that, although technically a part of the CIA, was independent. Further, according to Loftus, as the army began discovering more and more of the OPC's Nazi networks, the OPC had already decided they would make the CIA a scapegoat for illegal Nazi immigration.

The deception that they planned was one that the Nazis had used when they'd realized they would lose the war. The strategy involved having each Nazi make two visa applications. The first denied Nazi affiliations and was given to the CIA, who would then hire the agent. The second application admitted Nazi membership and was kept by the OPC at the State Department, away from CIA eyes (Loftus 2010, 45). This technique was designed to embarrass the CIA and also "destroy any criminal case against the Nazi for perjury, fraudulent entry, or withholding material facts from the US government" (Loftus 2010, 45).

As the reader can see, there is no easy answer as to which parts of the CIA and other governmental and corporate institutions have been doing what with mind control. No doubt it will take many decades to sort this out and to fully understand which globalist groups are doing what. My aim is to provide information and resources so the reader can begin to make his or her own exploration.

In the following section, my aim is also to open up the reader's mind to the widespread use of mind control and how it may manifest in the therapist's office as dissociative identity disorder (DID)—without the therapist understanding mind control is involved.

RA, MIND CONTROL, AND DELIBERATELY CREATED MULTIPLE PERSONALITY

Many writers and speakers detail how this process is done. Colin Ross's book *Bluebird: Deliberate Creation of Multiple Personality by Psychiatrists* is a good overview of mind control programs. A ten-page summary of the book can be found at *www.wanttoknow.info/bluebird10pg*. The following is from this summary:

According to my definition, the Manchurian Candidate is an experimentally created dissociative identity disorder that meets the following four criteria:

- Created deliberately
- A new identity is implanted
- Amnesia barriers are created

- Used in simulated or actual operations

That the CIA created Manchurian Candidates is a fact ...

> BLUEBIRD blows the whistle on extensive political abuse of psychiatry in North America in the second half of the 20th century. Many thousands of prisoners and mental patients were subjected to unethical mind control experiments by leading psychiatrists and medical schools. Organized academic psychiatry has never acknowledged this history. The network of mind control doctors involved in BLUEBIRD has done a great deal of harm to the field of psychiatry and to psychiatric patients. My goal is to break the ugly silence.
>
> The participation of psychiatrists and medical schools in mind control research was not a matter of a few scattered doctors pursuing questionable lines of investigation. Rather, the mind control experimentation was systematic, organized, and involved many leading psychiatrists and medical schools. The mind control experiments were interwoven with radiation experiments, and research on chemical and biological weapons. They were funded by the CIA, Army, Navy, Air Force, and by other agencies including the Public Health Service and the Scottish Rite Foundation.
>
> The psychiatrists, psychologists, neurosurgeons, and other contractors conducting the work were embedded in a broad network of doctors. Much of the research was published in medical journals. The climate was permissive, supportive, and approving of mind control experimentation. *(https://www.wanttoknow.info/bluebird10pg)*

The best-known modern form of trauma-based mind control was developed, at least in part, by the Nazis (Dizdar; Springmeier; Gunderson; Sullivan; O'Brien; Svali; Rosio; Rutz). If one understands history, it is not a stretch, knowing the ever-increasing numbers of multiple personality victims showing up in therapists' offices who say they are victims of ritual abuse, to believe there is a link between the imported brand of Nazi mind control with the million or so Germans who immigrated 4 generations ago into the United States after World War II, and these therapy clients whose stories are often similar. In addition, many recruits outside of these bloodlines have also been mind controlled through extensive governmental and non-governmental networks.

CULT ABUSE OUTSIDE OF GOVERNMENTAL MIND CONTROL

Many are unaware there have been practicing Satanists in every culture throughout history. Child sacrifice is common in these cults. If one reads carefully through the Old Testament of the Bible, one can see the ongoing problem of Baal/Moloch/Asteroth worship throughout. Children were sacrificed, and ritual sex was featured.

Though my familiarity is strongest with governmental mind control and Satanism, there are many cults with varying agendas, often tied into power and control. Satanism and other dark cult practices including intergenerational witchcraft are forms of mind control that aim to bind people forever into a dark system out of which they can never escape physically, psychologically, or spiritually. Susan's history demonstrates a possible history of ritual abuse, but at the time therapy was terminated, there was no definitive information pointing to governmental mind control.

Anne Johnson Davis's book, *Hell Minus One: My Story of Deliverance from Satanic Ritual Abuse and My Journey to Freedom*, is a corroborated story of ritual abuse. In an unusual set of circumstances, Anne's parents confessed to subjecting her to hideous satanic rituals and torture when she was a child. The horrific tortures reinforced in Anne that she would be killed if she ever told. However, the rituals in this case were not apparently connected to mind control implementation.

Ritual abuse provides the necessary trauma and horror to cause dissociation and is therefore a perfect base for installing governmental-type mind control programming. Because of this, RA has provided a natural pairing with trauma-based mind control. It is thought that early governmental mind control programmers in the United States deliberately kept a database of pedophiles and intergenerational Satanists and paid them to turn over their children for "experiments" while at the same time threatening to blackmail them if they did not. The agreement was the pedophiles were free to continue to offend and were given instructions on how to abuse their children to prepare them for mind control training and usage.

Given the massive trauma that goes into creating these living slaves (and they are that, with robotic, nonthinking personalities programmed to do whatever their handler/puppet master tells them to do, no matter what), it is hardly surprising that many of them have ended up in therapists' offices across this country and throughout the world. As I have mentioned, other groups have used various forms of RA and other occult practices as part of their trauma-based mind control programs as well.

This strange and horrible cultic side of the New World Order (now called the Great Reset) has been emerging through the stories, memories, and dreams of these horrifically abused persons as shared in therapists' offices everywhere. The stories they tell are outside of what any of us therapists learned about in our typical graduate and postgraduate training. A whole generation of therapists was thrown into a brand-new, steep learning curve in the 1980s and the early 1990s when these patients began appearing with greater regularity in their offices. This pattern has only increased since then, for we are now in a fourth generation of deliberately created multiples since World War II. Further, most training in dissociative identity disorder, even advanced training, includes little or no mention of mind control. How can we as therapists help our clients if we have no understanding of what we are seeing?

The following points are relevant to understanding the link between WWII and RA/mind control victims showing up in therapists' offices.

(1) Dizdar found in his research, as mentioned in his *Belly of the Beast* podcast series, that there were approximately forty-five million practicing Satanists in Germany by the end of World War II.

(2) The Lebensborn-program children were bred, conceived, and born with occult rituals done by the SS; they were Aryan and born to be supermen. The youth corps was also satanized, as were the four hundred thousand kidnapped children who were given to the SS.

(3) The Nazis, the SS, and the Thule Society had been preparing for a German messiah. They saw Hitler as that messiah. Hitler saw himself as a channel for Lucifer. actively seeking possession through rituals. The Ahnenerbe and their families were deeply immersed in a tradition of doing satanic rituals and demonizing their children.

(4) The mass importation of Nazi scientists, doctors, and top leaders into the United States occurred via Project Paperclip through the OPC and into other countries around the world through similar programs.

(5) There was a huge immigration of Germans into the United States after the war.

(6) The ratlines were escape routes by which many Nazis were smuggled out of Germany and helped to establish in other areas of the world. Both American intelligence and the Vatican were

involved in various of these ratlines (Levenda, 2012).

(7) The CIA, US military, and other US governmental groups have been doing extensive mind control research and operationalization since the 1940s and have created multiple personalities to serve at every strata of society. There was also intensive research done on psychic powers and the occult, including remote viewing and psychic killers.

Is it really so farfetched to consider the satanic rituals and deliberately created multiple personalities clinicians are seeing in their offices in record numbers, are real and a part of a globalist program to take over the world via the New World Order? This is the agenda many of the recovering victims are describing, through their writings and public speaking, as they deprogram and discover these alters and programs within them. I have attempted to provide extensive references in this ever-growing literature for those readers who wish to explore the subject further.

The global Covid-19 lockdowns and vaccine mandates are part of this controlled move towards an authoritarian takeover under a scientific dictatorship. I will come back to this point later but it is important to recognize that the current World Economic Forum push to have all countries cede their sovereignty to the World Health Organization (WHO) in health matters to them is not only unconstitutional but also a nefarious and dangerous world power play. *(https://www.independentsentinel.com/the-who-plans-to-strip-194-nations-and-the-us-of-sovereignty-may-22/).*

There is no doubt the United States has researched and operationalized mind control in many formats. Walter Bowart, in *Operation Mind Control,* written in 1988, documents many of the programs. He is said to have noted that the CIA bought up most of the copies of this brilliant book when it was published, as they did not want the information to get out. It is available today on Kindle and on the Internet. Even today, in 2023, the information in *Operation Mind Control* is powerful and gives the reader a glimpse into the scope and purpose of that world.

Bowart's research focused on the period when US government agencies were developing sophisticated mind control and political psychological operations, from 1938 to the present. During this time, he says, the goal of what he calls *"Operation Mind Control"* has been to take humans, including US citizens and citizens of both allies and enemies, and make them into "unthinking, subconsciously programmed 'zombies'

> …motivated without their knowledge and against their wills to perform in a variety of ways in which they would not otherwise willingly perform. This is accomplished through the use of various techniques called by various names, including brainwashing, thought reform, behavior modification, hypnosis, and conditioned reflex therapy. For the purposes of this book the term "mind control" will be used to describe these techniques generically.

> Mind control is the most terrible imaginable crime because it is committed not against the body, but against the mind and the soul. Dr. Joost A. M. Meerloo expresses the attitude of the majority of psychologists in calling it "mind rape," and warns that it poses a great "danger of destruction of the spirit" which can be "compared to the threat of total physical destruction." (Bowart 1978, 145–46)

Bowart goes on to discuss how mind control was developed by psychologists, psychiatrists, chemists, and others who worked under government contracts in isolation. "Need to know" was the guiding principle, so each person was allowed to know only what he or she needed to know to complete his or her segment of testing or research. Since the contracts were issued through any number of foundations and agencies, both government and private, the researchers were largely unaware of the intended use of their research. If we take a closer look at many of the more recent mass shooters, it is undeniable almost all of them have a zombie-like quality to them, with bugged-out eyes and a strongly dissociated quality to their presence.

Since 1978 when Bowart wrote *Operation Mind Control,* the technology of mind control has shifted from primarily trauma-based methods into electronic means, combined with the use of drugs. Ken Adachi, in *"Mind Control: The Ultimate Terror" (https://www.educate-yourself.org/mc/)* gives a good overview of the development of mind control since the 1940s. There are many resources listed at the back of the article. His focus, like many writers', is on what is known—that is, Nazi mind control. It is thought the United States was intensively developing its own brand of mind control (e.g., the work of Dr. George Estabrooks and Dr. Ewen Cameron, who worked in Canada under auspices of McGill University) that was combined with the Nazi type, perhaps during the war and definitely after. Adachi makes the distinction between trauma-based mind control and electronic-based mind control. Trauma-based mind control involves massive psychological and physical trauma, often beginning in infancy, and is designed to shatter the mind into alter personalities to be programmed to perform any function the programmer wishes, such as spy, assassin, sex slave, and so on. Rape of the subject is frequent, again often beginning in infancy. Rape of a young child by an adult splits the mind. The alter personalities are often hidden behind codes that only the programmer/handler knows, and the front personality is unaware of these personalities. Certain triggers can be programmed into the system to call out a particular alter. Ken Adachi mentions the Montauk Project as an example of electronic-based mind control. The Montauk Project started at an underground base using trauma-based techniques but later developed an electronic induction process that could be "installed" in a person in a matter of days or hours.

As previously discussed, Mengele and other leading Nazis were brought into US government programs through Project Paperclip. Mengele is purported to be a primary developer of the US mind control program. Mind control was developed in secret underground military bases, among other places. Adachi, Springmeier, and others talk about how these underground bases were home to many thousands of kidnapped American children (with some estimates as high as one million per year) who were put into stacked cages. These children were used, not unlike in the concentration camps, to perfect Mengele's mind control techniques. Some of them would be programmed as mind-controlled slaves to be used for tasks ranging from sex slavery to assassination. A certain portion of these children were murdered in front of the other children to further reinforce total submission. This is a technique well known in ritual abuse as well.

USE OF MIND CONTROL PROGRAMMING TO DELIBERATELY HIDE PERSONALITIES AND TRAUMAS BEHIND AMNESIC BARRIERS

Researchers and programmers have long since known how to create amnestic personalities and parts accessible only with the proper code. In his article *"Hypnosis Comes of Age"* in the April 1971 issue of Science Digest, Estabrooks stated that by the 1920s psychiatrists knew how to split certain complex individuals into multiple personalities like Jekyll and Hyde. He says, *"Once a deep hypnotic trance is achieved, it is possible to introduce posthypnotic amnesia so that [a subject] … would not know … he had been subjected to hypnosis, to drugs, or to any other treatment."* His 1943 book *Hypnosis* talks about the successful use of multiple personalities with amnesic barriers in intelligence work. He worked with the OSS and promoted the use of hypno-programmed spies, assassins, and messengers with amnesic barriers to reinforce resistance to interrogation. These mind controlled people were placed in high levels in all governments to secretly take control of those governments. He stated these programs were operational on our side during World War II. Some suggest the British and Germans even used mind-controlled soldiers during World War I.

Many people have risked their lives to describe their lives under governmental mind control, which includes sexual abuse, sexual slavery, and the deliberate creation of multiple personalities through rape, torture, drugs, hypnosis, and often, horrific satanic rituals. An Internet search on government mind control will bring up many resources. *The Control of Candy Jones* by Donald Bain is an early exploration of mind control done on top model and celebrity Candy Jones. Fritz Springmeier and Cisco Wheeler (a former mind control programmer) have written a number of volumes that are available free on the Internet. These volumes go deeply into how and why mind control programming is done. It is evil to the core. Kathleen Sullivan's *Unshackled* describes her abuse and attempt to free herself from the RA and mind control she was born into. Carol Rutz's *A Nation Betrayed* has a lot of valuable information about experiments on her and on unsuspecting citizens. She was sold to the CIA for cruel and horrific mind control at age four by her grandfather, a pedophile who was encouraged to sexual abuse her and use her in pornography. At age four, she was told she worked for the CIA. Cathy O'Brien, a former Presidential Model (as my client was), writes in *Trance Formation* of America about her life under mind control slavery.

The previously mentioned film *The Manchurian Candidate* as well as the *Bourne* movies give us a small glimpse into how deliberately created multiples may be used for political and governmental purposes. For example, a given mind-controlled person might have an alter deliberately created to be an assassin. When the handler gives that person a code to bring up the programmed assassin alter, the alter commits the murder he or she is instructed to commit, then goes back inside, with the person amnestic to the event. That part can only be brought up to conscious awareness only with the correct code, which only the handler(s) have.

Various occult groups throughout history have understood the value of dark ritual and trauma in creating multiple personalities for cult purposes. Seeking to be possessed by the dark gods is a common theme of occult groups and rituals throughout history. Springmeier does a good job of discussing in his book *The Illuminati Formula Used to Create an Undetectable Total Mind Controlled Slave*.

The available information on traumatic amnesia and the role of drugs, torture, rape and electricity in creating dissociative amnesia needs to be brought forward to the general public and integrated into the discussion of memory issues, traumatic amnesia, and amnesia created by hypnotic and drug barriers. Mind control programming is one of the deepest, darkest secrets around today, and all the world's citizens deserve to know and understand it. The former False Memory Foundation, with its many CIA founders and Board members, seemed to have been created to make sure these issues and subterfuges were kept in the dark.

Several volumes go deeply into how and why mind control programming is done from the point of view of the victim. It is evil to the core. Kathleen Sullivan's *Unshackled* describes her abuse and attempt to free herself from the RA and mind control she was born into. Carol Rutz's *A Nation Betrayed* has a lot of valuable information about experiments on her and on unsuspecting citizens. She was sold to the CIA for cruel and horrific mind control at age four by her grandfather, a pedophile who was encouraged to sexual abuse her and use her in pornography. At age four, she was told she worked for the CIA. Cathy O'Brien, a former Presidential Model as my client was, writes in *Trance Formation of America* about her life under mind control slavery.

The previously mentioned film *The Manchurian Candidate* as well as the *Bourne* movies give us a small glimpse into how deliberately created multiples may be used for political and governmental purposes. For example, a given mind-controlled person might have an alter deliberately created to be an assassin. When the handler gives that person a code to bring up the programmed assassin alter, the alter commits the murder he or she is instructed to commit, then goes back inside, with the person amnestic to the event. That part can only be brought up to conscious awareness only with the correct code, which only the handler(s) have.

Various occult groups throughout history have understood the value of dark ritual and trauma in creating multiple personalities for cult purposes. Seeking to be possessed by the dark gods is a common theme of occult groups and rituals throughout history. Springmeier does a good job of discussing in his book *The Illuminati Formula Used to Create an Undetectable Total Mind Controlled Slave.*

The available information on traumatic amnesia and the role of drugs, torture, rape and electricity in creating dissociative amnesia needs to be brought forward to the general public and integrated into the discussion of memory issues, traumatic amnesia, and amnesia created by hypnotic and drug barriers. Mind control programming is one of the deepest, darkest secrets around today, and all the world's citizens deserve to know and understand it. The former False Memory Foundation, with its many CIA founders and Board members, seemed to have been created to make sure these issues and subterfuges were kept in the dark.

Ken Adachi has some startling things to say about the Montauk Project:

> The lone gunman that we hear about in assassinations, assassination attempts, school shootings, etc. are often mind controlled individuals who had been "programmed" to carry out those missions. Ted Bundy, the *"Son of Sam"* serial killer David Berkowitz, Oswald, Timothy McVeigh, the Columbine shooters, Chapman, Sirhan Sirhan, etc. were mind controlled individuals who were programmed to perform these killings. Tens of thousands of young teenage boys were kidnapped and forced into the mind control training program called The Montauk Project starting around 1976. Al Bielek, under mind control, was involved in many areas of the secret Montauk Project. After slowly recovering his memories beginning in the late 1980's, he came to realize that there were at least 250,000 mind controlled "Montauk Boys" produced at 25 different facilities similar to the underground base at Montauk, Long Island. Many of these boys were to become "sleepers" who are individuals who were programmed to go into action at a later date when properly "triggered" to engage in some sort of destructive or disruptive conduct. Other Montauk Boys were woven into the fabric of mainstream American life as journalists, radio & TV personalities, businessmen, lawyers, medical professionals, judges, prosecutors, law enforcement, military men, etc. *(Adachi, 2016, https://www.educate-yourself.org/mc/)*

How many of our many shootings and bombings are actually carried out by mind controlled operatives, who, with a code or other means, are called into service to further a shadow government agenda? The term "false flag" is increasingly well-known, and many investigative reporters in the alternative media look into each mass casualty event for possible signs of false flag operations. Mind controlled Manchurian candidates are perfect for many of these operations. Though it is out of the scope of this book to go further into specific false flags, the reader may wish to do an internet search to learn more about admitted historical false flags.

SATANISM IN THE MILITARY

The US military used Dr. Michael Aquino in mind control programming. Aquino was a lieutenant colonel with top security clearances who established the Temple of Set (Satan). In his book *The Book of Coming Forth by Night (1985)*, Aquino speaks of his faith in the Prince of Darkness and how the devil gave him communications from hell. The military recognizes the Temple of Set, inspired by Aleister Crowley's Ordo Templi Orientis (OTO).

Aquino is supposed to have said there is a satanic grotto (coven) on every military base. The supersoldier of the military, with all his or her enhancements, is mind controlled, likely a continuation of the Nazi superman idea. Through satanic worship and all the rituals, mind splitting, and intense programming, the supersoldier was created to be a blend of human, the occult, and synthetic enhancements. These programmed multiples are mutant, much as was Hitler's superman, permanently altered from conception onward by demonic attachment and various enhancements and programming. You don't believe in that? It doesn't matter what you believe in that regard—what we need to look at here is what the programmers believe and the energies they invoke. Many people sincerely worship Lucifer as an angel they believe works for good.

The appendix to Fritz Springmeier and Cisco Wheeler's *Deeper Insights into the Illuminati Formula for Creating a Mind Controlled Slave (https://www.scribd.com/doc/8306247/Deeper-Insights-Into-the-Illuminati-Formula)* offers a number of names and sites involved with mind control. In order to keep the research secret, the NSA and the CIA divided their 149 subprojects up among over eighty universities and hospitals, foundations, and drug companies in the United States and Canada. Funds were often paid in cash to prevent them from being traceable. Researchers were free to do what they wanted, and most subjects of the often gruesome and horrific research were unwitting.

Springmeier talks about the development of mind control programming and Satanism in the United States since 1900, discussing such key dark occult persons as Aleister Crowley, Anton La Vey, and Michael Aquino. These latter two were fascinated and obsessed with Nazism. Aquino traveled the country doing military mind control on various bases. Springmeier wrote the following before Aquino retired:

> Like so many programmers, Aquino flies all over the country, and has victimized people in numerous states and military bases. Michael Aquino's programming is standard military-type programming. Aquino puts his own spirit guide into people. He likes to use his own version of Star Wars, with himself as Darth Vader, for his programming scripts. He programs in sexual and death (suicide) programs—such as the Rivers of Blood suicide protection program, and all the rest of the various types of programs …

> Michael Aquino is familiar with all the standard programming, the Wizard of Oz and the other fairy tale themes. He is very proficient at programming, having many years of experience. In 1981, he used Cathy O'Brien to make two HOW TO films for training military officers in the skills needed to program slaves. These two training films were entitled *"How to Divide a Personality"* and *"How to Create a Sex Slave."* (See Cathy O'Brien's monograph "Dick Cheney and Reagan's *'Hands-On' Mind Control Demonstrations"* written/released 6/92.) President Reagan respected Aquino and encouraged the military to learn his programming techniques.

> Aquino likes to work with Catholic mind control victims. He is proficient at manipulating the concept of hell and of doing satanic reversals like the Black Mass. (Springmeier, 2010, *http://whale.to/b/deeper.pdf*, *Appendix*)

Aquino was also fascinated by top German Nazi Himmler's Wewelsburg castle, built to be a hall for invoking Satan. Aquino went so far as to perform a dark occult ceremony that he called the Wewelsburg Working. In his paper entitled *"The Wewelsburg Working,"* Aquino described his purpose in doing the ceremony. Himmler had seen the castle as the center of the world, a central portal or gate for the invocation of demons, where rituals invoked possession by demonic spirits. Aquino stated that since Wewelsburg was the "Gate of that Center," his aim in performing a satanic ceremony there was to "summon the powers of darkness at their most powerful locus." The goal was to send these dark powers out over the world, especially so they could possess leaders, and he believes he succeeded (*https://ia801604.us.archive.org/16/items/LeftHandPath666/WewelsburgWorking.pdf*). Why was someone so prominent in our military involved so deeply with satanic rituals? He was also known for pedophilic initiations and occult ceremonies on military bases.

David Shurter, in his 2013 autobiographical account, *Rabbit Hole: A Satanic Ritual Abuse Survivor's Story*, talks about his sexual abuse by Michael Aquino. Shurter was involved in the Omaha sex trafficking that led to the Franklin abuse scandal where young boys were prostituted to the White House under George Bush Sr.

THE MIND-CONTROLLED SATANIC SUPERSOLDIER

Comprehensive information on the satanic supersoldier is in *The Black Awakening: Rise of the Satanic Super Soldier* by Russ Dizdar. Dizdar was well familiar and seemed to know more about the spiritual aspects of these "chosen ones" than just about anyone else I have found. Many therapists, unfortunately, ignore the spiritual aspects of DID. Dizdar's website, shatterthedarkness.net, has a wealth of information available in the podcast archives. Dizdar had a large educational reach nationwide in train people as to the phenomena and how to eradicate it in their communities. Unfortunately he and his wife Shelley died a few years ago after illness.

Based on his many years of experience as a police chaplain and in the ministry dealing with RA and on his prolific research, Dizdar estimated a minimum of five hundred million satanic rituals have been done since the 1940s. Many horrific rituals are held throughout the year. Any holiday becomes an occasion for a satanic ritual abuse holiday. In addition there are a number of other dates. An Internet website for survivors of mind control, torture, and rituals called *survivorship.org* has a detailed ritual calendar that tries to include the dates used by various cults (*https://survivorship.org/alt-calendar/*). Further, Dizdar estimated the average ritually abused child has experienced a staggering five hundred satanic rituals by the time he or she is thirteen. These are brutal, sadistic rituals of the darkest nature. Many of Dizdar's videos are available on the internet.

Another resource is *https://supersoldiertalk.com*, a website with information on supersoldiers and mind control. These supersoldiers are deliberately created multiples, programmed in their various personalities to carry out all sorts of heinous programs. Though electronic and chemical means may now be used to help create these "chosen ones," it is likely extensive trauma-based means are still used. The "soul" is shattered to break allegiance to God, the divine, and the higher self, leading all personalities in the system to turn to Satan as their only refuge. The dissociated parts are then programmed and used for covert purposes. They have artificially enhanced capacities.

There is a large and growing amount of material on the Internet documenting the CIA and other intelligence and military agencies' role in mind control programming of human slaves. Aquino was just one programmer out of many. To the world, these slaves look like you and me. Boys and girls, men and women, are raped, tortured, and abused and kept in a dissociated state as slaves to their governmental handlers. The cruelty to which they are subjected is beyond our ability to comprehend. Hollywood and the music industry are said to be full of MKUltra slaves. Roseanne Barr has gone on record saying "MK Ultra rules in Hollywood."

Ted Gunderson, now deceased, was an FBI chief who played a large role in speaking out about the CIA, Satanism, pedophilia, and mind control. An example of one of his talks can be found at: (*https://spotlightonabuse.wordpress.com/2013/05/30/ralph-underwager-the-paidika-interview/*). Before his death,

Gunderson requested that his physician do an autopsy upon his death. This autopsy said Gunderson died of arsenic poisoning. A video of Gunderson speaking out about some of what he had learned, together with Brice Taylor, a recovered presidential model who speaks very articulately of the tortures, abuses, and slavery she was subjected to from birth, can be found on YouTube: (*https://www.youtube.com/watch?v=YpoNSdS5TQo*) Many other videos of Gunderson's talks can be found with a simple Internet search.

FALSE MEMORY SYNDROME (FMS) AND FALSE MEMORY SYNDROME FOUNDATION

Can we ignore all this information that many brave people have risked their lives to make available? Will we stick our heads back in the sand collectively as we did in the 1990s when pressure from the now disbanded False Memory Syndrome Foundation (whose board was heavily laden with psychiatrists with links to the CIA or the military) and threats of lawsuits shut down the awakening to what was happening? Will we be fooled again or scared back into submission? Many therapists were harassed and threatened by the foundation.

As the saying goes, "Fool me once, shame on you. Fool me twice, shame on me." It is this writer's opinion that nothing less than the future of humanity is at stake as we come to understand the massive perpetration of the big lie. Dark forces that wish to keep us ignorant have severely compromised and shaped our knowledge of the world. Many people do not know that false memory syndrome is not an official psychiatric syndrome. It was dubbed as false memory syndrome by Jennifer Freyd's non-clinician parents, who created the False Memory Syndrome Foundation, using this nonexistent syndrome for their foundation title, as if one could designate a real clinical syndrome just by saying so.

While in therapy, Jennifer (herself a psychologist) spent a lot of time processing never-forgotten sexual abuse by her father. When she privately confronted her father (not with a lawsuit or with going public but just with her memories), he and his wife took the accusation public and created the False Memory Syndrome Foundation (FMSF), saying that therapists everywhere were creating false memories of sexual abuse in their patients. There is a great deal of irony in the case, as Jennifer maintained she had never had amnesia for her abuse. Further, her brother stated he was aware their father had sexually abused her in childhood.

Therapists at that time were being quite aggressive about retrieving memories. As mentioned earlier, digging for memories is NOT good clinical practice, and the focus should be on stabilization and boundary setting before any trauma work is done. Material will emerge in its own time and in its own way. Additionally, when used for memory retrieval, hypnosis tends to reinforce material seen under hypnosis, whether true or not. Therefore, abuse memory material discovered under hypnosis is considered inadmissible in court.

While there were indeed abuses by therapists, these were overestimated in pursuit of the driving agenda to shut down growing awareness of sexual abuse and mind control tactics. In the time since, guidelines and training for trauma treatment have been further developed and updated and developed to prevent leading and to promote ethical, cautious trauma work. The abuse and trauma treatment field has grown by leaps and bounds in the twenty-plus years since. Throughout this book, I have encouraged and taught appropriate client-centered means of working with very challenging material. The therapeutic goal is to stay client centered and allow the client's material to emerge and be processed in the client's own way. It is clear that unwelcome consequences can ensue from careless practice and technique and from unchecked countertransference.

Tactics by the FMSF to shut down therapists included threats of lawsuits, harassment, and other forms of intimidation. The board was full of CIA and military types—including such people as Dr. Martin Orne— who have the most to hide because of their extensive mind control operations in this country and others. Dr. Orne was an original member of the FMSF's advisory board. He was a senior CIA/navy researcher based at the

University of Pennsylvania's Experimental Psychiatry Laboratory.

The following quote by Alex Constantine takes a strong stance with regards to the FMSF:

The Foundation is dedicated to denying the existence of cult mind control and child abuse. Its primary pursuit is the castigation of survivors and therapists for fabricating accusations of ritual abuse …

But the CIA and its cover organizations have a vested interest in blowing smoke at the cult underground because the worlds of CIA mind control and many cults merge inextricably. The drumbeat of "false accusations" from the media is taken up by paid operatives like Dr. Orne and the False Memory Syndrome Foundation to conceal the crimes of the Agency.

Orne's forays into hypno-programming were financed in the 1960s by the Human Ecology Fund, a CIA cover at Cornell University and the underwriter of many of the formative mind control experiments conducted in the U.S. and abroad. Research specialties of the CIA's black psychiatrists included electroshock lobotomies, drugging agents, incapacitants, hypnosis, sleep deprivation and radio control of the brain, among hundreds of sub-projects …

Dr. Orne, with SEI funding, marked out his own mind control corner at the University of Pennsylvania in the early 1960s. He does not publicize his role as CIA psychiatrist. He denies it, very plausibly. In a letter to Dr. Orne, Marks once reminded him that he'd disavowed knowledge of his participation in one mind-wrecking experimental sub-project. Orne later recanted, admitting that he'd been aware of the true source of funding all along.

Among psychiatrists in the CIA's mind control fraternity, Orne ranks among the most venerable. He once boasted to Marks that he was routinely briefed on all significant CIA behavior modification experiments. (*https://constantinereport.com/the-cia-the-false-memory-syndrome-foundation-fmsf/*)

Orne spoke often as to how all multiple personality disorder was iatrogenic, that is, caused by the treating psychotherapist, a leading premise of the FMSF. One can see from the quote above he was extensively involved in research into mind control and the various ways it was being used. Appendix B lists a number of FMSF founders and board members together with their history of work in intelligence and mind control. The list is from the Institute of Globalization and Covert Politics and uses a lot of the information Colin Ross obtained through his many years of FOIA requests. For example, Ralph Underwager, a founder of the FMSF, was forced to resign from the FMSF (that he helped found) in 1993, because of a remark in an interview which appeared in Paidika, an Amsterdam journal for pedophiles. He said that it was 'God's Will' when adults engage in sex with children. He told a group of British reporters in 1994 that 'scientific evidence' proved 60% of all women molested as children believed the experience was 'good for them'" (*https://www.liquisearch.com/ralph_underwager/interview_controversy*). Appendix C has a list of the former FMSF Board Members and the work they were involved in.

To see all this information in one place in the appendix is rather persuasive as to the question of whether FMSF is a cover for intelligence disinformation. That a number of researchers (read: mind control programmers) are on the FMSF board saying that all or most DID is caused by therapists and that amnesia is rare for trauma in children goes well past disingenuousness and into deliberate deception. These are exactly the people who are most aware that mind control programming often includes deliberately creating DID with alters behind solid amnesic barriers —because they are the experts at creating mind control and DID.

Investigative journalist Jon Rappoport's talk "The CIA, Mind Control and Children" (transcript available at (*http://whale.to/b/rappoport_i.html*) gives details of experiments on children as well as some more information on the CIA assets who are on the FMSF board.

Mind control programmers creating multiple personalities are highly aware of the dissociative barriers that the mind spontaneously erects in response to trauma and/or drugs and, as I have shown, have been aware of this for some time. They deliberately use trauma, electroshock, spinning, rape, and violence as means to create dissociation so they can shape the newly formed personalities as they wish and keep them behind an amnesic barrier. Many have made sure not to leave any corroborating evidence and install suicide programming should the mind control victim ever begin to remember.

Do the CIA, NSA, military, and other intelligence organizations lie about their black ops mind control programs? The very nature of intelligence programs is constant deception, which makes the question seem irrelevant. The secret contracting out of programs makes tracking the number and nature of the programs impossible. Without oversight, what do the contractors have freedom to do? It might be anything they want to do. If the Senate Intelligence Committee were to do a review of the practices throughout the alphabet intelligence agencies and the military, they would, in this writer's opinion, be unlikely to find these well-hidden programs, which are often carried out by civilians who may not know who they are working for.

A secret New World Order takeover would hardly work if the mask of secrecy were removed and replaced by transparency and law-abiding means. The takeover of the media under CIA Project Mockingbird has been a powerful means of propagandizing the public and having them believe whatever those in power want them to believe.

CIA's Media Takeover

The goal of the CIA's Project Mockingbird, begun in the 1950s, was to gain control of the media. Bill Colby, ex–CIA director, once stated that, as of 1970, the US media was totally controlled, saying, "The CIA owns everyone of any significance in the major media." It was cynically said a journalist was cheaper to purchase than a prostitute. This influence over the media is much greater today, more than forty years later. What does that mean to us today? It means that anything those in power do not want us to know will not be revealed in major media. This has been so since at least 1970. We will not find truth if we look to the mainstream media.

In 1974, two ex–CIA agents, John D. Marks and Victor Marchetti, published a book entitled *The CIA and the Cult of Intelligence*. The book, among other things, exposed how the CIA was like a cult and how its control of the media kept the public from knowing the truth about whatever the CIA did not want us to know. This is far more true today, as the media is owned by only a few conglomerates.

As we have learned, however, there are opposing factions doing mind control, even within the CIA. This makes getting to the truth of these matters extremely challenging.

Walter Bowart, in his now-dated but still extremely informative look into the world of mind control in the US government, calls this "cult of intelligence" the "cryptocracy." In his research, he found that although the CIA was a lead funder of mind control research, most government agencies were involved, whether witting or unwitting. Bowart began his research believing a "cult of intelligence" lay behind the mind control program but found instead there are several leading forces. He says, "It is the plan of a secret bureaucracy—what I call a cryptocracy—which conspires against our laws and our freedoms" (Bowart, 9). The word cryptocracy comes from crypto, or "secret," and cracy, or "governing body."

Bowart's thesis revolves around the cryptocracy, or shadow government, which includes the NSA, the Defense Intelligence Agency, military intelligence, and the Office of Naval Intelligence, as well as private contractors, institutions, and religious organizations. Others implicated are persons within the GSA, the NSF, the Atomic Energy Commission, the VA, the Department of Justice, and major American corporations, including airlines, oil companies, and aerospace contractors.

The cryptocracy invades the privacy of citizens and corporations. It meddles, often violently, in the internal politics of foreign nations, and has hired, trained, and equipped mind-controlled assassins for the murder of heads of state. We have seen how the cryptocracy may have been involved in attempts to control U.S. elections. It also control key figures in the U.S. and world press.

The story within the story, I discovered, is an astonishing one of a psychological war waged by this U.S. cryptocracy against the American people. The scientific reports and histories place the story in time, and at the government's door. However, the literature of the cryptocracy ignores the very real human factor. There is no written record of the mental anguish, the torture to the soul that comes from loss of memory and the resulting identity crisis. That mental anguish is the human story of mind control. (Bowart, 1978, 9–10)

Unfortunately, many of those who have suffered under the depravity are innocent children; their childhoods stolen from them so they can become weapons in America's secret war against its citizens. The book *Secret Weapons: Two Sisters' Terrifying True Story of Sex, Spies and Sabotage* by Cheryl Hersha and Lynn Hersha details how these two sisters were abused from a very early age and trained as spies and assassins. As children, they had advanced military training and skills. They were part of Project MKUltra. Appendix B shows the levels of mind control programming. Each is kept separate from the other. The programming is complex and tortuous. In everyday life many of the victims are constantly tormented by inner programs designed to make them slaves for life, unable to remember or to escape.

MIND CONTROL PROGRAMMING AS PORTRAYED IN THE MEDIA

George Estabrooks said that as far back as the early 1900s psychiatrists and hypnotists were aware that, with the use of hypnosis, a person could be made to do something he or she would not ordinarily do and then not remember having done it. In other words, it was known over a hundred years ago that the mind can create an amnesic barrier behind which memories of events can be hidden. In his book *Hypnosis,* published in 1947 and discussing work dating back to the early 1930s, Estabrooks explains military and intelligence uses of hypnosis to create mind-controlled slaves. *The Control of Candy Jones* is an excellent book in which the reader learns about Candy Jones's programming during World War II as she uncovers it herself.

If we go back in time, TV shows from the 1960s and 1970s in the United States reveal that air force and space research very much focused on the creation of a mind-controlled female robot who would serve totally the will of her handler and be programmed to have amnesia for her actions when instructed to do so.

In the 1964 TV series *My Living Doll* starring Julie Newmar and Bob Cummings, Newmar is Rhoda, a mind-controlled robot, called Air Force Subproject 709. She is programmed to do her handler's bidding, no matter what it is. In episode 3 of season 1, her programming is failing, and she needs to be reprogrammed. The reason her programming fails several times is because she was exposed to words from *Alice in Wonderland* (a key story used in mind control programming) and it confused her circuitry. She has trigger points on her back that, when pressed, activate or deactivate various programs. (In creating mind-controlled slaves, triggering points are created on acupressure points on the body so that, when touched, the human slave/robot will do what it is programmed to do.) Throughout the series other aspects of her top secret mind control programming are shown.

I Dream of Jeannie was another television show in this same genre, with a beautiful woman being totally controlled and locked up by her air force master. "Your wish is my command" was her mantra, similar to Rhoda's mantra "I will do whatever you wish" in *My Living Doll*. In both shows, the obvious sexual implications of this "your wish is my command" programming were completely sanitized. As we know, however, sexual programming is often a key element of mind control programming, with sex-slave alters well trained in sexual expression of every kind. Much of this is done for blackmail purposes, as most sex with sex slaves is videotaped secretly.

Another very well known show that treated the subject of mind control programming and amnesia was the original *Charlie's Angels*. The villain in the episode "Attack Angels" (*https://charliesangels.fandom.com/wiki/Attack_Angels*) is shown programming a number of women through known mind control programming techniques of hypnosis, using strobe lights and a sensory-deprivation tank to induce hypnotic trances. The programming goal is to create dissociation and then create assassin alters in the women who will carry out the murders they are assigned to do. In each case, after the murders have been completed, the host personality is programmed to have complete amnesia for the murders or any instructions to commit those murders. One of Charlie's Angels is even programmed but is stopped before she completes the assigned assassination. She has no memory of attacking her would-be victim and vehemently denies she did, even though the attack just happened and another of Charlie's Angels witnessed it.

One of the most well-known examples of mind control programming in the media is the 1959 book *The Manchurian Candidate*, which became a movie in 1952 and again in 2004. The theme is the mind control of a main character, Raymond Shaw, who is programmed to commit murders, which he is then programmed to forget. Additionally, an entire platoon of US soldiers is brainwashed to believe something happened that did not happen.

Media programming has grown ever more extensive since those early TV years. Fritz Springmeier in his writings has taken a detailed look at Disney shows, which are often used for mind control programming.

My aim in this section has been to demonstrate blatant mind control programming in the US media as far back as the 1960s. This media programming shows there has been awareness that hypnotic mind control programming can cause amnesia and also that amnesic assassins can be programmed. Of course, the intelligence and military agencies have known this for seventy to eighty years or more.

In the next chapter, I will transition from this historical material into a more personal look at a few of the many ways this shadow government tried to kill, frame, mind control, and otherwise neutralize me for the simple "crime" of being aware of some of their heinous crimes. Though I am loath to get into the details, giving a few detailed examples may help the reader understand to what lengths I, an innocent citizen, was targeted by our shadow government for understanding what a mind-controlled assassin may look like.

There was no constitutionally mandated due process afforded me in these experiences. Most of them were unconstitutional to begin with. All processes went on in secret and against US laws.

I am alive by the grace of God, who, I firmly believe, seeks the restoration of our republic to God's laws, not Satan's. We can see what the spirit of Satan did to Germany in World War II. What dark destruction are we facing on our current path? As the saying goes, "Evil always carries within it the seeds of its own destruction."

The unveiling of the elite satanic/pedophilic/child trafficking/sex slave networks in the US and globally has been coming at a rapid pace in the few years since the initial printing of this book in the summer of 2016. Previous to that, there was little mainstream exposure in the United States, which made the information I was exposing on pedophilia and satanism very sensitive and treacherous to me.

The "open border" and "catch and release" policies during the Obama era made it easy for traffickers to smuggle children across the border. This was exposed after Trump came into office with his focus on building a wall and stopping illegal immigration. Biden reversed this policy, opening to borders to virtually anyone. On the Mexican side of the border, the cartels are in control, and are trafficking children at unprecedented numbers. (*https://lizcrokin.substack.com/p/joe-biden-americas-trafficker-in*) At bottom, the problem is spiritual, and is causing destruction in every area of our collective lives — the family, economy, education, industry, government and so on. With the 2016 presidential election in the United States came the revealing, through Wikileaks, of John Podesta emails that emerged as a scandal called "Pizzagate." Podesta was Chairman of the Democratic National Committee, and head of Hillary Clinton's campaign. Although the focus on one pizza parlor in DC was misleading, the Podesta emails show links to child sex trafficking in Haiti (*https://www.charismanews.com/politics/elections/61050-redditor-clintons-connection-to-laura-silsby-discovered*) ,and points to a large organized pedophilic network, satanism and child sacrifice at the very highest levels of our government on both sides of the political fence. A very well-researched article by Joaquim Hagopian, a mental health therapist and veteran, explores the emails and trails of evidence: (*http.//whale.to/c/pizzagate77.html*) Another link with much information is found at: (*https://dcpizzagate.wordpress.com/2016/11/07/first-blog-post/*).

International sex trafficking and dark spiritual practices are not a new problem. Nor is it a political problem, as it exists across party lines. It is ancient, and it is global. Pedophilic/child sex trafficking/ satanism networks have been exposed in the UK (Jimmy Saville as a procuror of children for the royals and more), Belgium (the Marc Dutroux affair), Australia (which also took in a number of Nazi war criminals; the Psychiatric Association is led by programmers), Nigeria, China, Central America and more. Since 2016, we have seen the arrest and supposed suicide in jail of Jeffrey Epstein. The exposure of his pedophilia and association with a number of world leaders put organized pedophilia on the map. Ghislaine Maxwell, who procured girls for him, said they had videotapes of everyone, most likely for blackmail purposes. It is very unlikely Epstein was working on his own. Because of the many connections to politicians such as Clinton and corporate heads such as Bill Gates, it was likely part of a much larger blackmail network, designed to compromise politicians and heads of state. Some indicators are that he may have been working for Mossad, as did Ghislaine's father. Clearly he was a threat to those high-level persons who had been caught in his trap.

We have seen evidence of pedophilia in the Catholic church, the Baptist church, even amongst the Amish. We have seen the trials of the now convicted Olympic gymnast doctor Larry Nassar who abused many young girls over years. Jerry Sandusky was convicted of rape and sexual abuse of athletes at Penn State. The Boy Scouts recently (February 2020) declared bankruptcy because of the expensive lawsuits against pedophile scout leaders. The list goes on. We hear of these kinds of instances, seemingly isolated in nature — are they part of something much bigger?

WOULD YOU PUT IT PAST THE NAZIS?

To sum up, the Nazis planned ahead for the end of WWII and seeded themselves in every major country in the world, planning for the Fourth Reich which would be implemented by covert means through infiltration and take-over of all the major institutions including military, educational, governmental, medical, corporate and so on. The spiritual force which drove them was, as documented, satanic. The satanism developed through rituals, which include child sacrifice, pedophilia, bestiality, sex trafficking and demon possession and it was carried on inter-generationally through breeding. Many of these Nazis and allegiant Germans immigrated into our country, into Britain, into Australia and many more countries after WWII.

What if this worldwide global network of satanism, pedophilia, ritual abuse and sex trafficking (which the Nazis were involved with) was tied to the Nazi plan for the Fourth Reich? What if they are actually succeeding in their plan? Can we afford to turn a deaf ear and blind eye to what we are seeing? Will a false allegiance to political parties keep us from seeing the problem that is growing like a very fast-spreading cancer nationally and globally, going by the names of globalism, the New World Order or the Great Reset? What if all our leaders since Kennedy have been compromised by the series of internal coups that are a plague on us all, the Fourth Reich so carefully plotted out by the Nazis? Jim Marrs' book *The Rise of the Fourth Reich* speaks to the financial and political dynamics of this rise. Their Satanic roots express themselves in these global networks. Did they not have the means to do so and did they not tell us the Fourth Reich would be covert? If we put together the jigsaw puzzle pieces, what picture emerges? Doesn't it look very much like what they may have planned, and wouldn't they have done it if they could? Our lack of education on these issues will not serve us well as an excuse if we continue to look away from what causes us discomfort, enabling them to complete their dark global takeover.

All of these problems must be carefully and soberly examined by the light of day — but until the underlying spiritual problem is fully seen, the problems will only increase. We must wake up spiritually and use our discernment to understand the big picture. We may not want to see what is going on, and we may be afraid to see — this will only destroy us in the end if we do not understand why our media has been virtually controlled since 1970 (Project Mockingbird) and has been lying to us.

REPEAL OF THE SMITH-MUNDT ACT.

In fact, the 2012 National Defense Authorization Act (NDAA) authorizes the US government to use lies and propaganda against Americans, literally "fake news." In a stranger than fiction amendment to the 2012 NDAA, Obama signed into law HR4310, allowing propaganda to be used on its own citizens repealing the Smith-Mundt act which restricted the use of propaganda to those abroad. This legalized a level of lying in the media never before seen, which has figured into elections, the Covid-19 and vaccine.

> The amendment sanctions the US government, without restriction, the use of any mode of message to control how we perceive our world." (*https://www.occupycorporatism.com/2013/07/22/ how-the-ndaa-allows-us-gov-to-use-propaganda-against-americans/*)

From the same article:

> The amendment, which was hidden within the NDAA, has remained relatively unnoticed. However, it empowers the State Department and Pentagon to utilize all forms of media against the American public for the sake of coercing US citizens to believe whatever version of the truth the US government wants them to believe. All oversight is removed with Amendment 114. Regardless of whether the information disseminated is truthful, partially truthful or completely false bears no weight.

This is absolutely chilling, and sets a new low for standards of journalism in the United States. All citizens need to be aware that being lied to by the government is now not only an undercover secret CIA program (Project Mockingbird), but it is now also official policy. This policy does not bear any resemblance to reasonable standards of ethics and integrity in the media, and reflects a dark spiritual foundation. Additionally, the passage of the 2017 NDAA (sponsored by John McCain and passed on Dec. 13, 2016) created and funds what Zero Hedge called a "de facto Ministry of Truth" which gave the government, without restriction, the means to "counter foreign disinformation and manipulation" which is can be used on anything that doesn't go along with the official government narrative or which criticizes the government. It horrifyingly rescinds our First Amendment rights and deepens our descent into totalitarianism.

Since Trump's election, we have seen in full display a controlled and censored media which continually puts forward false narratives. Talking points across the various media networks are synchronized. Censorship of opinions and facts that go against the official narrative has been rampant. Twitter, YouTube and Facebook widely censor speech which is not in alignment with the accepted narrative, as do the television networks. (It remains to be seen how Twitter will develop under Elon Musk. His choice of CEO has many worried she is allegiant to the cabal.) What is not seen and rarely discussed is Project Mockingbird and now the NDAA— and how the media has been increasingly controlled, leading to a misinformed public susceptible to government lied.

This should concern everyone, regardless of political persuasion. We should be alarmed that the CIA and other intelligence agencies are in control of what we hear and read, and moreover, what we believe. This has been a progressive long-term program of brainwashing which has gone on for so long, and which has reached into every institution in our society so deeply, that much of what we think we know and believe has been manipulated. The field of journalism itself has been radically transformed. Glenn Greenwald is a journalist who has been acutely aware of and reporting on the propagandizing of the media:

> "It's not prohibited in American corporate journalism to spread false stories and conspiracy theories," Greenwald asserted, adding "In fact, that's the only way you can thrive in journalism."

> "The people who have lied the most, and who spread the most conspiracy theories, are the ones who have been promoted and enriched most within corporate journalism," he further urged.

> "The difference is, the way to advance in journalism is to tell lies and spread conspiracy theories on behalf of the CIA, and that advance the interests of the U.S. government. That is not only permitted. That is required to be promoted," Greenwald emphasized. (Glenn Greenwald System Update, Rumble May 23, 2023)

Greenwald went on to say that what you can't do is report on narratives that go against the US security state. Tucker Carlson's removal from Fox News when he was reporting against the "party line" is an example of this. UN, WHO and World Economic Forum Agenda 2030: Global pandemics and the sexualization of children Calin Georgescu, a former UN Executive Director, in a conversation 2022 with the International Crimes Investigation Committee says the oligarchs who rule the world are pedophilic and tied to the pedophilic system and agenda. He says 8 million children disappear each year with no trace, a number equal to the entire population of Austria. He says Trump was the first time one of their selected candidates did not win, which disrupted the Agenda which Hillary was to direct. A pandemic was planned for 2015; 2020 was to be a disaster with food and water, now pushed up to 2023 and beyond.

The WHO has planned a series of pandemics through 2030 to help install their worldwide dictatorship. Bill Gates in this video talks about the second pandemic and how brutal it will be compared to Covid. (*https:// www.globalresearch.ca/plan-who-ten-years-infectious-diseases-2020-2030-leading-world-tyranny/5803048*). WHO's director Tedros has said we should prepare for a deadlier pandemic than Covid.

Pedophilia, which I have discussed frequently in these pages, is an agenda which they are pushing. Don't believe me? Read the following which , in their words, describes their "aims to equip children... to develop sexual relationships."

This evidence report reveals how the World Health Organization and United Nations are sexualizing little children in primary education worldwide, for the purpose of normalizing pedophilia. This report consists of nothing but solid evidence, with many official documents, videos, books, archives, etc.

Little children are sexual beings who must have sexual partners and begin with sex as soon as possible. For this reason, kindergartens and elementary schools must teach children to develop lust and sexual desire, learn masturbation, build same-sex relationships, use online pornography, and learn different sexual techniques such as oral sex.

The above is a paraphrased summary of the official guidelines issued by the World Health Organization and the United Nations to educational authorities worldwide. Meanwhile, judicial organizations are issuing statements that sex between little children and adults should be legalized, while media outlets and political parties are calling for the acceptance of pedophilia as a "normal sexual orientation". (*https://stopworldcontrol. com/children/*)

If little children are sexualized, it is only a small step to the acceptance of pedophilia. These are the UN recommended educational guidelines for sexualizing children:

- Children between 0 and 4 years must learn about masturbation and develop an interest in their own and others' bodies.

- Children between 4 and 6 years must learn about masturbation and be encouraged to express their sexual needs and wishes.

- Children between 6 and 9 years must learn about sexual intercourse, online pornography, having a secret love and self-stimulation.

- Children between 9 and 12 years should have their first sexual experience and learn to use online pornography.

The sexual agenda extends of course to transgenderism. Many companies have embraced this agenda in their advertising, and are losing great amounts of money from consumer response. Target lost a whopping $10 billion in 10 days after their transgender/pride/baphomet tee shirts for children were publicized. Bud Light has also had huge losses after featuring a transgender model on its ads.

Perhaps we as a culture are finally waking up to the tyranny being imposed on us in ever increasing amounts? It is not too late to say "No" to being sexualized, poisoned, brainwashed and otherwise controlled. It is our voice, our "NO" that is enduring and powerful. They are few, we are many. And we have God behind us.

CHAPTER 17

DANGEROUS TIMES

For we are not ignorant of the devil's devices.

—2 Corinthians 2:11, ESV

No one will enter the New World Order unless he or she will make a pledge to worship Lucifer. No one will enter the New Age unless he will take a Luciferian Initiation.

—David Spangler, director of Planetary Initiative, United Nations

He that dwelleth in the secret place of the most High shall abide under the shadow of the Almighty. I will say of the LORD, He is my refuge and my fortress: my God; in him will I trust. Surely he shall deliver thee from the snare of the fowler, and from the noisome pestilence. He shall cover thee with his feathers, and under his wings shalt thou trust: his truth shall be thy shield and buckler.

Thou shalt not be afraid for the terror by night; nor for the arrow that flieth by day;

Nor for the pestilence that walketh in darkness; nor for the destruction that waste that noonday. A thousand shall fall at thy side, and ten thousand at thy right hand; but it shall not come nigh thee. Only with thine eyes shalt thou behold and see the reward of the wicked.

Because thou hast made the LORD, which is my refuge, even the most High, thy habitation; There shall no evil befall thee, neither shall any plague come nigh thy dwelling.

For he shall give his angels charge over thee, to keep thee in all thy ways. They shall bear thee up in their hands, lest thou dash thy foot against a stone.

Thou shalt tread upon the lion and adder: the young lion and the dragon shalt thou trample under feet. Because he hath set his love upon me, therefore will I deliver him: I will set him on high, because he hath known my name.

He shall call upon me, and I will answer him: I will be with him in trouble; I will deliver him, and honour him.

With long life will I satisfy him, and shew him my salvation.

—Psalm 91, KJV

Whoever makes a practice of sinning is of the devil, for the devil has been sinning from the beginning. The reason the Son of God appeared was to destroy the works of the devil.

—-I John 3:8, ESV

D r. Colin Ross disclosed many programs in his book Project *Bluebird: Deliberate Creation of Multiple Personalities* by CIA Psychiatrists but said they stopped in the 1970s (when my father was CIA General Counsel). However, as I mentioned earlier, my dad told me the bulk of the records subpoenaed by Congress were destroyed by Richard Helms. As such, it was abundantly clear to my father and myself back then that the programs would not stop because they were hidden and Congress never knew about most of them.

Because it was public knowledge that most of the documents never saw the light of day, it always puzzled me that people thought the programs stopped in the 1970s. It is true President Ford ordered these programs stopped, but without any evidence of their existence, why would the CIA, which was so determined to continue the projects that Helms ordered all records destroyed, stop what was still secret and which they saw as key to fulfilling their New World Order agenda?

Because of my many discussions with my dad when he was General Counsel, the issue of mind control and the CIA was heightened for me while he was still working for the agency. After that, the subject faded to the back of my mind as I went on to two graduate schools and the beginnings of my career. My training and career focus on religion, spirituality, dreams, and psychology was in the opposite direction from the military and intelligence career my father had pursued.

If the surveillance that had shown up periodically throughout my early life was still going on, I was unaware of it. Now, looking back, there are incidents that I find curious in retrospect and that might have been CIA-related. I will likely never know. My focus was on the pursuits of a young professional. I became involved in a life apart from these dark shadows.

When my dad and Colby were let go by President Carter, Dad took some time off, during which he got sober and stayed that way. His alcoholism had increased greatly during those last, very tense CIA years and during his first year of retirement. I am amazed he was able to withstand the pressure. With my help, he went into treatment for his alcoholism and got involved in a recovery program with AA. That was the last of his drinking career. At the time of his death, he had been sober for thirty—three years. After gaining a year's sobriety, he went to work as an estate attorney in a private law firm on K Street in Washington, DC. This was a relatively pleasant and lucrative period of his life.

We had discussed his being let go by the CIA and how he felt betrayed. The General Counsel position had never been a political position, although the CIA directorate was. His friend Colby was let go as director by Jimmy Carter. In an unprecedented move, Dad was also let go. Imagine being a founder of an organization to which you have given lifelong loyalty, only to discover their many illegal and horrifying black ops programs, and to be fired. Perhaps it was retribution for his not towing the party line; perhaps they wanted someone in that position they could control better. He never knew. After that, we rarely talked about his CIA days; he had moved on, and I didn't look back.

WHAT I WAS NOT GOING TO WRITE: WRITING TO SAVE MY LIFE

The book I originally wrote did not include Section V. I had no wish to discuss the information. I especially had no wish to talk about what I am about to say, even though much of my experience over the past decade has been colored by it.

Events outside of my control forced me to reconsider my position. A murder attempt as I was finishing up the book appeared to be designed to prevent the book from ever seeing the light of day. I will discuss the details later in this chapter, after I take the reader through a chronology of events.

I have been a threat to the powers that be because of specific details I know of global sex trafficking, mind control, ritual abuse/satanism and pedophilia at the highest levels. This was before the current awareness of sex trafficking and widespread pedophilia. Epstein was still unknown as was Harvey Weinstein, NVIVM, pizzagate, and the widespread sexual abuse of children in Hollywood. The profits made from sex trafficking run the dark cabal which has run our world; it is more profitable than drugs. Children can be used over and over; drugs cannot. I had details of Presidents and heads of state involvement. No doubt my relationship with my father was of great concern. All of this is information I never had any intention to share publicly. I am a therapist, not a whistleblower. My primary purpose is as a healer. I wanted to keep on in that arena of work. Further and very importantly, I did not have permission to share specific client material.

THE LAST STRAW

Had an assassin not come after me on my writing retreat, I would not be sharing any of this, but after so many years of this, I am angry, sad, exhausted and fed up. I have the right to share my story and how I have been affected by the years of intrusive, illegal trespasses into my life and work since my father's death. I am beyond weary of being threatened with death, rape, torture, murder, and mind control.

I made a previous decision not to disclose which was, erroneously, for my safety—as in "be quiet, and no one will bother you." This strategy turned out to be a spectacular failure. I grew sick of a criminal government organization that operates on lies, deception, abuse, and murder acting as if it is accountable to no law and is a law unto itself. It took me a while to understand there was no safety in keeping information to myself: they just keep coming after you even when they tell you they won't.

In this writing I am standing up for the principles this country was built on, the God-given inalienable freedom of speech and the rights of life, liberty, and the pursuit of happiness. These rights are not given to us by our government but by God. Our government has no right to take away from us those rights that God has given.

With the years of constant surveillance and many plots against me, I sometimes wonder how much wasted taxpayer money has been spent to deprive me of all of the above. I am just one fairly unimportant person, trying to live a quiet, purposeful life helping others. How much has been poured into this never-ending surveillance and destruction strategy? The attitude seems to be "Just kill them; get rid of the problem." This is not the country I thought I lived in; in the shadows it has been taken over by a criminal organization that acts collectively as a psychopath on the loose.

The mass mind control of America was perfected through control of the narrative via Project Mockingbird, and more recently, the 2012 and 2017 NDAA. In Mockingbird, the CIA was violating its own charter, which explicitly states the CIA arena of operations is not to be domestic. Of course, murder of an American citizen without due process is also unconstitutional, whether or not President Obama gave himself that power by executive action. (He did: _https://www.theguardian.com/commentisfree/2013/feb/05/obama-kill-list-doj-memo_) Can you imagine the irony and horror for my father had he been alive to see the agency he helped found hunting down his daughter as if she were an animal?

How did I arrive in this situation? In the writing of this volume, I have come to understand that my personal journey and the journeys of those whom I am helping are often inextricably intertwined on a number of levels. Even though I started out writing this book with the intention of keeping my personal journey and experiences mostly to myself, I have discovered one story cannot be told without the other. My clients have taught me more than I ever thought possible, and my personal journey has many intersecting connections.

As a child of the 1960s witnessing my father's military and intelligence career, I was determined, from a very young age, to follow a radically different path than his. My high school psychology teacher, Mr. Lee, helped inspire me to follow a career of helping people work through their traumas and difficulties. I never dreamed my path, directed in a completely different direction than my father's career, would intersect so profoundly with my father's.

SURPRISING EVENTS THIRTY YEARS LATER

I will now fast-forward more than thirty years, to events that happened from 2006 until the first publication of this book. In 2006, I was working as a psychotherapist in private practice in Falls Church, Virginia. I had worked long-term with many people who remembered being victims of ritual abuse, child trafficking, and pornography. I had also trained extensively and developed skills in treating dissociative disorders and had experienced a number of treatment successes. My name was on lists in the DC area for people who treated dissociative identity disorder. Being that Washington DC is the country's political center, perhaps a higher percentage of these people lived in the area.

Estelle found me on one of those lists. Her psychiatrist/therapist was looking toward retirement, and though he could still help her with medications, he asked her to find a new therapist. He was well known in the DC area for working with mind control victims and, like me, had been in attendance at the Greenbaum speech. This psychiatrist had worked with Estelle for many years and assured me she was indeed a "presidential model." He said that the unusual history she presented was sadly true. She had been groomed from conception to be a servant to Lucifer as a mind-controlled sex slave, courier, breeder, spy and more. Her sexual abuse had begun right away, as had her training and exposure to rituals and torture to split her mind and make her into a mind-controlled slave.

Estelle was brilliant. Now in her mid-sixties, she was still being actively handled, meaning she was brutally raped and tortured regularly, to keep her dissociated, sick, and disempowered. She was weakened and her body very sick, but her mind and her spirit were brave and strong. Over many years, she had come a long way in remembering her past and how she had been used; she had become aware of having many alters used for many different purposes, most especially as a sex slave since childhood to presidents and heads of state (Marilyn Monroe was a Presidential Model). Apparently there is nothing quite like blackmail to keep politicians in check, and it is used extensively, as is likely with the Epstein case. Some say blackmail is how Washington, DC is run. These sexual encounters are often videotaped; key people are offered whatever sexual encounters they like. Estelle was highly prized even above other Presidential Models, as she had been a favorite of JFK. Because of this, she was highly sought after by other Presidents and heads of state. Also because of this, she was closely handled, tortured, raped by her everpresent handler and surveilled. As soon as she began therapy with me, unknown to me at first, I also became under close surveillance.

Even those with decades of hard work in therapy, and as is the case with many mind control victims, much of Estelle's mind control programming was intact. Programmed alters would open the door at night for her handler even though other parts took extra precautions to make sure she was safe. Other alters, also unknown to her, would report anything she did or said. Others would strike her ill or give her great pain for revealing secrets.

As her therapist, there was little I could do except to support her and empathize with her. Though I was skilled in working with DID, I knew nothing about deprogramming. Estelle gave me many volumes written about governmental mind control similar to what she had experienced, saying she needed me to read them so that I would better understand her and what she had been through. These books included all of the volumes by Fritz Springmeier and Cisco Wheeler (an ex–mind control programmer and victim), all available free online, including *Thirteen Bloodlines of the Illuminati, The Illuminati Formula to Create an Undetectable Total Mind Control Slave,* and *Deeper Insights into the Illuminati Formula.* She also gave me a copy of Svali's *Svali Speaks* (Svali was an ex–mind control programmer who writes about how she did programming; this volume is also available free online) and Brice Taylor's *Thanks for the Memories.*

I had dealt with many victims of ritual abuse and mind control at this point, but this was on an entirely different level. Ritual abuse is unimaginably awful no matter what. Staying present to hear her stories challenged me to the maximum. I was new to this level and magnitude of organized, programmed abuse and had a lot of resistance to hearing what she had to say. The readings helped educate me to a whole other dimension of reality. The reader may be experiencing some of this same resistance with this material.

One day when I was not at work, Estelle, without my knowledge or consent, inexplicably sent a suitcase full of papers to my office. They were old love letters from her to JFK. They had spent much time together. She had fallen in love with him and believed he loved her as well. In fact, she had gained a lot of attention for his feelings for her, as she had been deemed his favorite. For this reason, she became highly sought after sexually by extremely prominent persons. I took a quick look at the contents, then put everything back in the suitcase and in the trunk of my car to give back to her when I saw her next.

I did not want to be responsible for her personal papers. I thought nothing more of it, as since everything was in her handwriting, her deep love for this president could be denied as the delusional fantasies of an aging woman. Nothing here seemed a matter of national security to me.

DAWNING REALIZATION OF COVERT OPERATIONS

I kept a spare house key hidden in a magnetic container underneath the air conditioner in my backyard, in case I locked myself out. One day my front door closed while it was locked when I was outside. I was locked out! When I went to get my spare key, I found, to my chagrin, the container had been left partly open, and the key inside had been taken. I knew I did not do that. I had suspicions someone had been coming in and out of my house, as things would sometimes be different than I had left them. I had no idea who it might be or why. Why had the container been left open?

At first I did not know for sure if the person going in and out of my house when I wasn't there was my neighbor Stephen, but I figured it out eventually. He had previously told me that he was retired from the CIA and had been CIA special forces and a mercenary. He was not retired, as he later admitted to another neighbor.

In an in-person conversation, perhaps trying to win my trust, Stephen told me how he had not only seen but touched a CIA torture manual—written by Dr. Joseph Mengele. He told me this during the time of Abu Ghraib. The torture techniques Estelle and others reported Mengele using on them struck me as strikingly similar to those reported at Abu Ghraib and Guantanamo, especially because of the sadistic humiliation, rapes, and spiritual abuse. Mengele, of course, had lots of practice with all of these techniques in the concentration camps.

As far as I know from media reports, FOIA searches did not produce this manual. The Senate Intelligence Committee Torture and Interrogation Report (released December 2014) details horrific abuses by the CIA, including many unethical practices such as rape, threatened rape of a loved one, and rectal feeding—practices that are assessed to not have produced any valuable intelligence.

These practices are heinous, unquestionably unethical, and immoral. They are also the same types of practices used on the estimated more than ten million mind control victims in our country. Interrogation centers at military bases and other facilities across our country are also reportedly regularly used for mind control programming. This programming involves torture, rape, use of drugs, and even bestiality. We have taken on dark Nazi practices and made them our own, having utterly lost our moral compass. I know what I am saying sounds impossible to believe; I have had the same reaction many times over.

SURVEILLANCE AND INTIMIDATION

Those monitoring Estelle's every move and mine began acting as if they believed I was plotting to be a whistleblower. Someone began breaking into my house regularly, leaving small things changed as if to let me know someone had been there. This is a known method of intimidation.

It appeared they were paranoid about what I'd learned from my client and what I might do with it. Indeed I learned many very disturbing secrets, things that would horrify anyone who heard them. It certainly would have caused damage to the pedophile/mind control agenda. However, I am by profession a therapist, which means keeping confidential what I learn. I had no fantasies of going public with any of Estelle's information; it was hers only to share.

PSYOPS

Part of psychological operations (psyops) can involve intimidation; they let you know in every way possible that you are always being watched, that you have no privacy, that they can and do enter your home whenever they want, and that there is nothing you can do about it and there is nowhere you can go where they cannot find you. Many people, including targeted individuals (TI's), who are stalked, socially isolated, harassed, and intimidated, their lives invaded, have written about this. Many people are electronically targeted for various tortures.

Many kinds of intimidation tactics are used. Tactics include leaving an object the target individual does not own in a visible place in the home, thus letting the TI know someone was there; another can be taking an object not necessarily of financial value but that the person will eventually miss. The point of all of it is intimidation. Another common intimidation tactic is to send people wherever the TI goes, people who will do something to let the TI know they are stalking him or her; sometimes they will act as if they are going to walk (or drive) right into the TI. The point of this Stasi -like technique is to let the person know there actions and whereabouts are always know. Your tax dollars at work.

All of the above and more were used on me. A screw or a brand new pack of screws would be left in my front hallway to remind me metaphorically I might be raped or gang-raped if I did not watch myself. Something in my house might be moved to another location. These kinds of intimidation and harassment techniques were widely used in the Cold War and are often used with mind control victims and targeted individuals.

At one point, my passport was taken from the folder where it was always stored, just before I was to depart on an international trip for a conference at which I was scheduled to speak. It was a holiday, and State Department officials were unavailable to help me get an emergency passport. Fortunately, the conference was in Montreal, and since I lived in DC and a driver's license was still accepted for travel between the United States and Canada, I managed to drive there.

When I got home from that weeklong trip, to my horror, I found a small camera hidden in my shower. Enraged, I impulsively grabbed it and threw it down the toilet, hoping they would get an image of their camera going down the drain. I knew from this that surveillance equipment had been placed in my house when I had been gone. I went in person to meet with a company who would do an electronic sweep of my home to find any recording devices. I knew at this point every email and every phone conversation of mine was being closely monitored.

Unfortunately the company foolishly called me, against my express instructions, letting me know they could not come on Thursday as we had planned — and that they would come on Friday instead. Now Stephen et al. would know. The element of surprise was ruined.

Stephen would of course try to remove the equipment ahead of time, while I was gone. I was powerless to stop that, as I would be at work and they were able to get into my house despite security precautions I had taken. They would not want me to have evidence of surveillance. I now wished I had saved the camera I'd found in the shower.

That Thursday when I came home, the front door was unlocked, despite my having been careful to lock it in the morning. That evening, it was still light as I watched two men in a black SUV come to visit Stephen. One by one, he very gingerly carried and handed off two black packages. You could tell the contents were delicate by the way the men handled them. Stephen had never had any friends visit him; both the meeting and the exchange were odd. My guess was he was handing off the surveillance equipment, right on time. I knew now that when the company came to find surveillance equipment the next day, they would not find anything. They did not.

I learned a valuable lesson from this. In the future, whenever I suspected surveillance equipment had been placed in my home or office, I would convey by phone or e-mail to someone that I was going to do an electronic sweep. This tactic would set a reaction in motion whereby there would be another break-in and the equipment either removed or disconnected, saving me the trouble and the expense. There were always telltale signs of the break-ins. I followed up with sweeping the place.

A Thwarted Attempt

I experienced many instances of stalking and intimidation. Always I had guidance from God to help me escape the fate intended for me. The story I am about to tell gave me the shivers when I realized the possibilities of what was intended for me. However, more so than that, this experience helped me see God was protecting me always, in every detail. It made me very thankful to God for that protection. Through the many years of this now, I have not spent much time worrying about being harmed, for inevitably the Holy Spirit or one of God's helpers, often my dad, has been able to step in and miraculously guide me to safety.

My house in Virginia was a two-story house with a full basement. My bedroom was upstairs at the back of the house. I kept the light on downstairs in the living room until I retired for the evening. In more than a decade of living there, I had never turned the light off and fallen asleep on the sofa downstairs. Instead, it was my habit to deliberately keep the light on until I headed upstairs, to encourage me to head for my bedroom rather than sleep downstairs on the sofa.

This night in particular, I uncharacteristically turned the light off and then stayed on the sofa and napped for some hours. I awoke after midnight, wide awake, and heard a voice in my head sternly warning me, Don't turn any lights on. I didn't understand but had long since learned to pay attention to such messages! I slowly climbed the double flight of stairs in the dark, with continued guidance that I was not to turn any lights on upstairs.

I went back to my bedroom in darkness. Because there had been no lights on indoors for almost three hours, anyone outside observing would likely think I was asleep and in bed. As I approached my bedroom in the dark, I saw a light shining outdoors in my private backyard, which had only woods behind. I went to a window and looked out back. A light was shining steadily at my basement window, marking it! The light was coming from the side and front of the house. Something was horribly wrong here.

I needed to see what was going on. Still in the darkness, I went to the upstairs window at the front of the house. There I saw my neighbor Stephen with a man who matched the description of Estelle's brutal handler, trained by Mengele. Stephen was holding a flashlight and shining it at my back bedroom window, as if to show him where they would be entering my house.

You can imagine my horror at seeing them there. It was clear they were planning something very serious for me. This was a major step up beyond the ongoing intrusive surveillance and intimidation tactics and was clearly meant to cause me some kind of physical harm.

It also seemed clear this would not be happening the same night, for if it were to be the same night, they would have headed back there rather than standing in front talking about it. This appeared to be a coordinated plan to get into my house while I was sleeping. My best guess was this night's activity was a planning night, which included casing my house. The next night would most likely be the night they planned to get in.

This looked very bad for me. Stephen already came in and out of my house when I was not there, and this was definitely not that. The options for what they wanted seemed few. Estelle's handler had been Mengele's protégé and was expert in rape, torture, and brutal mind control. I was horrified and chilled to the quick to consider what they had in store for me.

My inner guidance from the Holy Spirit reassured me I would be safe that night and that I could investigate the basement window and security system in the morning. I had learned to trust my inner guidance and went to bed. I don't know how I was able to sleep so well that night, but I did.

When I investigated closely the next morning, I saw my inside basement window security sensor had been disabled but made to look as if it were intact. Right away I called ADT. The technician came out that morning and inspected my security system. Somewhat disturbed by what he had found, he said the system had been rewired inside the wall at the kitchen control panel (during one of Stephen's criminal visits). This rewiring would ensure any intrusion would not be reported to ADT, but the alarm would still sound at my house as if it were fully operational.

My locks had long since been changed, but the basement window was apparently how Stephen was getting in and out. I reinforced the basement window with braces so that no one could come in or out without breaking the glass. I have learned that in order to keep the surveillance covert, it is rare that overt evidence of breaking in, such as a broken window or lock, is left. Breakage would alert the resident.

I do not know what they had planned, but at the minimum, it likely involved drugs, rape, torture, and mind control. Maybe they thought they could convert me to their darkness and use me for their dark purposes. When I went into the basement bedroom, I saw that a wooden chair, normally placed against one wall, had been placed in the corner, as if they planned to use it for me. It seemed to be part of the setup.

The next day, a neighbor called and said she had seen Stephen shining a flashlight on the back of my house in the middle of the night. I was glad for the witness. We met for coffee, and I explained the situation.

Afterward, while talking with someone on the phone, I laughed and said Stephen had blown his own cover the night before. I knew that he listened to all my phone calls and that he would hear what I said and feel humiliation at me laughing at him for blowing his own cover. I took the psychological advantage when I could. It would have to be very uncomfortable for him to be a known criminal operative living in a neighborhood where the neighbors were aware he was regularly breaking into my house.

Later that very same day, I heard from a neighbor that he'd told another neighbor, apparently to cover himself, that the CIA had just called him up and activated him again, putting him on assignment. Additionally, to cover for having been outdoors the night before with a flashlight, he told the neighbor he had been outdoors looking for a fox. I guess I was that "fox."

Since Stephen "worked" from home, he also would have seen the ADT truck at my house that morning. That would have let him know the security wiring was now corrected and the back window once more secured.

Help from a Friend

After the thwarted attack on me in my own house, I filed a police report in Fairfax County, complete with names. I did not expect this to help me in any way, but I wanted it to be on record. I knew something had to be done. I couldn't just wait for the next thing. The latest thwarted intrusion was very serious, and I had barely escaped whatever horrible fate they had planned for me.

I carefully thought about what course of action was available to me. To my surprise, I was strongly advised in spirit by God to visit a particular friend who worked as a private consultant in the intelligence field. I was told he would be able to help me. I was also given information to pass on to him, something which I did not understand, but which meant something to him. Prior to this advice, I would not have considered going to him for help. As it turned out, he was the absolute perfect person to both understand and help me negotiate my circumstances. I had no idea how deeply connected and respected he was as an honest man with integrity in the intelligence community. Later, I learned he was opposed to torture, and I thought he might be interested in hearing about the CIA torture and interrogation manual written by Dr. Mengele that my neighbor had claimed to see and actually touch. He was.

Full of trepidation about not being believed, I was a nervous mess when I met with him. I will refer to him as my ally from here on out to protect his identity. I told him my story with all the crazy details. He knew me well enough to have basic trust in me, and to my great relief, he did believe me. I was relieved to see how well he understood the tactics I described. He had once been on the Senate Intelligence Committee.

A major thrust of our discussion was that I had no wishes to be a whistleblower and no desire to become famous by sharing Estelle's story; a story that she shared with me in the confidence of our therapist/client relationship. I wanted only to be left alone and serve.

No Inclination to Be a WhistleBlower

It had never crossed my mind to be a whistleblower. However, I have learned many times in this life that thinking and acting a certain way does not prevent others from projecting content onto you that has nothing to do with you.

Some friends in Tucson had been checking my deceased parent's Tucson house every week for two years while I was still living in Virginia. One day I was prompted to ask Antoinette, my friend, if she had noticed anything odd in her weekly visits to the house. She said, yes, as a matter of fact, on her visit that day, a neighbor had come up to her and told her the garage door had been left up for three days. When Antoinette came, the door was down. The door clearly could not have gone up and down by itself.

Antoinette did a thorough search of the house and found three doors had been left unlocked. She had always been scrupulous about keeping everything locked, so it was clear it had not been her mistake. Someone had been in and was planning on coming back. In addition, there were scratch marks at a number of very secure doors where someone had worked very hard to get in, unsuccessfully.

Stephen had once told me that when he made trips, he drove his car to the airport and left it there, even though we lived a very short cab ride from Dulles Airport. I realized his car had been gone for four days, and it might be he who had broken into my Tucson house. What would he want there? To check it out, of course, but another highly likely thing would be to put in surveillance equipment, as he had in my Virginia house.

When I arrived next in Tucson, I called the police. A policeman told me a criminal's trick is to leave the garage door open if they are planning to go in and out of a home. The trick works in this manner: if the homeowner or a friend comes to the house during the period the garage door is left open by the criminal/spy, the homeowner or friend would of course then close the garage door. The criminal would then know not to enter.

My way of forcing Stephen to now take out any surveillance equipment was to briefly fill Antoinette in by phone as to what was happening to me in Virginia and to say I would be doing an electronic sweep of the house first thing once I moved to Tucson. Stephen would not want any equipment to be found. I knew he monitored my phone conversations, as the surveillance was constant and completely intrusive.

As part of my own psy-ops to intimidate Stephen (with the truth), I told Antoinette a few days later by phone that everyone in my Virginia neighborhood was now aware Stephen was breaking into my houses in both Virginia and Tucson. People had disliked him long before this, and now they despised him. I wanted them to know who he was so once I was gone they would be proactive about defending themselves if he decided to take something personally and turn on them. He had very dark parts that seriously put people off.

When I told my ally about the break-in into my Tucson house, he was alarmed, seeing they had no plans for stopping their pursuit of me. It took him time to arrange, but he did something for which I will always be grateful—he went to the CIA director and explained I was not a whistleblower, and had no wishes to be. He asked that all operations against me cease and desist. I am sure the fact that my father was a CIA founder and General Counsel, not to mention one of the top fifty CIA employees of the past fifty years, had an impact as well.

They must have been pretty eager to get rid of me before I moved to Tucson. I took one last trip to the beach before I moved. I was constantly followed, and sentries were set up in various places. It was totally creepy and a waste of resources for no reason whatsoever. When I checked out, the hotel manager behaved bizarrely, creepily saying that he knew who I was and that he had personally watched over my car all night. I had a very bad feeling about it, and was glad to leave.

My car completely broke down shortly after I arrived back home. The mechanic, who knew nothing about me, discovered my car had been tampered with so as to cause a fatal accident. He told me I had narrowly avoided the fate designed for me.

TWISTED NEW WORLD ORDER DECEPTIONS

Before I moved to Tucson, I went to visit my beloved maternal grandmother's grave in Arlington. Next to her grave, on the large corner spot that had always been bare, there was now a rather large above ground tombstone structure with a very wide painting that had obviously been commissioned. The painting was of the Last Supper and in many ways was very well done. I was horrified to see whose tomb it was—I'll get to that in a minute.

As I looked more closely, I looked at the figure of John the Beloved next to Jesus. Very markedly, John had the index and middle fingers on both his hands crossed, as if to say, "I was lying. God will not win." John is the author of Revelation, which predicts the apocalyptic unleashing of evil on the world, with the inevitable outcome of evil, or Satan and Lucifer, losing to God.

The grave was for Senator William Byrd and his wife. At the time, Senator Byrd was still alive. His wife was deceased and buried there. Byrd was said by many, including Springmeier, Cisco Wheeler, Brice Taylor, and others, to be a known Satanist and mind-control handler. Earlier in his career, he'd held high ranking in the

KKK. Hilary Clinton later eulogized him as a friend and mentor.

In the New World Order and satanic programming, of which Byrd was very much a part, there is a great deal of focus on the end times. Their "end times" programming of both individuals and of the masses, focuses on bringing forth the events in the book of Revelation—but not in God's timing, in theirs. John's Revelation reveals the ultimate problem for the shadow governments, for it states that despite the concerted attempts by the dark side to take over the world, long-term victory is resoundingly God's. That is what I believe also. Byrd's commissioned painting was in effect saying Satan, not God would win. I find it pathetic that what Byrd has to offer on his tombstone to negate John's two-thousand-year-old prophecies is but a feeble lie, depicting John *crossing his fingers*.

MOVE TO TUCSON

Once I got to Tucson, my ally told me it would take a while to find my file, and call off the operation against me. He told me he did not know how long it would take—maybe a few months.

The intensity of the surveillance and intimidation showed no signs of stopping once I moved to Tucson. I did not move because of what was happening; I had planned the move previously to go to this wonderful, beautiful place where I could be outdoors every day. I didn't think moving would stop my problem, but I also didn't expect that the problems in Tucson would start even before I moved there.

There was a murder attempt on me in my first week in Tucson. Fortunately, as always, I was well guided. This man was not one of the smarter ones sent against me. He latched onto me when I arrived at the central area at Sabino Canyon National Park to get a parking sticker. (I always went to Sabino on my regular visits to Tucson, so planning for this wouldn't have been a stretch.)

He started following me right away. He was in a pseudo park volunteer uniform without any identifying badges or identification. I decided to head back to the parking lot and my car as I was definitely not up for dealing with him. I watched as he walked in a very wide arc around the huge parking lot, with me as the fulcrum point, watching me. Was he so stupid that he thought I could not see him?

I figured he was pretty foolish and decided I could easily flush him out. I wanted to hike and was not ready to give up on the day just yet. My strategy was simple: I would act as if I did not realize he were there. I would head up a secondary wide path, where there were sure to be people, and go approximately one-tenth of a mile to the turnoff for a favorite trail. At that point, I would turn around very quickly at the turnoff and see if he had followed.

When I started the path, he was nowhere in sight. If he were to make a move, I would need to give him some rope to hang himself, so I did not turn around again until I hit the .10 turnoff mark. At that point, I suddenly and unpredictably whipped around.

What do you think I saw? He had to have walked very fast to get as close to me as he was (luckily he was still a safe distance away, and there were people around). Chillingly, he wore a very large fanny pack facing forward at his abdomen. It looked like it was full of all kinds of things. As I turned, he turned his face away from me quickly, so I wouldn't be able to identify him, and then walked away in the opposite direction—fast.

I knew I could go on my walk now. He wouldn't risk trying again now that I had identified him. Once I completed my walk, I went to the ranger's station and reported the incident. The ranger taking my complaint said there had never before been an incident in this national park. He assured me it was standard procedure for them to file any reports with the sheriff's office, so I did not have to do so. I figured the matter was closed.

Months later, I saw the same man, now in a volunteer uniform. Many seasonal volunteers come into Sabino National Park during the warm winter months. I went to the ranger's desk and told the ranger on duty this volunteer was the man in my report. He looked for a report and found nothing. It had been removed from the ranger's record book.

A year or so after that, I had the opportunity to speak with a friendly sheriff in a public place. I asked him to check if a report had been filed from Sabino Canyon on the incident. There was nothing in the Pima County Sheriff's Department records about it.

I took some time off from working after I moved to Tucson. Within a month, I involved myself in a total remodel of my home. It had been my parents' home, and the decor was dated. The project manager I hired, an interior designer, was very impressed with my choices and my skills. He offered to train me in interior design. I was thrilled. I wanted to get far away from working with DID and mind control. He would train me, and in a few years we would go into business together. It was fascinating to be training with him and to explore an entirely new field more in line with my aesthetic talents.

He knew of my problems with the CIA. He was an older man and wanted to get me started in a new field away from the trauma and threats on my life associated with my previous life. He was very kind to me, and I have a lot of gratitude for his efforts and attention. We met most days and I went with him as he worked on various houses. I was loving it.

Unfortunately, however, within two years' time, he fell seriously ill. He would not be able to help our business plans come to fruition. Fortunately, however, the surveillance and attempts on my life stopped shortly after my move to Tucson, as my ally had promised.

BACK INTO HELL

A few years later, a new round of surveillance, murder attempts, intrusions, and intimidation began. It happened after I wrote an email to a friend about a traumatic mass shooting in which the shooter, Jared Loughner, bore all the signs of having been mind controlled. He had posted about having been mind controlled and having a satanic altar in his backyard on social media. He also said he had been trained in Phoenix (in the army?)When you have trained and worked with mind control victims as I have, it is not hard to recognize the hallmarks of mind control in the many mind controlled shooters who have been activated. Most are programmed to kill themselves once they have completed their assigned killings or if they are caught—this one was stopped by the police before he could.

Even after everything I had been through, I was still naive enough to think I had the right to free speech in a private email. The truth, which I know now, is they may try to kill you based on the surveillance they always have on you—if you say something they don't like or if you see past the deception, they perpetrate.

An operation likely connected with the shooting, Operation Fast and Furious, had not yet been discovered. At the time, I knew nothing about it, nor did the public. Wayne Madsen, an investigative journalist, later said the false flag shooting came because Gabrielle Giffords and John Roll, who were both shot (Roll later died of his wounds), had become aware of the illegal gun smuggling that put firearms in the hands of Mexican cartel members in the as-yet-unknown Fast and Furious program being run by the DOJ/FBI in Arizona. Madsen said he had found evidence both Giffords and Rolls were aware of and researching the gun smuggling program. Tucson is not far from the border, so the gunrunning and provision of guns to Mexican criminals was an issue that impacted Tucson. A border patrol agent, Brian Terry, was killed with two weapons that were traced from the Mexican cartel back to the Justice Department's Bureau of Alcohol, Tobacco, Firearms and Explosive. This caused a huge furor, and the Fast and Furious investigation began in earnest.

Madsen says a hit was put on him for his research findings. For his safety, he left the country for a while after the shooting. Once he published his article and the information became public, thus helping to ensure his safety, he came back to the United States. (A video on this can be found at: (*https://www.youtube.com/watch?v=w9mijTufMaI)*)

Fast and Furious has also been linked to the 2016 Paris attacks in which one of the terrorists had a gun which tied back to Fast and Furious *(https://www.newsmax.com/Newsfront/fast-and-furious--paris-attacks-gun-terrorist/2016/07/05/id/737087/)*. There have been a number of reports that Fast and Furious continued to be active and involved with giving guns to ISIS and other terrorist groups. It is beyond the scope of this book to get into this subject in more detail, other than to say that perhaps there was a great deal more to hide about this gunrunning operation, which might have motivated an attack on Giffords and Roll, as well as eventually on myself. Dizdar often talked about of mind-controlled shooters and included Jared Loughner as an example in many of his podcasts.

I can only speak to what is my experience. That experience was that after I said in an e-mail that I thought Loughner was a mind controlled shooter, it took no longer than a few days before the next murder attempt on me, described below.

I spent the better part of the next five years with them coming after me, often with daily intense surveillance and intimidation tactics, in addition to multiple murder attempts. They also sent men to date me, without success. My ally had warned me that dating would be off limits, unless it was a friend of a friend, as sending someone as a date is a common espionage tool to gain access to the targeted individual.

Continuation of Round Two

One day soon after I wrote the e-mail about Loughner, I was hiking one of my favorite trails, Finger Rock Trail. This trail was familiar and beautiful, one I had hiked many times. At about forty minutes in, I often took a little side trail where I would sit on a big boulder and rest and enjoy the beautiful view. Interestingly, I often called this canyon the Mary canyon because on the cliff face is a huge natural carving that reminds me of Mary, mother of Jesus. The place where I would sit off the side trail is directly below the Mary cliff face, a place that has always felt protected and safe.

On this day, my familiarity with and love of that spot saved my life. As I was hiking, at about thirty minutes in, I heard footsteps rapidly approaching. As a lifelong hiker, you get used to footstep sounds and learn to read them. This was not just some random fast hiker; it is hard to explain, but to me, his footsteps resonated of not only strong determination but also of predation. My instincts told me I was in big trouble. He was quickly overtaking me.

Obviously I had no choice but to deal with the situation. Facing possible danger is the only way you have a chance of getting out alive.

I rapidly (and unexpectedly for him) swung around and faced him. He quickly turned his head away so I wouldn't have facial recognition of him, something these CIA predators /hit men always do. He quickly walked away from me, in the opposite direction, and was then hidden behind boulders. Clearly, since he had turned and hidden from me, the evidence supported my instinctive reaction that this was no ordinary hiker. I knew I was in deep trouble.

I had no choice but to keep moving deeper into the trail. I was unable to turn around and head back the half hour or so to my car because that was where he was. Throughout my life, in life-and-death situations, my instincts kick in, and I get very focused on what needs to be done. There is no time for any experience of fear; there is only action fueled by adrenaline.

Fortunately, I was not far away from the little side trail where I often went to relax. No one ever seemed to go back there; it was off the main trail. I knew there was a very good hiding place off that side trail. I kept walking, headed there with my sole focus on finding a good temporary hiding place.

Then, out of nowhere, I felt a sting in my right butt cheek. To my utter dismay, I felt myself starting to lose consciousness. Whatever it was that had stung me was powerful and was quickly overtaking me. There was no doubt in my mind that I had been drugged. (CIA use of tranquilizer dart guns became public with the Church Committee investigation in the 1970s.)

In a flash I assessed my predicament. Succumbing to the drug was not an option—it would mean certain death. From deep within my core, I marshaled all my personal will to fight against the rapidly encroaching unconsciousness and say an overwhelming "Noooooo!" to the drug. (I am reminded of ordinary citizens who, when a loved one is in danger, can lift a car because of the adrenaline that pumps out during the crisis.) I was also moving somewhat fast, and my increased circulation might have hastened the metabolizing of the drug.

It seemed to work, because the feeling of being drugged disappeared pretty quickly after that. I thank God for the jeans I was uncharacteristically wearing while hiking that day, for the double thickness of the denim back pocket may have prevented some of the drug from entering my body.

I had surprised him in the act of sneaking up on me. There was no doubt in my mind that the attempted drugging was a part of his preparation for the next attack. I had no illusions that his retreat was anything but temporary. It had given him the opportunity to attempt to drug me, but that was not where it would end.

(Later, when talking over the event with a sympathetic policeman, the policeman told me that when a hit is ordered, the instructions are, first and foremost, "Failure is not an option." An initial failure is to be met with increased resolve but never with giving up. Once the target knows someone is attempting to murder them, it is considered critically important to the assassin to finish the job.)

Fortunately, with his retreat and with the divine grace that attended me that day, I was far enough ahead of him that I had enough time to get to the side trail and find a very good hiding place. I prayed I was far enough back and well enough hidden he would not find me if he did come back on the side trail.

In the dry desert air, sound travels far and clearly. From my hiding place, my heart sank as I heard his footsteps approach the fork where the main trail climbs in a series of switchbacks. The smaller side trail off of which I was hidden goes to the left. Right away, he took that side trail. This was really bad news for me.

He came back a bit on the side trail and paused. It was as if I could imagine his train of thought—if he wasted time back here, on a path that appeared to go nowhere, then if I were on the main trail, I might be able to get away, and he couldn't risk that. I gratefully listened to his footsteps as he turned around and headed for the main trail. I soon heard him climbing the switchbacks up the main trail. There were no other discernible sounds.

There was no time to feel relief. After he had climbed the switchbacks for a short while, I knew I had a window of maybe ten seconds to get out from my hiding place and head back on the trail. He would soon reach a vantage point where he would be able to visually see I wasn't on the main trail, and he would then come back for me. If I did not get out quickly, I would be trapped. Though I am fit, I was dealing with adrenal fatigue and I had no doubt he was faster than I. All I knew at the time was I had to move, and I couldn't afford to think about what might happen.

When I felt the "go" signal inside me, I gathered up my courage and quietly moved out from the side trail. Once I started the way back on the main trail, I knew it would be a very long thirty minutes at a fast pace until I could get back to my car. If I had thought about it at the time, I would have realized he could easily overtake me—even with the lead I had. But I didn't and couldn't think about it; I just moved.

And then a miracle happened. Literally out of nowhere, two extremely loud and very fast women walkers appeared one hundred yards or so behind me, also headed back toward the parking lot. Why had I not heard them when I was hiding? The trail ran in multiple switchbacks right above my hiding place—as loud as these women were, I should have been hearing them for quite a while in the dry desert air.

Their appearance was my miracle ticket out of this intended date with death! I knew that the would-be assassin would not want to risk being seen by getting in between me and the two women, and what I had to do was go as fast as I could, staying ahead of the women but within earshot. He would not attempt to harm me with them as witnesses.

Gratefully, and against all the odds, I moved as fast as I could and made it out safely. By the time I got to my car, I was numb. I breathed a huge sigh of relief. In my numbness, I was unable to think clearly of the implications of what had just happened. I know now I was in shock: it was like everything had been a dream. It would take me a few days to metabolize the experience, put together in my mind the pieces and magnitude of what had happened and to process my emotions.

What would he have done with a drugged, tranquilized me? Would he have thrown me off a cliff, to make it look like an accident? Whatever it would have been, I doubt I would have survived.

During those next few days while I recovered from the trauma, I mulled over what to do. I needed to tell people, and get the word out to friends and family all over the country, with instructions as to who to contact in case of my death. I also shared with them the reason this thug had been sent after me. I sent private letters as well as made phone calls that were of course surveilled. It was important that those surveilling me understood that a lot of people knew and that I would be a lot more trouble dead than alive. Both traditional and alternative media contacts now also had information about me and the situation.

It was important I made sure people knew that if anything happened to me, though it might look like an accident, it would not be an accident. Further, in case they tried to set me up as an apparent suicide, I explained I would never commit suicide.

I concluded I had been right about the shooter and the false flag. Had I been wrong, none of this would have happened. Clearly they had something to hide and did not want public awareness directed toward their criminality. Wayne Madsen's report had not yet come out. All I knew is I recognized the signs of a mind-control shooter in the many details of the shooting and his private life.

I had no desire to be a whistleblower but realized that didn't matter to them anymore; they were only interested in getting rid of me so they could keep their dirty secrets. When it came to my most private communications, there was no semblance of free and protected speech. They had surveilled me illegally, keeping constant surveillance on me. To me, this murder attempt was evidence of a tyrannical and out-of-control government using surveillance to crush the truth and anyone who knew it. Those who say we need a surveillance state to protect us are sadly naive about the totalitarian aim of total control.

I suppose maybe they thought they also needed to get rid of me so they could keep the gun smuggling and money confiscation quiet. But it wouldn't stay hidden, and once the story came to light, Fast and Furious dominated the headlines for quite a while.

ANOTHER ENCOUNTER

I was to see this killer again soon. Because he had turned his face away from me on the trail so quickly, he must have thought he was safe from recognition. But little did he know that when he'd turned his head away from me so quickly, I'd studied the back of his head, which was very distinctive! I could best describe his hair as an unusually thick thatch of straw, all one length and down to the nape of his neck. When he turned away from me on the trail, this striking image of the back of his head burned into my mind. Additionally, he had an unusual and distinctive body build.

I was pretty sure my narrow escape was not the end of my problems and was keeping a watchful eye. One evening, I received a message from the Holy Spirit saying to watch very carefully for people in the neighborhood who did not belong there. The proof is in the pudding, as they say, and whenever I receive warnings from the Holy Spirit, I try to at least stay open to the possibilities.

The next morning as I was driving up the street from my house on my way to my exercise studio, I saw a man walking down the street in a utility vest. My gut instinct was there was something wrong about him and the marking instrument he held. He was acting as if he were using it as he walked down the street, but it was clear to me he had no relationship whatever with that device. It seemed more like a prop than a tool.

In retrospect, I should have turned around and gone back to my house rather than to go on. But I didn't. My house was triple secured and had an alarm system. I had worked with the security company to identify and correct vulnerabilities. On top of that, I had added a number of extra precautions. Because of this, I reasoned it would be okay to go on, because even if this man did try to break in, I knew he couldn't get in without breaking something and triggering the alarm system. As previously mentioned, I had also learned they don't like to leave break-in evidence such as broken windows because then you are alerted to whatever they might have put into your house that they don't want you to know about, like surveillance equipment.

When I came back from exercise, I showered and made some phone calls. It was a cool day outdoors. As the afternoon wore on, I began to feel chilly in my house. Puzzled as to why it was so cool when the heat had been on and working early that morning, I went to the thermostat. The heat was not working; the temperature was several degrees below the set temperature, and I could not get it to blow heat. I called a heating contractor, and he was fortunately able to come out that day.

The contractor went out to the utility closet. In Tucson, which rarely gets cold for long, furnaces are often kept in an outdoor utility closet. The heating contractor then came to my front door, chuckling, telling me one of my kids must be playing a prank on me. I told him I did not understand and asked why he'd said that. He said the fuse (which had to have been there earlier that day because without it the heat wouldn't work) was missing from the closet. This large fuse in the utility closet controls the furnace, and it had disappeared. Fuses don't just walk, especially from a closed closet. It had apparently been there that morning in order for the furnace to work.

Now I was concerned. I remembered the suspicious man I had seen near my home that morning. I walked around the house and found signs of an attempted break-in. A jimmy stick had been left on a window ledge where apparently he had tried to get in. This was not good. Why would he have taken the fuse?

I asked the heating contractor to look at everything very carefully, showing him the evidence someone had tried to break in my house that same day. I was concerned something had been tampered with. As it turned out, I was right.

The heating contractor did as I asked and went over everything with a fine-tooth comb. He then came to the front door, this time with a rather grim face. He told me he had found something: wiring in the utility closet had been tampered with so that when he replaced the fuse to start up the furnace, the tampered-with wiring on the plug would start a fire in my house, at first slow and then bursting into a conflagration that would likely burn down a lot of my house. Thank God he found that wiring before he put the fuse in!

It appeared that, failing to break into my house, the criminal had gone to plan B of burning my house down. Twice within ten days I had experienced major criminal actions against me. What had our country come to that it launches these kinds of actions against an innocent woman just because she could see through official lies? Whatever happened to due process? What had America become?

I took my time to recover from the incidents, staying away from people for a few days to process the trauma. I decided it was time for me to buy a gun to protect myself. I went a week or so later to a gun store to buy one. As I spoke with a sales clerk and looked at different guns, I saw a man in the store whom I knew I had seen before. I heard in my head: "just stare at him." Paying attention to this voice, I kept my gaze fixed on him, almost as if it were a game of chicken. After a few moments he startled. His shocked look said to me, How did you recognize me?

THIS MAN'S IDENTITY

I now recognized him. He was the suspicious man with the utility vest who had been outside my house a few days before, less than a week after the murder attempt on Finger Rock Trail. I was facing the man who had almost successfully burned my house down. There was something peculiar about him that shone through both times I saw him. (He showed up later as well.) Although he was in minor disguise both times I saw him, his oddity and the fact I had become excellent at facial and other recognition (perhaps because my life depended on it) helped me to realize who he was. This was corroborated to my satisfaction when he startled as he realized I recognized him.

Inside my head, I now heard: "look around him; see who he is with." That seemed like very good advice, so I did. He and another man were standing in front of a large wall of glass windows overlooking the shooting range. Very fortunately for me at that particular moment, the man with him was facing the shooting range, looking away from me. All I could see was his body and the back of his head.

That was all I needed at this perfect moment. Unmistakably, this head bore the same distinctive thatch of straw that had indelibly burned itself into my brain during the Finger Rock Trail murder attempt. He had the same physique too, and the same baggy blue jeans.

The arsonist did not know yet I recognized his pal. I was busy putting the pieces together in my mind, for though I had encountered each one of them individually, I had not seen them together before. I now understood they were working together as a team.

I watched as the arsonist brought his partner around the gun store to another spot. He and his partner exchanged some words, and then the partner slowly turned his face around and looked at me so I would see his face. The arsonist was testing me: he watched very carefully to see if I recognized his partner. Though I hadn't seen my would-be assassin's face before, I stared him down now, memorizing his nondescript features. Now I also could ID him by his face. My staring him down was also my way of letting them both know I knew exactly who they both were.

When they realized I recognized them both, they ran out of the gun store like their pants were on fire! I have to admit I felt some satisfaction at seeing them flee like the criminal cowards they were. They would have figured out that gun stores always have video cameras running. They also knew I had marked them with my eyes by staring at them both. I had the gun store send the police the surveillance videotape that had captured these criminals with a description of the two and where they had been standing.

I called the Pima County Sheriff's Department. I had a lot of evidence from the break-in and arson attempt on my house. I had the jimmy stick underneath signs of a disturbed window, the tampered-with plug, and now a videotape. When I called in to check on the progress of the case, a Pima County sheriff said to me, "You have a lot of evidence, far more than we usually get on a case."

I did have a lot of evidence. But somehow and for some unknown reason, the case was closed immediately. It didn't take much research to find out the Pima County Sheriff's Department takes direct orders from the presidency (or Eric Holder and Obama's Department of Justice, which was deeply involved in Fast and Furious).

It's much harder to kill someone when you have to make it look like an accident. If they outright murdered me, all eyes would focus on them, as many people around the country had information including some identities and addresses, and instructions on what to do if I was harmed. They turned to different methods.

The following experience, which happened within a month or two of the Finger Rock Trail murder attempt and the attempted arson, illustrates the power of dreams, which in this case warned me in advance of another operation against me. Each operation against me showed me the depth of the treachery to which I was being exposed, and yet in that truth lay my way out.

A DREAM THAT SAVED ME FROM HARM

The following is an example of a dream that revealed to me ahead of time one way they were going to try to get to me. (To do what? Frame me, kill me, drug me and begin mind controlling me? Perhaps it depended on what opportunities availed themselves.) The dream occurred on a Saturday night. I had plans to go with a girlfriend the next day to an outdoor blues festival.

In the dream I was at an outdoor park setting where there was music and people were dancing. A man with a distinctive hat was dancing with me. An authoritative voice told me, "This man is a spy."

The scene then changed, and I saw a visual of a large black circle. I watched as the black circle totally filled with gold. I was told that just as the circle once filled with black was now 100 percent filled with gold, that this man whom I was to meet and who was depicted in the first scene was 100 percent a spy.

Within the dream, I still struggled with believing what I was being told. Almost as if the person speaking knew my doubt, an authoritative voice again very emphatically said 'this man is a spy."

The dream was very vivid and stayed with me long after I woke up. I had no idea what the dream meant, but I figured I might soon find out. I was struck by the fact that I had been warned three times within the dream about this man: the first time verbally, the second time both pictorially and verbally, and the third time verbally. I was left with little doubt that if I did see the man from the dream, I would need to beware. Almost every warning dream I'd ever had had come the night before the event being warned against, so I thought that I might be facing this trouble at the blues festival. I had never been there before, so I was not sure if the setting would look like the one in the dream.

When Phyllis and I went to the park where the blues festival was held, there was an area where people were dancing that looked just as had been portrayed in the dream. We laid out a blanket and got up to dance. Within a short while, a man approached me who looked exactly like the man in the dream. Even more incredibly, he was wearing the identical distinctive hat as in the dream, different from any hat I had ever seen. (It turned out to be an Australian hat that had strings with small corks tied onto them dangling from the front—these corks constantly move and are designed to keep flies away.) I made a decision to play along with him. We were in public, and nothing untoward would happen here. I was careful and did not want to arouse his suspicions that I knew he was very possibly a spy. I was reality-testing, curious to see what kind of stunts he would pull.

He stuck with me like white on rice throughout the afternoon. That stick-to-it-iveness is a trait I have learned to associate with operatives. Since they are assigned to you, there isn't the normal back-and-forth testing a person would do to assess whether this is a good match—they just focus exclusively on you, as if the match had already been decided before they met you. It would be flattering, I suppose, if it weren't so transparent!

It was also interesting that he didn't seem to care that my girlfriend and I often had two male friends sitting with us on our blanket. He would be there too. At the end, he walked us to our car and got my number.

I knew, of course, that this was the man I'd seen in my dream. I had enough curiosity and desire to test the reality of the dream to want to see how he played out the next step or two. It was my contention that the more I learn about how these operatives work, the better off I would be. If I were wrong, I would find that out also. Mostly, I study them while they study me. He—I'll call him Peter—called the next day and asked me out.

I knew it was risky for me to meet with him, but I felt I needed to. I would meet him at a public place. Because there was a risk of being drugged, I would not ever leave my food or drink to go to the restroom. I couldn't call or e-mail anyone to tell them what was going on, for I knew my emails and phone calls were closely monitored.

My plan was to watch carefully for tells. I have learned from experience there are always "tells." All the many operatives I have encountered always betray themselves one way or another. You just have to watch them closely. I didn't have to wait long.

Peter asked me to choose a restaurant where we could meet. My sense of irony was apparent in my choice: I suggested we meet at a local restaurant named Risky Business.

I was understandably nervous. These are very dangerous people. Peter's assignment could well have been to kill me. (It is interesting to note that he worked at the main post office in Tucson, the Cherrybell station. I guess that was his cover job. We hear about our mail being monitored by the CIA…) At this point, however, I had met quite a few spies, and I had an idea how they acted and how to conduct myself. He would want to get me into a private setting before he would do anything, and that would not happen.

As we talked, he said he wanted to spend the night with me. He further said that since he didn't have to go to work the following day, he could spend the entire next day with me. It was all rather robotic and out of context, as there was no chemistry or connection whatsoever between us. I declined his offer.

In my nervousness, I was wringing my hands. I was trying my best to be brave, but it was an anxiety-provoking situation. Peter commented on my nervous hand-wringing. He put his hand on top of mine and held it there. He said, smiling, "I know why you're nervous."

I played along, curious as to what he would say. I said to him, also smiling, "Tell me then: Why am I nervous?"

If this had actually been a first date and not a CIA operation, there could be a lot of reasons to be nervous, including "How will it go?" "Will I like him?" "How will he like me?" and so on. Normal reasons. What he said next was hardly one of those normal reasons.

Almost unbelievably, Peter provided me the tell I was looking for: "You're nervous because you have been spied on." His intonation carried the implication that this had happened quite a bit. This was the tell I had come for. Who would say something like that? This bonehead thought he was being clever. My dream had correctly warned me ahead of time. I played along with him, acting as if he were very wise to have guessed my secret. I asked him, "How did you know?" He made it seem that he too thought he was clever in how he was building my trust and impressing me.

It was time to wrap up the meeting. I had gotten what I came for, and I needed to get out of there safely.

I went to my car, which I had carefully parked nearest the restaurant, under lights. Peter said he would call me.

Peter texted me several times later that evening, bizarrely saying he needed psychotherapy. I did not respond. At first I did not know what in the world he meant by that, but then I remembered how one of the ways therapists who understand something about mind control and ritual abuse are prevented from helping these victims is by being framed. Patients can be plants who then turn against the therapist, suing them with false claims. This technique has derailed the careers of more than a few well-known therapists working with multiple personality disorder and mind control, including a couple personally known to me. It can get very ugly.

I also imagine these operatives come in with a variety of options of how to handle the situation, depending on how things go. The intent seemed to be to neutralize the problem I was causing by my existence. Murder seemed always to be on the table. In this case, he overplayed his hand; showing himself to be a bumbling operative.

It was pretty clear to me Peter was testing to see my response. I didn't respond. He called several times, and I did not respond. Now I had the problem of how to get rid of him.

My girlfriend Phyllis, who had gone to the blues festival with me, had no idea of any of this except she knew Peter wanted to take me out. She called me the next day, as girlfriends do, and asked me if I'd gone out with him and, if so, how the date had gone.

Understanding that my phone was always actively monitored, I quickly considered whether I should tell her the whole story over the phone. I decided it would be a very good idea to tell her, because I knew once those monitoring my conversations in real time heard me tell the whole story, including the dream—once they knew Peter had blown his cover—I would no longer hear from Peter. That would be an ideal way to get rid of him.

I told Phyllis the story of the dream, how the dream had told me three times emphatically that Peter was a spy and how Peter looked exactly like the man in the dream down to the unusual hat. I told her we'd met under the same circumstances as in the dream, dancing in the park. I also told her about our "date," what he had said, and how I now believed he was a spy, just like the dream had said he was.

I didn't hear from him again. It worked! No doubt he was notified right away that the operation was blown. That warning dream had been of tremendous help to me. Over time, I learned how to recognize the men they sent to date me pretty quickly. Even Phyllis grew excellent at seeing them coming, sometimes recognizing them before I did. As I mentioned already, a curious thing about all of them was their complete and unwavering focus on me, very unlike chance meetings with most men. This was, of course, because I was their assignment. It never seemed to matter what I said or did; it was as if the match were predetermined. I never went out with one again.

As mentioned, my ally had instructed me it was not safe to date during these years, because sending an operative in to date someone and gain control of, frame, or murder that person is one of the most commonly used espionage techniques. And it was commonly used with me, whether in Washington, DC; Tucson, Arizona; or Holland. None of them ever got anywhere with me; it was as if they had a smell I learned to identify.

WHACK-A-MOLE

Within two months after the Giffords shooting, a new neighbor moved in a few doors up. Because they had moved a CIA special ops agent next to me in Virginia, I was highly attentive when the house went up for sale as to who would move in. However, because I did not understand they would keep coming after me, it didn't register as a strong possibility another spy would be moved in. All this spycraft costs a lot of time, money, and resources.

Unfortunately, the man who moved in behaved in a manner that aroused my suspicions immediately. Every time I saw him reinforced my first impression that he was likely a spy. Over the years, I have come to appreciate that I have solid instincts for detecting spies immediately when I encounter them. I facetiously call it my "spydar," a term I coined modeled after the term gaydar used for people who can intuitively or through observation detect gays. My spydar meter went off like crazy every time I saw him, for any number of reasons.

When I walked by him on the street as he was landscaping his front yard, he tried so hard not to engage or even look my way that it struck me as studied and trained behavior. I mused that, since Stephen in Virginia had blown his cover and some agency secrets to me in befriending me, this next spy neighbor might well have been instructed to keep to himself.

BACK IN PRIVATE PRACTICE

After a few years' retirement in Tucson, I wanted and needed to get back to work. Because of my interior design mentor's illness, he would not be able to go into business with me. It seemed I had no viable alternative but to go back into practice as a psychotherapist. I had always done well with my own business, so I decided to build a private practice from scratch.

I decided it was best to not work with dissociative identity disorder; this would hopefully help me avoid the problems associated with that. I wanted to help people and was good at it. There would be no shortage of other types of issues I could help with. Things had settled down in recent months, and I was hoping I could move on with my life, no longer concerned with people who wished to harm me.

There had long been an intimate and often near-immediate connection between what I wrote and how a given operative would respond. Every word I wrote on my computer and all emails and texts and phone calls were monitored—not just for time and date but for content. People need to understand the invasion of their privacy is beyond comprehension and without regard for laws. I will address this further in the next chapter.

I had become aware there was a central person who seemed to coordinate events and surveillance and to direct operations against me. (What do they call these people assigned to destroy a person's life by invading every part of it, finding out that person's weaknesses?) In Virginia this person was Stephen, for he was always home and knew all my comings and goings, as well as my habits. I did not yet know who now assumed this central role in Arizona, but I was speaking to that person when I wrote, "Although I can do nothing about the intense surveillance under which they have kept me, neither can they escape being under surveillance themselves. For as surely as they are watching me, their every move is also being watched. Those watchers have been quite talented at getting the necessary information to me—in the best way possible and at the right time—to keep me from harm." I did not say who those watchers were; they were God's army and the Holy Spirit.

My goal in writing this was to demonstrate how the playing field was more level than they understood. I knew what I was writing was going to make at least one main person watching me very uncomfortable thinking that he too was under surveillance. With all their technology and money and spies and lies, they could do nothing about the fact every plan and move they made against me was seen by God and God's angels, my invisible helpers. A for sale sign went up on his house almost immediately. This was an impossibly quick time in which to get a house ready to put on the market and find a new home. A surveillance camera suddenly appeared on his roof, pointed at the street. The spook was spooked!

It was very odd that he would suddenly move because, within recent months, he had put a full-size lap pool in his backyard, an expensive item that suggested he planned to stay. This man was registered as a real estate agent, and as such, he would well know that in the Tucson market a pool is not something you put in to increase property value. They are expensive to put in and maintain, and often buyers don't want a pool. Putting in a pool just a few months before a planned sale would be foolish, as the cost of the pool would not be covered in the sales price. Potential buyers who don't want a pool might be able to negotiate a lower sales price for the house. It very strongly seemed this move was not planned.

I strongly suspect being a real estate agent was his cover, for a friend familiar with real estate business checked and pointed out my neighbor had only two listings, one of which was his own. Further, the photos in his listing were of poor quality, as if he were inexperienced. He had a blog on his website with three entries for March 2011, when he moved in (right after the Giffords shooting in Feb.!), and no others before or after. In his blog he talked about how much his wife and he wanted to live in this neighborhood as they downsized and how they had tried to buy in this neighborhood before. The perfect cover, right? But with no other entries in the months and years previous and subsequent, the lone blog looked suspicious, as if it were disinformation.

Once secure in his anonymity as he surveilled me and planned for my destruction, he was now in full flight mode. Isn't it funny how brave men are when they are hidden behind their four walls and their exalted technologies, but not so much when they are discovered for what they are? The high-tech camera suddenly appearing on his roof after 4 years and just before he moved seemed bizarre. As far as I know, my community has had virtually no crime other than CIA people breaking into or attempting to break into my house, so there was really no need for this and other high-security measures he took. In my experiences, spies are always the most paranoid, for they know what they do to others.

The secret was out. By his own actions, he had implicated himself and blown his own cover. There had been many attempts and constant stalking in 2011 and 2012—all of this must have been orchestrated by him. He must have taken great pleasure in all the dark plans to destroy me. How does a man like that live with himself? Oddly enough, he left no forwarding address with the HOA. Does he believe he is doing right, or does he even care? Maybe he's just a mercenary (I am told the word for this now is "contractor", as if to prettify something so ugly), selling his soul to the highest bidder. Is this now the American way?

ATTEMPTED REVENGE

I intuitively knew the first week after the psychopath moved out of my neighborhood would be very dangerous for me. (I only found out later that both he and his wife made a number of very negative impressions in the neighborhood.) This was a man driven by his lower self and his personal ego, and no doubt he was narcissistically enraged he had to move. My psychological assessment of him was that he would be motivated by revenge over the loss of his expensive lap pool, which he might be paying for over some years. I told a friend the week after the perp moved would likely be very dangerous for me.

The first day after he moved, I was ill and stayed home from work. That illness likely saved my life. The second day was quite another story. My schedule was full for the day with the exception of a noon appointment that my client had canceled in person the previous week. I have always kept my schedule on paper and not digitally; there would be no privacy if I kept it digitally. If someone had been watching me over time, they would know I was usually in my office at this time.

Since I had been sick the day before, I thought I would stay in my office and use the time to rest. God had other plans for me, however. In my head, I was commanded loudly, "Go out—now!" Even when I doubt that what I hear is true, I have learned it is better to act now and question later. I picked up my keys and purse and walked toward my car. I had no idea where I was going, I was just obeying spirit.

As I crossed the large parking lot to the back toward my car, a man in a dark car drove up perpendicular behind my car and blocked it. That was strange, especially since there were no other cars around and plenty of spaces for him to park. He was fooling with something in his hands, and I had a creepy feeling about him. Why had he driven up to my car? What was he doing there? Why was he looking at my car?

I got in my car and needed him to move so I could get out. He seemed extremely reluctant to move. That seemed strange, as there was lots of room in the lot. Had I interrupted something?

He made a left turn going south on the main road. Letting go of my thoughts of something being wrong, I turned right and headed north. I had not gone more than half a block when I felt something. I turned around to see he had made a very quick three-point turn and was now following me in the left lane, traveling in my blind spot. All my senses came to full alert as I realized he had altered his course to follow me. This was not good.

I remembered the policeman had told me one time after an attempt on my life: that if someone is assigned to do a h_t, they are trained that "failure is not an option." He further explained that meant the person is to keep coming after the target until he or she succeeds. Period. Once the killer begins the kill, he or she needs to finish by whatever means.

I was very uneasy with this scenario. I did not like that this man was pursuing me by traveling in my blind spot on the driver's side. He reached over to his right on the front seat. All the while he was staring at me with total focus and a very hateful look. There was no chance this was not about me. In my mind's eye, I saw an image of a gun, and knowing better than to second-guess myself, I said to myself, "That is not going to happen." I braked (there weren't any cars behind me) almost to a stop in my right lane, while he was then forced by the traffic behind him to keep moving past me on my left.

I watched as he demonstrated his utter confusion and ineptitude all over the road ahead of me. He crossed over into the next left-turn lane and then back onto the main road and then back again into the left-turn lane and then back onto the main road we had been traveling. He was looking pretty crazy to me by this point. Between the three-point turn and now being forced ahead of me, he clearly didn't know what to do.

He had to stop at a red light on the main road, and I pulled in behind him. Conspicuously, I wrote down his car make and model, as well as his license plate. I knew he could see me in his rearview mirror. I wanted him to feel the heat.

When the light turned green, I stayed behind him for a while. I had no intentions to create a new situation, but I also wanted him to understand the tables had turned. I planned to turn left at the next light, but then he moved into the left-turn lane. I decided to continue on my course: I wasn't going to follow him, but neither was it time to let up. I guess the pressure got to him, because instead of taking the left turn, he made a U-turn. What was distinctive about this turn was that he watched me as he turned and continued to give me his ugly stare as he drove away, craning his neck around to stare as he passed me and beyond.

The situation had happened fast. The way I saw it he had gone from predator/murderer to scared and confused: everything had been turned inside out, and he was fleeing the scene (just like my neighbor who had sent him had fled). This complete reversal struck me at the time as very funny: when he made his retreat by U-turn, I laughed out loud. He saw me laughing, and in that I had satisfaction.

My pitiful ex-neighbor appeared to have had someone come after me again in revenge after all; I had read him correctly. The one he'd sent had seemed very desperate to get me. I am happy the effort was another rather spectacular failure. I took the opportunity to send emails about the many felonies my neighbor had attempted on me, reminding those surveilling me that if I am harmed, many people have his name.

A couple of small things happened that helped to confirm the situation in my mind. First, as I was driving into my neighborhood in my neighbor's last week here, he turned his head ninety degrees to avoid looking at me at such a speed he surely must have gotten whiplash! Secondly, at a community HOA meeting, a board member spoke of who had moved out and who was moving in. This person thought it was odd this neighbor had not left a forwarding address, as everyone else always has. It made perfect sense to me.

I'm sure the reader will understand when sometimes I resorted to dark humor to deal with the situation. From that perspective, sometimes I laughed looking at the situation as a little like playing whack-a-mole (pun intended). Every time I thought the situation was successfully handled on one front, up popped another mole somewhere else with yet another plan for my destruction. A seemingly endless supply of spies willing to violate my constitutional rights for what reason? The only thing that made sense to me is they were desperate to keep their pedophilia/sex trafficking/ritual abuse/mind control secrets hidden. Where on this earth does a person turn when the government illegally and surreptitiously comes after him or her? I will discuss the larger implications of this surveillance state unconstitutionally turned on its citizens in the next chapter.

FAITH AND DIVINE PROTECTION

Faith kept me strong and aware. Just as God told me so much earlier in my life, before my around-the-world trip, that I would be protected, I received continual reassurances that I would always be protected and that the operatives would never lay a hand on me.

I know, from these many experiences alone, that God wants me alive. After everything I have been through and all that I have been told in spirit, I feel very loved and very protected from above. I cannot know God's mind as to why I have experienced and survived so much, but I do know I was guided and protected through every danger. It is not ego but hard-won spiritual knowledge with which I face them when I say, to paraphrase Jesus, "If He wills that I live, then what is that to you?"

I have been blessed with spiritual gifts that, combined with God's help, enabled me to escape the large range of plots directed against me. Though I have little true comprehension of the relentless and cruel nature of these operations or of the motivations, I have been gifted with a natural resiliency of spirit that carries me through every situation and never leaves me despairing. My daily walk with Jesus nourishes my spirit and informs me of what I need to know.

Jesus was always there and helped me through many situations. I am immensely appreciative and in awe of the help he and others gave me. I know Dad has pride in me as his daughter for overcoming these obstacles and finding the voice to speak out on subjects he could not, if from a very different perspective.

Dad in some way seemed to be my lead guardian angel when it comes to operations against me. I was guided expertly and perfectly through every threat. It was interesting to see Dad work with Jesus, who is always present and in whose name Dad works. I don't really understand these things but what I do know is I owe my life many times over to God and I am extremely grateful. As mentioned, I hear a voice in my head guiding me through every situation. I call this the voice of the Holy Spirit.

I was extremely fortunate in that I walked through every situation with ample guidance to either uncover the plot ahead of time or to deal with it as it unfolded. My dreams often gave me the details I needed to know ahead of time, giving me the advantage in being able to identify and get out of a given situation. God came to my assistance whenever I needed it. I knew Jesus was always in charge. I did not live in fear. My father was with me every day, supporting me and reassuring me they would never get me. It was not God's will for me to die or to be mind controlled. And there was nothing they could do about it. The more I escaped their heinous attempts and plans, the more eagerly they seemed to come after me, as if it were sport from the Hunger Games.

In the meantime, I repeatedly asserted my innocence at every turn. I questioned, in e-mails I knew they would read, what lies had they told to get so many people to come after me so eagerly, to destroy me and intrude on my civil rights. Since I had not done anything wrong, the operatives involved must have been lied to about me and any possible threat I represented. I hoped to get them to at least think about that possibility.

I have also not been shy about pointing out that although I can do nothing about the intense surveillance under which they have kept me, neither can they escape being under surveillance themselves, that God is watching their every move. The necessary information is communicated to me—in the best way possible and at the right time—to keep me from harm. Sometimes the warning was ahead of time, as in a dream; other times it was guidance at the time of a situation.

Sometimes I was led to take steps I would not otherwise take. For example one time before a planned trip, I had a nightmare in which I watched from my hotel room as the hotel manager accepted a bribe and allowed my killer into my room. I knew in the dream I would die.

I woke up from that dream convinced I would meet certain death if I did not change my plans. I canceled the trip, as the certitude of my murder in the dream seemed a chance not worth taking. That early dream in which I was warned not to bike ride to work because of danger and the resulting murder that occurred in that place and time taught me to take these warnings seriously. They are great gifts.

The same man who was my would-be murderer in the dream ended up coming after me in waking reality in Tucson during that same time period I would have been away. However, I had been warned by seeing him in the dream, and I was able to confront and dispel the dangerous situation.

I wrote that if they came after me again, there is no doubt in my mind they would fail again (in fact there were a series of recent attempts, and they did fail each time). At the time, I said the more they came after me, the more information I would disclose. I was beyond weary of the appalling threats of rape, murder, torture, and mind control by my own government. I was charged with no crime. How many crimes did they attempt against me?

I feel angry and very sad for the many people who are being so used and abused in governmental mind control, pedophilia, sex trafficking and ritual abuse. Especially the children, who are seen as commodities to be used and sometimes cruelly murdered and cannabalized. Sometimes organ harvesting is involved, this is a growing international enterprise. My experience is but the tip of the iceberg of a very ugly global problem operating in the shadows in every city in this country and around the world. If our own government's part in it were clearly seen by the light of day, the world would revolt in horror.

The problem described with Edward Snowden's grim revelations about the surveillance state goes far deeper. There are countless black ops programs operating in the shadows without supervision or oversight, programs that violate the dignity, lives, and minds of private citizens with no ties to terrorism. Do citizens have the right to not have their minds controlled by covert, intrusive means? Does the government have the right to assassinate its own citizens for any reason it wants? Does an unconstitutional law or executive action overrule the Constitution? Of course not; a law that violates the Constitution is no law at all.

A New "Contractor"

Did this neighbor moving out solve my predicament? Unfortunately not at all. Astoundingly, and defying all reason, it appears the same house was used by yet another "contractor." I guess they didn't want to lose the house, conveniently placed where all my comings and goings can be seen. No doubt there was all manner of fancy surveillance equipment there. It hadn't crossed my mind they would put another "contractor" in the same house.

One day my new neighbor looked up at me as I drove by. I felt he "recognized" me. As our eyes met, my being was overcome with the intuitive knowledge that he knew me, that he knew a lot about me. This was my spydar operating at 100 percent. There was nothing I could do and I had no proof. I kept my house well secured as always but beyond that did not worry. Very shortly after he moved in, my computer was mysteriously wiped clean. My email account, which I had had since the 1980's, was at the same time wiped of all my emails. AOL said this was not possible but it was possible: the emails were gone.

There were a number of incidents after Michael moved in, including my being poisoned when I was eating out. Not food poisoning—rather, according to my doctor, chemical poisoning. The soup tasted off, and I didn't eat but a few bites of it. I started feeling horrible immediately, with multiple gi and other symptoms. I was crashing quickly, and gave all my things to Dennis so I could go to the bathroom. I was not at all clear from the sudden onset and severity of my symptoms that I would return, so I wanted him to have my keys, phone and coat. I didn't make it but a few steps.

When I came to, I was lying on the restaurant floor, surrounded by paramedics who were fortunately having dinner at the restaurant. I was diaphoretic. My stomach hurt a lot and there was a lot of activity. Fortunately for me, I had been on a pureed soup cleanse for a number of days and was pretty cleaned out inside. With my diaphoresis, the paramedics believed I had had a heart event. I said no, this was gastrointestinal, not cardiac. They helped me up and waited at the door as I went to the bathroom. Whatever had been in my stomach went right through me, and I passed it out. The poison must have passed through me extremely quickly, for as soon as my bowels moved, I felt better. If I had not been cleansing, it is likely the poison would have stayed in my system and affected me, as it did a friend whose ex-wife poisoned him. He was not on a cleanse and the poison stayed in him and absorbed into his organs, damaging them to the point he had to eventually go on disability. He was hospitalized for suspected cardiac problems. Afterwards, Dennis said he had dipped a french fry in the soup to taste it, and said he too thought it tasted funny.

In other related incidents, a stalker suddenly appeared everywhere I went at the nearby park where I exercise in the morning. I vary my paths and over the years have never run across the same people even twice in a row unless I stay on the same path, which I rarely do. Safety is a major concern for me, and I have learned to be quite vigilant. Yet for four or five times in a row, even with me varying my paths, he was everywhere I went. It seemed well beyond coincidence. He had a very creepy, very non-hiker "feel" about him. He seemed much too focused on me. I stopped going to that park for a while and varied my exercise routine. After a few months off, I tried the paths at the park again and did not see him again. As this book got closer to publication, the efforts to get rid of me intensified. There was another one after I had a very positive radio interview about the book.

EXPOSURE NECESSARY

A wise friend named Ron Sable had worked as a top aide to President Reagan for seven years. Because of this and some personal experience of the dangers, he understood something of the way dark things happen in Washington and how people are threatened if they know too much. He told me that I needed to disclose as much as I could without endangering anyone. This was 2014. Ron told me that in order for me to find safety, I must write the book and expose the material. He further told me that because of my background and the credibility of my voice, I was the one to do it. There was no safety in remaining quiet. (Spoiler alert: when the book came out, all activities against me immediately stopped. Once the information is out in the open, there is no need to pursue the writer.)

I had started this book many years before, never envisioning this Section V. It had never been my intention to write about this material; however he was right: my being quiet about everything kept a target on my back. With all the craziness, I had let my book go and not worked on it further. I realized I had to do as he said; to add a Section to this book to describe what was going on. And how my work with sexual abuse, pedophilia, ritual abuse, sex trafficked individuals tied in to this global order.

THE LAST STRAW

Apart from the poisoning and my emails "disappearing" right after the new neighbor moved in, things quieted down for a short while. I had more time and energy available for creative pursuits. The decision to rewrite the book, adding Section V was made. I made a reservation at a hotel to spend a quiet week writing. Unfortunately, my reservation was canceled at the last minute. Since it was October and therefore prime vacation time in Arizona, I had a very hard time getting another reservation. I ended up reserving a cabin at a location outside Sedona, quite a bit more remote than the spot I had originally reserved, but with others around who shared meals at a common center.

Everything went wrong on the way there. Perhaps it was God's way of warning me. I took a bypass that headed me in the wrong direction. Instead of arriving before dinnertime as I had planned, it was late night by the time I arrived. But there was nowhere else to stay, and I definitely wanted to work, so I decided to make the best of it.

It was a new age place; Sedona has a number of them. I try to stay away from them, but there was no choice in this instance. The cabins were nice despite not having bathrooms, which were down the road a bit. I had been through a lot, but apart from sharing some of the information I had learned from my father about the CIA, I had no plans to write any details about mind control as it relates to RA and pedophilia. Those plans quickly changed.

I worked hard in the morning of my second day there, and fell into a deep sleep in the afternoon. I didn't want to wake up, but internally I "heard" that it was time to wake myself up and take a walk before dark. It was about an hour before dark. With repeated urgings, I reluctantly stirred. It would be good to stretch my legs and get some exercise before dinner. I planned to walk along the main road, a dirt-and-gravel road with beautiful overlooks onto the Sedona valley.

I pushed myself to stir and get going. I started walking toward the main road. However, once I got there, I was guided to walk down an unmarked side road in the national forest. It was a long, deserted road, but it was still light. I never would have gone there had I not been guided to do so.

Along the way there were campsites with pull-offs for parking located every few hundred yards or so. The campsites were fifty to a hundred yards off the road. At the first campsite, a hundred yards off to my left, I saw a man stringing up a blue tarp like a hammock to a tree. He did not look my way, but I had the feeling he was aware of my presence. He looked very fit and was wearing camouflage pants. He struck me as a special forces type, highly aware of his surroundings and spring-loaded for action. Although it was chilly and going to be cold that night, in the forties, he had no firewood or fire. Further, he had no provisions, blankets, or heavy clothing. He was wearing a short-sleeved T-shirt with the camouflage pants. He had olive skin. His short beard was meticulously groomed.

Nothing felt right about this. All my inner alarms were going off. I was puzzled as to why there was no car in the pull-off associated with the campsite. As I walked further, I saw a car hidden behind bushes. That was odd, and combined with everything else, I decided to walk over to it to take a look. It was a brand-new high-end

Mercedes and was very clean—which was strange enough in this dusty part of Sedona. The license plate was from New Mexico. I was horrified when I saw what the plate said: "BULLET." What was this about and what was he doing here? And what did he do to be paid so handsomely?

I kept on down the road, trying to dismiss my reactions and instincts. After all, things had been quiet for almost two years. As I walked down the road, I saw a common sight of tents and campers and dusty people. As I am wont to do if alarmed, when I decided to turn around and walk back to my cabin, I did so suddenly and without warning.

To my great surprise, off to my right and partially hidden in the tall grass and trees was the man who had been at the campsite. Apparently he had been stalking and following me for quite a distance. When he saw me turn, he turned around quickly and ran into hiding. He had been covertly following me and was now running to hide from me. This was really bad news. I had let my suspicions go, but now I was on full alert again.

In order to get back to my cabin, I had to walk past his campsite. I was grateful for the occasional car or camper that went down this dirt road, as it was insurance to me that if he meant me harm, he would not hurt me when conditions were unpredictable and he could be discovered. As I walked past his campsite, the other end of the tarp he had been putting up was now tied to a tree. He was lying in it as if he were relaxing.

Given that I had seen him a few minutes before hiding from me at a distance in the brush, his pose seemed studied to me. He had probably just gotten back. His pose seemed designed to throw me off. He probably didn't know I had seen him running away from me in the bushes. It was dusk now and chilly; still he had no blanket, no fire, no provisions at the campsite—not even a sweater or jacket. This man was no camper. My assessment was this was a bivouac site for him, a place for him to get situated before he commenced whatever he had come there to commence.

There was nothing I could do but go back to my cabin, have dinner, and relax for the evening. Despite everything, I am not paranoid by nature; I made a decision to be careful, but since I had no reason to think they were coming again after me after all this time, I tried to forget about it.

My cabin was at the end of a line of five or so cabins, each separated from the others with a small piece of land. Across from the cabins was a wooded area in front of a creek, and the national park was on the other side of the creek. I had sat on my porch for two previous evenings and enjoyed the quiet and the very dark skies. Sedona is designated as a dark-sky location, meaning there is very little light pollution and the dark skies there are exceptional for stargazing. In addition, the moon was less than a quarter full and would not rise until well after midnight. The stars shone, but without a moon, the landscape was extremely dark.

It was not long before I began seeing something unusual. In the wooded area opposite me, in front of the creek, was a steady, dim neon-green light rising up about three feet or so. It struck me as odd because there had been no lighting there on previous nights. Further, I was struck by how the light rose those few feet in a rectangular pattern. That seemed very unusual, as most light emits a round pattern. I hadn't seen this color of neon-green light before. Over the evening, I gazed at it, wondering what it was and why it rose in a rectangular shape.

I studied it for a while and contemplated whether someone was out there. There was no natural light source in the woods; I concluded the neon-green light had to be related to some human activity. If there had been a moon in the sky or more light pollution, I doubt I would have been able to see the neon-green light. It made me very uncomfortable, but I could not put my finger on what it was or why. I went in for the night and locked my door.

Amazingly, I fell into a deep sleep for a few hours. Sometime around three or four in the morning, I was awakened by a horrible nightmare. In this nightmare, I saw the man I had seen on my walk. He was the one situated in the woods in front of my cabin. I was "told" he was obsessed with killing me and, while doing so, drawing it out in the most horrific way possible. I could feel the monstrous, rapacious energy emanating from him and invading my dream.

The only way I know how to describe the killer energy that came through him into my dream is to say that it was demonic. It was crazed, psychotic, murderous, vengeful, rapacious—all those things. I did not feel any humanity in this spirit. Was this one of the demonically charged multiples? It was the closest I had ever come to experiencing demonic energy. This thing I was experiencing through the dream was unlike anything I had ever encountered. I woke up on full alert, knowing without a doubt that this man intended to murder me and that the nightmare came to warn me.

I also woke up with the sudden "downloaded" understanding that the rectangular neon light in the woods was a night-vision monitor. I had no idea there was such a thing and wasn't sure what one would look like. Although I did not have phone reception in my cabin, I did have Wi-Fi. Chilled by my nightmare, I looked up night-vision equipment on the Internet. I was stunned to see the exact color of dim neon-green lighting I had been watching that night was specifically associated with night-vision devices. The distinctive light was the exact color I had been observing! Monitors were of various shapes; some were rectangular. In more-normal nighttime areas, not a designated dark-sky area like Sedona, it would be unlikely that a person like me, at a distance, could see the low light emission. However, in the moonless dark skies of Sedona, the slightly eerie, dim neon-green light was visible.

Suddenly everything came together in my mind. They must have been worried about what I would write. It seems they decided to kill me rather than wait to see what I might write. If people don't understand the surveillance state is turned on the American citizen, it's time to think again. That was years ago and the agenda was not yet in full force. The goal is total control of the populace and has nothing to do with protecting our safety as innocent civilians.

It was not my first time dealing with life-or-death decisions. I knew from experience that in order to make sure he succeeded in killing me ("Failure is not an option"), he would likely spend a night before the killing night casing the area to observe who was out when and determine the likely foot-traffic patterns around my cabin in the middle of the night. There could be no witnesses or interruptions.

I was grateful I had memorized his car's make and model as well as the alarming license plate. I also had a good physical description of the man. I did the only thing I knew how to do to protect myself: I wrote an email to close friends explaining the situation. I told them if anything happened to me, it should be easy to find my killer with the identifying information and license plate number I was giving out.

I surmised these emails would be all I would need for the threat to swerve, for the last thing they would want would be an investigation into the owner of that car. The email recipients knew my history, having listened to many of my stories over some years. One had even helped me understand some of my warning dreams. She had the e-mail addresses and phone numbers of people to contact if I were harmed.

The next night and all subsequent nights, there was no green light coming from the woods. The danger had passed. There were no more horrible nightmares and no more strange sightings.

Why did I have to go through this madness yet again? Was I to be killed for something I might write? How psychopathic are these people who order and execute these hits? Or perhaps it is the controlled parts of these people? It is often the case that the programmers are also victims of mind control, so they have dissociated, programmed parts as well.

As someone who sees myself as somewhat ordinary, I didn't understand the value I seemed to have to them. My father was gone from this earth, his secrets safe with him. As for myself, for every word I under these circumstances felt forced to write, I held back far more. Even then, I didn't fully appreciate the immense magnitude of their pedophilic/sex trafficking/mind control/perverted globalist desire to control the world.

The gambit had worked. I was safe. To help secure my future safety, I spoke with many people about what had happened. The physical description of my would-be killer, as well as his car's make and model and distinctive license plate, were in the hands of many. Unfortunately, any record of the license plate soon disappeared.

It is sad to say there were so many of these attempts I lost count. Thank God for the protection afforded me and for the good sense God has given me in these challenging situations. I should not have had to endure any of this. But I did and am alive to tell the tale. And perhaps that is a reason God kept me alive.

After this event, there was no way I could any longer be quiet. Any safety I felt in not speaking about certain subjects evaporated. I had falsely hoped it would all just go away if I did not write of those things—but it did not go away. Judging by everything I'd witnessed, this last would-be assassin showed an intense level of determination in the desire to exterminate me. Why? This chapter and the preceding one were not even a thought in my head.

It is clear this kind of persecution is not just my isolated experience but also that of other innocent citizens, for whatever reasons. "Arkancide" and the "Clinton body count" are familiar terms denoting those who are killed for political reasons. Obama legitimized citizen assassination. What had become of our country, as this giant totalitarian surveillance machine begins to feed on its citizens, cannibalizing itself?

How many others are there who have not been so lucky? When the mere possession of knowledge creates this kind of Stasi-state reactions, the structure we call our (shadow) government has far overstepped its constitutional mandate and no longer represents the will of the people. The encroaching totalitarian state was out of control. Who can a person go to to stop the madness? Those who are willing to give up their liberties for the illusory "safety" are deluded. They will have neither.

PROCESS DESCRIPTIONS

After that October surprise, I was again hopeful all operations against me had ceased. After all, I'd caught them in the act and had a license plate number plus a car make and model. Sure, they could scrub the records (as they did). My human tendency toward denial of continued operations against me was supported in my mind by the absurd record of them going at me for the better part of eight years for no legal reason whatsoever. I was a small potato. Didn't they have bigger fish to fry? Actual criminals and terrorists, perhaps? Someone who had actually done something wrong?

In those eight years, they had surveilled me, had come up with dozens of attempts to kill or otherwise harm or neutralize me, had moved a CIA agent next door to me in Virginia, two more a few doors away from me in Tucson, had followed me all over Holland, and had tried to harm me on pretty much every trip I made within the United States. They even poisoned my father's magnificent grapefruit tree when I gave a public talk on what was happening to me. The arborist who regularly fertilized the tree said the tree, which suddenly died, had most definitely not died of natural causes. He said only: "Do you have enemies?" I guess the poisoning was meant to discourage and dishearten me. It was staggering and unimaginable. I had done nothing wrong. But where to turn? I had no choice but to hang in there and continue to fight.

When several incidents were directly or indirectly hurtful to my friends, I had to pull back from them somewhat. I try very hard not to harm others and did not want to be even indirectly responsible for another's pain. I had learned early in life how loved ones may be threatened and targeted. I could not risk others because of something I was forced to go through. I had friends and family but managed to steer clear of any deep involvements that would jeopardize them. As horrible a time as I was having, I couldn't let these desperate measures get me down for any length of time—I could not afford to lose focus. Though I had been repeatedly traumatized, I learned how to isolate myself after an incident and take time to heal psychologically, physically and spiritually. I focused on God's promise to me to keep me safe, and never questioned it.

When I decided to describe in this book some of the events from which I'd escaped, I had to make a decision how much of my internal process I would describe. I was not sure I wanted to give away my secrets while I was still under illegal pursuit. Finally, though, I realized it would be best to describe my spiritual guidance. For without an understanding of the guidance given me so that in every case I knew what to do and when, my responses and escapes seem implausible and incomprehensible. Those who understand God's miracles will see his spirit in action in my stories. I realized I needed to explain my experience of God's presence in every situation, guiding and protecting me.

Fortunately, through a series of events and reactions, I was able to identify and expose the new neighbor after him living here only a few months. His patterns drastically changed once I exposed him. Instead of being at home all the time, suddenly he was gone from Sunday night, through the workweek, not returning until the next weekend. I exposed him the same way I did with the previous ones, using the knowledge of the continuous surveillance on me to communicate with them through my emails to others. In these emails I exposed his name, address, and the specifics of my experiences, tying them to him. Of course, if he or the ones before him were not listening to my phone calls or reading my emails, they would not be uncomfortable, feel exposed, or show such intense need to flee from the neighborhood. It's a bit like cockroaches: they scurry away when exposed to the light. I also reminded him via email that following unlawful orders is not considered a legal defense, that I am in no way a terrorist, and have not broken any laws. I hinted that some neighbors were suspicious of him.

If anything were to happen to me, many people had his name and address, and he would be the immediate target of suspicion. These "contractors" well know that if they are exposed, they will be cut loose or "burned." Their employer will deny there is a connection between them, and they will have to face any legal consequences on their own. Thus, in exposing the names of the 3 persons in Virginia and Arizona who were assigned to me, I reduced their potential lethality. Anything that would happen to me would have to look like an accident and like it was unrelated to them. I used their names often, with each attempt, tying the incidents to them, so they would lose hope they will not be implicated.

This newest neighbor moved out after only a few months. Coincidence? Unlikely.

Hope and Faith

I have learned in a very powerful way through these experiences that my true hope and faith is with God, who delivered on his promises to protect me. I was assured that not a hair on my head would be touched. And I am safe. There are a hundred miracles right there. I have continually been amazed at the help and guidance given me and how effective the results were. We don't always know what God's purpose is for us, especially in times of trouble, yet through my experiences, my understanding of my purpose has grown deeper. It has been made abundantly clear to me and hopefully now to those watching me that it is God's will for me to be alive at this time. I imagine my continued survival has caused considerable distress and consternation to some.

By the grace of God, this book was printed. Even in that process there were extreme obstacles including the publisher refusing to publish at the last moment. This was resolved when the Vice-President of the publishing company intervened. Secondly, the well-reputed marketing company I had hired bailed at the last moment. According to an insider, neither of these things had ever happened before. If anything happened to me, there were people who had copies of the manuscript and would release them. Immediately with the printing of the book, the 3rd contractor put a "for sale" sign on his house and moved out. It is now four years later and there have been no incidents. After 10 years of dealing with this horrible nonsense, I have been wondrously free to live my own life.

Just as I didn't understand the true magnitude of their globalist satanic order and why all this attention was focused on me from the CIA and whomever else is involved in this madness, I was not able to understand why I was blessed with so much help and support from above. Certainly my dad in heaven, as author of the National Security Act of 1947 and of the CIA charter, would not want his creations to destroy another of his creations (me), of which he is much more proud. I can only imagine his horror at the out-of-control, depraved, and demented monsters coming after his daughter to murder her or mind control her.

But since life is ultimately about God's will, it was God's will that I live. The scenarios I have had to deal with have been extremely complicated and involved, and yet at every step I was given all the help I needed, sometimes in the most surprising of ways. I also experienced at a deep level of my being that I was safe and that the next event would take care of itself. I did not lie awake at night worrying, nor did I spend much energy anxious about the next thing that would happen.

A DREAM AND VISION

A dream fragment combined with a vision I had during a particularly rough period gives a clear depiction of this feeling of safety I carry with me despite everything going on. This has always been true for me, but this dream and vision are illustrative, so I will include them here.

Within the dream fragment, I woke up, my eyes still closed as I lay in bed. I felt exquisitely and totally safe and protected. That sense of safety and protection was profound.

As I pondered the dream, I realized the feeling of safety and protection was a spiritual one. I was being reassured I am being guarded and no harm will come to me.

The next morning, I was sitting on my back patio, staring at the beautiful mountains and contemplating the delicious feeling of the dream fragment. As I looked up at the sky above the mountains, I saw a vision of many very large hands, one after the other, hands from heaven, hands present to help me, support me, and love me. In my vision, I saw a multitude of angels, like something out of William Blake's art. The vision was profoundly moving and gave me full reassurance I would continue to walk in safety and in love.

JOHN'S VISION

John's inspired writing in the book of Revelation encourages us to have hope and faith throughout whatever profoundly disturbing challenges we face both individually and collectively. Contrary to Senator Byrd's dying hope—as portrayed on his gravestone—John did not lie. The New World Order/Great Reset is ultimately doomed to fail, as is the mind-controlled enslavement of the people with which those dark elements hope to achieve it.

If God can protect and save me from horrific fates designed for me, can he not help others who turn to Him? I hope by my words and my story to inspire others to always reach for the Highest.

I could not have been more thrilled when this book was published and all operations against me ceased immediately. That was almost 7 years ago now, and there have been no further incidents. It has been wonderfully freeing to have my life back again without that very dark cloud hanging over me.

My walk with Jesus grew on a daily basis during that time, and I learned to rely on him and the Holy Spirit. He was always with me, of that I have no doubt. He was always there. Words cannot express the depth of my gratitude. Since that time, I have continued my walk and deepened my faith through Bible studies and friendship with a life-long pastor, Carl Hogue, D.D., who taught me so much.

In the next chapter, I take a broad look at the implications of mind control and a total surveillance society in which ordinary citizens are targeted without restraint. Edward Snowden's revelations of spying in real time on everyone sent shock waves around the world. Snowden has commented on the naïveté and massive complacency by even the most-well-educated people who say, "I haven't done anything wrong, so I don't mind the surveillance." I couldn't agree more strongly with him. In a world in which the plan for the New World Order includes total control of what is left of the masses, the shadow goal of surveillance is total control.

CHAPTER 18

CROSSING THE RUBICON

Where the spirit of the Lord is, there is Liberty.

—Corinthians 3:17, ESV

You have rights antecedent to all earthly governments; rights that cannot be repealed or restrained by human laws; rights derived from the Great Legislator of the Universe.

—John Adams, second president of the United States

Study the Constitution! Let it be preached from the pulpit, proclaimed in legislatures, and enforced in courts of justice.

—Abraham Lincoln

Any society that would give up a little liberty to gain a little security will deserve neither and lose both.

—Benjamin Franklin, sometimes attributed to Thomas Jefferson

In the process of dealing with the many unconstitutional violations of my rights and the murder attempts, there were times when I thought the whole dreaded ordeal was over. After all, I reasoned, I had done nothing wrong, had no thoughts of being a whistleblower (a "crime" obviously punishable by death without trial), and was trying as hard as I could to lay low and live my quiet life in peace. I was mostly confused as to why these obsessed people continued to track me closely and try to kill me or mind control me. The persecution of whistleblowers has been mainstream news for a long time. Prominent examples are Julian Assange and Edward Snowden. Assange is famous for releasing emails from John Podesta, Hillary Clinton's Campaign Advisor, to other high-level persons regarding child sex trafficking, pedophilia and torture, creating an international awareness of sex trafficking in the US This was before Epstein. Assange has been imprisoned since 2012.

The fact that my father had been author of the National Security Act of 1947, which had created the foundation and structure of the nascent security state, and had been a charter writer for the CIA could be a reason for the focus on me once I started working with the CIA's mind control victims. Many of them had been enslaved since early childhood, victims of ritual abuse, sex trafficking, torture, mind control and more. But since I was a therapist with no inclination to publicly share this information, the obsessive pursuit had made little sense. I was not in any way a terrorist and had never had any violent or criminal affiliations. My mind had a hard time wrapping itself around how I—or, rather, the goal of controlling me and murdering me—had become so important to them. They had now moved a total of three agents into my neighborhoods in Virginia and Arizona so they could obsess over and surveil my every move and thought. Imagine having someone move close to you so they could focus on destroying you with all the latest surveillance and personnel resources available. How much are these people paid just to ruin me and live near me? And for what?

Early on, I realized my task was to stay sane and centered throughout the insanity. Sometimes it was extremely difficult because, as I have mentioned, the stalking and surveillance drove me to isolate and pull back from friends and loved ones, who would otherwise have been at risk of being harmed. It got very lonely. There were always friends to hang out with, but I could not risk intimate relationships. Temperamentally an introvert, I have the capacity to adapt to solitude and even thrive in it for short periods—but it is not my choice. I wanted to be partnered, but could not risk it. The isolation was extremely painful, but I did the best I could under the circumstances. The aftermath of each traumatic attempt was very challenging. My mind went into shock after each one, and it took days to work through the inrush of feelings and piece together all the details of what had happened.

To say the inmates are running the asylum hardly does justice as a description. With the massive surveillance opportunities could not all congressional representatives and senators be compromised either by their actions or by being framed? Henry Vinson, in his book, *Confessions of a DC Madam*, talks extensively about how our politicians are controlled by blackmail, often because of their sexual activities. At that national level, sex slaves are offered—any age, any sex, any perversion. Drugs are offered as well. What those partaking of these enticements do not understand is they will be videotaped (even at so-called "safe" parties) and otherwise recorded and will then be subject to vicious blackmail. Epstein's arrest brought public attention to the blackmail, and Ghislaine Maxwell said they had videotapes of everyone.

The surveillance is used to control, not protect. Do we want our country to be run by the use of the surveillance machinery and blackmail? Do we not have enough proof that the intrusive surveillance has invaded our lives and has not yielded significant intelligence advantages? Why do TVs, computers, and phones and now even refrigerators, dishwashers, and other appliances have the capacity to spy on us? There is no neutrality in a totalitarian surveillance in which black ops mercenaries are free to crush those who dissent. The surveillance pretexts of preventing terrorism have enabled the destruction of the Constitution and civil liberties in many significant ways. It is not a secret that the massive dragnet has not successfully prevented any terrorist attack. But it has been our shameful national secret that the dragnet and the programs that feed into it serve to terrorize, mind control, and murder many innocent civilians.

The following quote, taken from a 1957 CIA Inspector General Report assessing the benefits of mind control research in the CIA of another era, could as well be said of today and expanded to include the various intelligence agencies:. "Precautions must be taken not only to protect operations from exposure to enemy forces but also to conceal these activities from the American public in general. The knowledge that the Agency is engaging in unethical and illicit activities would have serious repercussions in political and diplomatic circles and would be detrimental to the accomplishment of its mission" (quoted in Rutz 2001)

Compartmentalization is the means by which secret programs are carried out and by which plausible deniability is maintained. In 1976, the Senate Intelligence Committee concluded the CIA used compartmentalization to conceal their "unethical and illicit activities." Church said, of CIA activities in the 1950s and 1960s, that the agency was a rogue elephant.

CONSTITUTIONAL LAW

The US Constitution is the supreme law of the land, and any statute, to be valid, must be in agreement with the Constitution. It is impossible for a law that violates the Constitution to be valid. Marbury v. Madison (1803) clearly states, "All laws which are repugnant to the Constitution are null and void." Further, in Miranda v.

Arizona, the ruling was "When rights secured by the Constitution are involved, there can be no rule making or legislation which would abrogate them" (Miranda v. Arizona, 384 U.S. 436, 491).

Further case law on unconstitutional law states, "An unconstitutional act is not law; it confers no rights; it imposes no duties; affords no protection; it creates no office; it is in legal contemplation, as inoperative as though it had never been passed" (Norton v. Shelby County, 118 U.S. 425, 442) and "No one is bound to obey an unconstitutional law and no courts are bound to enforce it" (16 Am. Jur. 2d § 177).

The Nuremberg trials were established to bring Nazis to an International Court of Justice. Out of those trials it was determined, "The fact that a person acted pursuant to order of his Government or of a superior does not relieve him from responsibility under international law, provided a moral choice was in fact possible to him."

It can be readily seen from the above rulings that one cannot legally legislate or issue executive orders that contradict the Constitution. Is it any surprise that those in the United States who consider themselves strong constitutionalists are now increasingly being seen as terrorists? Beginning in 2009 when the DHS Office of Intelligence and Analysis issued a report on "Right-Wing Extremism," it was claimed that those who use the term constitutionalist are a threat. Even more bizarrely, returning war veterans were labeled as potential threats.

UNCHECKED POWER, THE FOUNDATION OF TYRANNY

In this section, I will review various articles of the Bill of Rights of the US Constitution guaranteed to US citizens as they pertain to both my own personal experiences and to those many persons subject to mind control against their will.

> Amendment I (1791): Congress shall make no law respecting an establishment of religion, or prohibiting the free exercise thereof; or abridging the freedom of speech, or the press; or the right of the people peaceably to assemble, and to petition the Government for a redress of grievances.

When my email was read, a hit put on me, and an operative moved into my Tucson neighborhood to find a way to control and then kill me, the entire surveillance apparatus fed into a black ops program. Since my opinion about Loughner being involved in a false flag was apparently, if judged by their rather immediate reaction, true, those in power in the shadows chose to try to deprive me of my life in order to protect their criminal secrets of the mind controlled shooter and of their illegal gun running.

> Amendment IV (1791): The right of the people to be secure in their persons, houses, papers, and effects, against unreasonable searches and seizures, shall not be violated, and no warrants shall issue, but upon probable cause, supported by Oath or affirmation, and particularly describing the place to be searched, and the persons or things to be seized.

The CIA operative next to me in Virginia, Stephen, was in and out of my house all the time. I didn't know about it at first but gradually figured out from the many break-ins who he was. Everything I had was gone through, and until I figured it out, there were cameras everywhere. There were multiple attempts to get into my Tucson home (one successful) and multiple break-ins into my Tucson office until I figured out to key the office off the master key, with a different locksmith. I was not secure in my person, houses, papers, and effects against unreasonable searches. There were no warrants and no probable cause. Every keystroke on my computer, every phone call, every text, and every email was monitored. For the better part of 10 years, I lived in a fishbowl of complete surveillance, in each case by a psychopathic mercenary obsessed with killing or otherwise neutralizing me. And this is in the name of national security? No, these are the means used by a fascist, totalitarian state to crush dissent. As another major whistleblower, Snowden, revealed, the extensive US surveillance program is focused on each and every one of us, in virtually all we do. Our phones are portable tracking devices which we voluntarily carry.

Amendment V (1791): No person shall be deprived of life, liberty, or property, without due process of law.

Amendment VIII (1791): Excessive bail shall not be required, nor excessive fines imposed, nor cruel and unusual punishments inflicted.

Life under a microscope by hostile entities trying to eradicate me is a very cruel and unusual punishment when I have been accused of no crime. Julian Assange and Edward Snowden are high-profile figures whose lives have been severely disrupted for telling the truth. How many others are there? I tell my story as an example, for how many more are out there who told the truth and paid with their lives, property or livelihood? Kevin Shipp (fortheloveoffreedom.net), a former CIA high-level employee was forced into being a whistleblower by life-threatening poisoning of his entire family. Later, as he bravely fought the CIA with a lawsuit, and with his family sickened, his hard-earned pension was taken from him. Kevin has been a prolific speaker on the deep state and shadow government and how it operates. His excellent talk on the deep state, what it is and how it operates is available at (*https://www.youtube.com/watch?v=rQouKi7xDpM*). Kevin speaks of a global crime syndicate run out of the FBI and DOJ. Many whistleblowers have come out in recent days (2023) testifying to a deep web of corruption.

Amendment XIII (1865)

Section 1. Neither slavery nor involuntary servitude, except as a punishment for crime whereof the party shall have been duly convicted, shall exist within the United States, or any place subject to their jurisdiction.

Section 2. Congress shall have power to enforce this article by appropriate legislation.

Civil libertarians do not talk about this amendment as much as the others, as it is assumed there is no slavery in the United States today. This is far from the truth. Those who are subjected to mind control as children in the ongoing heinous programs are kept and used as slaves throughout their lives, often from birth or childhood. As mentioned earlier in this manuscript, the numbers of those who are bred and whose lives are enslaved through various mind control means to serve the desired New World Order are estimated to be approximately forty million in this country alone. The numbers who are conscripted as unwitting adults are unknown—modern electronic and chemical measures in mind control do not require childhood years of the most horrific traumatization and can be used to develop mind-controlled slaves from adulthood.

RELEVANCE OF THE LITTLE-KNOWN PIKE COMMITTEE FINDINGS (1976)

A very interesting piece of information emerged as I was doing my research for this book. At the same time the well-known Church Committee was doing its research into alleged CIA abuses in the mid- 1970s, the House of Representatives had the lesser known Pike Committee investigating the CIA. It was trying (unsuccessfully) to look at the CIA budget. The Pike Committee came at the CIA in a very contentious manner, yet out of it they grew to understand major CIA operations were done at the behest of the president. This information from the final Pike report was divulged in January 1976, saying that oversight of the CIA budget was virtually nonexistent.

Interestingly, the Pike Committee's final report lay more blame on the White House than the CIA for its illegal actions:

> The CIA does not go galloping off conducting operations by itself ... The major things which are done are not done unilaterally by the CIA without approval from higher up the line ... We did find evidence, upon evidence, upon evidence where the CIA said: "No, don't do it." The State Department or the White House said, "We're going to do it." The CIA was much more professional and had a far deeper reading on the down-the-road implications of some immediately popular act than the executive branch or administration officials. ... The CIA never did anything the White House didn't want. Sometimes they didn't want to do what they did. (*https://www.cia. gov/static/CIA-Pike-Committee-Investigations.pdf*)

Whether this is true in the modern era of the massive deep state is unknown. As mentioned, the black ops mind control projects are hidden from sight. The current Trump administration has been continuously targeted by the deep state, which aligned itself against the administration in a series of lies and illegal coup attempts, including the failed impeachment.

CIVILIAN ASSASSINATIONS

My dad was asked by the William Morris Agency to write a pilot for a show on the CIA. This was in the 1970s, around the time of the highly popular FBI show with Efrem Zimbalist Jr., a show that aired for nine seasons. Dad's pilot was deemed unacceptable; they wanted a lot more of agents going off on their own and doing spectacular things. Dad wanted nothing to do with this, saying the CIA did not go off and do missions on its own as might be portrayed in popular media. He was, as I have said, both naive and unaware of many CIA operations.

I would like to pose to the reader the following hypothetical scenario for consideration. The executive branch and Department of Justice in 2017 gets involved in some criminal activities to push forward some dark agenda they want to keep secret, something like the illegal gun running to the cartel done by Fast and Furious. What powers might they use to get rid of anyone who might catch on, so they can maintain their operation? Might they use mind controlled shooters to get rid of the opposition? (The mind control technology has been there and used for a hundred years now. No one should be surprised about this if they have gotten this far in reading this book.)

Would they use the pretext afforded by citizen assassinations? It is critical to note there is no jury, no trial—only an accusation and secret murder, often disguised to look like an accident or heart attack. Perhaps, as the Pike report suggested, the president orders the CIA to do the kills. What is the citizens' recourse? Perhaps the president has assassins at his disposal from a number of sources?

What is to stop a president from going after political enemies and potential whistleblowers? If you were comfortable with Obama as a Democrat making these decisions because you are a Democrat, will you feel comfortable with a Republican president also having the absolute power to kill whomever he or she wants just because he or she says so? What happened to our collective moral and ethical compass?

In the excellent February 5, 2013, Guardian article "Chilling Legal Memo from Obama DOJ Justifies Assassination of US Citizens," constitutional lawyer and journalist Glenn Greenwald comments:

When the New York Times back in April, 2010 first confirmed the existence of Obama's hit list, it made clear just what an extremist power this is, noting: "It is extremely rare, if not unprecedented, for an American to be approved for targeted killing." When the existence of Obama's hit list was first reported several months earlier by the Washington Post's Dana Priest, she wrote that the "list includes three Americans."

What has made these actions all the more radical is the absolute secrecy with which Obama has draped all of this. *Not only is the entire process carried out solely within the Executive branch—with no checks or oversight of any kind—but there is zero transparency and zero accountability.* The president's underlings compile their proposed lists of who should be executed, and the president—at a charming weekly event dubbed by White House aides as "Terror Tuesday"—then chooses from "baseball cards" and decrees in total secrecy who should die. The power of accuser, prosecutor, judge, jury, and executioner are all consolidated in this one man, and those powers are exercised in the dark ...

In sum, Obama not only claims he has the power to order US citizens killed with no transparency, but that even the documents explaining the legal rationale for this power are to be concealed. He is maintaining secret law on the most extremist power he can assert. (Greenwald 2013; italics mine)

The checks and balances between the executive, judicial, and legislative branches are upset if the executive branch holds the power of life and death over a given individual—just because the president says so. Greenwald further states, "In sum, Obama not only claims he has the power to order US citizens killed with no transparency, but that even the documents explaining the legal rationale for this power are to be concealed. He's maintaining secret law on the most extremist power he can assert" (Greenwald 2013).

Greenwald cites the authoritarian conflation between the government saying someone is an appropriate target for assassination and valid proof of guilt. "Political leaders who decree guilt in secret and with no oversight inevitably succumb to error and/or abuse of power. Such unchecked accusatory decrees are inherently untrustworthy."

The constitutional argument is that citizen assassinations are a violation of due process guaranteed by the Fifth Amendment. Again from Greenwald:

The core freedom most under attack by the War on Terror is the Fifth Amendment's guarantee of due process. It provides that "no person shall be ... deprived of life ... without due process of law." Like putting people in cages for life on island prisons with no trial, claiming that the president has the right to assassinate US citizens far from any battlefield without any charges or trial is the supreme evisceration of this right ...

During the early Bush years, the very idea that the US government asserted the power to imprison US citizens without charges and due process (or to eavesdrop on them) was so radical that, at the time, I could hardly believe they were being asserted out in the open.

Yet here we are almost a full decade later. And we have the current president asserting the power not merely to imprison or eavesdrop on US citizens without charges or trial, but to order them executed—and to do so in total secrecy, with no checks or oversight. If you believe the president has the power to order US citizens executed far from any battlefield with no charges or trial, then it's truly hard to conceive of any asserted power you would find objectionable. (Greenwald 2013)

We are now seeing a very large imprisonment of citizens over the J-6 event at the US Capitol. They have been imprisoned for 2 plus years in horrible conditions, the video evidence of their innocence having been covered up by the government until it was revealed on the Tucker Carlson show, shortly before he was fired. The very idea of citizen assassinations or false imprisonment abhorrent and repugnant.

My story of being surveilled, gang stalked, harassed, intimidated, and having everything in my life subject to their tromping on would be bad enough, but the truth is someone ordered a hit on me and put considerable resources into ensuring I would die an untimely death. I am clear the CIA was involved in Virginia. I cannot say who ordered any of this, whether in Virginia or in Tucson. The assaults spanned two presidents, one Republican and one Democrat. Does the CIA assume illegal authority to order a hit on someone in their hidden black operations? Who else in our government claims the power to carry out citizen assassinations and does so? As far as I know, it is only the president of the United States, but there may be many independent black ops involved from any number of agencies with no accountability.

What is also clear to me is I had information on pedophilia, sex trafficking of children, ritual abuse, mind control and cannabalism at the highest levels. Knowledge of criminal actions by the government at the highest levels (even without intent to whistleblow, not that this should matter) is not a valid reason for a citizen assassination. The knowledge of global widespread sex trafficking of children was as yet unknown publicly, (Epstein's global sex trafficking had not yet become news) and no doubt provided a major impetus for trying to quiet me.

What kind of depraved criminal deep state would allow this? How many people in the United States would be comfortable knowing any words they say in private communications could be used as pretext for their murder or the murder of a loved one, without them ever knowing why? What if you write a private e-mail, as I did, and someone watching doesn't like what you say and targets you for assassination? Would this not have a chilling effect on free speech and even thought? Should we as a society allow anyone this intimate access to our private correspondence or conversations? Can it be stopped? We have been far too complacent and naive.

All people out there who are naive enough to think the entire unconstitutional surveillance program is not a problem because they have done nothing wrong and have nothing to hide have missed the point entirely. It has nothing to do with whether you have done anything wrong or whether you plan to do anything wrong or whether you have anything to hide. My story is but one example of a hidden criminal faction in our government that will do anything to prevent its illegal actions and agenda from being discovered—anything. These people have no moral or ethical bounds and do anything they think they can get away with. They can come after you for any reason whatsoever—they can, just as they did with me, project onto you that you might in the future think of disclosing their criminal secrets. In their psychopathic world, that is all they need to put a hit on you. It is beyond insane and far from the ideals and principles on which this country was founded.

Who had the authority to order this ongoing assault against my person, my property, and my liberties? And against how many countless others? The national debate is focused on mass collection of phone records, but as my experience suggests, there are many black ops programs (unlimited secret funding and accountable to no one in terms of what they do) that illegally feed into the existent surveillance network and use it to keep track of personal information and to invade a person's home and private life. Where was the court-ordered subpoena to break into my homes and office and put in surveillance equipment? Where was the authority to gang stalk, harass me and try to kill me? What legality accompanies moving agents into my neighborhoods in Virginia and Tucson to monitor my every move and conduct these illegal operations against me? Who is the terrorist here? How do we stop this?

There is an obvious need in this country to dramatically rethink the surveillance programs and take a deep look at the mind control programs run by the defense and intelligence agencies as well as by the military, and even by religious institutions. As citizens, we are extremely vulnerable to the many black ops programs that feed into and utilize the surveillance grid for their own nefarious purposes. The more AI is used, it can be trained to work against humans.

With so many things serving as surveillance tools, such as phones, TVs, appliances, security cameras, and video gaming, there are endless opportunities for these dark programs to invade our everyday lives in ways we cannot even possibly imagine. Before I forced my Virginia spy neighbor to remove all the surveillance equipment from my house by planning to sweep my house, I even found a camera in my shower! The psychopathic mercenaries the CIA or others hire are allowed to do whatever depraved things they want to as long as they keep focused on the target. Imagine having cameras surreptitiously planted all over your house and them watching your every move and listening to your every sound or reading your every communication. And you have done nothing wrong. This is what they do. And we do it to ourselves by using Siri and Alexa, devices that spy on us 24/7. There must be many in this country who have thus far been dealt the same treatment as me and many more who were not nearly so lucky as to survive the many attempts. How many tens, hundreds, thousands, tens of thousands, hundreds of thousands, or millions thus far?

Many have risked their lives to write about the horrors they have experienced under these programs; the information is out there and has been increasingly so in recent years. In this book, I have tried to reference the best of this rapidly growing literature and body of videos. These black ops mind control programs feed into the surveillance grid so they can continually tighten their grip on innocent citizens. As long as all our information is being surveilled, it can be hacked. Kay Griggs, in her lengthy ten-hour interview often titled "Sleeping with the Enemy," talks with a pastor about what she learned as the wife of the head of special operations under NATO Admiral Kelso. She shares very chilling information both about the surveillance state and military black ops goals and operations. (*https://www.youtube.com/watch?v=hzvMv3jtjUU*).

Wherever there is an opportunity for abuse of the surveillance, you can be sure that opportunity is or soon will be utilized in the service of the underground dark agenda of total control of the populace. Think it won't happen here, in the United States? It has been blatantly rolling out since Covid-19. Kay Griggs enlightens us about many of the dark ramifications. The tragic truth is we are far down the rabbit hole already. Many of us are like frogs put in temperate water that is very slowly heated to boiling—slowly enough that we get acclimated to the increasing temperatures and have no idea we are in danger. If we sense no danger, we make no attempt to jump out—and thus die in the boiling water.

It is not too late, but it is dangerously close to the tipping point for humanity. In addition to the surveillance agenda of knowing everything we do, the dark spiritual agenda that is interwoven into the surveillance agenda is horrifying. We ignore it at our peril.

Those who understand the dark spiritual aspect of the agenda know that the goal is, through rituals worldwide, to release dark energies throughout the world. These demons and dark energies are summoned to enter through various portals and rituals to take over Satan's army so the army in turn can take over the world. Yes, it's crazy, and it's not important whether you or I believe in the occult—what's important is that they believe it and have been working nonstop toward this goal at an increasing pace for many decades. Will we wake up to what is happening before it is too late? The Germans in World War II had been dealing with the gradual encroachment on their liberties since the 1930s and were caught unawares by the big lie. Will that be our fate as well?

Springmeier and Cisco Wheeler's books, Svali's writings, Russ Dizdar's podcasts and book *The Black Awakening*, Ted Gunderson's many videos, Kay Griggs's interview, Cathy O'Brien's book *Trance Formation of America* (*https://trance-formation.com/*) and many other books mentioned previously go into detail of how and what is being planned and operationalized on the spiritual side of the planned military and corporate globalist agenda through the use of mind-controlled slaves. The robotic aspects of mind-controlled slaves are characterized and popularized in modern American culture by the immense popularity of the zombie phenomenon—soulless dead people whose only purpose is to prey on anyone who is alive and not a zombie. From *dictionary.com,* a zombie is "the body of a dead person given the semblance of life, but mute and will-less, by a supernatural force, usually for some evil purpose."

Whereas an academic approach to surveillance and mind control issues in modern American society may yield a great deal of information, there is a dreadful lack of awareness of the implications of current policy and practice. I have striven in these chapters to give adequate research background so as to make my experiences intelligible in the light of current systems of dissent and truth suppression by whatever means possible. We live increasingly in a black ops/assassin culture. Our TV shows and books are full of assassins and special ops killers. What is all this killing about and why are we being desensitized to it? It is my hope that my experiences will give an immediacy to the reality and scope of the problem. How would you feel if your daughter or wife or husband or son were targeted? What would you do? What if it were you being targeted, and there was no government agency which could help you?

It was a horror show—and I am one of the lucky ones. I strongly feel God kept me alive in part so I could get some of this information out. If these programs are not reviewed by the light of day and seen for the criminal activities that intersect with them in dark, hidden ways, our freedoms will be irretrievably gone, perhaps forever, surrendered to a technocratic fascism. How many have, are, or will suffer under this despotic, tyrannical system? How many children have had their innocence stolen forever through their use as sexual slaves, experiments, and more? How many people's lives have been lost? How many have lost the right to live their lives in privacy—that most important right? It is all of us. Make no mistake: everything we do, say, and write is recorded.

CHAPTER 19

UPDATE: A GLOBAL PROBLEM

"We'll know our disinformation program is complete when everything the American public believes is false".

—William Casey CIA Director (1981)

"The oligarchs run the United Nations...The problem is that ... all of them are related to the system of pedophilia. We know that there are more than 8 million children per year which disappear. 8 million does mean the entire population of Austria. They disappear without any information, simply like that."

——Calin Georgescu, Former President of The Club of Rome and former executive director of the United Nations

Several years have passed since the original publication of this volume, which documented a decade of my life being terrorized by pursuit, gang stalking, break-ins to my homes and offices, 24/7 surveillance and multiple murder attempts by multiple means. I have, beginning with and as a result of the publication of this book experienced a wonderful cessation of all these activities against me. It has a been a true blessing from God, the culmination of many miracles which protected me from these agents of evil. I have had several years to heal, to feel the freedom of daily life without the need for constant watchfulness of my every step.

I had gotten too close to deep secrets of the globalists aiming to bring in the New World Order. They have been in full control of the mainstream media for many years now, something essential to the mass mind control of the population. Earlier I discussed the total media control which began with Project Mockingbird in the early 1950's, and also with the 2012 and 2017 National Defense Authorization Acts which sanction government lying and manipulation through the media and which is used to counter any criticism of the government, however valid. These globalists rule in the highest offices of our nation and our world by secrets too dark to be believed: child sex trafficking, pedophilia and child sacrifice are at the very core; mind control was at every level of society but particularly at the very top; there was deep corruption and enslavement of the very souls of our leaders to Satan through the most perverse worship. In order to get to the top, one had to be conscripted voluntarily or through blackmail. I learned of many leaders of our world who were involved. The secrets of massive global child sex trafficking, pedophilia and Satanism were mostly well preserved at that time. This was before the time of Epstein/Maxwell, the exposure of a number of cults doing sex trafficking, including Keith Raniere's NXIVM, and John of God in Brazil, and Wikileak's exposure sometimes called Pizzagate. These secrets to which I was exposed were/are essential to the maintaining of the deception by which the Illuminati and their minions rule the world.

My client had been bred though many generations of bloodlines to serve at the very top. From infancy onward, she had been brutally raped, tortured and mind-controlled. She was "designed" through the cruelest of means to be the perfect seductress from early childhood onwards. Her different alters/ personalities were trained as a spy, assassin, messenger/courier, breeder and much more. Her double Merovignian bloodline, prized as the highest of all bloodlines, is said to be the one out of which the Anti-Christ will come. She was bred with a number of American royalty, and was highly prized as a sex slave with Presidents and heads of state internationally. Her story was shocking and mostly unbelievable to me when we met. Knowing this would be the case, as I mentioned previously, she provided me at the outset with a number of volumes, including all of Fritz Springmeier's writings, which explained how the globalist used mind-controlled slaves such as herself to service many leaders and Presidents, who themselves were also mind-controlled. Brice Taylor had a very similar role and history as my client, who gave me a copy of Brice's shocking book *Thanks for the Memories.*

I learned from her and the ongoing research upon which I embarked, that the goal of the New World Order is to control the world through infiltration and deception through every means possible: the media, financial, religious, medical, political and governmental, educational and so on. Fear would be the central focal point around which everything else would be organized. Through fear, blackmail and payoffs governments gain power and control. Their goal is at some point to launch the Antichrist on the world who would bring about their own version of the end times. The reduction of the world's population is a key component of the plan, as portrayed on the (recently destroyed) Georgia Guidestones: to "maintain humanity under 500,000,000 in perpetual balance with nature." Given that the world's population is almost 8 billion, that would be an astonishing reduction in population of approximately 7, 500,000,000. The timeline for the completion of the Illuminati global takeover seemed well in the future to me at the time, in 2008. Its goals included destruction of Christianity and in its place a One World Church headed at the Vatican, destruction of all national governments in favor of globalism; no more private property and inheritance; destruction of patriotism; state control of children and of religion, and the creation of a world government. The United Nations goal is to implement world government by 2030 through the 2030 Agenda for Sustainable Development.

Again, the timeline for the implementation of all of this seemed far away. At the time I was meeting with my client, George Bush Jr. (whose father George Bush Sr. had openly spoken of the New World Order) was President. I later learned on that there was a 16 year plan for the takedown of America and bringing it into the NWO, beginning with Obama. The United States is seen as the shining jewel in a dark world, for its representative government made it stronger and more free than any other country. Therefore, the takedown of the US was a prerequisite for the globalist world domination goals. The US would be at the center of the NWO.

The assignment of Barack Obama was to weaken the US internally and globally in his 8 years as President and that Hillary would destroy the USA and bring in the NWO in her 8 years. (*https://www.youtube.com/ watch?v=r2IAmjoPgZ8&ab_channel=TruthificationChronicles*). Trump with his focus on nationalism and on the eradication of child sex trafficking (*https://townhall.com/ columnists/lizcrokin/2017/02/25/why-the-msm- is-ignoring-trumps-sex-trafficking-busts-n2290379 ; https://lizcrokin.substack.com/p/revisited-trump-sex- trafficking-and?s=w)* interrupted these globalist plans. His efforts at eradicating child sex trafficking were ignored by the mainstream media. It appears Biden is hurriedly trying to implement them and make up for lost time.

AN ORCHESTRATED CRISIS TO BRING IN THE NEW WORLD ORDER (AKA THE GREAT RESET, AGENDA 2030)

It was planned that an orchestrated crisis would be the means by which the globalists would bring in the NWO. David Rockefeller said in 1991 to a UN Business Conference: "We are on the verge of a global transformation. All we need is the right major crisis and the nations will accept the New World Order." Some researchers believed it would be via medical tyranny. Dr. Rima Laibow, interviewed in 2009 by Jesse Ventura in his show *Conspiracy Theory* with Jesse Ventura, Season One, Episode Five, 'Secret Societies' shared insider information from a head of state patient, who said in 2003 that in a short time the US would be facing compulsory vaccination as part of the planned "great culling" of the earth's population. The plan was to put people in FEMA camps for refusing the vaccines. (Note: in Australia many people have already been put in such camps.).

A ray of light came into this dark conversation. When Laibow, who fled the US to live in Panama some years before, met Ventura on an airfield for the interview, she was asked about the power elite who make such decisions and how powerful they are, she said: "Not as powerful as we, the people, in the aggregate are. When we raise our voices, every single time they step back. The problem is, the dirty little secret is that we have that power. They don't want us to know that we have that power." More on this later.

The Rockefeller Foundation, which has been leading the charge fort he NWO and eugenics for many years, published *Operation Lockstep* in 2010, describing a planned dystopian future of a top-down coordinated global authoritarian leadership, using an engineered virus to induce fear and terror in the population as the method for instituting unprecedented governmental control. Lockdowns, forced vaccinations, false statistics about case rates and deaths, enforced mask-wearing, censorship and stigmatization of dissidents, dismissing of side effects of the vaccine, increasing control over the population, martial law and much more were in this plan. Event 201: A global pandemic exercise, held just before the Covid-19 outbreak, and sponsored by John Hopkins, Bill Gates and Claus Schwab's World Economic Forum (WEF) simulated dilemmas and cooperative institutional responses associated with a hypothetical pandemic. It was held in October 2019, just before the pandemic broke out. *Coincidence? Covid 19: The Great Reset*, is a book by Charles Schwab. It is a call for global governance, a technocratic totalitarianism to be instituted in the wake of Covid-19, using Covid-19 as a launchpad for transhumanism and to remake everything into a global state of communism in which no one owns anything. He does not see Covid as a particularly deadly pandemic compared to others over the past 2000 years such as the Black Plague, but nonetheless sees it as a perfect opportunity for the *Great Reset* (*Schwab, The Great Reset, 2020*).

It is not my purpose in this section to delve deeply into the details leading up to the pandemic, nor into the planned and globally coordinated responses. There is a great deal of information available. The movies *Plandemic* and *Indoctornation (Pandemic 2)* (*https://plandemicseries.com*) go into this in some detail. Dr. David Martin has done intensive research into the planned development of Covid-19 over the past 20 years (*https://www.bitchute.com/video/wrkDc0YdfCcI/*) and also into the development of the vaccine beginning in 2015 (*https://rumble.com/vote83-dr.-david-martin-arming-the-public-with- important-information-nov-2021. html*).

Archbishop Vigano appeals to the world: a spiritual perspective

Archibishop Vigano has written a series of bold letters denouncing the pandemic and the associated measures. He has a big picture understanding of the interlocking of the political with the spiritual that few people have. Referring to Rockefeller's comment about needing the "right crisis" to get people to accept the New World Order, he says in his Aug. 21, 2021 letter:

> Today we can affirm that this 'right crisis" coincides with the pandemic and with the
> 'Lockstep' outlined since 2010 by the Rockefeller Foundation document 'Scenarios for the Future

of Technology and International Development,' in which the events we are now witnessing are all anticipated. In short, they have created a false problem in order to be able to impose population control measures as an apparent solution, cancel small and medium-sized businesses with lockdowns and the green pass to the benefit of a few international groups, demolish education by imposing distance learning, lower the cost of manpower and employees with 'smart working', privatize public health for the benefit of Big Pharma, and allow governments to use the state of emergency to legislate in derogation of the law and impose so-called vaccines on the entire populations, making citizens traceable in all their movements and either chronically ill or sterile. Everything the elite wanted to do, they have done. (Vigano, Letter #100, Tuesday, August 31 2021)

In an earlier open letter to President Trump, he wrote from a spiritual viewpoint as the "voice of one crying out in the desert":

...this historical moment sees the forces of Evil aligned in a battle without quarter against the forces of Good; forces of Evil that appear powerful and organized as they oppose the children of Light, who are disoriented and disorganized, abandoned by their temporal and spiritual leaders.

Daily we sense the attacks multiplying of those who want to destroy the very basis of society: the natural family, respect for human life, love of country, freedom of education and business. We see heads of nations and religious leaders pandering to this suicide of Western culture and its Christian soul, while the fundamental rights of citizens and believers are denied in the name of a health emergency that is revealing itself more and more fully as instrumental to the establishment of an inhuman faceless tyranny.

A global plan called the Great Reset is underway. Its architect is a global élite that wants to subdue all of humanity, imposing coercive measures with which to drastically limit individual freedoms and those of entire populations. In several nations this plan has already been approved and financed; in others it is still in an early stage. Behind the world leaders who are the accomplices and executors of this infernal project, there are unscrupulous characters who finance the World Economic Forum and Event 201, promoting their agenda.

The purpose of the Great Reset is the imposition of a health dictatorship aiming at the imposition of liberticidal measures, hidden behind tempting promises of ensuring a universal income and cancelling individual debt. The price of these concessions from the International Monetary Fund will be the renunciation of private property and adherence to a program of vaccination against Covid-19 and Covid-21 promoted by Bill Gates with the collaboration of the main pharmaceutical groups.

Beyond the enormous economic interests that motivate the promoters of the Great Reset, the imposition of the vaccination will be accompanied by the requirement of a health passport and a digital ID, with the consequent contact tracing of the population of the entire world. Those who do not accept these measures will be confined in detention camps or placed under house arrest, and all their assets will be confiscated...

You are well aware of the means that have been deployed to sow panic and legitimize draconian limitations on individual liberties, artfully provoking a world-wide economic crisis. In the intentions of its architects, this crisis will serve to make the recourse of nations to the Great Reset irreversible, thereby giving the final blow to a world whose existence and very memory they want to completely cancel.

He adds there is hope as:

This Great Reset is destined to fail because those who planned it do not understand that there are still people ready to take to the streets to defend their rights, to protect their loved ones, to give a future to their children and grandchildren. The leveling inhumanity of the globalist project will shatter miserably in the face of the firm and courageous opposition of the children of Light. The enemy has Satan on its side, He who only knows. how to hate. But on our side, we have the Lord Almighty, the God of armies arrayed for battle, and the Most Holy Virgin, who will crush the head of the ancient Serpent.

If God is for us, who can be against us? (Rom 8:31). (Vigano, Open letter to the President of the United States Of America, October 25, 2020)

An additional concern is the WHO's current push to have all countries become signatories to their treaty which would cede their sovereignty in any medical or climate emergencies. The constitution of the signatory countries would take a back seat to the WHO 's dictated policies during a pandemic or climate emergency. We would lose our independence as a nation in responding to crises, which they may well initiate. We are currently being warned by Fauci and the like of another pandemic. It's important to put the pieces together. This is the vehicle they are using to create their satanic New World Order/Great Reset.

CATHY O'BRIEN ON COVID-19: AN MKULTRA MIND CONTROL PERSPECTIVE

Cathy O'Brien was sexually abused and mind-controlled from birth. She was used as a Presidential Model, used by many Presidents and heads of state, much as my client was. She describes herself during those years as a controlled robot unable to think for herself because of the extremely heavy trauma and mind control to which she was subjected. Like my client, she had Dissociative Identity Disorder. Many of her alters were created to carry out specific tasks for which she would have amnesia afterwards. Her book *TRANCE Formation of America: True Life Story Of A Mind Control Slave*, co-written with Mark Phillips, the man who helped her escape from the mind control, tells her horrific story and the unbelievable traumas to which she was subjected. Although Mark has died, she has bravely gone on to find hope in her new life and to help other survivors. She recently did a video interview on Covid-19 & the *Trance Formation of America* (*https://beforeitsnews.com/health/2021/11/cathy-obrien-phillips-covid-19-the-trance-formation-of-america-3042918.html*). Because of her life experience with MKUltra and having been privy to the details of the dark agenda, she sees through the fear and the propaganda surrounding Covid. She offers her own perspective on how the same powers that abused her for so many years are continuing the degradation of society through using the "ultimate mind control," fear, to control the globe. She calls Covid "mind control masked as a virus" and says the agenda is to create a slave society (much like the world in Schwab's dystopian "Great Reset.")

Cathy states that the overarching goal of MKUltra is the mind control of humanity. One purpose of the vast pedophilia and sex trafficking agenda, of which we have seen only glimpses, (the Catholic pedophile scandals, Epstein and Maxwell, Wikileaks and Podesta) is to traumatize children and impair free thought. In an online article, O'Brien lists how sex trafficking, mind control and the NWO work together hand in hand.

> Sexually abusing a child prior to age 5 creates a dissociative disorder basis of mind control; mind control is being used to usher in their New World Order slave society; sex trafficking children is the most lucrative business in the world and funds the NWO agenda; children are trafficked for blackmail purposes to compromise judges and promote pedophilia; pedophilia perpetuates sexual abuse of children. Sexually abusing a child prior to age 5 also results in heightened sexuality and gender confusion which fuels the sex industry and perpetuates human trafficking. (*https://trance-formation.com/human-trafficking-has-many-faces/*)

In an already traumatized population, a key way MKUltra is orchestrated is through the controlled media, its coordinated talking points and the drumbeat of fear which is laid down 24/7 through repetition. I shared earlier how, through Project Mockingbird, the CIA and the deep state have been in control of the media since 1970. Repetition is a key feature of mind control. MKUltra is laid down, whether in individual or in societal mind control, through creating a base of fear. A fearful mind cannot think clearly and will grasp for solutions that may not serve. O'Brien describes a Covid Cult manipulated by fear, with the repetition of "get the vax" as strong in every venue through constantly heard programming. Further, masks are used in MKUltra programming to depersonalize and deprive of oxygen. Science tells us the virus molecule is much smaller than the holes in the mask, and even the mask box warns masks don't protect from viruses. Nonetheless mask wearing is widely mandated and is seen as "virtuous". Media censorship allows no alternative viewpoints. O'Brien says this constant bombardment has an impact on people who know better (it permeates the unconscious mind), and further says it is using the same play as in the Nazi era. Her suggestion is to ask self at a soul level "is this what I really think?" As someone who has come out of complete robotic mind control, she understands better than most that we are all vulnerable, and that anyone can be influenced. O'Brien maintains that we need to arm ourselves with knowledge about mind control, that this is crucial to restoring brain function in a world where we are bombarded by lies daily.

Further, like Archbishop Vigano, O'Brien sees the pandemic as a battle between Good and Evil, a battle for the soul of humanity. Ultimately, O'Brien is hopeful that through public awareness, change will come. She sees a great awakening happening where people are reclaiming their free will and thought and are reaching out to each other. For example, the lockdowns have given parents an opportunity to learn what their children are being taught about the rewriting of history and the pedophile agenda, and they are fighting back against corrupt school boards which insist that parents should have no role in determining their child's education.

MASS FORMATION HYPNOSIS: A PSYCHOLOGICAL PERSPECTIVE

Professor Desmet of Belgium is a psychologist who has extensively researched totalitarianism. He describes the societal conditions leading to Mass Formation, a type of collective hypnosis in a traumatized population. He says that in any general population, 30% are hypnotizable, and 40% somewhat so. The other 30% are not.

He says mass formation hypnosis is a precondition for totalitarianism in which people are willing to give up their rights. Certain conditions need to be met for mass formation hypnosis. One of them is the lack of societal bonding, like the social isolation and lack of community on a mass scale during the lockdowns. People without work or social bonding experience their lives as meaningless or senseless. (Even in normal times, more than half the population see their work as meaningless). This leads to widespread anxiety and discontent, out of which arises free-floating aggression and frustration.

Desmet says that when these conditions are met in a large portion of society, "they are ripe for mass formation hypnosis. All that's needed now is a story in which the source or cause of the anxiety is identified and spelled out, while simultaneously providing a strategy for addressing and neutralizing that cause. By accepting and participating in whatever that strategy is, people with free-floating anxiety feel equipped, finally, with the means to control their anxiety and avoid panic. They feel like they're in charge again." (*https://www.technocracy.news/mass-formation-the-applied-science-of-social-engineering/*)

Once in that process of mass formation, there is a loss of reason, a buying into an illogical narrative. Isolation is replaced by a group identity and group think which allows for no individual thought. In the case of Covid-19, the opposition to the centralized media mind control has been suppressed and widely censored. Effective treatments were suppressed and demonized, and dangerous treatments were mandated as hospital protocols by the NIH. Voices of doctors who opposed Dr. Fauci, the CDC or the WHO were widely censored as the controlled media created a cohesive unipolar point of view about the virus, always promoting fear; PCR tests were used which couldn't differentiate between the flu and Covid (hence the "disappearance" of the flu and cold for a year until the CDC withdrew the test, admitting it could not differentiate between the flu and covid) and which created, according to the CDC, huge numbers of false positives. All of this and the constant fear-mongering via the media kept the population in a state of fear and terror with highly inflated case numbers. The drumbeat towards taking the experimental gene therapy (which is not a vaccine as it neither prevents illness nor transmission) was globally coordinated, even though almost all age groups have lower risk from getting the disease than from taking the jab. The risk statistics of taking the shot were suppressed; people have been deliberately kept unaware of the large numbers of deaths and adverse events.

Desmet says in a totalitarian society about 30% of the people are under a hypnotic spell and another 40% may be unconvinced but go along with the program. Only about 25% are willing to go against the crowd. Hitler's Germany is a prime example of the "idiocracy" and how most are willing to go along with the program whether they believe its for the greater good or not.

Dr. Larry Burk gives an excellent analysis of this process:

At Nuremberg Hermann Goering said, "It is always a simple matter to drag the people along, whether it is a democracy, or a fascist dictatorship, or a parliament, or a communist dictatorship. Voice or no voice, the people can always be brought to the bidding of the leaders. That is easy. All you have to do is to tell them they are being attacked, and denounce the pacifists for lack of patriotism and exposing the country to danger. It works the same in every country.

Anthony Fauci has been compared to Josef Mengele, the notorious Nazi doctor known as the Angel of Death for his unethical medical experimentation. As documented in Robert

F. Kennedy, Jr.'s new book, *Fauci* has been responsible for blocking safe, cheap and effective early anti-viral treatments for the past 2 years in favor of experimental, profitable and unproven injections resulting in thousands of preventable deaths. His misleading and conflicting health policy recommendations have been gaslighting the entire world.

It is a testimony to the depth of the fear trance that millions of intelligent people will uncritically accept the pronouncements of unelected authority figures from the NIH, CDC, FDA and WHO who claim to be following the science, but are actually following the money. Such a malicious magic trick would not be possible without the uniform collusion of the mainstream media moguls. (*https://larryburk.substack.com/p/mass-hypnosis-2001-2021-wake-up-now*)

Another psychiatrist, Dr. Mark MacDonald, Board Certified in both child and adolescent psychiatry, and trained in adult psychoanalysis, agrees that the real crisis is not medical in nature, but is the fear which has morphed into mass delusional psychosis due to their delusional fear of Covid. "Even when the statistics point to the extremely low fatality rate among children and young adults (measuring 0.002% at age 10 and 0.01% at 25), the young and the healthy are still terrorized by the chokehold of irrational fear when faced with the coronavirus." (*https://www.eviemagazine.com/post/americans-are-suffering-from-mass-delusional-psychosis-because-of-covid-19*). In the same article, masks are used as an example: "In our society today, fueled by the COVID-induced delusion, it's acceptable to kick a toddler off a plane for not wearing a mask when there's evidence that toddlers rarely spread the virus." Pre-mask mandates, I had a man follow me around the grocery store accusing me of being selfish that I was not wearing a mask. If he believed his mask would protect him then how was I endangering him, especially since he was literally stalking me around the store and I was trying to stay as far away from him as possible!

Dr. Robert Malone, inventor of the MRNA technology of the current shots, has been speaking out with great impact. In an interview with Joe Rogan on Dec. 31, 2021, he said: "We have never seen this level of media coordinated propaganda." Further, he said of the illegality of this totalitarian state:

Our government is out of control on this [Covid response] and they are lawless. They completely disregard bioethics. They completely disregard the federal common rule. These mandates of an experimental vaccine are explicitly illegal. They are explicitly inconsistent with the Nuremberg code. They are explicitly inconsistent with the Bellmont Report.

They are flat-out illegal and they don't care… They are lawless. They completely disregard bio-ethics. They've broken all the rules that I know, that I've been trained on for years.

He elaborates on mass formation hypnosis:

What one observes with the mass hypnosis is that a large fraction of the population is completely unable to process new scientific data and facts demonstrating that they have been misled about the effectiveness and adverse impacts of mandatory mask use, lockdowns, and genetic vaccines that cause people's bodies to make large amounts of biologically active coronavirus Spike protein.

Those hypnotized by this process are unable to recognize the lies and misrepresentations they are being bombarded with on a daily basis, and actively attack anyone who has the temerity to share information with them which contradicts the propaganda that they have come to embrace. (Rogan interview, Dec. 31, 2021)

The delusions deepen as the process continues:

> The endpoint of this mass delusional psychosis is a totally controlled society, where an experimental shot is a requirement to participate, regardless of whether it actually protects or not. Endless unconstitutional rules and mandates are created ostensibly 'for the greater good' but really furthering the interests of the globalists. There is no end to this mass paranoia unless people wake up, speak against the narrative, and allow diverse points of view from the medical arena. Many brilliant doctors who do not go along with the official narrative have been censored, even despite their adding good solid scientific information. (Dr. Robert Malone, *https://rwmalonemd. substack.com/p/mass-formation-psychosis*)

CARL JUNG AND PSYCHIC EPIDEMICS: DEPTH PSYCHOLOGY AND THE COLLECTIVE UNCONSCIOUS

The famous psychologist Carl Jung addressed essentially the same phenomenon, using different terms. According to Carl Jung, we are our own worst enemies; the greatest threat to civilization lies in our own inability to deal with the forces of our psyche. "Indeed, it is becoming ever more obvious that it is not famine, not earthquakes, not microbes, not cancer but man himself who is man's greatest danger to man, for the simple reason that there is no adequate protection against psychic epidemics, which are infinitely more devastating than the worst of natural catastrophes." (Jung, *The Symbolic Life*). Jung cites Nazi Germany as an example. After a stage of panic and terror in which a person's reality is shaken and confused, comes a descent into delusion in which society, under mass mind control, focuses on a common enemy, the solution to which problem is to follow the dictates of the psychopathic leaders.

As stated earlier in this book, the Nazis never lost the war; they went underground globally and are now raising their heads with the attempt to create an all-enveloping New World Order globally, also known as the Fourth Reich. The New World Order was Hitler's dream. Jim Marrs wrote about this extensively in his brilliant book *The Rise of the Fourth Reich*. They have had many years to plan how to do it, using the best of the brainwashing tools they developed during Nazi Germany and in all the years afterward. It can be said that what we are seeing with Covid-19 today is a deliberately manufactured psychic epidemic (mass formation hypnosis) paired with the bioweapon virus and "vaccine." The common enemy to be rallied against is the virus; the endless media brainwashing has its goal of convincing the world that the vaccine is the way of stopping it. This is despite many studies that show that a majority of the 2022 hospitalized are fully vaccinated. Nonetheless, after 24/7 terrifying media coverage for several years, the population has become submissive to an agenda not about medicine or health; but rather about establishing global domination and drastic depopulation. The psychotic delusion is that safety lies in obeying authorities who are actually determined to depopulate 95% of the world by 2030. (Agenda 2030). No amount of vaccines, boosters, lockdowns, masks and vaccine passports will do anything to stop the madness of the psychopaths in charge who delight in the submission of the masses. They have no concern for public health; it is a ruse. Vaccine passports will be used as a increasing form of social control as they advance their murderous agenda.

We are in the midst of the modern version of Hitler's "Big Lie": "In the big lie there is always a certain force of credibility; because the broad masses of a nation are always more easily corrupted in the deeper strata of their emotional nature than consciously or voluntarily; and thus in the primitive simplicity of their minds they more readily fall victims to the big lie than the small lie" (Hitler, *Mein Kampf*)

Carl Jung talked about the spiritual problem of modern man brought about by a combination of the decline of religious beliefs and communities; together with the diminished importance of the individual such that they feel themselves insignificant and impotent. Jung maintains the individual is on the way to "State slavery" when he is overwhelmed by his puniness and sense of impotence. When this process occurs on a mass scale, society is very vulnerable to the rise of tyranny. This was demonstrated multiple times in the totalitarian regimes of the 20th century.

Jung describes how, without a spiritual or religious focal point, the State becomes the highest reality, the God:

> Instead of the concrete individual, you have the names of organizations and, at the highest point, the abstract idea of the State as the principle of political reality. The moral responsibility of the individual is then inevitably replaced by the policy of the State. Instead of the moral and mental differentiation of the individual, you have public welfare and the raising of the living standard. The goal and meaning of individual life (which is the only real life) no longer lie in individual development but in the policy of the State, which is thrust upon the individual from outside...The individual is increasingly deprived of the moral decision as to how he should live his own life, and instead is ruled, fed, clothed, and educated as a social unit...and amused in accordance with the standards that give pleasure and satisfaction to the masses. (Carl Jung, *The Undiscovered Self*)

A SPIRITUAL SOLUTION

The central spiritual issue of meaning or lack thereof factors into the number of totalitarian takeovers of the 20th century. Jung suggests that man resolving his spiritual issues is a way to begin to come out of the pathological dependence on the psychopathic State.

> To me the crux of the spiritual problem today is to be found in the fascination which the psyche holds for modern man...if we are optimistically inclined, we shall see in it the promise of a far-reaching spiritual change in the Western world. At all events, it is a significant phenomenon...important because it touches those irrational and—as history shows — incalculable psychic forces which transform the life of peoples and civilizations in ways that are unforeseen and unforeseeable. *(Jung, The Spiritual Problem of Modern Man.)*

In other words, he is speaking of a spiritual renewal which would occur from turning inward into the richness of the psyche/ God rather than outwards towards the collective, the State. One can see evidence of a strong turning to God as the solution to the absolute mess being created by the seemingly omnipotent global New

World Order. Many are assessing the magnitude and the global orchestration of the problem, and realizing a turning to God is necessary. In the past few years since Covid began, a huge 44% of Americans see the pandemic and global meltdown as "a wake-up call for us to turn back to faith in God."(*https://www.jpost.com/opinion/ millions-of-americans-say-coronavirus-a-wake-up-call-from-god-623320*)

Many are reading the Bible more than ever, many non-Christians are turning to the Bible and online sermons. Dr. Zelenko (recently deceased) is a Jewish man who, in the wake of the suppression and outlawing of effective treatments for Covid, developed an effective natural protocol (Zstack) to enhance the immune system as a means of avoiding Covid or at least minimizing the impact. He too described the mass psychosis and likens it to World War II "where normal decent people were transformed into… just following orders type of people." (*https://rumble.com/vrk95h-covid-genocide-dr.-zelenko-slays-globalists-with-veritas-bombs.html*). He agreed with O'Brien, Desmet and others who see the key in recovering from this great evil "is to bring to the awareness to the consciousness of humanity, of decent people, the psychodynamics of what is going on and give them the tools to combat it." Further, he adds: "Ultimately I think its a test from God…who are ultimately you going to look to for protection?"

He elaborated in an inspirational manner, stating that Carl Jung says:

> The degradation of a society begins with the degradation of the individual; the spiritual elevation of a society begins with the elevation of the individual. If each individual one of us makes firm resolutions not to give in to the fear; to connect deeper in our faith to the one God and to stand firm with your principles and not submit to anyone who is trying to suppress your free will and your consciousness of God, we will win. Because there are many more of us, and God is stronger than them and he's testing us. He's waiting, I believe, for people to choose him.

CRIMES AGAINST HUMANITY

The national death rates, according to the CEO of OneAmerica insurance company, Scott Davison, are up a whopping and unheard of 40% in working age people from pre-pandemic levels. Most of these deaths are not from Covid. (*https://rwmalonemd.substack.com/p/what-if-the-largest-experiment-on*). Have the workplace mandates of the toxic vaccine driven what Dr. Malone calls "a true crime against humanity?… All major mass media and the social media technology companies have coordinated to stifle and suppress any discussion of the risks of the genetic vaccines AND/OR alternative early treatments."

There is a lot of material available in alternative media from reputable doctors about the dangers of the experimental gene therapy, never before tried on a human population. The animal trials were discontinued because the animals died, not directly from the vaccine but from a well-known immune response called "antibody dependent enhancement" or ADE. ADE is when, rather than enhance your immunity against the infection, the vaccine actually enhances the virus' ability to enter and infect your cells, resulting in more severe disease than had you not been vaccinated. Dr. Lee Merritt says vaccine trials for Sars/COV virus have never been successful in animal studies because of ADE, and it has never been tried on humans before. *Dr. Lee Merritt, (https://varjager. wordpress.com/2021/01/30/dr-lee-merritt-in-animal-studies-after-being-injected-with-mrna-technology-all- animals-died-upon-reinfection/*).

Dr. Mike Yeadon, former chief science office and Vice-President for Pfizer says "I have absolutely no doubt that we are in the presence of evil – not a determination I've ever made before in a 40-year research career

– and dangerous products." (*https://coronanews123.wordpress.com/2021/04/04/former-chief- science-officer-at-pfizer-says-he-now-fears-massive-depopulation-may-be-underway/*). He states: "It's my considered view that it is entirely possible that this will be used for massive-scale depopulation."

RECOVERY: A PSYCHOSPIRITUAL SOLUTION

The psychologists, scientists, doctors and mind control survivor discussed above agree on basic points: that we are in a battle for our very survival as a human race; that the nature of the battle is between Good and Evil; that recovery from the mass hypnosis is by speaking up and bringing awareness to the consciousness of humanity; that it is necessary to not give in to fear but to connect with our faith, with God and with our inner being rather than in dependence on and submission to the State. Those controlling the global narrative are few in number compared to We the People and they know it and ultimately fear us: it is through our individual and collective awakening, our prayers, our speaking up and standing up for the truth and for our rights, and our getting involved in community solutions that we can overcome this cancer that threatens the future of humanity.

After this look at this cancerous hellhole growing amid us, I now escort the reader into lighter, significantly brighter material. I will take a look at positive spirituality in dreaming as it may manifest in treatment. Spirituality can be an important component of trauma treatment, informing and supporting the work. As I go more deeply into the material, I will also look at some rather miraculous events of physical healing that occurred through dreaming.

SECTION VI

SPIRITUALITY AND DREAMS

CHAPTER 20

SPIRITUALITY AND DREAMING

SPIRITUALITY IN TREATMENT

I know turn to the first chapter of several on a much brighter subject: positive spirituality in psychotherapy. Spirituality in psychotherapy can take many forms. When people who are traumatized dissociate from their inner experiences in order to not feel the pain of those experiences, the gradual reestablishing of that connection can be a most valuable step in exploring both their psychological and spiritual beings. That connection can be developed through many means, including through exploring feelings, dreams, journaling, meditation, prayer, art, dance, music, and other creative means. The process is one of soul making, of understanding the deeper aspects of one's nature through one's own creative process. Each person comes into the search in his or her own way.

A young teenage girl, Vanessa, came into my office and on the first visit told me she did not believe in God. Her mother, a dedicated Catholic, said she was very concerned for her daughter's soul. She saw her daughter as being in a state of sin because she did not believe in God. It was clear that she and the daughter had struggled in adversarial roles on this question, with the daughter feeling judged and alienated for her conviction.

Over the course of several sessions, Vanessa and I spoke at some length about her beliefs, since they were a major issue in her relationship with her mother. She had many questions about God, Jesus, and the efficacy of prayer. It was clear to me that she was on a genuine spiritual search. I had no doubt this search would take her eventually into a very firm and grounded faith, because her faith was being so carefully seeded. I could give the girl no answers, but I did validate and affirm her search and reassure her that in being true to herself and what she believed, she was giving God the greatest hearing of all. Vanessa seemed genuinely relieved to have her personal search for meaningful spirituality validated.

REVISIONING PSYCHOTHERAPY AS SPIRITUAL PSYCHOTHERAPY

We make a somewhat arbitrary division in our culture between what is psychological and what is spiritual. In many other cultures, there is no dividing line between the two areas, and to consider one without the other would not make sense. The Buddhists, for example, are superb psychologists who were thousands of years ahead of their time in some of their very astute observations about the human psyche and its workings. Their take on personal spiritual development is very inclusive of day-to-day thoughts and actions and does not exclude any aspect of life. Their religion might more aptly be called a science of mind, as the focus of the work is on observing, controlling, and using the mind for good, rather than on some outside deity who can make good things happen. Mircea Eliade's classic work *The Sacred* and the *Profane* explores a number of preindustrial cultures and demonstrates how it was the rule, rather than the exception, that all aspects of life, including what we would now consider profane and secular, were considered to be within the realm of the sacred whole. The division of our lives into "psychological" and "spiritual" is relatively recent in the course of history.

Thomas Moore, in his best-selling work *Care of the Soul*, discusses in rich detail the attentive listening and nurturing of self necessary to cultivate the care of the soul in a day-to-day, creative yet grounded fashion. He offers thoughts on how the split between the secular and the sacred manifests in our daily lives in this modern world and puts forth many ideas on how to overcome the split. He is very emphatic in his views on the need for psychology to be re-visioned so as to be inclusive of spirituality:

> In the modern world we separate religion and psychology, spiritual practice and therapy. There is considerable interest in healing this split, but if it is going to be bridged, our very idea of what we are doing in our psychology has to be radically re-imagined. Psychology and spirituality need to be seen as one. In my view, this new paradigm suggests the end of psychology as we have known it altogether because it is essentially modern, secular, and ego-centered. A new idea, a new language, and new traditions must be developed on which to base our theory and practice. (Moore 1992, xv)

A crucial feature in 12-step recovery programs is the integration of assistance and support from one's higher power, without which it is believed there can be no sustained recovery. Alcoholism and other recovery programs provided momentum during the 1970s and 1980s in bringing spirituality into psychotherapeutic treatment.

Many clinicians today are finding it extremely valuable and important to allow for the exploration of spirituality and religious belief within the therapeutic hour. Clients can be encouraged to cultivate a form of spiritual work that appeals to them, whether that be meditation, dreamwork, creative work, prayer, journaling, workshops, involvement in an organized religious or spiritual community, and so on. A growing number of graduate-level programs exist today in areas such as transpersonal psychology that teach the combining of psychotherapy and spirituality in practice. Carl Jung was an early pioneer in this area, believing every psychological problem is also a spiritual problem. I agree fully. A complete healing is one that occurs on both psychological and spiritual levels.

DREAMS AS VEHICLES FOR DIVINE EXPRESSION

Dreams are vehicles through which what we disown about ourselves, whether it is our horrible childhood experiences or our intrinsic spiritual natures, can manifest. To the extent we are cut off from our feelings and our past, *we are cut off also from our experience of ourselves as spiritual beings. Our divine nature lies within our unconscious, in our shadow side.*

For a person who has experienced significant trauma and who has cut off from feelings associated with that trauma, one common dream includes imagery of a threatening figure stalking or chasing the dreamer. Often, the stalker represents an emerging awareness of past trauma or issues. The issues feel very frightening as they emerge; over time, they have gained in power because the dreamer has not faced them. The normal reaction we have to such material emerging from the unconscious, material that we are literally in the dark about, is to feel afraid, because it feels menacing. We fear the unknown; we sense it as our enemy. The normal reaction we have to the subject of our fear and, in this case, to that which in its emergence feels as if it is pursuing us, is to avoid it—to run.

When the dreamer understands that the stalker represents his or her fear of the unknown and that the unconscious material is not inherently dangerous material or the enemy, the dreamer can more comfortably allow that which is hidden to come into the light of day.

To the extent we are not consciously aware of our relationship with God, our awareness of our spiritual nature lies hidden in the unconscious. Who of us is perfectly aware always of our relationship with God? In the same manner as that which is painful in the dreamer's past is brought into awareness through the dream, the unconscious, being the ultimate source of our spiritual awareness, brings forth dream material to help us understand our wholeness and spiritual nature. I will speak in more detail about how this emerges in subsequent chapters. Next, however, I will give some general background information on dreams and spirituality.

DREAMS AND VISIONARY EXPERIENCE

The Bible is replete with examples of revelation that came forth through dreams. There are numerous accounts in the existing dream literature today that document the many dreams in the Bible. Well-respected religious scholars have written on dreams, discussing the dream as the realm through which the sacred may reveal itself (Sanford; Kelsey; Taylor; Bulkeley; Savary and Berne; and so on). This revelation of sacred truths in dreams occurs today, as it has throughout history.

G. Scott Sparrow, EdD, in his book *I Am with You Always: True Stories of Encounters with Jesus,* documents a number of modern-day dreams and visions people have had in which they had an encounter with Christ. Sparrow wrote a follow-up book, *Blessed among Women: Encounters with Mary and Her Message,* that contains modern encounters with Mary, many of which are also in dreams. Of the sample of Christ encounters that Sparrow collected, more than half of them came as dreams that Sparrow describes as "unusually deep and clear dreams." Such encounters are typically described as having great power on the individual who had them and can be quite transformational in the effect they have on the individual. I quote from I Am with You Always:

> It is probably true that most of us give waking visions more credence than dreams. We are somehow reassured when a person tells us he was on his feet with his eyes open when it all happened.

> However, dreams have not always been considered less real or meaningful than waking experiences or so-called waking visions. Morton Kelsey's analysis of both the Old and New Testaments reveals that dreams and visions, or rather the singular concept of the dream-vision, occupies a central place in the Judeo-Christian tradition. Actually, Kelsey points out that the ancient position was to regard the dream as the state in which a vision naturally occurred. The vision, according to this view, is the content of the dream. Although the vision can intrude upon waking awareness, the dream was considered the natural state in which visions were experienced.

> Kelsey is fond of displaying a Bible from which all references to dreams and visions have been removed: There is simply not much left …

> The belief that dreams are inferior to waking experiences still prevails. To give dreams a fresh chance, we might do well to look at the extent to which the dream involves the person in a dynamic and rich interaction with Christ and with the thrust of his message. By looking

at it this way, the dream-based Christ encounter may emerge as an experience on an equal footing with waking encounters. Indeed, we might even conclude that the capacity of dreams to symbolize complex truths may better serve the purposes of the Christ encounter in many instances. (Sparrow 1995, 21–23)

I Am with You Always contains many fascinating encounters with Jesus. One particularly powerful dream was one a woman had when she was six years old. This dream had a very strong positive power for this woman throughout her life. She grew up in a home where her father was both physically and verbally abusive.

In the dream below, only the girl can see Jesus, as if to say that the others are so caught up in their cycles of abuse and suffering that they lack the spiritual perspective this dream affords the girl.

I had my own personal encounter with Christ in a dream at the age of 6, the night before Easter. The dream has stayed with me my whole life and is as real as it was then.

I dreamed that I was in the living room of the house my family lived in then, when Jesus appeared to me. I was so awestruck, and my heart was touched because he had shown up for me. I immediately ran into the kitchen where my father, brother, and my new stepmother were. I told them that Jesus was in the living room, so they followed me back there, but he wasn't there, so they returned to the kitchen. When I turned around, there he was again. I ran back into the kitchen screaming to my family once again, "Jesus is in the living room." They were reluctant to leave the kitchen this time but did so at my insistence. And again, Jesus was nowhere in sight. Again my family made fun of me, and this time they seemed really angry with me; they returned to the kitchen again.

When I turned around, there he was again. He lovingly told me that only I could see him, not my family. Then Jesus took me by the hand to the kitchen to show me something. Jesus pointed out to me the Easter eggs that my parents were decorating and getting ready for Easter. My parents were carefully putting poison in the eggs that were to go in my Easter basket for Sunday. I was stunned with what I saw; the sadness was so much that I could hardly breathe. Jesus then told me lovingly that I would be all right; and he instructed me just not to eat the eggs.

The next day was Easter, and my parents did not understand why their little girl would not touch the truly beautiful Easter eggs my mother had made during the night.

This dream helped me so much as I was growing up. My father was very violent and both physically and verbally abusive in the extreme. This dream made me see my parents as the disturbed people they were, and I did not take the harmful things they said about me as truth. So I grew up feeling that there was something inherently wrong with my parents—unlike most abused children, who end up feeling, as the result of habitual abuse, that there is something wrong with them. Though I have needed therapy because of this tormented past, I was able to develop into a healthy adult, psychologically, as a result of my encounter with Jesus.

I feel I was spared years of therapy that would have been otherwise necessary to put back together a shattered personality, if indeed this could have been done at all. The presence of Christ has been with me my whole life. I'm now 45. I feel so grateful. (Sparrow 1995, 173–74)

The encounter this girl had with the divine in her dream, in the person of Jesus, helped to give her detachment from and perspective on her abuse that a young child would not ordinarily have. She could feel the certain, unconditional love of Jesus when the world around her was violent and unpredictable. The message Jesus gave her and the feeling she had within the dream of his loving presence helped her to develop a protective psychological boundary around her sense of self. This protective boundary helped keep her from being shattered and overwhelmed by the ongoing terror and brutality of the abuse.

Dreams of the numinous and of the divine tend to place one's experience on earth into a larger context, which in this case is within the unconditional love of Jesus. Alternatively, this can be viewed, in the Jungian sense, as an experience of the deeper self breaking through to provide a steady center of light and love within the girl's heart, to which she could return and to which she could retreat for shelter in the storminess of the life around her.

Dreams, therefore, can serve as tools for connection with the divine, however our deeper selves envision it. Spiritual dreams often use symbols within one's own belief system but may incorporate symbols from other belief systems to make a point or bring in a particular energy.

For example, a woman who had been struggling with freeing herself from the alienating image of Jesus from her early religious indoctrination had a dream that helped her. At the time she dreamed it, she was working on identifying manifestations of divine energies within her. In the dream she saw herself walking in her neighborhood. She was herself, and at the same time she was also Jesus.

The dream was very affirming for her, helping to bring her understanding of Jesus and the inner divinity into her own heart. It was helpful in healing some of the spiritual trauma she had experienced around the historical religious figure of Jesus. In another dream, she saw her fun-loving husband as Zorba the Buddha, incorporating both his wisdom and fun-loving nature into her spiritual view of him.

CHAPTER 21

SPIRITUAL DREAMS AT VARIOUS STAGES OF THERAPY

Since dreams are a statement of the emergent concerns of the dreamer, they serve to show the dreamer what he or she needs to attend to in order to heal and create a new level of wholeness. These areas of concern may vary according to many factors, including one's emotional, physical, developmental, cultural, environmental, and spiritual states. The dream, coming as it does from the center of the self, pushes the dreamer to a new awareness and to new elements or energies that, when assimilated, contribute to a new wholeness.

Each person comes into their inner journey in his or her own way. For many, the opening into the inner world is a monumental step into discovering their personal truths. For some, that will lead into that which is more commonly understood as spiritual or religious. For these people, dreams can provide a profound inner connection with the higher self and the transcendent realm. Often, the manner in which emergent spiritual material introduces itself during treatment is through the dream. In this chapter, I will discuss spiritual dreams that occurred at various stages of treatment and that helped the dreamers to work through problem areas at both psychological and spiritual levels.

Before I get into the actual dreams, I want to bring up Carl Jung's conception of the transcendent function. In Jung's thought, the tension between consciousness and unconsciousness can cause to arise a psychic function that supports the union of the two. What does that mean? Let's say someone has been very depressed and hasn't known why. Jung said that in order for the transcendent function to develop, the person needs to become aware of unconscious material. That may occur through a dream or a fantasy. For our example, let's say it happens through a dream. At that point there is a tension between the unconscious material (dream) and the conscious ego. Those are the two equal opposing forces.

> Once the unconscious content has been given form and the meaning of the formulation is understood, the question arises as to how the ego will relate to this position, and how the ego and the unconscious are to come to terms. This is the second and more important stage of the procedure, the bringing together of opposites for the production of a third: the transcendent function. At this stage it is no longer the unconscious that takes the lead, but the ego. (Jung. 1969, "*The Transcendent Function*", par. 181)

In this quote from Jung, "once the unconscious content has been given form and the meaning of the formulation is understood" means in our example that once the dreamer has dreamed the dream and worked to understand its meaning, then the issue is bringing together the conscious stance with the dream material, and the transcendent function emerges. "From the activity of the unconscious there now emerges a new content, constellated by thesis and antithesis in equal measure and standing in a compensatory relation to both. It thus forms the middle ground on which the opposites can be united" (Jung.1971, par. 825)

The first dream below occurred pretreatment and was brought into the first therapy session. It was a spiritual dream that involved a Christ encounter and that had a significant impact on the teenage girl who dreamed it.

ON THE WINGS OF CHRIST

I began seeing a young girl of fifteen, Kelly. She had been in therapy the year before with another therapist. She had seen this therapist over some months for depression. As often happens with teenagers, Kelly had not been ready at the time to use the sessions. Because of her minimal participation, she had gotten very little out of therapy. She had terminated with this therapist. During the summer before she came to see me, she'd had another, more serious bout with depression. This bout had brought her to her knees. She had not been able to get out of bed for months.

In the midst of her depression, she had a powerful dream. The dream had a big impact on her, helping her come to the decision to begin working in therapy. The dream and its subsequent impact are a perfect example of how the transcendent function works. The spiritual dream below led her conscious mind to open herself to taking action by getting back in therapy. She reported the dream to a new therapist, who did not know how to proceed with it.

> I'm at a relative's home with a girlfriend. All my relatives are there, as is a 17-year-old boy whom I've never met before. My family and my girlfriend go out. I am left alone at the house with the boy. I try talking with him, but at first he doesn't seem at all interested. I talk with him about my favorite band, and he starts getting more interested. He tells me about his favorite band.

> Then he says something unexpected to me that moves me deeply. I have no idea why he says this.

> (He speaks to me in the first person now, as if he were me.) He says to me, that when I (Kelly) was buried alive, Christ carried me out on his wings.

When Kelly reported this dream to me, it was clear she believed it to be very important. She expressed disappointment that the previous therapist, whom she had seen for only a few sessions, had not been able to help her with it and had apparently not resonated to its importance. She believed this therapist's style was more distant than what she needed. Teenagers strongly need a therapist who can be real with them and who can be very engaged and present in the therapy process. What works for adults often does not work for teenagers. Kelly had asked her mom to find her a therapist she felt she could connect with better.

I was moved by the dream. The tears in Kelly's eyes as she told it to me gave me an idea of how deeply she had been, and still was, moved. I asked her about the tears. She said she was remembering how excruciating the depression felt.

On a hunch, I asked her if the depression was anything like she imagined being buried alive would be. This clicked with her immediately, and she said yes, that was probably a very good way of describing how it felt to be depressed—she had been buried in her overwhelming thoughts and feelings. The dream now made more sense to her. I saw on her face that "aha" experience that often happens when a dream that was previously mystifying suddenly makes sense to the dreamer.

Kelly was puzzled how in the last part of the dream, when speaking of being buried alive and of being carried out by Christ, the young man had spoken as if he were she. The dream had shifted as if it were now her experience.

I explained to her that in dreams, a woman's inner self is often represented by a masculine figure (what Carl Jung called the animus). Might this young man represent her depression? Could this be why she blended with him at the end of the dream? Kelly thought this fit.

She was intrigued by the beauty of the phrase "Christ carried me out on his wings," a phrase she had never heard before. I asked her what she made of this. I asked her about prayer and her relationship with Christ. It seemed difficult for her, as a fifteen-year-old speaking with a virtual stranger, to articulate such things. She said, however, that when she had been at the worst of her depression, she'd prayed every day. She'd prayed for God to deliver her out of it.

Following her associations and dream material, I asked her if she felt there was a chance that Christ had, indeed, as the dream stated, carried her out on his wings. She smiled and said she believed this might indeed be the case. Kelly believed spiritual assistance had been given to her to lift her out of the depths of her despair and to give her hope. She saw this dream as the evidence of that which she could not touch on a tangible level. Although her depression was not yet healed, she had been given hope that it might be healed someday. This hope lifted her up to the point where she was willing to try again, with a different therapist, who turned out to be me.

Imagine the power of such a dream to a fifteen-year-old girl, who feels she has been touched and healed by a caring, loving Christ who valued her enough to respond to her pleas for help and to assist her! The magnitude of having a spiritual intervention in one's life leaves an impression not easily forgotten. Further, I believe that the act of my hearing this dream with her and being able to see it through her eyes further enhanced its value to Kelly, who now had an adult who could accept and validate her experience.

Kelly did not believe this dream relieved her of her responsibility to help herself; rather, it encouraged her. Even though Kelly did not fully understand the dream until we worked with it, she was nonetheless affected by it in a very powerful way. The dream, as she experienced its meaning, informed her divine help was given to lift her out of the depths of her depression and open her up to a more receptive state. As help came from a divine source (the transcendent function), she became more, rather than less, receptive to help.

It is significant that Kelly did not have to be fully conscious of the meaning of the dream in order for it to have an impact. As Sparrow states in *I Am with You Always*, "We can see that even children who receive such instruction seem to know how to interpret and apply Jesus' symbolic communications. It may be that this knowledge is imparted to the recipient during the experience itself" (Sparrow 1995, 174). By the time Kelly had a fuller conscious understanding of the dream, she was already engaged in the psychotherapeutic process.

The dream informed her she was not, and is not, alone: she is loved. As Sparrow states, based on his survey of Christ dreams, "In almost all of the cases, Jesus seems to manifest himself to communicate above all else the simple fact of his love for the person during a difficult time in his or her life" (191). He also points out how the encounter with Christ typically serves to point the way for the individual to work his or her way through an impasse, and to provide balance to a situation that is out of balance. This girl was moved by the dream to a new place of understanding, even without having the advantage of being able to, at the point when she dreamed it, fully understand the dream. She knew, however, that the dream was very beautiful and made a strong impression on her. It is a dream she will likely remember for the rest of her life

We cannot know what is conveyed emotionally or spiritually within the imagery a dream provides. We can only look at the results and the dreamer's reports and wonder about the inner power of the dream and what might have been conveyed that was not articulated or seen. Many people have had the experience of going to sleep mulling over a problem and waking up with the resolution to that problem, even without any awareness of having dreamed. Many dreamworkers attribute this to the power of the dreaming mind to work through the various aspects of the problem during the sleep state. An answer is given, without any memory of how the person arrived there. No conscious understanding of the process is needed, as the dreamer need only act on the result. Other times there is a dream that might provide some information to work with in the attempt to solve the problem.

THE CHRIST WITHIN

In Jungian psychology, the symbol of Christ is seen as a metaphor, or an archetype, for the larger, fuller self within us all. (The Self archetype could also be represented in dreams by other religious figures or symbols, depending on one's cultural and religious background.) It is that divine self within us, which we may occasionally access, that Jesus fully actualized while in human form two thousand years ago.

Jesus taught that through him and by trusting that the kingdom of heaven was within, all could share in his nature and his gifts. The following quotation from the Bible speaks to this issue, which can be understood both theologically and psychologically. Jesus begins by saying, "I am the true vine" (John 15:1).

Abide in me, and I in you. As the branch cannot bear fruit by itself, unless it abides in the vine, neither can you, unless you abide in me. I am the vine, you are the branches. He who abides in me, and I in him, he it is that bears much fruit, for apart from me you can do nothing. If a man does not abide in me, he is cast forth as a branch and withers; and the branches are gathered, thrown into the fire and burned. If you abide in me, and my words abide in you, ask whatever you will, and it shall be done for you. (John 15:4–7)

From a Christian perspective, these words are taken literally. From a Jungian perspective, cleaving to and abiding in Christ is analogous to following the promptings and dictates of the inner spirit. With prayer and meditation, we become attuned to the callings of our deeper self, apart from the ego-ridden drives and motivations that push and pull us in our everyday lives. With the assistance of prayer and reflection, we gain detachment from that which is small and base in ourselves and open ourselves to listen to spirit. We appeal to spirit by "abiding in the vine."

If we recall the dream of the girl severely abused by her parents who created the lovely but poisonous Easter eggs, the loving presence of Christ and the comforting words he spoke to her enabled her to "abide in him"—that is, to retreat into her deeper, higher self, where she met Jesus and received his love and wisdom. Kelly's dream informed her that Christ had delivered her from the depths of her depression. She saw her healing as a response to her prayers and believes Christ cares deeply about her and gave her help. She understood her dream as Christ literally healing her. Each individual will understand his or her dreams in his or her own way. It is very important to respect the understanding the dreamer has of his or her own dream. Attempts to psychologically analyze what the dreamer believes is essentially a spiritual experience are not helpful.

INITIAL DREAMS AND TREATMENT GUIDANCE

As I have repeatedly stated, the most effective and safest treatment is informed and guided by the client's inner self. This guidance may manifest as a dream that occurs at a critical juncture in treatment. Dreams often guide both client and therapist as to the direction treatment should take. Such dreams often give clues as to the underlying nature of the problem or impasse and can point the way for avenues of exploration. The initial dream a client brings into treatment often identifies the major issues or themes of the treatment and the major obstacles along the way.

Dreams may or may not manifest as overtly spiritual dreams but come as a form of guidance from the individual's higher self. Dreams frequently introduce multiple dimensions of the problem at hand, including the spiritual. The kinds of problems that bring clients into treatment, such as depression and addictions, are often part of an unconscious process of seeking healing of both the human heart and spirit. Different aspects of this unconscious search frequently emerge out of dreaming life.

Mike began treatment with me after being in therapy with several different therapists over a long number of years. He had a clear agenda of issues he wished to work on. He seemed pleased to have a forum to discuss his dreams. In our initial session, he recounted a recurrent dream he had dreamed many times, with minor variations, over a period of some years.

The recurrent nightmare would begin with a female who had drugs or sold drugs. It was unclear to him whether he had killed her or was afraid that he had, but the dream theme was that he was a fugitive, on the run, because of this horrible thing he had done.

When we discussed his associations to the dream, it became clear he had abused alcohol and drugs over a long period. In part, he was abusing these substances to numb out from the internal pain he carried after a childhood full of physical abuse and abandonment. The woman he'd killed or harmed in the dream was his own internal self, his anima, whom he had knocked out with alcohol, drugs, and pornography—all means of avoiding the self. When we explored the dream, it became clear that his recurrent dream pointed out that he was in reality a fugitive from his inner self. He was running from his feelings and his childhood experience because of his fear he could not possibly face—or heal—the pain. This recurrent dream, which had mystified Mike for many years, finally made sense to him.

The next weeks of our early therapeutic journey were very difficult, for a number of reasons. For a while, it seemed Mike would be terminating treatment. His alcohol abuse was a major factor standing in the way of his healing. We somehow got through this very difficult period, and he reported the following dream.

I am in a foreign country I do not recognize, perhaps Sudan. I am on some kind of journey. I make a stop in a small town, and go into a convenience store. At the back is a shop where they sell pornography.

Now I am with a female, who is accompanying me on the next leg of the journey. We travel for a while, and encounter a god and goddess along the way. We meet up with a man who joins us on our journey down a river. We reach a wall, and then travel by land, tracing back the route that the river traveled. At some point, my traveling companion has a large blue dragonfly above her head.

I visualize this as client and therapist being at 2 points on the base of a triangle, with the apex being Christ, the pure sacred healing power of God.

In his dream, Mike first stopped in a convenience store and then in a pornography shop. Mike's association to the convenience store was it being the place he goes to buy cigarettes and alcohol—that is, where he feeds his addictions and avoidance of the self. Pornography is a debasement, essentially stripping human beings of spirit and soul and reducing them to their purely material and sexual aspects. As a symbol in his dream, pornography represented a demeaning and devaluing of the feminine principle— that is, a demeaning and devaluing of the internal relationship Mike had with the feeling and nurturing aspect of himself.

After this initial part of the dream (therapeutic) journey, Mike encountered positive male and female divine figures who help him in his journey. One is a god, and one is a goddess. His positive relationship to these divine energies in this stage of the dream is in sharp contrast to his devalued relationship to himself and others via his addictions and pornographic obsession. The female with him is his anima guide, representing his inner self who, like Persephone, will show him the way through his unconscious mind.

In the psychology of individuation, the issue of the relationship between the inner male and female is important. Wholeness in both men and women calls for the recognition and honoring of both one's feminine and masculine sides. When men identify themselves with a one-sided masculine psychology, as is often the case in modern American culture, they can lose touch with their inner feminine aspects, which Jung called the anima. Jung said it is the anima that leads men to their souls. The anima makes contact with the unconscious and places a man in touch with energies that can help balance and round out his masculinity. (In women, the inner masculine is called the animus and is represented by males in dream. I personally believe, as is demonstrated in Mike's dream, that both men and women have both anima and animus figures, whether positive or negative.)

Mike felt very positively about this dream, feeling it signaled a transition in our work. He later said that I was the woman who accompanied him, representing, he felt, that I would accompany and assist him as his therapist and guide on this sacred journey. I noted that he was now actually on the journey, since in his dream he was no longer running, as in his previous fugitive dream series; rather, he was now consciously on his path.

This spiritual dream not only gave great encouragement about the therapeutic journey as a whole but also strongly validated the steps Mike was taking to move away from his self-destructive behavior patterns. The dream noted that client and therapist were working together for a common purpose, to attain this sacred goal. There was now a therapeutic alignment between us, even at the deepest levels of the unconscious. This dream was to remain strong in both our memories, providing hope and reassurance for both of us in the very tough times that followed.

My understanding of the therapeutic alignment between therapist and client is as one in which the two are working together in the service of the client's higher good. I visualize this as client and therapist being different points at the base of a triangle, with the apex being God, Christ, or whatever one wants to call the pure benevolent and safe power of the sacred. This visualization and invocation is the inner conceptualization that I use to guide and inform my work. Although there is an inherent power imbalance in the client-therapist relationship, I believe it is crucial that the work be balanced by surrender to the service of a higher good. The relationship between client and therapist is a sacred trust, and I actively (privately) ask God to allow me to be a vehicle through which the healing may occur. The therapeutic process is intrinsically a mystery journey on which both client and therapist are embarked together. Neither can possibly know where it will take them.

A Guidance Dream in Mid-phase Treatment

Many of the dream examples I use in this manuscript are from the middle phase of therapy, the stage where a closer look is given to historical material, to understanding any trauma and unconscious determinants of present behavior and emotions. This is the stage where the client is making significant connections with his or her inner self, through memories, flashbacks, dreams, feelings, and so on. During this time, a more meaningful spiritual understanding may develop out of the enlarged view of consciousness that comes through allowing unconscious material to emerge, honoring it by looking at it, and learning to trust the deeper self.

The dream example I share now occurred at a critical point in treatment and helped both the dreamer and me recognize what course the treatment needed to take. This dream was not what would typically be considered a spiritual dream but nonetheless appeared to have come from a detached-observer place in the dreamer's psyche, where her reality was witnessed from a different perspective than her waking ego. Jung called this witnessing point the transcendent function, for it gives us an accurate and objective view of the situational dynamics. The dream gave us a big picture view of what clearly needed to be seen and addressed.

Nina was a very bright, articulate woman in her late twenties. She had a very complicated history and had worked hard to stabilize her life and moods. One day she told me that since the problem areas in her life had now calmed down, she was ready to quit therapy or at least to begin talking about termination. She had stabilized, the work of the initial phase of psychotherapy, but had not done significant depth work on the traumas that caused the symptoms she manifested. With a complicated background like Nina's, general psychotherapeutic theory would support that healing is not complete without resolving major traumas; unresolved symptoms are likely to break out again destructively in stressful times.

Different people, however, have different therapy goals. Some want mainly symptom resolution, and some want or need to resolve the underlying issues. Some may want to stop for a while and come back later to do another piece of the work. It is important that the therapist respects the client's decision, even when there is disagreement.

I supported Nina's desire to look at termination, and we had an initial discussion of the pros and cons. I added that though I would support her decision, now that she had stabilized, it might be the perfect time to go inside and work on some of the issues that had created the crises.

Nina reflected on this. She expressed concern about not knowing how to go inside, and additionally she was afraid of what might lie there, buried under layers of protective defenses. I empathized with her fears and shared with her that many others experience the same trepidation when it comes to looking within. At this point, I brought up dreams in general and an earlier dream in particular that had helped both of us understand unconscious dynamics motivating her puzzling behaviors. I reiterated how dreams could help to provide the way in.

At this point, she suddenly recalled a dream from the night before. I often call these dreams that occur the night before a therapy session "therapy dreams." They often contain very informative material important for the session that follows the next day. In her dream, Nina was in my office when she began experiencing back pain.

I took aspirin before the therapy session began. I was certain I would need more pain-killing power to get through my work shift, which began right after the session. In the session, I say I can call a friend to bring me some extra strength Tylenol.

To my surprise, Carol told me to go ahead and call him. I did, right there in the middle of the dream therapy session. My friend's wife answered the phone. There were some very awkward moments before and after he came to the phone.

As I talked with him, knowing Carol was watching and listening to me, I realized, within the dream, how inappropriate it was for me to be relating with him in this manner.

As we worked with this dream, Nina had a number of associations to the dream material. She was married and had a history of acting out while in a committed relationship. She'd had an affair while dating her husband-to-be. The affair had been long over by the time her then-husband had found out about it. Nonetheless, when the affair had come out into the open, it had almost destroyed her young marriage. It had taken a long time to work through the pain and upset feelings it had caused. Sometimes it had seemed they would never heal sufficiently to allow them to be truly present and loving with each other without constant painful intrusions of hurt from their past.

Now, in the present, the dream helped Nina to see she was still acting out in a sexualized manner with her male friend. Even though there was no sexual contact between them, there was a sexualized element in her interactions with him that repeated her earlier pattern. As Nina talked about the dream, she remembered a dream we had discussed a number of months before that had focused on her unconscious pattern of diverting the anger she felt in her intimate relationships. The dream had shown her how, instead of dealing with the anger in the relationship directly, she suppressed it. The anger was then unconsciously channeled into sexualized relationships outside of the marriage. This dream (details lost) had provided a talking point for several therapy discussions because it had zeroed in so aptly on her unconscious pattern.

Now, this newer dream helped Nina to realize that, although she was not having a sexual relationship with her male friend, she had managed to achieve the recent calm in her marriage by diverting her anger toward her husband, in a sexualized manner, into this relationship with her friend. Nina associated the back pain in the dream, for which she felt she needed more than the normal dose of medicine, to the anger she felt toward her husband. This anger often seemed so powerful to her that she had no idea how to manage it or if it could be managed within the marriage. The medication she asked her friend to bring was a metaphor for her asking him to collude with her in the inappropriately sexualized relationship between them in waking life. It was a temporary but inappropriate salve for her marital pain.

As she worked with the dream, Nina could see she was unconsciously using her friend to meet needs not met in her marriage. As she realized what she was doing and why, she knew two things: (1) she did not wish to use him in this manner, and (2) she had to deal with the real issue. By the time she had finished processing the dream, it was clear to Nina the dream was a strong message that some important work needed to be done before termination of therapy.

Strictly speaking, this was not a spiritual dream in the sense in which we are accustomed to thinking of such dreams. It is, however, an example of the emergent transcendent function showing Nina new information, in the middle ground between her unconscious desires to act out and her ego, which wanted to help heal her marriage. It was an urgent message from her higher self for us both. Its impact was strong and immediate.

There is another noteworthy aspect to this dream. Dreams involving the therapist are usually significant; this one is no exception. The insight that took place within the dream occurred because the therapeutic relationship between client and therapist was one of trust and safety. My dream role was of being a caring, non-judgmental witness to her drama as it played out. She recognized her inner truth within the dream as I sat with her. In this accepting atmosphere, Nina could make her own explorations and come to her own conclusions. I as therapist/witness represented not only myself as the person outside of her who was engaged with her on this healing journey and also the inner therapist/healer/transcendent part of herself. This part of herself could not only observe and make sense of her behavior but also could provide her with the unconditional acceptance and love she needed to be able to tolerate the discomfort of looking at this dark and disowned part of herself.

Dreams in which the therapist plays a part, whether positive or negative, often speak to the core of the healing matter. The appearance of the therapist in the dream can represent the actual person of the therapist and/

or the inner therapist/healer of the client. In this case, I believe my appearance in the dream represented both myself and the inner therapist of the client, the internalized "Carol."

A client's associations to the dream will often help in sorting through the dream material. It can be important, where appropriate, to underscore to the client that the therapist in the dream is also an internalized part of him or her. This helps the client to recognize the wisdom source within him or her, which will always be with the client, long after the client-therapist relationship in the outer world is completed.

In this dream, the therapist's office symbolized the healing field, that psychological and spiritual space in which healing can take place. Within that healing field is an unconditional acceptance, where one's deepest and darkest self can be accepted, forgiven, and then transformed. Dr. David Allen, in the lecture "The Role of Narcissistic Injury in the Development of Depression," given in Washington DC in 1995, spoke of the true hurt in child development as being the loss of unconditional love. When we leave the embracing, soothing environment of the womb, we are from that point on subject to the various hurts and wounds that life inflicts on us all. As Dr. Allen stated, "the resolution of this hurt is through unconditional love."

This dream gave Nina, in a dramatic and compelling way, an example of the wisdom of her own inner guidance. It helped her to look at dark aspects of herself while standing in the healing field of the light of her own soul. This dream showed her that inner work, though frightening, would occur at a pace she could tolerate. The dream challenged her but not too much, providing help at the perfect therapeutic window.

To recap, Kelly's dream appeared pretreatment and indicated a spiritual healing. The dream helped motivate her to obtain appropriate treatment. Mike's Africa dream occurred at the beginning of treatment and provided us with a road map of the therapeutic journey to come. We referred back to this dream during several extremely difficult spots over the years. It gave us a positive vision of a therapeutic alliance that continued to move forward. Each time it was helpful in giving hope and strength to sustain the arduous emotional and spiritual journey. Nina's dream occurred in the mid-stage of treatment, when she was prematurely considering terminating treatment. The dream took her a few steps further into her unconscious, where she could look at and work with some of the deeper issues underlying her behaviors.

LATE-STAGE SPIRITUAL DREAMS

The next dream occurred when Ann was near the end of her therapy. Ann had been severely depressed eight years before, to the point of being bedridden and unable to function in her daily life. She had grown up in an extremely dysfunctional alcoholic family, where there had been considerable physical brutality at times. The very sad feelings she had from the many losses, abandonments, and betrayals she had experienced as a youth, came crashing down on her after the birth of her first child in the form of a severe postpartum depression. She did not believe treatment could help her, but her distraught husband helped her to come in. It is the complete loss of hope in severe depression that is most disabling: one is certain that hope will never be restored and that life will never again be good.

Ann felt depressed and hopeless for a long time, but she worked hard, took antidepressant medication, and gradually progressed. She began to feel better than ever before. She applied to and got into medical school, a huge accomplishment. In her final year of medical school, though she was having a difficult time managing the many aspects of her life, she now had hope for herself and for her family's future.

However, there were some very significant stresses on her, and she relapsed back into depression. Relapse is a risk for long-term depressed clients who are recovering from depression but who are under severe sustained stress. Ann wisely sought to prevent relapse into deep depression and get extra support to help get her through this tough period. During this period, she brought the following dream into her session:

> I'm at medical school, in one of the buildings. I look down at my hands, and see that I have stigmata on them. They are bleeding significantly. People around me see the blood, and ask me what I want them to do. I tell them to call one of the Jesuit priests at Georgetown University. I think maybe a Jesuit will know what to do.

> I look out onto the street, and see a man who is bent over and crippled with arthritis hobbling down the street. Somehow, I know that I can heal him of his affliction. I know inside myself that in order to do this, I have to take on his disability. I also know somehow that as frightening as it might be to take on this disability, that Christ will heal me.

Ann had rarely discussed dreams in our therapy sessions, but she was impressed by this one and brought it up. Her associations to the stigmata were to the wounded Christ, who had carried so much sorrow and pain in his experience on earth. She related some of her waking-life experiences when she felt sad and overwhelmed both for herself and for some of the extremely disabled children with whom she was currently working. She had visited a hospital the day before the dream and talked with a doctor about a child who had been healthy and normal but who had suffered severe brain damage after a vaccination. The child had become a complete vegetable as a result and had been this way for some time. The hope for recovery for the child was nil. Ann's initial feeling about the dream was that it related to her tendency to empathize strongly with those she saw who were in pain, and she felt this crippled man somehow related to the child she had seen.

As we delved a little bit further into the dream, I questioned Ann about the spiritual aspects. Ann was not Catholic, which made her dream reference to the Jesuits somewhat mystifying to her. She said she prayed regularly, especially now that she was dealing with children disabled by vaccines whose personal tragedies saddened her. As we talked, it became clear she had recently been feeling the need for a spiritual connection, and she said she had been considering going to church. She wanted to make it a family venture, believing this kind of spiritual undertaking could be very healing and offer support for her family unit.

I asked her what aspect of her was like the crippled man in the dream. (Gestalt therapy started this technique of looking at every aspect of a dream as a part of oneself, and many dreamworking styles have incorporated this technique. It can be very powerful in looking at disowned parts of oneself.)

Ann looked surprised by the question, thought about it for a while, and then looked at me and said, "That's a really good question. I wouldn't have looked at it that way. I had seen him as something external to me. But now that I think about it, he could be the part of me who feels so handicapped by my sadness, depression, and personal problems."

From here, the conversation progressed into a discussion about the need to fully own the disabled side of her, rather than to try to keep it at a distance out of fear she would regress into deep depression. The dream reassured her that, in taking on the man's pain, there was healing through Christ. She understood it as healing that would come through the stronger relationship with Christ she was yearning to make in her life. This dream indicated a problem that required help from a higher source. The dream not only pointed out the need for help but also pointed out the way to find it. As therapist, my role was to serve as a guide and support for my client and to encourage her movement in the direction of the dream.

It was important that she recognized, as she did in the dream, that she, in her identity as female, mother, wife, and medical school student, was separate from those parts that had been identified with the "crippled" self.

In the dream, this separation between the healthy functioning self and the disabled self was clearly demarcated, as seen in the contrast between the dreamer as medical student who was experiencing her divine nature through the stigmata and the part of the dreamer who was like the man who could barely walk down the street because of the crippling effects of his disease.

Depressed people commonly identify with the pain they feel and which they have known for so long. Separation of the healthy part of the self from the depressed part does not feel possible. "I am my pain" and "I have no self apart from my pain" is how it feels. When the depression occurs or recurs, it seems that it is one's fundamental self. Change, and getting better, may be feared because in the unconscious lies the belief "If I let go of my pain, then I will also lose my identity." Therefore, in the irrational world of the unconscious, depressed people often hold on to that which they know to be true, their tortuous pain.

This dream explicitly pointed out to Anne the separation between these two parts of herself while also telling her she is not her affliction. Yet, paradoxically, the dream seemed to say Anne must also fully accept and take on her affliction in order to heal, something that would take a great deal of courage. The dream told her she would be able to do so after seeing her essentially divine nature and by knowing the divine Christ within would restore and heal her. She became hungry for a divine connection, and sh eand her family began going to church.

Ann had spent several years in her depression, in the underworld of the psyche, experiencing the pain of the many losses, abandonments, and betrayals she had experienced in her early childhood. She'd spent many hours and oceans of tears grieving these losses and mourning for that which she had never had but had needed so desperately as a child. She had come out of her depression while in medical school and was mystified by its reappearance.

Dr. David Allen, in the workshop *"Loss, Grief and Depression"* held in Washington, DC, on November 4, 1995, described the depression recovery process as a descent into the underworld of the psyche to face our losses and to grieve them. This is the essence of Persephone's journey. Dr. Allen spoke of the heart, where both hurt and love are stored. He further described the recovery process by saying that, as we unleash our losses from the deep recesses of the psyche where they are bound and grieve them, we are led to love. He stated repeatedly, and I believe this to be true, that since hurt and this love are tied together in the human heart, "one can love only as deeply as one can grieve." He quoted John Bradshaw, who said that "grieving is the healing field."

We see this principle of grieving leading to love in Ann's dream. She had done much grieving work already. She emerged out of this grief with a deep and profound sense of love and compassion for others. Her powerful empathy and compassion for disabled children can occur because in her grief work she learned to be compassionate toward herself. If "grieving is the healing field," then it was in fully taking on the afflictions of her own wounded inner male self, or animus, that led her into her own further healing. This dream, and the associations she had to it, bore witness to the considerable work she had done and to the task still ahead of her. Her heart was transformed by the depression. In learning to love the wounded and abandoned part of herself, she was learning to love.

CHAPTER 22

RETURN TO THE SELF: THE COURAGE TO LOOK WITHIN

"The Self is the slow, gradual realization of a divine cosmic center in the unconscious psyche of the individual. "

—William Walker, DMin, "The Nuts and Bolts of Jungian Psychology and Spirituality," *explorefaith.org*

In this chapter, I will take a more in-depth look at splitting off from God (or the higher self) as it occurs in trauma survivors and at the importance of addressing this split for the healing process.

Though the examples are of trauma victims, I believe that being cut off from one's inner experience of God and one's higher self applies to some degree or another to all of us who live in this externally focused, materialistic culture and who experience the many woundings life has to offer. I also explore the idea that our conceptualization and experience of the divine parallels the stage of our emotional and cultural development.

For example, in our materialistic, patriarchal culture, God is seen as external to us and is male. Our inner knowing and spiritual experience are devalued, for we are told we need priests or ministers to access God or to be forgiven by God. To the extent that we internalize this belief system, whether consciously or unconsciously, we are cut off from the possibility of direct, non-mediated spiritual experience.

The stories of the people in this chapter demonstrate how, as they turned inward in their healing process, they spontaneously experienced healing aspects of the divine, which nurtured them and helped them move forward. Their healing challenges all of us to move into our inner spiritual experiences and into a more balanced understanding of the masculine and feminine energies.

RAGE AND CUTOFF FROM GOD IN ABUSE VICTIMS

In the psyche, the inner connection to one's feelings and even memories is not the only casualty of trauma. The abused child, at some level, often feels that God has forsaken him or her, having abandoned him or her completely. Common reactions include anger and rage at God for not having protected him or her, for having abandoned him or her and caused such pain. Anger and rage at God are often relegated to the unconscious, for a conscious stance of anger at God often is too frightening to the child's (or, for that matter, the adult's) mind.

Charlene went to parochial school. She remembered vividly the nuns often told her God protects good children. How then, when she was sexually abused as a child, was she to understand herself and to understand God? The conclusion she came to was that she must be a "bad" child, for otherwise God would have protected her.

In my first few years of working with Charlene, the issue of a rejecting God came up in therapy through her dreams. We worked with her dreams and with her strong suspicions she had been sexually abused as a child. She had massive amnesia for childhood and had many of the symptoms common to an abuse history. She recognized through her associations to her dreams that she carried deeply within her a fear that if she were to remember that she had been sexually abused as a child, God would now abandon her for having been so "bad." On an unconscious level, her amnesia served to shield her against her fear of God's critical and judgmental stance. We looked closely at this fear, for her dreams presented this as one of the psychological obstacles that was keeping her from remembering her past.

On a conscious level, Charlene had rejected God, believing that if God truly existed, he would not have allowed the bad things she did remember to happen to her. Yet it became clear that, on another level in the unconscious, Charlotte still believed in God and needed a spiritual connection. She was unconsciously terrified to look inside, because if she found she had been abused, as she strongly suspected, she feared she would be exiled from God. (This fear of rejection and abandonment if she found out she had been abused was a projection of her self-rejection. She was fearful her husband and family could not accept her if she had been abused. These related issues also had to be worked through.)

Charlene recounted that, as a child, she had two separate reactions to the spiritual teachings she received from the nuns at school, in the light of what was going on at home. One, mentioned above, was that she accepted the teachings about God protecting good children literally: her reaction was that since he did not protect her from the abuse, she must be bad. A further reaction in this line of thinking was that God might have punished her for her "badness" by allowing these awful things to happen to her.

The other reaction, which stands separate and is often associated with abuse, was that she felt that since God did not protect her, there must not be a God. Her conscious faith in a benevolent divine being was lost, along with her ability to trust that the adults in her environment who were supposed to protect her would do so. At the same time, since God did not protect her and so she must be bad, she lost faith in herself.

To sum up these common unconscious reactions to abuse: (1) The sexually abused child internalizes that he or she must be bad, because this abuse would not be happening if he or she were good enough. (2) In addition, just as the abused child suppresses and splits off much or all the rage he or she feels toward the abuser, because it would be dangerous to express it, the child splits off and suppresses his or her rage at God for allowing it. This spiritual issue can be a very important and a very critical issue in recovery, in the healing of the whole self, but it is often ignored. How does one express rage at God when there is fear of retaliation by this apparently unjust God? (3) The abused loses faith in self, in others, and in the divine.

Each person has his or her own conception of God or the divine, which may change over time. For a child in our Western culture who has been taught that God can and does intercede in one's life, it does not make sense that God would allow unspeakable abuse to occur. Adults with fully developed cognitive and emotional capacities have trouble enough understanding how such horrendous actions can happen. Many survivors of the Holocaust felt utterly abandoned by God in their hour of greatest need. How, then, does a child who is sexually abused come to terms with the idea of a God who is supposedly loving, benevolent, and just but who seems apathetic and unconcerned in the face of the most cruel occurrences? The solution for many is, consciously or unconsciously, to reject this God or to experience rage at his indifference and cruelty.

In chapter 7, I wrote of Michelle, who lost her adored father in her early teens and whose life then turned upside down. Not only did she lose her father, but also her mother was emotionally unavailable from that point on, perhaps depressed. Michelle was expected to fend for herself and to help take care of the younger son. From that point onward, she colluded with this caretaking role, realistically seeing it as the only way she was going to gain positive attention in her family.

When she first presented to me, she was emotionally exhausted. She had focused on caring for others and had denied her own needs and her own feelings for so many years that she no longer knew what she felt or what her needs were. At some point well into therapy, she expressed rage at God for having abandoned her. She told me how she had cut herself off completely from any faith at that early age. If God could do this to her and allow this tremendous pain and suffering to come up in her life, then she would absolutely not have anything to do with him and wanted no part of a spiritual life.

This was the first time I had seen her anger and rage. She blamed God for her pain and for her father's death. Here, in the realm of her spiritual beliefs, the full intensity of her affect, especially her rage, was first accessed. We could truly see the complex intertwining of the emotional and spiritual developmental lines. In her rage at God, she raged at her deepest self. The self-hatred is internalized in a parallel line to the rage at God, for it is internalized as "I must be bad; something must be horribly wrong with me that this would happen to me."

To phrase it another way, the same cognitive distortions that occur in the developing child's conception of self with his or her experience of trauma or abuse also occur in the child's conception of, and relationship with the divine. These distortions must be addressed and explored in the therapeutic context in order for the fullest healing to occur. This truth is most strongly evident in victims of ritual abuse for the savage disruption of access to the self and to God.

If one accepts that we are souls who have taken on flesh and who are here on earth to fulfill some purpose, no matter how great or small, then it is a corollary to this belief that our psychological well-being cannot be separated from our spiritual well-being and the search for meaning. Unfortunately, in much of modern psychology, this is how the client is approached.

THE PROBLEM WITH THE EXTERNALIZATION OF GOD

The idea of God as a remote masculine being in the sky who carries ultimate authority and power has spent itself for many of us. Many people today are looking for a meaningful and more relevant understanding of the divine and spiritual, a God with whom they can be in relationship. This externalized conception of God parallels our projections of power in the outer world, in which we collectively, over thousands of years, have accepted and sustained the patriarchal system.

In the patriarchal religious system, men have traditionally carried the power and authority. Women's roles have been seen as subordinate and lesser. In this kind of religious system, the external voice of authority and rules becomes the measure by which we evaluate ourselves. We learn to depend on priests and ministers to tell us what is right for us rather than learning to tune in to our own conscience and the voice of the godhead within. The inner voice, the feminine receptive tuning inward into the world of feelings, dreams and spirit, is devalued and subjugated to the outer male principle of obedience to authority. Both male and female lose immensely in this system, for we lose our connection with the ever-flowing river of life that streams within us that would take us to our true spiritual home in God.

In ritual abuse, this loss of connection is deliberately cultivated, for the rituals and deliberate programming of multiple personalities are specifically designed to keep the victim from ever finding their true self or a relationship with a benevolent God. The brutal, sadistic ways the victim is split off from God in mind control programming could take a book to write. For further information on this topic, I again refer the reader to Alison Miller's two volumes, *Healing the Unimaginable* (written for therapists) and *Becoming Yourself* (written for RA mind control victims).

The massacre that was the Holocaust was an ultimate expression we have seen thus far of the depraved extreme to which humanity can go when the patriarchal and authoritarian system is taken to is outermost limits, unbalanced by the receptive, nurturing spirit, heart, and wisdom of the feminine. All emphasis in the Third Reich was on blind obedience to the external authoritarian, patriarchal voice. There was no evaluation of, or compassion for, a human being by looking within to a person's heart or soul. All measurement and judgment were done based on rigidly defined external values. Complete obedience to the value system of the power elite was not only expected but also demanded. The suffering and murder of millions was justified and demanded by the particular autocratic dictates of an evil man and his henchmen, heartless and cruel beyond belief. Absolute power corrupts absolutely.

The role of women within this system was strictly confined to service of the male and to the reproduction and rearing of children. Independence of thought and action was not tolerated. The act of listening to the inner voice of conscience and heart within each human being (the receptive feminine stance) was threatening to the totalitarian regime. A terroristic state developed in which individuals became afraid to voice their thoughts, to feel their feelings, and even to dream their dreams.

A very informative older book, *The Third Reich of Dreams* by Charlotte Beradt, assesses over three hundred dreams from people living in Germany during this period. These dreams, compiled in secrecy by Beradt, point out the terrorist quality of everyday life in this regime, in which even personal thoughts and feelings that were contrary to the accepted doctrine felt absolutely forbidden. The dreams reflected a great deal of anxiety that authorities would know one's innermost thoughts and feelings. (Does not our current surveillance state and the ardent prosecution of whistleblowers produce the same effect?)

Many simple everyday objects in these dreams would somehow become alive and traitorous and would report the dreamer's forbidden thoughts to the Nazis. As one man reported, "It was forbidden to dream" (Beradt 1966, 52). This despotic regime tried to control feminine receptive consciousness, insofar as it denied the expression of turning inward and expressing true thoughts and feelings about the horrendous world around these people. Satanic mind control programming, which came out of this system, does the same, with horrific consequences programmed in for remembering and for telling.

The Taliban and its repressive regime in Afghanistan is a recent example of the regressive pull to patriarchal consciousness in its extreme form. Similarly, al-Qaeda and Isis are also examples of the regressive domination of the male principle, lacking balance with the feminine principle. It can also be said that our increasingly totalitarian state, in which even our TVs, phones, and other appliances spy on us, is stripped of the feminine principle.

TURNING BACK INSIDE FOR BALANCE

At the conclusion of World War II in 1945, the world had faced its most gruesome disaster in all of history. The dynamics that supported it paralleled those that much of patriarchal culture and organized religion had been developing for thousands of years. With nuclear weaponry and the real possibility of the annihilation of the human race came the dawning of the realization there has to be another way. Collectively, we share the realization we have moved into a new time in history. We now have the potential to obliterate our world. It seems as if we are on the brink of destruction.

We share the collective responsibility for allowing the development of the values that have brought us to this edge of destruction: We need to find a way out of this dilemma, or we will not survive. This dilemma has ushered in the dawning of a time when the old, externalized religious stance has begun to lose its powerful sway.

People have now begun en masse to turn inside to meet God, connecting with spirit or the kingdom of heaven within, through the receptivity of the feminine principle. Unfortunately, there is more spiritual deception and occultism in the New Age movement being promulgated than ever. Many are caught up in it, not aware of the grand scale of the deception. There has been a return to God as the many deceptions of the plandemic and the gross corruption surrounding it come to light, and as our freedoms were increasingly curtailed.

Interestingly enough, there was a huge proliferation of occult and new age–style writings in Germany after World War I, unparalleled except by the proliferation of occult and new age writings in the United States beginning in the 1960s. In Germany, those writings helped set the stage for the massive occult influence in the Third Reich, in the SS, in the training of Hitler's youth and troops, and in the Lebensborn program. I talked in an earlier chapter about the occult in Hitler's Germany and how it was brought over to our country and countries all over the world through the Nazis' underground satanic practices and mind control programs.

Renowned modern writer and speaker Andrew Harvey has written a powerful book on the subject of the need for humanity to return to the understanding and cultivation of the feminine in our daily lives. He speaks passionately and eloquently about the need to integrate the feminine into our deeply masculinized and patriarchal culture and attitudes. He also speaks of how all organized religions have failed us by emphasizing what is outside of us rather than what we find within our own hearts.

> The tragic imbalance of the masculine has brought humankind to the point of disaster, and unless we recover the feminine powers of the psyche, the powers of intuition, patience, reverence for nature, and knowledge of the holy unity of things, and marry in our depths these powers with the masculine energies of rule, reason, passion for order and control, life on the planet will end. This sacred marriage of the masculine with the feminine has to take place in all our hearts and minds, whether we are male or female. (Harvey 1995, 17–18)

Harvey speaks of the stages of history and how we have gotten to our present position. As discussed earlier in this book, the patriarchal stage began in ancient Greece, with the rejection of the old goddess archetypes. I discussed this rejection and its implications at some length in the chapter on Persephone.

> This stage saw a crucial and terrible thing: the dismemberment, division, and destruction of the feminine, in the human psyche and in the growth of an almost universal oppression of women … Humankind left the womb of the Mother and developed extraordinary powers of manipulation and domination of nature.

> But there was illness at the root of the enterprise, there was madness at its root. It depended for its energy on the denial of our fundamental connectedness to each other and to the world, and took on an increasingly schizophrenic rejection of all of those values of nurturing, intuition, unity, tenderness, and bliss associated with the abandoned Mother. Nature, soul, matter, the body and its instincts, and the imagination were all in the process devalued and desacralized. This led inextricably to the creation of the worldwide psychic Auschwitz we now inhabit, in which nature herself and everything natural in us is in danger of being tortured to death.

> We are now, I believe, on the threshold of a third stage which I call the stage of the sacred marriage. This is the only position we could possibly take and still survive. This is a stage beyond

both matriarchy and patriarchy. It involves the restoration to human respect of all of the rejected powers of the feminine. (Harvey 1995, 221–22)

If we accept that our true natures, our souls, are ultimately divine, it follows that we can connect with our divine natures in the deeper layers of our psyches through our inner lives, through dreams and prayer, through meditation and inner work, and through our creativity. As we connect in a personal and intimate manner with the divine through our inner work, we can each come to our own individualized understanding of and personal relationship with God. This God within is the immanent God of which Jesus spoke when he said, "The kingdom of heaven is within."

Two thousand years later, we are now finally beginning to come to this realization in a more collective manner. Perhaps the tragic lessons of both our personal and our collective histories are contributing to the increasing number of people who recognize we risk all in turning to outside authorities for our spiritual truths. However, there is more spiritual deception afoot now than ever: churches water down their messages, witchcraft is publicly promoted, and many turn to the theosophists and other occult influences (Helena Blavatsky's *The Secret Doctrine* was key) that brought the worship of Lucifer to Germany and, from there, to much of the world, through the underground rituals held everywhere.

Is it a coincidence that the Holocaust and the ongoing Middle East crises are ostensibly "religious" wars? Is the crisis in the Catholic Church, with its pedophiles and cover-ups, an unfortunate accident, an inevitable result of a system that depends on obedience and trust in an external male authority, or is it perhaps the result of the infiltration of darker forces into the Vatican?

Both our psychological and spiritual health are dependent on our learning to tune into and recognize the ability of the higher self /Holy Spirit to guide us through our inner voice. As I have discussed, development of normal trust is arrested for abuse survivors. They develop suspicion and fear toward others, for others have been the perpetrators of such great pain. In much of our Western culture, we tend to view God as a male authority, outside of oneself, who gives or takes according to some unknowable plan. The abuser in childhood sexual abuse is frequently male (though I believe that the instances of sexual abuse by females are greatly underreported and unrecognized). In those cases where the abuser is male, the spiritual relationship of the child with our Western notion of God as patriarch is in double jeopardy. In addition to the father or uncle or priest having betrayed and emotionally abandoned the child, the damage is replicated and further realized by the perceived rejection and abandonment by God the father. In either case, whether the abuser is male or female, the feeling is that God has abandoned the victim, for why would he allow such horrible things to happen?

As I have mentioned, the internal feeling experience of the abuse victim becomes cut off to a greater or lesser degree. The feelings of pain, horror, and rage are dissociated or buried in an adaptive attempt to survive. This leaves the victim in a double bind of the worst nature; those in the outside world cannot be trusted, because they have repeatedly betrayed the victim, and the inner life cannot be trusted because the feelings and experiences that have been split off are so huge and threaten to overwhelm.

I have also discussed how this cutoff from inner experience is true to some extent for all of us, who, having grown up in this culture, are trained to focus on the outer world and what it has to offer. We all struggle with the same dilemma; it is just a matter of degree. Men, particularly, are acculturated to shut off from their inner life, such that, unless they have an unusually good, balanced upbringing, by the time they are six to eight years old, they are emotionally shut down (Kindlon and Thompson 2000).

I have described how terrifying one's inner life can feel for the abuse victim, for it is full of terrifying experiences, memories, and feelings. Many of my abused clients report to me that before they began to come to terms with their abuse, they kept themselves endlessly and obsessively busy, never allowing themselves a quiet moment alone. Those moments alone were full of fear of the threat of that which they did not wish to know.

If one's emotional life is too terrifying and the inner recesses of the psyche seem to promise only pain, then why would anyone want to take the time and energy needed to find the possibility of a rich spiritual life? How many of us who consider ourselves "normal" are able to be comfortable with solitude and with quiet? We too are almost instinctively afraid of what we might see. We hurry to fill ourselves with something or someone to distract us from ourselves. When connection with inner feelings are made, through the therapeutic process or otherwise, the possibility is opened for a rich spiritual life.

At one of the early International Association for the Study of Dreams (IASD) conferences, held at Marymount, Virginia, a therapist named Patricia Reis and her client Susan Snow (who happened to be an artist) jointly gave a talk. The two detailed the course of the therapy, in which Susan recalled a number of incidents of molestation by her father. Dreamwork was an extremely important component of this work. Often the abuse memories were presented in a dream. The remembering and piecing together of dissociated incidents happened very gradually and with the agonizing pain characteristic of working through profound trauma.

Susan and Patricia found a repeated pattern in the work. Susan had a number of eloquent and beautifully moving spiritual dreams in the course of her work. Often in these dreams a circle of women, whom she trusted completely, surrounded her. The women and their protective, nurturing stance toward her conveyed to her a feeling of great solace and spiritual strength. These dreams would sustain her for a long period thereafter. Often she drew or painted these dreams as a means of honoring and further learning from them.

Susan found that one of these dreams would always come before another wave of remembering abuse, with all of its agony. It was as if they came to give her strength and solace for the time to come, when she went through the next stage of remembering and working through the abuse. She drew the dreams that indirectly or directly were associated with the molestations she had endured. She showed many of these drawings and paintings to the audience. I remember being extremely moved by this talk and by Susan's description of her process. Patricia sensitively and appropriately helped Susan to work with and honor her dreams. In doing so, Patricia helped Susan to reconnect, at a much-deeper level, with the various parts of her psyche. In the darkness, in the unconscious, lay both immense pain and spiritual joy, which gave her great strength upon being brought into consciousness. The material was later made into a moving book, *The Dreaming Way: Dreamwork and Art for Remembering and Recovery* (2000). I saw the pair of them again at a later IASD conference and was once more impressed by the solid work they had done together.

It is not that victims of abuse cannot or do not have a spiritual life until they have worked through their abuse issues in treatment. However, the full richness of the inner life can become extremely split off because of abuse, trauma, or other familial, interpersonal, or cultural dysfunction. Spiritual issues naturally come up in treatment when a client is in recovery. A skillful handling of these issues can help clients negotiate critical turning points in their recovery. Further, therapists can help their clients to make links between their abuse-and-trauma issues and their wounded spirituality.

WHEN ABUSE AND SPIRITUALITY ISSUES COLLIDE

Hope had been sexually and physically abused over a period of many years. She came to see me the day after a major holiday. She was upset and wanted help in sorting out something that had happened the day before. She had invited several family members to her home for a holiday meal. She had also invited a man whom she'd met through a friend, because he had nowhere to spend the day and she wanted to do the right thing. She had planned on an early-afternoon meal. He called in the morning when she was out and said he would be there at five, long past the appointed mealtime. He left no reason on the message nor an acknowledgment this might not be okay with the hostess. She tried to accommodate him and asked her guests if they could eat later, but they had other plans, so she kept the time the same.

One of her friends told Hope she thought this man was not being respectful. Then there were some phone calls back and forth between the man and Hope. Something did not feel right to Hope. The man could not seem to make it until later, but his reasons were flimsy. If he came at his proposed time, Hope's other guests would be leaving shortly after he arrived. Hope felt uncomfortable with the idea of being alone with him and canceled his invitation.

She was upset about it and was worried she had done the wrong thing. I asked her to elaborate, and she said she had wanted to do the "Christian" thing, the "right" thing. She felt she had been selfish. After all, it was a major holiday, and she believed she should help those less fortunate. She felt that Christ might disapprove of her actions. She was genuinely in torment over this conflict. I knew it was important to address it fully, from all sides, as Hope's spiritual life is very important to her. I thought we needed to look at her feelings both about her religion (which I knew that she experienced as external to herself) and about this man in order to get to the heart of this issue.

It may be difficult for someone who has not been abused and tortured over many years, with the brainwashing that goes along with it, to understand and be patient with Hope's dilemma. However, this kind of dilemma is indicative of the arrest in emotional development that can occur with prolonged abuse and needs to be treated sensitively and thoroughly. Abuse victims often have a very difficult time believing they have a right to be safe.

When I asked Hope about her image of Christ, she said that she wished she had some internal image or feeling of him but that all she had was a picture in her bedroom. She had nothing inside her that referenced to him to which she could connect and ask what felt right. She wanted badly, she said, to develop some kind of inner spiritual wisdom and reference point but just did not seem to be able to find it. This issue was critical, for she viewed her religious reference point as someone external to her, someone who might encourage her to do something that she was not comfortable doing. This was the crux of how her spiritual and emotional issues intertwined; her early abuse had trained her to please her abuser at great cost to herself. This history provided the imprint for her spiritual belief system.

We discussed her abuse history and how she had been trained to accommodate the needs of others at her own expense. We discussed the considerable trouble she had gone through at the last moment in her attempt to accommodate this man. She had tried to rearrange a large holiday meal, including asking guests if they could change their plans, for this man, a virtual stranger, who had offered no reason or apology for his sudden change in plans.

I asked Hope about her feelings about this man. She had some trouble identifying them, except to say that she was somewhat uncomfortable with his sudden shift in plans. She had met him only twice previously and did not know what she felt about him.

At this point in the session, she suddenly remembered a dream she'd had several days before the holiday. In the dream, this man was in her home, in her den. He sat on a chair and then went over to the sofa and spread himself out on it. She told me that her initial read on this dream was that his appearance in her home meant she should invite him over to her home for the holiday.

Something felt disconnected to me in her initial interpretation. Knowing that feelings can often provide the vital link between a dream symbol and its meaning, I asked Hope to tell me how she'd felt in the dream about what he was doing. She thought about it and said clearly, without equivocation, that she'd felt very uncomfortable about his behavior, that something about it had felt sexually inappropriate. She'd felt a similar discomfort on the holiday itself, when he'd changed his plans. She'd felt he might have had ulterior motives for arranging to come later, but she had discounted her feelings. We talked about this and how her subconscious mind might have noticed some signals about him that she had consciously missed.

(Missing signals is typical of abuse victims, who have been trained by their experiences to disregard their feelings about their abuse and their abusers. This discounting of feelings is also common to the patriarchal culture in which we live, in which the feminine principle generally and connecting with one's feelings specifically are discounted and devalued.)

Hope admitted she had been worried. She'd felt very vulnerable about the possibility of being alone with him in her house. I reminded her she had once told me she wished she had an inner spirit to show her the right thing to do. I pointed out to her how her dream had done exactly that; it had shown her trouble might be brewing and how, in her feeling self, she was uncomfortable with this man. Her dreamwork assignment then became to act on her feelings and to protect herself.

We talked about how doing the right thing means protecting her own safety first, something she had not learned as a child. In her emotional development, doing what the other wanted had always come first, regardless of her needs or feelings. We can see now how her spiritual development paralleled this emotional developmental line. Her relationship with the divine by her interpretation of her religion was one of submitting to an external, controlling male figure. This is an excellent example of how a person's emotional and spiritual development and developmental arrests proceed in lines parallel to each other. This kind of relationship with an external, authoritative divine is, as I have mentioned, often reinforced in the ways that religion is taught and indoctrinated. Those teachings are in turn based on the emotional and spiritual level of development and understanding of those who are teaching.

As we processed the dream, Hope could accept the need to look out for herself in this case. However, she strongly felt she wanted to help others in some way during the holiday period. I helped her to look at other ways she might help those in need by volunteering her time and energy in a safe environment, outside of her home, where her own well-being would not be jeopardized.

SPIRITUAL DREAM HELP IN HEALING SEXUALITY

Rita came into my office for an emergency visit, stating that she had regressed over the past few days to what she had been at an earlier stage of her recovery. She had been angry, throwing things around the house (not at anyone, but just to ventilate her anger), and doing a lot of yelling (again, not at anyone, but just to ventilate). She felt she was deteriorating and was frightened by the intensity of what she called a "relapse."

At this point, we had been working together for several years. Rita had been sexually abused as a child, over a long period of time, by a close relative. In her adult life, she had found a great deal of solace in her spiritual beliefs. Mentally, however, she separated completely from her spiritual and physical nature. Her spiritual belief system had no room for acceptance of the human body and its deeply sexual nature. This was a consequence both of her upbringing about sexuality and the sexual abuse she had suffered. The religious teachings that she had been indoctrinated with and that she studied on her own as an adult reinforced a negative view of human sexuality. When she was meditating or praying, she felt "pure" and "spiritual." Throughout her marriage, which was now ended, she had been mostly split off from her sexual nature.

As she proceeded in therapy, Rita's attempts to reconnect with her sexuality felt as if she were doing something terribly wrong. She felt horribly betrayed by the men in her life, feeling she could not conceive of trusting any man as a lover. Her attempts at masturbation as a way of experiencing her sexuality in a safe and private manner gave her some relief but also left her fraught with guilt, wondering if she was doing something terribly wrong. She struggled with her sexual feelings.

During this period of internal struggle, Rita had a vision of Christ. She said he was radiant, with divine light exuding from him. In front of him, however, there was a dark area. Rita felt this darkness did not belong to him, nor was it in any way connected to him. She was puzzled as to what it meant and why it was there. She thought perhaps it might have something to do with her own dark side; perhaps he had come to her in this vision to help her.

During this time, when Rita was feeling particularly frustrated and cut off from her sexual nature, she prayed for help with accepting and understanding her sexuality. The fantasy that came to her surprised her greatly. Because it seemed to come in response to the prayer, she allowed herself to go with the fantasy, despite her initial reluctance. In this fantasy, Jesus came to her as a lover. He was the most tender and gentle of lovers; she felt she could trust him completely. She realized he was the only man she could trust to love her and not betray her. Rita was afraid to tell me of the experience, having spoken of it to no one. She was ashamed of the experience and felt that she was bad or that this experience was somehow "the work of the devil."

I asked Rita, in an attempt to help sift through her mixed feelings about the fantasy, how she felt during the fantasy. She said the fantasy had been sublime and tender. She believed the fantasy had been a healing response to her prayer, and it had been very healing for her. I asked her if there had been any sense of darkness or wrongness in the fantasy itself. She said no, she had experienced only love and tenderness. It was as if something inside her had been healed and made whole.

Only after the fantasy had Rita been plagued by guilt, fear, and other negative thoughts. As we continued to talk and process the experience, Rita realized the major trigger for her relapse was this fantasy and its emotional aftermath. Her internal voices from her personal upbringing and abuse history, which identified sex as bad, had kicked in with full force after the healing fantasy. The internalized voices from her religious training, which held spirituality and religion as pure and completely apart from the realm of "sinful" sexual nature, convinced her of how terrible a person she must be to have had, and to have enjoyed, the fantasy.

We had tried earlier in the session to identify the triggers to her regression without success. Now, as she talked of her extreme upset, Rita realized her rages and her tears were a result of her horror and shame at having had this pleasurable fantasy. She was thoroughly confused about what was true and what was right. In her upset, she railed at God as much as she self-castigated. She was ashamed of herself for yelling at God too, for telling him that she hated him. Her dilemma felt absolute. If God could send her this fantasy, then why would he allow her to feel so awful about it? Moreover, if it wasn't from God, then how could he have allowed her to have it almost immediately after her prayer for healing of her sexuality, in seeming response?

As her therapist, it was not my role to decide for Hope whether her fantasy was right or wrong. After all, I was aware of a long tradition of nuns who married Jesus, their bridegroom. (The 2017 movie *Novitiate* explored the romantic side of nun's relationship with Jesus). My task was to avoid religious commentary or judgment and to allow Rita the space to work with her very uncomfortable feelings about this fantasy that had felt so healing to her. If she had been talking about demons or other types of spirit lovers, I would have taken a different stance, as these are different phenomena entirely.

Sometimes when healing occurs, a backlash of old negative voices and feelings come up from the unconscious, threatening to annihilate the newly integrated and newly formed conscious stance. The waves of these backlashes can be quite difficult to ride out. I have found that the greater the power of the positive integrating experience, the greater the power of the negative backlash. As I spoke of the backlash effect, Rita remembered and told me a dream that had moved her greatly. She had dreamed it shortly before she'd had the fantasy, when she was struggling to find a way to accept her sexual nature.

> I am sitting on a mountain top. Then it is time to descend from the mountaintop. I look down. The way down is extremely steep, and very terrifying. It is a long way down, and I know I must go.

> I look down below, where I see a lush green valley of extraordinary beauty. I know I will make it down, but I also know the descent will be exceptionally difficult. As I begin to make the descent, I look down at my path and am terribly frightened.

Rita said she'd experienced a great deal of terror in the dream, both at the thought of the descent and as she'd begun to descend. She reported she'd also felt much serenity within the dream. She'd felt serenity when looking at the gorgeous valley and in the certainty she would make it there. She said there had been a sublime or spiritual sense about the valley. She knew that once she forced herself to overcome her fear and to not only begin but also to get through the ordeal of the descent, the treasures and beauty of the valley would be hers to enjoy.

As Rita described the dream and the feelings she had experienced within it, I was struck by the parallel between the feelings she'd experienced in the dream and those she'd experienced in connection with her fantasy experience. Rita had described feeling discontent to be cut off from her sexuality. This could be understood metaphorically as sitting on a mountaintop, high above the reality of her sexual, physical nature, represented by the rich, lush valley below, which was populated and very appealing and had a sublime and spiritual feeling that was missing on the mountaintop. As we worked with the dream and the feelings involved, she noted the similarities. She felt the feelings associated with the perilous descent could represent the feelings of danger and treacherousness that had gotten stirred up during her fantasy.

Now, as we worked with the dream imagery, the experience of the healing fantasy and the subsequent relapse came into a new, more objective perspective for Rita. The dream seemed to be pointing out Rita's initial psychological position, the work that needed to be done, and the difficult feelings to be stirred up in the process. It also seemed to reassure her she would make the perilous journey successfully and would arrive at a very beautiful and desirable location.

Dreams can be very important prognosticators of psychological trends and directions. It is also possible, in addition to foreshadowing future psychological trends that are already patterns in the psyche, dreams carry within them the function of psychological integration and healing. Whatever the case may be, since this dream reassured Rita of her safe arrival at a beautiful location, it seemed to point out that the extremely difficult psychological process she was undergoing was purposeful and necessary to arrive at a newer, healthier position. Rita could feel the truth of this as we processed the dream and the contents of her experience of the previous few days. This helped to calm her fears about the psychological battle she was undergoing.

We went on to talk about Rita's difficulty intellectually processing what she had found to be an ecstatic spiritual and sexual experience. Rita's shame around the prolonged sexual abuse to which she had been subjected and the feelings she had internalized about the "badness" of her physical nature had been reinforced by her religious upbringing. Although the experience of Christ as the divine, healing lover had been an extremely positive experience for her, afterward she'd told herself she was shameless and evil for having dared to create this kind of "degenerate" fantasy experience.

We talked of religious traditions where the height of spiritual experience is found in the intimate union of lovers. This blending of sexuality and spirituality, which is widely accepted in some Eastern religious traditions, is foreign to most of the dichotomous teachings of the West. In much of Western organized religious tradition, spirituality is polarized and considered as pure and not of the body; it is seen as opposite from the bodily nature. The tradition of the virgin birth seems to highlight this split.

There is now increased understanding in the West that the body is a temple through which the divine is expressed in us, including our sexuality. However, the integration of our physical and spiritual natures has been a very difficult task for us in this culture. We seem to go from one extreme to another when it comes to sexuality. The recent hunger in the West for breath-based meditation, yoga, tai chi, martial arts, acupuncture, chiropractic, and other disciplines through which the body and spirit can be experienced as one is part of a culture-wide need for integration of body and soul.

Rita was interested in these ideas. She said she needed to broaden her intellectual base in order to provide room for the inner emotional expansion. The dream and the dreamwork gave her a more complete understanding of her experience. When Rita left my office, she was still upset. However, she called back within a short period and said she was feeling much calmer and more accepting of her experience. The dream experience was far more helpful than anything I could have told her, for the dream was a product of her own psyche and showed her clearly and without judgment the nature of the process she was undergoing. The spontaneous sexual fantasy of Christ as the tender lover can also be seen as the inner archetype of the Christ, who emerged out of her own psyche as the divine animus figure she can accept and fully trust.

CHAPTER 23

THE THERAPIST'S JOURNEY

Sometimes a client will, seemingly out of nowhere, ask me, "How do you do this work, hearing so much about people's problems and trauma every day?" Sometimes the person will add, "I don't think I could do this work." Sometimes I will start my reply with the typical therapist response "Why do you ask?" and go from there. People might be concerned that their problems will bore or overwhelm me or that I might not have enough emotional energy or compassion left over for them. Sometimes they are expressing empathy for what they understand to be the difficulties of my line of work.

My response is tailored to their particular concerns first, and then I share my feelings about what I do and how I do it. I tell people that I love what I do and consider myself very fortunate and even blessed to work in such a trusted position with people, where I can be a part of helping them to learn about themselves and to heal. It is a source of ongoing joy to me to see people learn, grow, and heal. I also share that I learn a great deal from my clients. If the situation warrants, I share a little about how I manage it, which is by practicing good self-care, including three-day weekends every weekend (a must for me, I've found!); regular exercise in the outdoors whenever possible; quality time with family and friends (including fun); time for hobbies such as writing, dancing, and reading; dreamwork, meditation, and other spiritual work on a regular basis; healthy eating habits; gardening; and getting enough sleep and lots of water. I also limit the amount of client hours per week.

Because I work hard to keep life outside of work balanced (easier now that my life is back to normal) I can be present for my clients and genuinely glad to spend the time with them. I feel strongly that my personal emotional and spiritual work have contributed much to my effectiveness as a therapist.

In this chapter, I discuss therapist feelings about spirituality and how they may influence our work with clients. Further, I go into the importance of self-care, personal psychological work, and spiritual development, paralleling that which we teach our clients. Some of the early information in this chapter is geared more toward therapists but may be of interest to the non-therapist as well.

Much of this book focuses on dreams and what they teach us. In this section, I focus on therapist dreams about clients and the power they have to instruct and to heal both ourselves and our clients. In one particularly powerful dream I had of a client, the universal theme emerged of the fear of looking within, a fear that ties all of us together, no matter what our station in life. This theme is a thread that runs throughout this book. Those of us who are clinicians in the field of psychotherapy have spent many years developing our theory base, methods, and various tools. Many of us have struggled with concern that including spiritual issues as a part of treatment may jeopardize our professional credibility. Perhaps some think these issues are not particularly relevant to the work, and maybe there is a feeling of general discomfort with this subject material. If our clients bring this material into the treatment hour and we disregard their concerns or pay them less than adequate attention because we are uncomfortable with these discussions, what kind of message do we send?

It has been my contention in this book that one need not be an expert in spiritual matters in order to help a client to develop at least a working comfort level with exploration of his or her own spirituality. It does not matter if one's religious or spiritual beliefs are radically different from those of the client. What is important is that the therapist helps the client to explore his or her own material and what it means to him or her. We do not have to be in the position of understanding what a particular manifestation means, but we do need to be sensitive to issues raised in treatment and to be present for the client as he or she explores their meanings.

If a therapist cannot be present for spiritual material and shows discomfort by shifting the subject or by otherwise demonstrating he or she is not particularly interested in exploring the material, the client will experience the therapist as abandoning. How is it that we are trained to hear and deal with the most intimate details around sexuality, but when it comes to spirituality, we have little, if any, training and can feel at a loss?

If the client is particularly sensitive to approval and abandonment issues, as virtually all trauma and abuse victims are, then avoidance on the therapist's part could easily be read as discouragement and disapproval rather than as a reflection of the therapist's discomfort and feeling of inadequacy in a given area. Of course it is important to make referrals as appropriate to clergy or other spiritual advisors, but that does not preclude the need to stay open to guiding clients through their own material when it emerges.

The caution here is that it is important to not impose one's value system on a client. Several clients have come to me from Christian counseling centers where therapists imposed judgments and ideas on them, which made them feel very uncomfortable. This is very different from the client-centered process I have described throughout this book.

THERAPIST WOUNDING IN THE SPIRITUAL ARENA

More than likely, it is not only the client who has wounding in the arena of spirituality. The therapist may bring into the therapeutic setting spiritual issues and wounds of his or her own. The therapist may come into the work with spiritual trauma. Spiritual trauma is common and may come from a variety of sources, including encounters with organized religions, religious leaders, or our personal indoctrinations in the area. The horrific trauma the therapist hears from clients may have an impact on him or her in such a manner that the therapist's own spiritual beliefs are affected. This is an aspect of vicarious traumatization. This then can have an impact back on the clients.

A number of trauma therapists have written about vicarious traumatization. Laurie Anne Pearlman and Karen W. Saakvitne discuss this concept at some length in their recent book *Trauma and the Therapist: Countertransference and Vicarious Traumatization in Psychotherapy with Incest Survivors*. They define and describe vicarious traumatization and its impact on the therapist as follows:

> Vicarious traumatization is a process through which the therapist's inner experience is negatively transformed through empathic engagement with client's trauma material ... The therapist is a witness to his clients' traumas, through their vivid descriptions of traumatic events, reports of intentional cruelty and sadistic abuse, and experiences of reliving terror, grief, and yearning. He is both a witness to and a participant in traumatic reenactments within and outside of the therapy relationship.

Vicarious traumatization results in profound disruptions in the therapist's frame of reference, that is, his basic sense of identity, world view, and spirituality. Multiple aspects of the therapist and his life are affected, including his affect tolerance, fundamental psychological needs, deeply held beliefs about self and others, interpersonal relationships, internal imagery, and experiences of his body and physical presence in the world.

Vicarious traumatization is a natural response to a very specialized kind of highly demanding work. Just as survivor clients have developed various styles of protecting themselves as a result of childhood victimization, so do therapists develop styles of protecting themselves from repeated exposure to trauma material and traumatic reenactments in the work. Unfortunately, these adaptations are not necessarily all in the best long-term interest of the therapist, the therapy, or the client. (Pearlman and Saakvitne 1995, 280–81)

Therapists carry into treatment situations their own particular backgrounds, with their own coping styles and manner of relating internally to their own psychic material. They may also be survivors of various forms of abuse and trauma. They also are impacted by the brutal descriptions they hear of the many variations of unimaginable abuses inflicted upon their clients. It can be difficult to sit in a session and be fully present for a client who is reliving his or her abuse experiences. A therapist can be so overloaded and overwhelmed that it is almost automatic to try not to absorb the full impact of what he or she is hearing.

When I was first dealing with ritual abuse in my clients, the details reported by my clients were so horrific and brutal that it was hard to stay present. I found that having a balanced schedule of three and a half days of work and then three and a half days off gave me maximum time to rebalance and recharge my batteries. Whatever my level of health, I found time to exercise at some level most days, helping to keep my body strong and my spirit resilient. I also spent time with friends and family, had a meditation and prayer practice, and kept a dream journal. I worked with my dreams on a daily basis, and they helped to keep me aware of any imbalances.

When I first started working with Estelle, the Presidential Model, I was woefully unprepared for the ongoing horror story she had to tell me. Her programming was advanced and deeply sophisticated. She was being actively handled, meaning she suffered rape and various means of torture most nights to keep her dissociated and compliant. She had a lot of credibility, having at one point testified before Congress as to her abuse and governmental mind control programming. Obviously it hadn't helped her case much.

I know Estelle was bonded to me and appreciated our meetings and my belief in her. When someone is still being handled as she was, it is almost impossible for a therapist to offer much permanent relief, unless the person who is being accessed can be moved to safety. Under these circumstances, my task was to hear her and to remain open and empathic when I was internally recoiling in horror and disbelief at the magnitude of the lies perpetrated by our government on innocent victims. (A well-respected psychiatrist in the DC area who had significant experience in working with governmental and military mind control, and who had worked with Estelle for many years, assured me Estelle was the real thing; she was not confabulating.)

Therapists need to be fully present to the client to help contain their own reactions; if both client and therapist are dissociating from the painful material, the therapeutic work is seriously impaired. The message that the client might then internalize is "No one can bear to really hear and understand what happened to me. How can I possibly tolerate it?" This might evoke, for example, within the session, the transference of the non-abusing parent, who could not bear to see the abuse that was going on and who, either consciously or unconsciously, turned away from the scene of the horror. Practicing psychotherapists hear about abuse and almost unimaginable evil, often on a daily basis. Without adequate supervision, personal psychotherapy, and a committed spiritual practice, it would be easy for us to fall into numbness and despair over the cruelty of the human condition.

It is vital that therapists practice the self-care and self-nurturing they actively teach their clients. Ample time for friends and family, rest, play, hobbies, laughter, exercise, meditation, prayer, and so on, is important in the ongoing renewal process therapists all need in order to maintain the necessary emotional availability for the therapeutic work. Pearlman and Saakvitne describe many self-care methods in their volume.

The presence of boundaries in treatment facilitates and protects the therapeutic work. Boundaries also protect both the client and therapist from the acting out of transference and countertransference issues. For the clinician, good boundaries help prevent burnout and minimize vicarious traumatization while protecting the therapist's private time. Yet there is another side to the boundary issue. In the following quote from a letter to the editor in the November/December 1995 issue of *Common Boundary,* psychotherapist Linda Heller speaks eloquently on her personal struggle with effective boundary setting in trauma work and some unforeseen consequences in her own personal spiritual life:

> As a psychotherapist whose practice includes many adult survivors of childhood traumas, I have found the "language of boundaries" tremendously helpful as well as restrictive and confusing. I have found myself striving to maintain a delicate balance with my own boundaries. If I go too far one way, I feel numb and distant. If I go too far the other way, I become like a sponge flooded by the traumas I bear witness to …

> Over the past decade while I have done this work, my sense of spiritual connectedness, in the way I knew it, has all but disappeared. Troubled deeply by this, I re-entered my own therapy and consulted with spiritual teachers. It wasn't until I heard one rabbi speak of the "boundarylessness of the divine" that it clicked for me. I had been defining all forms of "boundarylessness" as abusive and had cut myself off from the experience of union that I believe to be crucial to living a grounded spiritual life. (Heller 1995, 9)

Heller concluded her letter to the editor by stating her thoughts that too much attention to this issue of boundary maintenance can have a negative impact on therapist spirituality. Union with the divine in a prayer, meditation, or dream experience can be wondrous. However, it requires a willingness to let go of one's limited personal definitions of self. One must be willing and able to surrender to a power higher than oneself, to an unknown over which one has no control.

Perhaps a key word in the above quote is grounded when discussing spiritual life. A grounded spiritual life is one in which the individual maintains a strong integrated connection with his or her body, with the earth, and with his or her own psychological issues in addition to any spiritual practices. It is not a spacey spirituality but a spirituality that infuses and informs rather than remaining separate from the personality. Maintaining this balance requires a well-integrated personality, which in turn requires ongoing attention to, and work on, the self.

In order to be able to be emotionally healthy and available to their clients, therapists need to make a commitment to work with their own inner material on a regular basis. Just as the myth of Persephone provides a model for the client journey, it provides a model for the (hopefully!) ever-growing and deepening psychotherapist psyche. It is vital that therapists experience their own psychotherapy/personal growth programs. Psychotherapy teaches us about ourselves and the impact our experiences have on our lives. It helps us to make fully informed choices. Also very importantly, it helps teach therapists about the psychotherapist role. Regular supervision supports the psychotherapy process and is an important part of being an effective therapist. It helps to ensure that personal issues do not intrude inappropriately in the therapy.

THERAPIST DREAMS OF CLIENTS

For the therapist, much as for the client, journaling and working with one's dreams provides a means of connecting with feelings and other material that might otherwise be unconscious. Doing so can also warn us about where we are going wrong with a client or with ourselves and can point us in directions we might not otherwise have considered.

Typically, however, therapists have been erroneously taught that if they dream about a client, this means they are over-involved or have countertransference issues. This false belief that dreaming about clients means something negative about the therapist binds the dreamer with shame, keeping him or her from being open to the valuable treatment information that may be contained in the dream. It is true that some (but not all!) dreams about a client can show us where we may be over-involved or where our own issues are triggered in the therapy. These dreams can be very helpful in assisting us to take a step back from the therapy and sort out our feelings before they intrude or seep into the treatment.

Unfortunately, since client dreams have come to be negatively stigmatized as signs of the therapist's over-investment, the value of these dreams has rarely been openly discussed. Dreams about clients can be of great importance to treatment, on many levels, and come under a variety of circumstances.

I was working with Paul, a single male client who had been laid off. He was continuing his insurance coverage through COBRA. We made a payment arrangement in which he agreed to maintain his COBRA while unemployed. However, he slipped into his typical avoidant patterns, neither looking for work nor keeping up the insurance, which paid 80 percent of my bill. When I found out through an insurance- payment denial that his coverage had lapsed due to his negligence, I gave him a bill for the full amount due up until that point. It was a significant amount for him but only a few hundred dollars, not that much. I knew he could put it on a credit card. I also knew that forcing him to face this financial reality might help motivate him to follow up on some of the excellent job leads he had been given. Since he was an alcoholic, I knew that my not enabling him was important to his treatment. Once I sent the bill, however, feelings of doubt set in, and I wondered whether I had been too harsh.

That night, I had the following dream:

> I'm driving a car, with three women in the backseat. Paul gets in the backseat with them. He looks quite ill, and I know he is not doing well.

> He begins talking with me about the bill. I know he is going to try to talk me out of him having to pay up front. He begins by saying, "About that bill you want me to foot—" I have a strong and immediate reaction to Paul and interrupt him before he gets any further, saying emphatically, "You mean that bill you want me to foot." I'm a bit shocked at myself for interrupting him, but within the dream both of us realize this is exactly what he is asking me to do.

I woke up knowing I was doing the right thing in this situation. When I saw how physically ill he was in the dream, I was reminded that Paul and I were dealing with a very serious illness, his alcoholism.

Deirdre Barrett, PhD, discussed therapist dreams in a paper she presented at the International Association for the Study of Dreams conference held in New York in June 1995. One of her findings was that dreams about clients can also point out directions and interventions that the therapist might not otherwise have thought about. She gave several powerful examples where these kinds of dreams provided insights into a particular client's therapy and moved the therapy along, out of a stuck place and into a positive movement. In the example above, the dream reinforced my decision and highlighted the severity of the problem I was treating.

A Corrective Diagnostic Dream

I sometimes have dreams about clients. Some of these dreams have pointed out my countertransference issues and have helped me to analyze my own feelings and involvement and correct my position vis-à-vis the client. Some, such as the payment dream about Paul, supported my conscious stance and helped keep me from getting caught in a countertransference issue. Some have been diagnostic in nature, while others have pointed out helpful interventions.

One dream clearly presented to me an essential diagnostic aspect of a client that the medicating psychiatrist and I had missed. I had worked with Deborah for several years, and though her severe depression showed some signs of easing, she continued to trigger into complex, irrational hopeless states where she wanted to die. These states could last from three days to weeks, during which time she was non-responsive to intervention. Afterward, she was unable to articulate what had happened to trigger the state or what had happened during the state. I was feeling frustrated at my inability to help or sufficiently understand what was happening to Deborah when she was in the grip of these depressive states.

It was during this time of feeling frustrated about Deborah's treatment that I had a dream about her. The dream started out with a direct verbal message to me. It then shifted into a psychotherapy session with Deborah, in which I interviewed her in a specific way. I then obtained information from her that she had not known how to communicate to me or the psychiatrist.

> I'm told directly that the psychiatrist and I have really missed the boat with Deborah in our diagnosing. We have diagnosed her with major depression, but we have missed that she also suffers from severe post-traumatic stress disorder (PTSD).

> I am now in session with Deborah. She and I are reviewing the episodes she has suffered from for many years. I take my time and, step-by-step, go over with her how she is triggered. It is very clear from her responses to this line of questioning that she might be calm in one moment and then some stimulus will set her off with a series of intrusive recollections of the massive trauma that she endured in her earlier life. It is at this point, with the intrusive recollections, that she falls into her hopeless states.

The dream was clear and straightforward. Deborah's responses in the dream clearly indicated the presence of PTSD. Needless to say, the dream had an impact on me, and I decided to explore this information with this client. Sure enough, in our next session, an appropriate opening came up. The session unfolded just as it had in the dream.

I then told Deborah about the dream and went over the symptoms of PTSD with her. She thought the description of PTSD fit her well. She expressed relief to finally have some kind of framework for viewing these episodes that had always puzzled her greatly. She had not previously known how to articulate the intrusive recollections, characteristic of PTSD, that seemed to bombard her when she was triggered. Her meltdowns continued, and the psychiatrist and I struggled to understand and help her.

Bessel van der Kolk, a leading researcher on the psychobiology of trauma, whom I have quoted earlier in this work, explains this aspect of PTSD:

> Research into the nature of traumatic memories indicates that trauma interferes with declarative memory (i.e., conscious recall of experience) but does not inhibit implicit, or non-declarative, memory, the memory system that controls conditioned emotional responses, skills and habits, and sensorimotor sensations related to experienced.

> … When people are traumatized, they are said to experience "speechless terror"; the emotional impact of the event may interfere with the capacity to capture the experience in words or symbols. (van der Kolk in Alpert 1996, 41–42)

Part of the biological and psychological impact of the trauma, which Deborah had experienced from early on in life, interfered with her ability to describe or give words to her internal experience. When she had these intrusive recollective episodes as an adult, she still had no words to express her state. She was not able to explain what happened to her to me or to the psychiatrist. Indeed, as we talked further, it seemed that she was suffering from what is known as complex post-traumatic syndrome, a syndrome created, in her case, by ongoing intrafamilial abuse. This syndrome involves "chronic affect dysregulation, destructive behavior against self and others, learning disabilities, dissociative problems, somatization, and distortions in concepts about self and others" (van der Kolk in Alpert 1996, 40). The treatment for post-traumatic syndrome includes some different types of work than that which is typical for recurrent depression. Having this knowledge about the client was vital for all of us in moving forward with her treatment.

When a therapist stays in touch with his or her own dreaming life, it is one important way to stay connected with his or her own feelings and unconscious currents, whether or not they have a direct impact on the therapy. The healing field of psychotherapy is relational; it is through the relationship that the work is done. A therapist's issues naturally emerge in response to the often intense relationship dynamics and demands of psychotherapeutic work. Ongoing self-exploration and self-monitoring help keep a space open for gaining awareness of unconscious responses. Sometimes dreams about clients can help the therapist explore self in quite unexpected areas and ways.

PERSONAL GROWTH THROUGH A DREAM OF A CLIENT.

The appearance of a client in a therapist's dream might provide the therapist an opportunity to reflect on an aspect of self mirrored by a similar quality in the client. This can help the therapist in his or her own growth and self-understanding. This awareness can also help the therapist maintain appropriate emotional boundaries through the recognition of the connection.

As an example of this mirroring function, I will cite a dream I had about a client that, on the surface, appears to be of no more than moderate significance. As I worked with it, however, I found that it had major significance for me. It contained within it the theme of avoidance of self, which ties this book together from the beginning to the end. It also pointed out to me my own participation in this avoidance of self.

> I am out somewhere, having just seen a movie. My car is in the back of the theater, in a parking lot. I walk up to it. On the windshield, under one of the wipers, is a note from a man who has been stalking me over a long period of time. From what I can gather from the note, he is with me always. He tells me he loves me. He does not say who he is, but my first guess is that he is a particular client of mine. I feel very endangered and threatened. I do not know how to get away from him.

> Now I am sitting a block away, in the backseat of my car, reading over the note. I am not sure what to do next.

In the first part of the dream, I had just seen a movie. In my personal dream vocabulary, the symbol of seeing a movie comes up when I am projecting my own personal issues onto someone else. Therefore, this symbolism alerted me that I was dealing with a personal projection. My movie-watching dreams often come to inform me how and on whom or on what I am projecting some aspect of my own intrapsychic issues into my waking life.

Dreams of being chased are among the most common of dreams, both among children and adults. Stalking dreams in general, and for me in particular, usually have to do with some unconscious element that is trying to emerge into consciousness and that feels very threatening.

I began my dreamwork with owning that the stalker was an aspect of myself. In my dream, I wanted to avoid the stalker aspect of myself. I did not know who this stalker was and was afraid he meant me harm. He left a note that said he loved me always, but I did not trust his love. My association to the dream was that the harder I try to avoid this aspect of myself, the more threatening it feels, because it gains inpower with my fear and my flight. (It is often the avoidance itself that makes the emerging material feel so threatening. However, pain and grief are also involved in the processing of the contents.)

My first thought in the dream about the identity of the stalker was that he was a particular client. In waking life, I did not feel threatened by this client. However, as I thought further about him, I got my first clues as to the issue within me that the dream was addressing. This man had been struggling with a terrible fear of looking inside, afraid of the seemingly never-ending grief he had felt. Because of his avoidance of himself, he had shut off a deep spiritual connection. As I continued to work with the dream, I better understood that parallel between us, even though we were in different stages of our respective journeys. Soon after having this dream, I had an unusual experience. In this experience, I felt that I had somehow reached the center of my being, as if I had penetrated through the various layers of the psyche and arrived at my core. I do not know how to adequately explain the feeling, but it seemed I was at dead center. In that space, I experienced a deep and heavy sadness. In its depth, intensity, and bigness, this sadness seemed strikingly archetypal in nature. The encounter did not seem related to any particular content or experience, though by its nature was related to much of what I have experienced. Because of the close connection I maintain with my dreaming life and because of my many years of working on and sorting through my issues in both formal analyses and self-analyses, I am usually able to sort things through fairly well. I often find a number of layers in a given experience.

The sadness seemed to touch on all my experiences of pain and loss. However, it also seemed to filter down and through to something much larger, as if it were a direct experience of an aspect of the collective unconscious. The deep general archetypal feeling of sadness reminded me of the Buddha's conclusion that, by its very nature, all of life is suffering. The sadness seemed pervasive, weighty, and impersonal (even though it included my personal experience). There was no accompanying anxiety. Rather, it was a very still sadness.

This unusual feeling accompanied me throughout the evening. It is very difficult to describe—it weighed me down but not like depression. I had never experienced anything quite like it and was puzzled. It was almost as if this darkness was the abyss of my human nature at its core, unredeemed by spirit.

The previous day, on the persistent urging of several dreams, I'd picked up a copy of Blaise Pascal's *Pensées* at the bookstore. I knew nothing about Pascal, except that he was a mathematician from hundreds of years before, in the 1600s. Why would my dreams would speak strongly of the importance he would have to me in my thoughts and writings? However, since my dreams have taught me so much and have led me in such fruitful and positive directions, after the second or third dream about Pascal, I'd overcome my hesitance and bought the book. I discovered that Pascal had a conversion experience in a vision and that his most famous writing is a philosophical treatise on religion and human nature.

The night of my experience of deep sadness, before I went to sleep I began reading Pascal's work. I was fascinated by some of his ideas, especially in light of my experience that evening. Pascal wrote of the basic unhappiness of man's nature and how much energy we spend diverting ourselves in outside activities, trying to anesthetize ourselves and avoid looking within. In a provocative statement, he asserts, "I have often said that the sole cause of man's unhappiness is that he does not know how to stay quietly in his room" (Pascal 1966, 37).

Although Pascal's language is quite different from our modern psychological language, his ideas are relevant to the theme of this contemporary book. Pascal asserts how, at his or her center, a person without God is "wretched," or miserable and unhappy. He speaks at length of the various means people have used over the centuries to avoid facing what is inside, in the attempt to acquire "elusive" happiness for themselves on the outside. "If our condition were truly happy we should not need to divert ourselves from thinking about it" (Pascal 1966, 19).

Pascal's writings reminded me the avoidance of self is universally true. I pondered the many ways I'd seen this played out over the years, both in myself and others. I began my book with thoughts on this theme, which has continued throughout the book. Now, as my writing of this book was drawing to a close, my dreams pointed me to Pascal, a writer heretofore unknown to me. It could not have been a mere coincidence that I was led to this book in which he so strongly and eloquently discussed the avoidance of self! I resonated personally to the material, especially given the stalker dream, which I was working on understanding.

In a section in his book on diversion, Pascal makes a number of points that hit home to me on many levels. I also found what he had to say was strongly reminiscent of Buddhist philosophy. The Buddhists strongly believe that it is through our attachment to our desires and impulses that the ongoing round of existence continues. We endlessly pursue these attachments in the outer world in hopes of escaping the pain of our existence. However, our only hope is to escape this endless cycle of pain through looking inside to find detachment and through the subsequent development of wisdom and insight. The Buddhists speak of our desirous nature; Pascal speaks of our basic wretchedness and our need to find diversion to try to escape our basic nature.

Mark Waldman, in his book *The Way of Real Wealth*, states:

> All of the great spiritual paths and teachers tell us this spiritual truth: The first step on the path is to stop avoiding ourselves. The pain that lies at the root of much of our behavior can

be our greatest teacher. It can be our guide to the specific personal and spiritual barriers we must overcome to experience the Divine Presence in our lives. (Waldman 1993, 130)

To continue, I quote from Pascal:

But, after closer thought, looking for the particular reasons for all our unhappiness now that I knew its general cause, I found one very cogent reason in the natural unhappiness of our feeble mortal condition, so wretched that nothing can console us when we really think about it ...

What people want is not the easy peaceful life that allows us to think of our unhappy condition, nor the dangers of war, nor the burdens of office, but the agitation that takes our mind off it and diverts us. That is why we prefer the hunt to the capture.

That is why men are so fond of hustle and bustle; that is why prison is such a fearful punishment, which is why the pleasures of solitude are so incomprehensible ...

So, while the present never satisfies us, experiences deceive us, and lead us on from one misfortune to another until death comes as the ultimate and eternal climax.

This her (man) tries in vain to fill with everything around him, seeking in things that are not there the help he cannot find in those that are, though none can help, since this infinite abyss can be filled only with an infinite and immutable object; in other words by God himself. (Pascal 1966, 37–45)

In other words, our desiring nature drives us onward into these diversions that yield us nothing in the end except the continued avoidance of self. The answer lies in turning within.

Fascinated, I continued reading. I saw my struggles in these words from long ago; I also saw the struggles of those whom I have known and worked with. I saw how similar we all are, regardless of our histories.

Man's greatness and wretchedness are so evident that the true religion must necessarily teach us that there is in man some great principle or greatness and some great principle of wretchedness. It must also account for such amazing contradictions.

To make man happy it must show him that a God exists whom we are bound to love, that our true bliss is to be in him, and our sole ill to be cut off from him. It must acknowledge that we are full of darkness which prevents us from knowing and loving him, and so, with our duty obliging us to love God and our concupiscence leading us astray, we are full of unrighteousness. It must account to us for the way in which we thus go against God and our own good. It must teach us the cure for our helplessness and the means for obtaining this cure. (Pascal 1966, 46)

As I read these words, the meaning of my stalker dream came alive. In any dream, a single character can represent more than one person or set of attributes. The character who resembled my client represented the part of me, like that client, that was avoiding facing something within. We were both resisting a deep spiritual call. In both cases, we were resisting going through the pain we must feel in order to connect with the inner transformative power of the self archetype/Divine. Our particular struggles were very different. In my dream I see the universality of the human condition, as we flee from and avoid the existential pain of that unredeemed darkness inside. Yet in avoiding facing that pain, we inadvertently cut ourselves off from the divine within that beckons us and invites us to transformation.

How could I feel so threatened and frightened by this man, who said he was with me always and that he loved me? When I read over the words of my dream, I focused on the exact wording on the note: he said that he was "with me always." I remembered that these words appeared in the title of Scott Sparrow's *I Am with You Always: True Stories of Encounters with Jesus* (and in Matthew 28:20)/. When I made the connection, I realized that the stalker was not my client but rather the Christ within, calling me into relationship with Jesus.

When Jesus was suffering on the cross, he went into the depths of darkness. I believe something happened through which the darkness was fundamentally transformed. (I write about this in a slightly different form in my first book, *At the Feet of the Master*, in the chapter on the crucifixion.) After the resurrection and Pentecost, through the indwelling of the Holy Spirit, He can be with us always, as his Spirit is available to believers.

I now understood that my uncomfortable and painful experience of feeling that sadness was most likely the emergence of the Christ within. Perhaps in facing my fear of the stalker something inside was allowing a transformation to begin. Why was I so afraid? To the extent that I fear and run from pain, *I believe in the reality of death and give it power over me.* We all share this trauma of feeling cut off from our true spiritual nature, beginning in the womb and most certainly at birth, and we are all trying to find our way back home, to our true selves. Jesus's lesson to all of us, regardless of religious preference, is that our spirits, or our selves, are eternal; we do not die.

Upon reflection, I know I must rejoin this man of my dream and talk with him. I can leave if I think he means me harm, yet I know deep inside it is my fear and my avoidance that will cause harm, not the encounter. Jung, in a wonderfully rich and profound discussion on how the personality grows, has the following to say:

> Richness of mind consists in mental receptivity, not in the accumulation of possessions. What comes to us from outside, and, for that matter, everything that rises up from within, can only be made our own if we are capable of an inner amplitude equal to that of the incoming content. Real increase of personality means consciousness of an enlargement that flows from inner sources. Without psychic depth we can never be adequately related to the magnitude of our object. It has therefore been said quite truly that a man grows with the greatness of his task. But he must have within himself the capacity to grow; otherwise even the most difficult task is of no benefit to him. More likely he will be shattered by it...

> Christ himself is the perfect symbol of the hidden immortal within the mortal man. (Jung 1959, 120–21)

And thus, I've found in my dream of a client a wealth of information that has invited me into a deeper relationship with the Divine. This dream in many ways was an opening into my depths where I could access Jesus. For me, it was a deepening into knowing his love for me and experiencing Him in every aspect of my life. I could hardly have known at the time I had this dream how much need I would have of Him so many years later in my horrible ordeal, but it was, in retrospect, a vitally important step on my path. I had tried a number of churches and encountered many false theologies, none of which satisfied. But now, I was being called from within, from my depths, to grow a genuine relationship with Him. Although I did not understand it fully at the time, it was a much-needed opening, out of which would grow so very much over the years.

The dream also gave me an even greater respect for the fear and the terror that he, or anyone else, faces when confronting the magnitude of what is within. It has brought me face-to-face with my greatest fear and my greatest hope. The dream humanizes me and gives me hope. This dream of a client gave me helpful information about the client, about myself, and about the struggle we all face.

The dream of this client also kept me from an unconscious over-identification with him. Because I became aware of my previously unconscious identification with the issue, I was better positioned to sift through what belonged to me and what belonged to him. Our therapeutic relationship did not become contaminated by my unconscious projections, because the dream helped me face and own my issues.

Next, I close the book with three very powerful and beautiful examples of miraculous healings from physical diseases, two involving clients and a third my own. Dreams were involved in two of the stories; in one case the actual spontaneous, miraculous healing from advanced ovarian cancer was seen within a dream. These stories are testaments to faith and hope and prayer, the antidotes to the encroaching darkness.

CHAPTER 24

HEALING MIRACLES

A MIRACLE RECOVERY FROM DISABLING ILLNESS THROUGH DREAMING

In 1980, when China opened to tourism, my mother decided she wanted to go. This was a historic opportunity to see China. At the time, I was living on my own, working in an alcoholism inpatient unit. My mother asked my dad if he would go with her, but he was not interested, saying he had traveled a lot and was not interested in seeing China. Undeterred, my mother told him she would ask me to accompany her, which she did. I was thrilled for the opportunity. I had studied Mandarin Chinese for three years and had a strong interest in Chinese culture. It was an exciting opportunity to be able to see China at a time when the country was largely rural, before the massive industrialization that has taken place since.

We had to take smallpox vaccinations to go to China. Unfortunately, I had a terrible reaction to the vaccination. As a result, I lost fifteen prime years of my life to constant debilitating illness. Whereas before I had been very healthy and energetic, I was bedridden for many months. Getting up and going to the bathroom took all the energy I had. When I could begin to function in the outside world again, I was compromised by a severe auto-immune disorder. Additionally, I developed allergies to a hundred foods, to chemicals, and to just about everything in my environment. I succumbed to every flu or bug. Disabling migraines lasted two days at a time twice a week. I was now constantly ill and debilitated, reactive to everything. Life became a living hell. My time and energy was spent trying to figure out how to heal from these many terrible issues that had erupted.

Traditional doctors could not help me. I went from one alternative doctor to another. I did everything possible to try to restore my health, changing virtually everything in my life. It was overwhelming. As the years went by without significant healing, doctors said I would never be well. Once someone with my condition passed the ten-year mark, which I did, the chances of getting well were virtually nil. This was completely unacceptable to me.

No one knew how sick I was. My complaints were marginalized, and empathy was rare. People's reactions often made me feel worse, for I knew that, if anything, I greatly minimized the extent of my problems when I spoke to others.

After fifteen years of illness, I had reached the point where I felt I did not wish to live any longer with this consuming illness; I would rather be dead. (I wasn't suicidal, just fed up.) I had always been physically active and strong and couldn't bear to spend all my years so limited. My prime years were lost to ill health, as was my ability to carry a child and have a normal life because of my illness. Constant illness couldn't be my permanent destiny!

That New Year's Eve, I decided to devote all my dreaming to finding a cure until I was well. At this point, I had worked with my dreams for over twenty years, and I knew that the dreaming mind responds to intention.

I was very familiar with the ages-old tradition of dream incubation, described earlier in this book, in which a person asks his or her dreams for guidance and information on a given topic. I had successfully done dream incubation many times over the years and had always obtained very helpful information.

My perspective is that our higher selves/God within knows everything going on in our body minds. I believed it would be possible for my dreaming mind to access how to get rid of the illness if I were to ask for this help.

I was right. The amazing results of my dreaming over the next six months could take a book to describe, so I will stick with a condensed version. Within six months, as a result of following the guidance in the dreams that followed, I went through a very dramatic purge of the retrovirus that had colonized in my brain stem. I was shown in dreams that the problem was caused by a "retrovirus" which had lodged and colonized in my brain stem. The dreams showed me the retrovirus adhered to the brainstem via a sticky substance and had colonized there.

The first major dream snippet seemed, on the face of it, innocuous and non-meaningful. However, because I deeply believe the dreaming mind can connect with body wisdom to help heal disease—and because I knew from experience that in dream incubation all dreams are relevant to the incubation question—I took it very seriously. The snippet was very simple: I was in my condo, in my living room. I was sitting on the floor in front of my sofa, facing the coffee table.

I had no idea how to understand this dream, but I knew it could be very important to take it seriously. The only clue I could come up with was that it had something to do with "grounding," perhaps physical grounding.

A good friend of mine at the time, Kim, was an electrical engineer. I figured maybe she would be able to help me. First, I asked her what ground meant when it came to electricity. Kim said it meant neutral, with neither a positive nor a negative charge. I started thinking about how our bodies are complex electrical systems, so my next question to Kim was if she could think of any simple instrument that could measure human electrical current.

Kim thought about it for a while and then said she wasn't sure if it would work but told me of an instrument called a multimeter, which measures electrical current. She wondered what would happen if one of us held one of the electrodes in one hand and the other electrode in the other hand and then saw what registered on the multimeter. It seemed to us both it would definitely be worth trying.

I was an experienced meditator and for a number of years had been accustomed to experiencing a distinct feeling of connection when I reach what I call my higher self during meditation. My hypothesis was that when I reached that point of feeling connected with my higher self, then the reading on the multimeter, as I held one electrode in each hand, would be neutral.

One night when we went out to dinner at a mostly empty restaurant, Kim brought an analog multimeter with her. She showed me the instrument and how I would hold one electrode in each hand. I decided to try out my theory before we did any other experiments. When I felt the connection with my higher self, I would signal Kim and ask her to tell me what the reading was on the multimeter. I closed my eyes and within a short while signaled her.

I was right. The reading was exactly neutral when I signaled her. Now I could understand what "ground" felt like. We did a lot of experimenting on both of us to make sure this was not a normal reading. In ordinary consciousness, my readings tended to be just a bit on either side of neutral. I am, for the most part, a fairly even personality type. In contrast, Kim, who is bipolar, had readings that widely varied, in high positive or high negative territory, depending on whether her mood was hypomanic or depressed. (Note: the multimeter was analog; the digital versions do not seem to work as well.)

This was exciting—even if I had no idea how this could help! Now I had an idea of how to develop and sustain the grounding that I believed the dream was instructing me to do. I also now had a small, easy-to-carry biofeedback tool that could assist me in staying grounded.

I kept the multimeter with me throughout subsequent days and evenings. With the biofeedback readily available, I learned how to stay grounded or neutral for longer periods of time. It was my custom at the time to ride my bike daily and take a break in my favorite sunny meadow. There I would sit on the ground to pray and meditate. I continued this practice, keeping the multimeter with me to help me more quickly achieve and sustain that state of higher, grounded consciousness. It was fairly easy to do, as having biofeedback helped me strengthen my abilities.

Before long, I began to wake up in the midst of deep sleep, aware that I was deeply asleep yet also conscious. This is a phenomenon known for thousands of years by the Buddhists as witnessing. I knew as I stayed awake in this state that it must also be a grounded state, for it had the same vibrational feel. I stayed in it for as long as I could whenever this happened, keeping my consciousness focused so as to prolong it. At the same time, as I gained a little more confidence in my ability to stay stable in this state for more-prolonged periods of time, I did as much exploring of my surroundings within that state as I could.

Within a week or two, I was experiencing a grounded state around the clock for significant periods of time (probably never more than fifteen to twenty minutes at a time). I had no idea why this was important to my healing, but my dreams had emphasized the importance of grounding, and I had faith my dreams would heal me, even though it was a complete mystery to me. I was highly motivated to be free of my disabling illness and was willing to do what was necessary. I did not see it as a choice but a way to honor what was happening as part of the divine healing process.

It did not take long from there for things to start moving really fast. Another dream helped me understand at a deeper level what had been happening. I was shown a basketball hoop attached to a backboard on top of a pole. As I looked at the net attached to the hoop, I was told a retrovirus colony has adhered to the basket, covering the net and hoop. It did so by way of a sticky, adherent quality in the retrovirus.

When I woke up, I was struck by the term retrovirus, which was unfamiliar to me. I also awoke with the understanding the hoop and net represented my brain stem and spine. The brain stem sits right above the spine. I understood the hoop and net with adhered retrovirus colony to be the brainstem and the pole on which the hoop and net sat to represent the spine.

I looked up retrovirus and found that the AIDS virus is also a retrovirus. I discovered another retrovirus caused what I had, myalgic encephalomyelitis, an inflammation of the brain and spinal cord, also known as chronic fatigue immunodeficiency syndrome (CFIDS). My diagnosis had been CFIDS for fifteen years. I obtained a huge volume on myalgic encephalomyelitis, which contained many research articles. No one seemed to understand it well. However, it was seen as caused by a type of retrovirus. The retrovirus could colonize in various places.

My dreams were definitely zeroing in on something. What I was understanding now, as I did the research, was that it was likely, as my dream had suggested, that retrovirus had colonized on my brain stem, which was in line with what the research said about myalgic encephalomyelitis being an inflammation of the brain and spinal cord. This was getting very interesting.

Within several days of this basketball-hoop dream, and continuing with the biofeedback grounding work, I began experiencing severe pain in the top portion of my spine. It felt as if my spine were expanding and pressing outward from the inside, like a balloon filling with water. The pressure was great and very painful, and at times my spine felt as if it would burst. Over the next week or so, the pain shifted progressively down my spine, a little at a time. It is hard to explain, but it felt somewhat like it looks when you see a snake swallow its prey, the large lump slowly moving through the snake as the prey is digested.

As I noted the downward progression of the pain caused by the pressure, I speculated the retrovirus was beginning to move out of my body, down from the brain stem and then down and out of my spine. Perhaps the dream had come so I would be able to understand what was happening and would not panic. The pressure and pain continued, moving very slowly downward through my spine, for about a week.

I was just as unprepared for the next stage as I was for the first. I was out with my friend Kim. We were on Key Bridge heading into Georgetown from Virginia. I suddenly became overwhelmed and felt very sick. Fortunately we were near a gas station. We stopped there, and I ran as far from the car as I could. There I began what was to turn out to be a very long period of unrelenting projectile vomiting. I had never experienced anything like it. It just kept coming and coming!

When I could finally speak, Kim told me she was very worried at the severity and duration of the vomiting and wanted to take me to the hospital. Instinctively I knew that this violent purging was the answer to my prayers, that although I did not understand the details, I was in the process of getting rid of my illness forever. I was concerned whatever traditional medical treatment I might receive at the hospital would also stop the purging of the virus, so I told her no. Within an hour or so I was gratefully feeling much better.

Once the purging began, it took about a month to complete. The first five days or so it was mainly vomiting. The next five days it was copious diarrhea. I had to stay close to a bathroom. The cycles repeated in shorter versions during that month. I believed the retrovirus was releasing out of my body.

I shared the details of what was happening to me with an HIV positive doctor friend who agreed it could well be that my body was now ridding itself of what had made me sick. The violent purging was definitely making me stronger overall, not weaker, despite the electrolyte losses. This would be so wonderful if it were true! I had to trust the dreams and trust my process. I did not seek medical attention, for fear my body's natural healing mechanisms seemed to be working.

At the end of the month, when the purging had stopped, the feeling of a heavy weight in the back of my head that had been with me since I'd contracted the illness was now gone. I knew that meant I was now clear of the retrovirus. That ever-present feeling of a weight in my head must have been the retrovirus colony on my brain stem. Though my conscious mind had had no awareness of the nature of my illness, my unconscious mind clearly had had knowledge both of the nature of the problem and of the completely unforeseeable (to my conscious mind) method by which I was to become completely healed. There was no doubt in my mind at this point that the problem that had sickened me was now successfully resolved. I was very excited!

There was no time for celebration, however. My body had been severely ravaged by fifteen years of disabling illness. I surmised it would take at least a year to rest, renourish, and restore my depleted system. I was patient, not expecting too much of myself too soon. Every day that followed was another day of freedom. It was true; I had had my miracle healing! This brought me much joy and relief. It is now more than twenty-five years later, and there has been no recurrence of my illness. I am healthy and fit, and rarely catch viruses or colds.

More than a decade later, someone gave me a link to a 2001 article in *Nexus Magazine* by Donald W. Scott, MA, MSC, called *"Mycoplasma—The Linking Pathogen in Neurosystemic Devices."* (A copy of this article can be found by doing a search at *nexusmagazine.com*.) In the article, Scott talks of how mycoplasma has been bioengineered to be much more deadly (bioweaponized) since 1942. Further, he states:

> According to Dr Shyh-Ching Lo, senior researcher at The Armed Forces Institute of Pathology and one of America's top mycoplasma researchers, this disease agent causes many illnesses including AIDS, cancer, chronic fatigue syndrome, Crohn's colitis, Type I diabetes, multiple sclerosis, Parkinson's disease, Wegener's disease and collagen-vascular diseases such as rheumatoid arthritis and Alzheimer's.

> Dr. Charles Engel, who is with the US National Institutes of Health, Bethesda, Maryland, stated the following at an NIH meeting on February 7, 2000: "I am now of the view that the probable cause of chronic fatigue syndrome and fibromyalgia is the mycoplasma …"

> I have all the official documents to prove that mycoplasma is the disease agent in chronic fatigue syndrome/fibromyalgia as well as in AIDS, multiple sclerosis and many other illnesses. Of these, 80% are US or Canadian official government documents, and 20% are articles from peer-reviewed journals such as the Journal of the American Medical Association, New England Journal of Medicine and the Canadian Medical Association Journal. The journal articles and government documents complement each other. (Scott 2001)

A LITTLE MORE ON VACCINES

Just what was in that smallpox vaccination? As it turns out, retroviruses are a huge issue. The article *"Vaccines and Retroviruses: A Whistleblower Reveals What the Government is Hiding"*, published in Health Impact News (*https://healthimpactnews.com/2015/vaccines-and-retroviruses-a-whistleblower-reveals-what-the-government-is-hiding/*) gives a lot of information on retroviruses, their relationship to, and how Myalgic Encephalomyelits (ME), can be caused by them. A researcher named Dr. Judith Mikovits co-wrote with Kent Heckenlively the book *Plague: One Scientist's Intrepid Search for the Truth about Human Retroviruses and Chronic Fatigue Syndrome (ME/CFS), Autism, and Other Diseases* (Skyhorse Publishing, 2017.) She was fired from her federal government-funded position as Research Director and jailed for being a whistleblower about the weaponized retroviruses, how they found their way into vaccines, and about the subsequent government cover-up. She had presented evidence to the federal government about how a retrovirus not only underlies ME but also autism spectrum disorder.

It is outside the purpose of this book to discuss the US history of bioweapons research, vaccinations, and open-air spraying of pathogens. There is plenty of chilling information readily available with a simple Internet search. A few more examples which discuss this subject include: Carol Rutz's book *A Nation Betrayed: The Chilling True Story of Secret Cold War Experiments Performed on Our Children and Other Innocent People* and Gordon Thomas's book *Secrets and Lies: A History of CIA Torture and Bio-Weapon Experiments (2007).* John Marks' book *The Search for the Manchurian Candidate* is somewhat dated but nonetheless extremely well researched and informative as to the unethical research performed on unwitting victims. The CIA's use of LSD on many unsuspecting citizens was one of the lawsuits my father had to deal with as general counsel of the CIA in the 1970s with the death of Frank Olson. Mark's book has an entire chapter on the Olson case and much material on LSD research. Citizens of the United States don't want to think this, but the United States has done extensive unethical open-air and other research on unsuspecting citizens for at least seventy years. The use of bio-weaponized delivery systems is a huge moral and ethical issue that brings great shame to our country.

The Coronavirus grabbed the world's fearful attention with its fearful plandemic. There is scientific evidence this virus was bioengineered, and did not evolve in nature. Dr. Francis Boyle, a bioweapons expert who drafted the Biological Weapons Anti-terrorism Act of 1989, states in an interview the virus is designed for "efficient spreading" among humans, and has "gain-of-function" properties that make it a perfect bioweapon. Further, he says it was developed in the US and sold to China. (*https://www.walshmedicalmedia.com/open-access/coronavirus-is-a-biological-warfare-weapon.pdf*). It has been said that the bioweapon vaccine was the planned "cure" for the planned outbreak of Covid.

In early 2000, Fauci shook hands with Bill Gates in the library of Gates' $147 million Seattle mansion, cementing a partnership that would aim to control an increasingly profitable $60 billion global vaccine enterprise with unlimited growth potential. Through funding leverage and carefully cultivated personal relationships with heads of state and leading media and social media institutions, the Pharma-Fauci-Gates alliance exercises dominion over global health policy and our beautiful country.

This is not just another political book.

The Real Anthony Fauci details how Fauci, Gates, and their cohorts use their control of media outlets—both conservative and liberal leaning, scientific journals, key government and quasi-governmental agencies, global intelligence agencies, and influential scientists and physicians to flood the public with fearful propaganda about COVID-19 virulence and pathogenesis, and to muzzle debate and ruthlessly censor dissent.

In early 2000, Fauci shook hands with Bill Gates in the library of Gates' $147 million Seattle mansion, cementing a partnership that would aim to control an increasingly profitable $60 billion global vaccine enterprise with unlimited growth potential. Through funding leverage and carefully cultivated personal relationships with heads of state and leading media and social media institutions, the Pharma-Fauci-Gates alliance exercises dominion over global health policy and our beautiful country.

The Real Anthony Fauci details how Fauci, Gates, and their cohorts use their control of media outlets—both conservative and liberal leaning, scientific journals, key government and quasi-governmental agencies, global intelligence agencies, and influential scientists and physicians to flood the public with fearful propaganda about COVID-19 virulence and pathogenesis, and to muzzle debate and ruthlessly censor dissent. From the overview, (*https://www.barnesandnoble.com/w/the-real-anthony-fauci-robert-f-kennedy-jr/1142798123*)

To briefly return to and sum up my story, my dreams helped heal me, miraculously, from a disabling fifteen-year illness. They correctly identified the issue as a retrovirus problem. This miracle in my life opened me further to the possibility of other miracles. There have been so very many of them (two of which I will share in the following pages), and I am incredibly fortunate for the abundance of help I have received and have been able to give.

OUT OF THE DARKNESS COMES A MIRACLE

Bonnie began working with me for severe depression following the death of her mother and her separation from her husband of many years. She saw me twice weekly. About one year into the therapy, she becamevery concerned about her daughter, Jennifer, who was showing some unusual behaviors. Jennifer had retreated into herself; her usual sparkling personality had all but disappeared. Jennifer had always been beautiful and athletic, with a muscled body from the sports she excelled at doing. Now she was losing too much weight and was wearing mostly baggy, unattractive clothing. She had pulled away from her long-term girlfriends and in general just seemed down and "off." Some of these behaviors were possibly indicative of sexual-abuse problems. Mother and daughter had always had an unusually close relationship. Bonnie questioned her daughter as to whether anything was wrong. Jennifer adamantly denied problems.

Jennifer was entering adolescence. Her behavior could be related to adolescent issues, the recent separation of her parents, and her mother's depression. Jennifer was seeing a male psychiatrist and was also on medication he had prescribed for her. An older male relative was living in the home and appeared to get along well with Jennifer. Jennifer denied problems with him.

When Bonnie told me about Jennifer's behaviors, I told her I was concerned about the possibility of sexual abuse. Bonnie and I discussed the issue thoroughly. Bonnie had wondered over the years if her husband, from whom she was separated, had sexually abused her children, but she'd never found anything concrete to support her suspicions. Jennifer did not have current visitation with her dad. To her credit, Bonnie was receptive right from that first discussion to looking into the issue further.

Bonnie believed Jennifer might be reluctant to share intimate sexual issues, if there were any, with her male psychiatrist. She thought Jennifer might be more willing to talk with me, as a female. After discussing the situation with the psychiatrist, who supported Jennifer meeting with me for a session or two, we brought Jennifer into one of her mom's sessions.

Jennifer denied sexual abuse, but her mom and I were both left with a lingering feeling that she was holding back. I let Jennifer know if she ever wanted to talk about something with me, she should call me or let her mother know. In my own way, I let Jennifer know I didn't really believe her but that I would respect her decisions.

Several years later, Jennifer confessed to her mom that the male relative who had been living with them had been brutally beating her and sexually abusing her for many years. She had not disclosed this before because he had repeatedly threatened to kill her if she ever told on him, and she knew from his beatings of her he was capable of great harm without pangs of conscience. He'd also threatened to kill her mother. Since he was a violent psychopath under his friendly veneer, she believed that he might. Jennifer said she'd finally disclosed the abuse because she could not stand it any longer and wanted it to stop and wanted to bring him to justice. He was arrested.

Bonnie could not listen to the details of what had happened. Jennifer did not feel comfortable initially talking with her 6'4" male psychiatrist (who at this point was seeing her only for medications, not for therapy) about the intimate details. We all agreed she would come in to see me for several sessions to talk about it, since she was comfortable with me, while she and her mother decided what she wanted to do regarding a court case. The details were tragic and horrendous. Jennifer had suffered unbearably. She had also internalized a great deal of it, feeling that somehow she was to blame. Her main hope now was that her relative would be found guilty, which would give her some satisfaction that justice had been served.

The court case in Fairfax, Virginia, ended in a travesty of justice. Jennifer's rapist was acquitted and set free. A great deal of attention was focused on her mom's supposed failings as a parent and the aging judge's "feeling" that Jennifer had made up the years of abuse and torture. As Bonnie's therapist, I knew Bonnie was a good mother, and I believed Jennifer.

Jennifer was devastated. She had thought her rapist would finally get the justice he deserved. She could not fathom her relative being set free with no charges. She told me, "I finally told and did the right thing, because I wanted justice to be served, for all the years I was beaten and raped. Instead, my mom was blamed and my rapist set free." Speaking out had backfired on her.

Jennifer entered into a deep downward spiral of drug and alcohol abuse. She found a boyfriend who replicated her years of beatings by beating her further. She got into drugs, including cocaine. She was emotionally unreachable to both her parents. She eventually ran off to Florida, where she continued her self-destructive patterns. Even though she was underage, she worked at a strip club for a while and got involved with more drugs. During this time she was raped again.

Bonnie's grief was enormous. Her daughter was cut off from her, and she was understandably worried sick, unable to find her daughter and not even sure if she was dead or alive.

After a period, Bonnie terminated therapy and moved to Philadelphia to start a business. One day she called me and told me she had been in touch with Jennifer, who had finally asked to return home. Jennifer had said she was ready to start her life over and "face her past."

Bonnie was joyful but realistic. She said Jennifer could come live with her only on the condition Jennifer would get therapy in order to deal with the years of brutal abuse. Jennifer agreed. However, since adults' betrayals in her life had been so massive, Jennifer wanted a therapist she knew and trusted. She said the person she trusted was me. Maybe this was because I had guessed what might be going on years before.

Bonnie had always been willing to go the extra mile for her daughter, and now was no exception. Jennifer had lost her driver's license during her substance-abusing period, so Bonnie agreed to take one day off her day job per week to drive Jennifer the six-hour round-trip from Philadelphia to Washington, DC, to see me. This was an extraordinary step, but the circumstances were extraordinarily challenging. We all hoped the healing could now begin.

In our very first meeting, I asked Jennifer if she had gotten a gynecological exam. She had not. With her history of sexual abuse, I knew this would be a very important step. I encouraged Jennifer to see her gynecologist for a thorough exam. Mom had been urging this, and Jennifer now agreed.

Jennifer and her mom came together to my office the next time. They were very long faced and had some very sad news. They had gone to a gynecologist for Jennifer to have an exam. Unfortunately, the exam had shown something suspicious. A biopsy had revealed several large spots of ovarian cancer, a cancer with a very poor prognosis in one so young.

Shocked, Jennifer had gone for a second opinion. This next gynecologist had said she could easily see, with just a visual exam, three large spots of cancer on Jennifer's ovaries. According to the doctor, Jennifer had advanced ovarian cancer. The second biopsy had also revealed cancer. The prognosis was terminal. Jennifer's estimated life span was now six months or less.

Mother and daughter were both devastated. They sat in my office in a state of shock and disbelief. Jennifer commented on how her life had been "shit" and how ironic it was that now that she was again trying to make a fresh start, she was going to die. Bonnie was heartbroken and felt hopeless and helpless. I too was stunned and extremely saddened. At this point I had worked with this family for many years. I had a heartfelt connection with them.

That night, before I went to sleep, I included Jennifer and her mom in my prayers. I remember feeling so very sad for them. I asked God to help them. To the best of my ability to recall, I did not ask for any specific kind of help or outcome. During the middle of the night, I had the following dream:

> Mary, mother of Jesus, is descending from the sky. She is luminous and glowing, surrounded by the most beautiful ethereal blue light imaginable.

> As she floats down toward me, I see that she is dressed in a beautiful blue gown, perhaps with gold specks in it. She is so beautiful and emanates an incredible aura of peace and love.

> As I watch Mary, she outstretches her arms, palms upward. Three glowing globes of golden-white light issue from her palms. Each globe surrounds a spot completely. As I observe, I am given the information that each globe of light is surrounding one of the three cancerous spots on Jennifer's ovaries. As each spot is enveloped in light, it disappears.

> As I watch this amazing sight, I am absolutely certain that Jennifer is now totally healed of her cancer.

I cannot explain the absolute certainty I experienced both in the dream and immediately upon waking. Eventually I went back to sleep. In the morning when I awoke, I remembered the dream vividly and felt the same certainty of having witnessed a miraculous healing in the dream.

As the day went on, I thought often about the dream and tried to understand it. The memory of the strong feeling of certainty was there, yet now in my day consciousness I was having doubts. Maybe the dream had been a wish-fulfillment dream? I had known this family for a long time now and cared for them.

I wondered whether to tell Jennifer the dream. The last thing I wanted to do was to give her false hope. She had been through way too much already. However, if by some chance something so miraculous had happened, I strongly felt Jennifer should have the opportunity to investigate, if she felt so inclined. Maybe she would be touched that Mary would visit her in a dream, even if it wasn't her own dream.

I decided to go ahead and tell Jennifer, while cautioning her I did not know what the dream meant. It seemed to me in some way that I had no right to keep this dream from Jennifer, since it was about a visitation from Mary to Jennifer. In my mind, regardless of outcome, that was a very special thing.

When I spoke next with Jennifer, I cautioned her I did not know what the dream meant, but I told her that since it was about her, I wanted to tell her and believed it would not be right to keep it from her. Her eyes grew wide as I told her the dream. She immediately said she knew it was true, that she was healed and that Mary had healed her. Jennifer had been brought up Catholic, and Mary is a very important figure in Catholicism. Jennifer's simple but deep faith, after all she had been through, moved me greatly.

Jennifer went back to the same doctor who had told her the spots were readily visible to the naked eye. The doctor expressed disbelief that Jennifer was the same person she had seen the previous week. There was now absolutely no trace of any of the spots of cancer. A repeat biopsy verified that the cancer was completely gone. We were all thrilled and awed at what had happened. Finally, Jennifer had gotten a break in her short, intensely traumatized life, and a big break at that. She was determined to give back for this life she had been given and hoped someday to work helping victims of child abuse.

It is now more than twenty years since that dream miracle. Jennifer will have to be watched carefully for life. At five years past her miracle healing, she had a recurrence, but since she was being carefully monitored, it was caught early and treated. To my knowledge, there have been no further occurrences of ovarian cancer.

For a long time after that, whenever I pondered the dream, I doubted that what I had witnessed in the dream was the actual healing. Sometimes I told myself maybe it was just a metaphorical representation of the healing. Maybe it was my feelings of unworthiness; I do not know. At this point in time, however, I feel very honored to have been fortunate enough to experience the visitation by Mary and to witness her amazing healing powers. After much reflection, I now believe, in part because of the amazing spiritual energy in the dream, that I witnessed the actual healing through the vehicle of my dream. I cannot explain what happened, nor will I try. Many years have passed, and Jennifer is alive and well. That is enough for me. This experience has helped me believe in the power of prayer. I continue to pray for my clients on a regular basis.

BONNIE'S MIRACULOUS HEALING

Several years after this miraculous healing and after Jennifer had discontinued her therapy, Bonnie called me and asked to begin therapy with me again. She was still living in Philadelphia, but she was planning to sell her business and move back to the Washington, DC, area. Her business was overwhelmingly stressful to her, and she was physically ill. She had gained a lot of weight and had a number of significant health issues. We would do therapy by phone until such time as she would be able to come into my office in person.

The Bonnie I had known, back when she'd lived in Northern Virginia previously, had always been quite fit, with enormous stamina. She'd worked out regularly with a trainer and on her own. I had never known her to have any significant health issues. Now, by her report, she had odd lumps throughout her body, facial hair growth, and pain and swelling in her joints.

The woman who could previously ride her bike all day now had a lot of trouble going up and down stairs. She was fatigued all the time and was depressed at her disability. She had gained a lot of weight, which was uncharacteristic for her. Bonnie had many other symptoms that puzzled her and her doctors. She went from doctor to doctor for tests. She often felt dismissed by the medical establishment when they were not able to accurately diagnose her, and she grew discouraged as to the possibility of regaining her health.

I supported Bonnie in her attempts to find out what was wrong with her. In the meantime, we worked on developing stress-management techniques, on carving out time for recreation and relaxation in her busy schedule, and on helping her stand up for herself in a difficult relationship.

Bonnie grew worse and kept going to different doctors. Her frustration was understandably enormous. She finally found one who could diagnose her problem. At the time, few doctors understood the disease she suffered from, and fewer still specialized in treating it.

Bonnie was diagnosed with Cushing's disease, a relatively rare but debilitating form of Cushing's syndrome. In this disease, excess hormones are produced in the pituitary gland. In Bonnie's case, she had a tumor in her pituitary. Symptoms of Cushing's disease include weight gain, severe muscle fatigue, a hump on the back of the neck, and high blood pressure. It is difficult to diagnose, and at the time there were few treatment options.

Finally Bonnie had a diagnosis. Bonnie tried treatment with a doctor in Philadelphia but without success. Then, since she was planning to move back to DC, she found a specialist in the Washington, DC, area who put her on a medication protocol that had had limited successes with Cushing's disease. Unfortunately, this doctor's treatment did not work well for Bonnie. She hoped eventually a treatment would be found that would work for her. Because of her physical problems, her existence was miserable.

This doctor referred her to an ongoing National Institute of Health (NIH) study on Cushing's disease. In order for her to get into this NIH study, two doctors who were considered specialists in Cushing's had to recommend her and put her through a rigorous panel of tests and procedures to confirm the diagnosis. The reason for such a thorough screening was to make absolutely sure that all study subjects were correctly diagnosed. Although it was very difficult at the time to find two Cushing's specialists, Bonnie found them and went through all the requisite procedures and tests, which all confirmed she had Cushing's disease. She was accepted into the NIH study.

In the meantime, Bonnie sold her business and moved back to the Washington, DC, area. When she came into my office for the first time since I had seen her years before, she looked very different than I remembered. She had gained a lot of weight, was out of breath from climbing the stairs, and was without vitality. I was shocked at the difference in her.

In this first in-person session we talked about how disabled she was and how it dragged her down at every turn. Remembering her daughter's health miracle, Bonnie asked me to pray for her. I said I would.

When later I prayed, I "heard" in spirit an interesting response to my prayer. That response was that Bonnie would have to do this one herself, that her path included learning how to heal herself.

The next time I saw Bonnie, she was in a great deal of pain. I told her the answer I had received to my prayer. Then, an idea hit me. I had trained for a number of years in a healing technique called holographic memory resolution (HMR). (See www.healingdimensions.com for more information about this technique.) It is a client-centered healing approach, developed by an ex-priest named Brent Baum. I have found the technique to be extremely effective at healing trauma and physical complaints. When I utilize this technique, I am a guide helping the client to heal himself or herself. The technique is based on the belief that our traumas are stored energetically within the body. Unresolved trauma tends to create an energy block in that area of the body and can become a precursor to disease, whether psychological or physical. The technique, though still relatively unknown but growing in popularity, is the most effective trauma resolution tool I have found. I have used it over the years with great success. It is also something I can teach my clients to do themselves at home, which is a great benefit.

An interesting feature of HMR is that in the process the client is often asked to ask his or her higher self for an answer to a given question, and we then work with what is given. Using the metaphor of a computer, if one's psyche (the totality of the body and mind, conscious and unconscious) is the computer, then asking one's higher self for an answer is like doing a computer search. The information is there for the asking and proves on target time after time after time. Hypnosis accesses that deep inner wisdom through induction of a trance state. Dreams access the higher self as well through our sleep state. In HMR, the answer is sought directly, without the use of an induced trance or of the different brain wave states found in sleep.

I told Bonnie I had an idea and asked if she would be willing to try an exercise. She was. We spent the rest of that session using the HMR technique. In her mind's eye, I asked her to visualize the tumor in her pituitary. She did. Next, I asked her to ask her higher self to tell her when it began growing.

When doing HMR, a common question at this juncture might be "How young were you when the tumor first appeared?" The client asks his or her higher self for the answer, and an age comes to the client's mind. At that point a common HMR question would be "What was going on in your life at that age when the symptom first appeared?" At this point the client is usually able to identify a trauma or conflict that occurred at the given age. From there, the next part of the HMR procedure is to work through the trauma by revisualizing it in a resolved manner.

Bonnie's HMR would prove to be a challenge. When I asked her how young she was when the tumor first appeared in her pituitary, she stated it had started a year and a half ago. So far, so good. That was about when her symptoms had begun as well. When I asked her what was going on in her life at the time the tumor first appeared, she drew a blank. She could not identify anything related to the onset of the tumor.

I was left needing to do a work-around, as there was no identifiable trauma or conflict to resolve. I remembered from my advanced training with Brent Baum, the creator of HMR, that when this happens, you can directly work on resolving or eradicating the symptom rather than the usual focusing on the trauma or conflict that led to the symptom development.

Using the HMR guidelines, I asked Bonnie to imagine a way of removing the problem from her pituitary. She said she would have Jesus come and remove it. I gave her time to visualize this. We continued to work through the HMR exercise. When we finished, she said, "It's gone; it's not there anymore." That was interesting. Time would tell.

When Bonnie came in the following week, she was dramatically different. She said her symptoms were gone, and she was feeling herself again. Her blood pressure was normal, her pain was gone, and she had started to lose some of the bloat. I wondered if she might be in remission but still carrying the disease, though I did not say this to her. Her belief in her healing was what mattered.

Several months later, Bonnie reported to me that she had been released from the NIH study. With a big smile on her face, she told me she no longer had any of the markers of the disease, so there was no reason for them to keep her in the study. I was so happy for her; she had indeed healed herself, with a little guidance from me.

I do not understand how it is that I was involved in these two health miracles within the same family. I do know that these and my own miracle healing have given me a renewed appreciation for healing and miracles. No matter how dark it seems around us, no matter how hopeless and overwhelming the odds may be, there is still hope. I know that within each of us lies an enormous untapped power to heal ourselves and others. I am grateful to Jessica and Bonnie for their faith and the lessons they have taught me.

And so I end this book, a chronicle of many stories in the journey to the divine within. In helping others to heal and find their true selves, I discover my own. My clients have taught me well. Though each path may be different, we are all on the same ultimate journey. Though there may be many dark days ahead for humanity, it is possible for us to create a better future. God has kept me alive through so much for a reason; perhaps part of that reason is to spread renewed hope in the midst of darkness and to help us reach higher than we know we can reach.

CIA FOIA DECLASSIFIED
(SEPTEMBER 2014) DOCUMENT

INTERVIEW WITH FORMER GENERAL
COUNSEL JOHN S. WARNER

Unclassified

The Oral History Program

An Interview With Former General Counsel John S. Warner (U)

Editor's Note: The celebration in 1997 of the 50th Anniversary of the CIA served as a reminder of the Agency's fascinating history, with all its successes and its failures. Fortunately, it is still possible to speak with and learn from individuals who were present during the Agency's earliest years. One of those individuals, John Warner, provided to multiple interviewers his recollection of his time with CIA. Although Mr. Warner retired in 1976, he continues to write and speak about the issues concerning intelligence and national security law. He noted that his remarks are snapshots from the past and are illustrative of matters that arose in the history of CIA. One should not draw broad conclusions before exploring the full details of the incidents mentioned.

Photo: John Warner

John Warner served as the Agency's General Counsel from 1973 to 1976. He was present at the creation of CIA, serving as Deputy General Counsel in the Central Intelligence Group in 1946 and remaining in that post with CIA until his appointment as General Counsel in 1973. From 1957 to 1968, Mr. Warner served as Legislative Counsel while maintaining, for most of those years, his post as Deputy General Counsel.

Through the course of his career, John Warner witnessed--and frequently played an important role in--many of the major events and decisions that have shaped the Agency. From designing the legal framework for the Agency, through the evolution of the Agency's relationship with Congress, to Watergate and the damaging revelations of the 1970s, John Warner was on the scene.

Mr. Warner was born in Washington, DC. He began working in a bank when he was 16, and he worked his way through college and law school. He was finishing his master's degree when the Japanese attacked Pearl Harbor. The day after completing his degree, Mr. Warner enlisted as an aviation cadet, was trained to fly B-17s, and eventually completed 35 combat missions in Europe. While home on leave, Mr. Warner met James Donovan, General Counsel of the OSS, at a Washington cocktail party. The two hit it off, and Donovan arranged to have Warner transferred to the General Counsel's office of OSS in December 1944.

The following excerpts, preceded by brief introductions to the excerpted topics, were obtained from two interviews with Mr. Warner that were done under the auspices of the oral history program of the Center for the Study of Intelligence.

On the origins of CIA. *John Warner quickly befriended Larry Houston, another OSS lawyer, who went on to become CIA's first General Counsel. After the war, the two moved with the clandestine collection and support components of OSS, renamed the Strategic Services Unit, to the War Department until the Central Intelligence Group (CIG), was created in January 1946. Houston and Warner together drafted the legislative proposals to establish the CIA. These were to be a part of the National Security Act of 1947, but the Truman administration preferred to keep the CIA component of that Act more general. Their work was eventually encompassed in the CIA Act of 1949.*

John Warner (JW): [Thomas] Troy's *Donovan and the CIA* states [DCI Hoyt] Vandenberg commissioned preparation of a bill to create the CIA and sent it to Clark Clifford [then Special Counsel to President Truman]. Houston's recollection of this event is somewhat different. He recalls that he and I had written a substantial part, if not all, of the legislation prior to Vandenberg's arrival on the scene.

While working on other problems, I discovered a Federal statute, the Independent Offices Appropriations Act of 1945, which provided that a government entity set up by Presidential directive could not exist for more than one year without legislation. Technically, CIG was an entity without legal standing.... That's why we sat down and wrote as quickly as possible. In fact, I wrote the first drafts.

I was a young lawyer, never practiced, never been in government, and so what do you do? I went to the Executive Order, which established the CIG, to pick up what CIA was to be, and then I went to the OSS Appropriation Acts, because that was the only statutory thing about OSS. It was probably the smartest thing I ever did, because that was the guts of what later became the CIA Act of 1949.

On unvouchered funds. *One of the key provisions of the CIA Act of 1949 permitted the Director to expend funds "for objects of a confidential, extraordinary, or emergency nature" on his own authority without having those expenditures subject to audit by the GAO. These funds are known as "unvouchered" or "special" funds. Mr. Warner explains below that the Congress accepted CIA's need for unvouchered funds because the GAO had worked with OSS and understood that the Agency's mission required them.*

JW: The authority for unvouchered funds... that's the guts of the ability of CIA to do its work... to run espionage operations and covert action requiring the highest security. Every other agency in government, whatever vouchers they create are reviewed by the GAO, and they can take exception to it and so forth...

George Washington was the first one to get unvouchered funds. In fact, in the first Congress he said there ought to be a statute authorizing this, and there was. And it's been repeated over the years, except that CIA was the first Agency that got it up to 100 percent of its funds.

Because... the way things started, GAO was on the premises in OSS, and we learned to work with them. And [OSS General Counsel] Jim Donovan even submitted requests to them for an opinion. It was advisory only because it involved unvouchered funds. And there were other questions we would talk to GAO about. So when they were asked [by the Congress] for comments, they said, "Well, we would generally be against this kind of thing, but in view of the mission of CIA, we think it's necessary." Now that's a big step to get the Comptroller General to agree that at least half our money would not be looked at by him. It's also interesting [that] about the same time the Atomic Energy Commission, which was a separate agency, was asking for a big chunk of unvouchered money, and Congress said, "No" and the Comptroller General said, "No."

As you may or may not know, there were a couple of Communists who were members of the Congress, in the House, and they objected all over the place. They objected to the unvouchered funds, and they objected even to the concept [of the CIA].

On the DCI's authority to bring foreign nationals into the country. *One of the more controversial clauses of the CIA Act of 1949 gave the DCI permission to bring up to 100 foreign nationals into the United States each fiscal year, regardless of whether they qualified under the immigration laws.*

JW: Essentially, what happened is, [Senator] McCarran, who was head of Senate Judiciary, which has jurisdiction over immigration matters, said this is an impingement on the immigration authorities. [I explained] to him that this was not an immigration matter, that this was an operational matter to bring a very important alien into the country without regard to all the special provisions of the immigration laws and that probably, very rarely would we get to 100. As it turned out... for many years [there were only] seven or eight a year. But we had to report to McCarran. We said, "We'll give you a yearly report," and he said okay. That was the controversy. It wasn't on the substance of the thing, it was jurisdiction.

The Oral History Program   Approved for Release: 2014/09/10 C00872669   (b)(3)(c)

On the Office of General Counsel.

JW: I don't know how long it took us to get 10 lawyers [in OGC], but maybe five or six years. And there were no cases that brought us into court as a party, [although] we were increasingly involved with courts in one way or another. [In] private suits where someone was undercover . . . we would try to work arrangements with he judge or with opposing counsel. We'd clear the opposing counsel and brief him: "Look, it has nothing to do with your suite but would you respect this [operational equity]?" And they did. Running through all this, touching base with the judge or opposing counsel was the theme. Never put a false document into court. Never. If you had to take chances on the security involved, you'd do that, but you'd never put a false document, or direct an employee to put a false document. . . . We were lawyers, you just don't lie to a judge . . . .[S]omething that ran through most of our work was the question of preservation of security and compliance with the law. And, of course, the United States with all its laws is the most difficult country in the world. We have so many laws.

On agent contracts. Below, Mr. Warner discusses the case of an agent who sued the Agency for breach of contract. In the Totten case that Mr. Warner refers to, the estate of a Union spy sued the government, claiming that it breached a contract that had existed between the spy and President Lincoln. The Supreme Court ruled against the spy's estate, arguing that, "The secrecy which such contracts impose preclude any action for their enforcement."

JW: There's a long history on that, it's a Civil War case, *Totten*. Where a Union spy sued for back pay. And it went to [the] Supreme Court, and the Supreme Court said there is no basis for any such action. In the one case that came up, we cited the *Totten* case. There had been no citing of it for many, many years. Now there's a lot of them.

On the Marchetti case. *Victor Marchetti served with CIA from 1955 to 1969. Most of that time he was a Soviet military analyst, but, for the last three years of his career, he worked as a staffer in the DCI's office, including a stint as executive assistant to DDCI Rufus Taylor. It was from that vantage point that he learned much about the Agency's covert actions, which he sought to expose in a book after he left the Agency. Upon learning of Marchetti's plans to publish, the Agency on 18 April 1972 successfully sought an order in a US District Court forbidding him to disclose any information about CIA and requiring him to submit his manuscript for review before publishing it. John Warner wrote an article on this episode, and the article, "The Marchetti Case: New Case Law," was published in Studies in Intelligence in the spring of 1977.*

JW: A publisher came to us and said, "Here is a manuscript I think you ought to look at because it looks like it has some sensitive things in it." Prior to this, we'd often thought about what you do when someone threatens to publish or put out classified information. We thought that you would want to get an injunction to prevent him from publishing. Now to get a temporary injunction you've got to have a pretty compelling case....

Well, we had studied this in a theoretical way and looked at commercial contracts to protect proprietary information and thought we could go on a contract theory [arguing that a mutual agreement to protect classified information should be enforced] because everyone signed a secrecy agreement.... Colby called, he was Executive Director then, and [he asked] whether we ever thought about going to court [to prevent disclosure]. I said, "We sure have." . . .

[DCI Richard] Helms was concerned about being in court.... But Larry [Houston] and I went to see him and explained it. He went to talk to Nixon about it...and Nixon said, "Well, if it's that bad, or important, have your lawyers talk to my lawyers." So Larry and I went to see John Ehrlichman, and by then we had a pretty good reading from various directorates on how sensitive some of the material [Marchetti intended for publication] was.... Obviously, when we go to court [the Department of] Justice is our lawyer. And so we talked to Irwin Goldblum [a lawyer from the Department of Justice], and we prepared the necessary papers....

So what we have here is the first time that the CIA as a plaintiff went in to guarantee and protect its

11/12/02 7:34 AM

rights and we won. [E]very time you go in court you are losing something. But for me this Marchetti case is precedent shattering. We go in as a plaintiff to protect ourselves....

On the Snepp case. *After the Marchetti case, it was clear that CIA had the right, by virtue of the contractual provisions of the secrecy agreement, to review works that current and former Agency employees planned to submit for publication. The Agency knew that Frank Snepp, who had worked for the Agency from 1968 to 1976, intended to publish a book, and that he and his lawyer assured then DCI Stansfield Turner that he would submit his manuscript for review prior to publishing. He reneged on that promise, however. In the ensuing legal battle, the Agency successfully prevented Snepp from receiving his royalties from the publication of Decent Interval.*

JW: [In the Snepp case that followed Marchetti] for purposes of the trial, CIA's position was, "We are not alleging that there is any classified information in this book. We are just saying he violated his contract." He didn't submit [to the Agency the information he intended to publish], although he had signed a secrecy agreement.... The Supreme Court ruled [in favor of enforcing the secrecy and prepublication review agreements] and approved the forfeiture by Snepp of all profits from his book. So Marchetti and Snepp. I just felt these are tremendous victories the little old lawyers won.

The Freedom of Information Act. *The Freedom of Information Act, which Mr. Warner discusses, entitles anyone to request and receive copies of records in the possession of the executive branch of the Federal Government unless those records fall within certain exempted categories.*

JW: [W]e get to FOIA [Freedom of Information Act] [and] the FOIA amendments. These...impacted every government agency, but particularly the security agencies. The day after it became effective, Morton Halperin put in at least five letters [requesting information from] us, and seven or eight to others... and he was practically a member of Senator Kennedy's staff in getting the amendments passed....

Now [before the FOIA amendments became law,] we sa[id] this should be vetoed, it's unconstitutional.... It provides, if the Agency doesn't answer in 30 days, that they can file suit. You know, ridiculous. Then, of course, courts don't pay any attention to that, but it's wrong to put on the statute books something that no one is going to pay any attention to... so we recommended that the President veto it, and he did. And it was overridden.

On Congressional oversight: *Before the formation of the House and Senate Select Committees on Intelligence, formal Congressional oversight of CIA was performed by small subcommittees of the Appropriations and Armed Services Committees. These committees were among the busiest in the Congress, and their members occasionally did not have time to hold hearings on CIA, even on important matters like its budget. The substantive committees, such as the Senate Foreign Relations Committee, often asked for briefings on world events, but Warner notes that Agency officials would brief on operational matters only to the CIA subcommittees of Appropriations and Armed Services.*

JW: In the first few years I was there, I would...go to each of the committees [and say] "Please, will you hold a hearing so we can brief you." To our own subcommittees, [we briefed on covert action] and other operational matters. But...how well they were briefed is another matter because, if you only met with them once, and there was some event occurring worldwide, that [significant event] got the attention. We did not give them anything in writing. I don't think they had safes.

House Foreign Affairs, Senate Foreign Relations...they would call us... now and then for sensitive intelligence briefings.... We felt we were just as responsible to the Congress as we were to the President. The Congress created us, plus Congress gave us our money. In other words, we were realists. We drew the line when it came to operations.... It was never intrusive. They would ask for an explanation. They might halfheartedly "tsk, tsk," if you missed something...but they never jumped on us. Never.

[We were asked to give] a budget briefing, Sunday afternoon, in the House Office Building in the Capitol at 1 p.m. Okay, I said fine.... Sure enough, there we all are 1 p.m., Longworth Building.... It was sort of a crowded room and Clarence Cannon greets Dulles, "Oh, it's good to see you again Mr.

(b)(3)(c)

Secretary." He refers to [Secretary of State John Foster Dulles rather than DCI Allen Dulles] but he knows it is the CIA budget. [Allen] Dulles is a great raconteur. He can tell story after story. He reminds Cannon of this, and Cannon reminds him of that, and they swap stories for two hours. And, in the end: "Well, Mr. Secretary, have you got enough money in your budget for this year, the coming year?" "Well, I think we are all right, Mr. Chairman. Thank you very much." That was the budget hearing. Now [some members, including then representative Gerald Ford] were visibly disturbed by this.... So I pulled [them] aside and I said, "Gentlemen, would you like me to arrange a briefing either here or at the Agency on our budget?" And they... thanked me. And we did [have another briefing] without, obviously, telling the Chairman. And that's why I got to be such good friends with Gerry Ford.

When we began getting into a lot of matters before the Church and Pike Committees... there was a strong core of resistance in the Directorate of Operations. They didn't see why it had to be done. There is still that group that thought Colby did too much [in the way of providing information]. And they were wrong.

On the Church Committee: *On 22 December 1974, The New York Times published an article by Seymour Hersh that alleged CIA had seriously violated its regulations by conducting widespread, illegal operations against domestic dissident groups, such as the anti-Vietnam war movement. Other stories of a similar vein followed, and, in early 1975, the Senate voted to create the Senate Select Committee To Study Governmental Operations With Respect to Intelligence Activities under the chairmanship of Senator Frank Church. The House followed suit by establishing a similar committee under the chairmanship of Representative Otis Pike.*

JW: Church came out with that "CIA is a rogue elephant" statement before he ever had a hearing.... He was running for President.... So they got their charter and I remember vividly Colby and [I] went down to visit Church and his committee counsel.... The purpose of our going down was to establish agreed-on procedures for dealing with classified information, both in terms of personnel and in terms of documents. Church listened politely. Colby said, "We want your people to have standard kinds of safes, we will send security people down to brief your staff people on what kind of safe, or we will provide the safes. We will help you with your procedures for handling documents. We will ask your staff people to undergo investigation and sign secrecy agreements. Now, Senator Church, your clearance consists of the vote of your state that elected you." Patting him on the back.... Colby said, "I see no problem with that," despite the fact that Church had called the CIA a rogue elephant before the hearings ever opened.

The Church Committee issued a report and issued a later legislative proposal.... Very critical, but their report says, which Church signed as Chairman, "CIA has been responsive to the Presidency throughout." No rogue elephant. No one ever saw that in a headline. A lot of their recommendations, and proposed legislation, were ridiculous. This is again the staff. Senators don't read these reports in detail....

On MKULTRA: *MKULTRA was the principal CIA program for the research and development of chemical agents designed to control human behavior. Begun in 1953 out of fear that the Communist countries had made significant progress in mind control, the program lasted for 10 years and eventually focused on using LSD to obtain information from individuals and to control their behavior. On 27 November 1953, Dr. Frank Olson, a civilian employee of the Army, fell to his death from a New York City hotel window eight days after having been administered a dose of LSD by a CIA officer as part of an experiment. The program continued after Olson's death and included the administration of LSD to individuals.*

JW: [In many cases of high-profile flaps,] OGC didn't have the full, unadulterated story.... Because the operators, in part, partook of Helms's view of things. Don't get the lawyers in it. That's part of the operational kind of thinking.... About the Olson case.... The fellow that jumped out the window [allegedly because he was unwittingly administered hallucinogens by the Agency]...we didn't know it was part of a program that did this and did that, but it was quite clear that we had the essence of it that he had agreed that he would be a subject. And no one can say for sure whether this led him to jump out the window, but it was not unreasonable to suppose that it did.... [A]gain, we weren't told the entire story of the program. We were told strictly the elements around this one case. It never occurred to us to raise a question about the propriety of the program.

11/12/02 7:34 AM

The Oral History Program

(b)(3)(c)

I've often thought, without making a decision, that we should have been more proactive.... We never went looking for things that would raise questions. When things came to our notice we would act on it[, but we] never went looking for things, which is really an IG function.

On Watergate: *The five burglars who broke into the headquarters of the Democratic National Committee on 17 June 1972 all had CIA connections. Their leader, James McCord, had worked in the Office of Security, and the others, all Cubans, had worked with CIA on the Bay of Pigs operation. A longtime former Agency employee, Howard Hunt, then working for the White House, was also implicated in the burglary. It later emerged that Hunt had used CIA equipment in breaking into the office of Daniel Ellsberg's psychiatrist. Ellsberg had been the source of The Pentagon Papers leak.*

JW: The first time I got involved in Watergate, the US Attorney for the District of Columbia [Earl Silbert] asked if I would come by.... And so I went down there, by myself, and he was there with one other person...and started asking me these various questions.... Up to that time I had, in no way, been involved in anything relating to Watergate, nor did I know the Agency was in any way involved. So the question came as somewhat of a surprise.... Develop some film for Hunt? So I had these two pages of questions, I just can't remember all of them, but they were all, a number of them were things that had more or less appeared in the newspapers, so I knew what in the hell was cooking. I wrote this memorandum and sent it to the Director [Helms].... [Helms] addressed [a] meeting and expressed concern: "What are we going to do about this?" Not one person spoke out until I did. I said, "Dick [Helms], no matter what, we've got to respond to this. A US Attorney for the District of Columbia need answers. I haven't the slightest idea what this is about. None of these questions mean anything to me." [Helms] expressed his concern about involving CIA in the Watergate problem. I said, "Dick, we've got to respond. Now, if you've got some problems that I don't know about you may want to talk to the Attorney General, I don't know, but until I know more about it I can't give you any suggestions."... Eventually, the data was given to me in writing, and I put it together in some sort of package and took it back to the US Attorney.

On the need for secrecy.

JW: We overdid it some ways.... I think in some of our dealings with other [US Government] agencies we overdid the secrecy bit. We should have been more forthcoming.... There are a lot of reasons to be suspicious of CIA, or any government agency. I hear on television programs about this introduction of drugs in Los Angeles. But, on the other hand, what happened with DCI Gates, and others, is that they've opened up a lot of the Agency that they had to do, and should have been done earlier. Before, you go back to the 1950s, and everything is secret...the fact that we exist is almost secret.

Unclassified

Next   Previous   Contents

Appendix B

LEVELS OF MIND CONTROL PROGRAMMING

(based on *http://www.bibliotecapleyades.net/sociopolitica/esp_sociopol_mindcon02.htm*)

ALPHA—General programming includes the development of photographic memory (sometimes through a technique called brain stem scarring.) Also the development of substantially increased physical strength/visual ability. Alpha programming is accomplished through deliberately subdividing the victims personality.

BETA—Sexual programming eliminates all learned moral convictions and stimulates the primitive sexual instinct, devoid of inhibitions. "Cat" (Kitten) alters are Beta programs, which accounts for the pervasiveness of kitten and cat imagery surrounding models, actors, actresses, and musical artists.

DELTA—Killer programming was originally developed for training special agents or elite soldiers (i.e. Delta Force, First Earth Battalion, CIA/Mossad/MI6/KGB, etc.) in covert operations. At this level, there is optimal adrenal output and controlled aggression. Subjects are fearless and systematic in carrying out their assignment. Self-destruct or suicide instructions are programmed in at this level.

THETA—Psychic programming. Bloodliners (those from multi-generational Satanic families) are believed to have a greater propensity for psychic abilities than non-bloodliners ... Various forms of electronic mind control systems were developed and introduced, namely, brain implants, directed-energy lasers using microwaves and/or electromagnetics. These are used in conjunction with highly-advanced computers and sophisticated satellite tracking systems.

OMEGA—Self-destruct programming, Corresponding behaviors include suicidal tendencies and/or self-mutilation [cutting] ... These programs may be activated when the victim/survivor begins therapy or interrogation. They also manifest when too much memory is being recovered. The goal here is to prevent the victim from recovering or sharing information.

GAMMA—Deception programming is programmed to misinform and misdirect. This level is intertwined with demons and demonology. If one attempts to deactivate this programming, it is programmed to regenerate itself.

INFORMATION ABOUT FALSE MEMORY
SYNDROME FOUNDATION MEMBERS

[Reprinted with permission from Joel van der Reijden, Institute for the
Study of Globalization and Politics, *http://isgp.nl/FMSF_freaks*]

(Much of the intelligence/mind control information has come from Dr. Colin A. Ross, M.D., who received many
FOIA documents pertaining to US government mind control research.)

Dinges, David F., Scientific Advisory Board

Director of the FMSF who replaced Hyman. Faculty head (one of two) of the Unit for Experimental
Psychiatry at the University of Pennsylvania, together with Dr. Martin Orne (who founded the unit; died in
2000). Martin Orne, a member of Scientific Advisory Board of the FMSF, has been at the center of the creation
of a Manchurian candidate, has worked with Navy Intelligence, Air Force Intelligence, the Human Ecology
Foundation (a major CIA funding front for MKULTRA), and almost certainly also the NSA and Army Intelligence.

Freyd, Pamela, Founding Executive Director

Wife of Peter Freyd. Stood by her husband's conclusions that her daughter, Jennifer, was imagining her
childhood sexual abuse. Remained head of the FMSF after her husband resigned over the controversy.

Freyd, Peter, Founding Executive Director

Accused of childhood sexual abuse by his daughter Jennifer, who is a professor of psychology at the
University of Oregon. Jennifer: "My family of origin was troubled in many observable ways ... I refer to the
things that were never 'forgotten' and 'recovered,' but to things that we all knew about ... During my childhood,
my father sometimes discussed his own experiences of being sexually abused as an 11 year- old boy, and called
himself a 'kept boy'" Peter Freyd graduated to male prostitution as an adolescent. At the age of 13, Jennifer Freyd
composed a poem about her father's nocturnal visits. Part of it read: "I am caught in a web. A web of deep, deep
terror." The diaries of her youth chronicle the reactions and feelings (guilt, shame and terror) of a troubled girl
and young woman. "My parents oscillated between denying these symptoms and feelings ... to using knowledge
of these same symptoms and feelings to discredit me ... My father told various people that I was brain damaged."
Pamela Freyd turned to her own psychiatrist, Dr Harold Lief, another advisory board member of the FMS
Foundation, to diagnose Jennifer. "He explained to me that he did not believe I was abused," Jennifer recalls.

Dr Lief's diagnosis was based on his belief that Peter Freyd's fantasies were strictly "homoerotic." Of course, his daughter furrows a brow at the assumption that homoerotic fantasies or a heterosexual marriage exclude the possibility of child molestation. "At times I am flabbergasted that my memory is considered 'false,'" Jennifer says, "and my alcoholic father's memory is considered rational and sane ... I was at home a few hours after my second session with my therapist, a licensed clinical psychologist working within an established group in a large and respected medical clinic. "During that second visit to my therapist's office, I expressed great anxiety about the upcoming holiday visit with my parents. My therapist asked about half way into the session, whether I had ever been sexually abused. I was immediately thrown into a strange state. No one had ever asked me such a question. I responded, 'no, but ...' I went home and within a few hours I was shaking uncontrollably, overwhelmed with intense and terrible flashbacks." Jennifer asks herself why her parents are believed. "In the end, is it precisely because I was abused that I am to be discredited despite my personal and professional success?" Supposedly, in an electronic message from her father, he openly acknowledged that in his version of the story "fictional elements were deliberately inserted." "Fictional is rather an astounding choice of words," Jennifer observed at the Ann Arbor Conference. The article written by her parents contends that Jennifer was denied tenure at another university due to a lack of published research. "In fact," Jennifer counters, "I moved to the University of Oregon in 1987, just four years after receiving my PhD to accept a tenured position as associate professor in the psychology department, one of the world's best psychology departments ... My mother sent the Jane Doe article to my colleagues during my promotion year—that is, the year my case for promotion to full professor was being considered. I was absolutely mortified to learn of this violation of my privacy and this violation of the truth." (from Alex Constantine)

Lief, Dr. Harold, Scientific Advisory Board

Lief was the personal psychiatrist to the Freyd family who told Jennifer he didn't believe she was sexually abused from a young age by her father. Former major in the Army medical corps. Close colleague of the co-FMSF board member Dr. Martin Orne (the MKULTRA-connected scientist with many connections to different intelligence agencies and mind control research) and consulted with him on several studies in hypnotic programming and behavioral modification experiments at the University of Pennsylvania. Past president of the Sex Information and Education Council and director of the Centre for Sexuality and Religion. His academic writing reveals an interesting range of professional interests, including a study entitled "Orgasm in the Postoperative Transsexual." Ross: "Who is this guy Robert Heath? Well, we are going to see him in a future slide too. My secretary has actually interviewed him, and I might go down and interview him myself at Tulane in New Orleans. He did brain electro implant research for the CIA and he would put brain electrodes in human brains for non-therapeutic purposes, and he would pour in psyllicibin(sp), mescaline, LSD, and other chemicals to see what would go tingle-tingle in the electrodes. And I will tell you more about that. He's funded by the CIA and the military. In one of his papers, he thanks Harold Lief for referring in one of his brain electrode implant research subjects."

Loftus, Dr. Elizabeth, Scientific Advisory Board

February 11, 1996, Toronto Star: "She is a prolific research psychologist—with no clinical experience and no expertise in child sexual abuse or traumatic memory—who criss crosses the continent as a highly paid witness for the accused. A current Psychology Today profile practically drools with admiration, not least over her cream-colored Mercedes and fancy home. Some observers estimate that, according to her own boasts, Dr. Loftus must have earned between $3 million and $5 million as an expert witness—for hire—she even testified on behalf of mass murderer Ted Bundy." After 20 years she suddenly quit the American Psychological Association (APA) in January 1996, arguing that the association was moving "far from scientific thinking and more toward therapeutic and professional guild interests." Later it turned out that in November 1995 two separate ethics complaints had been filled with the APA against Loftus. Jennifer Hoult and Lynn Crook had recovered memories of severe childhood sexual abuse, found corroborating evidence, sued their fathers, and won. Hoult's father, who was defended by Loftus, appealed the case as far as possible, losing each time. Jennifer was awarded $500,000 in damages. The rule of the APA is that no member is allowed to resign while an ethics complaint is being investigated. Supposedly, Loftus didn't know about these complaints at the moment she resigned. Interestingly, Jennifer's father became an active member of the False Memory Syndrome Foundation after the trial.

McHugh, Paul, Scientific Advisory Board

Dr. Colin Ross, who received many FOIA documents pertaining to US government mind control research: "Chairman of Psychiatry at Johns Hopkins who says that 100% of cases of DID are iatrogenic and says that all the DID Units should shut down. He connects over to Walter Reed Hospital because when he was in the military he did research connected to Walter Reed Hospital that is listed in his c.v. which is a major site for military intelligence work, and is directly connected into the mind control network. Now why do I have Johns Hopkins connected to MKULTRA? Because a prior Chairman of Psychiatry at Johns Hopkins named James Whitehorn was on the Advisory Board of the Human Ecology Foundation. He had Top Secret Clearance and was Witting. The Human Ecology Foundation was actually a [major] funding front for MKULTRA. So one of his immediate predecessors was directly in network with Top Secret Clearance. The research in his c.v.—and I haven't actually got the papers out and read it—that he did in the military doesn't look like mind control research. But then the whole question becomes, what are the hypotheses that account for his behaviour? Here we have an apparently relatively bright guy who is the Head of the Department at one of the leading medical schools in the world, who just doesn't get it, he thinks that all DID is iatrogenic. Is this because he is not smart enough? Doesn't seem to be a plausible explanation. Well, is it because of some sort of peculiarity of his personal experience in his psychology that we don't know about? Maybe. Maybe it's disinformation. No way to know, no way to prove it one way or another. But this is the network for the creation and the denial of the creation of the Manchurian Candidate. It is a very funny little network."

Ofshe, Richard, Scientific Advisory Board

Dr. Colin Ross, who received many FOIA documents pertaining to US government mind control research: "In his book, *'Making Monsters'* where he ridicules me as a CIA conspiracy nut who believes that the CIA has been creating MPD (which in fact is a documented fact) … Margaret Singer publishes with Joly West, and Margaret Singer publishes with Richard Ofshe, who is an expert on coercive mind control and cult persuasion techniques." Ofshe is sharply at odds with much of the American Psychological Association (APA). He has filed a suit, with Margaret Singer, for $30 million against the APA for engaging in a conspiracy to destroy their reputations and prevent them from testifying in the courtroom. Both Ms. Singer and Richard Ofshe derive a significant part of their income as consultants and expert witnesses on behalf of accused child abusers. Their complaint, filed under federal racketeering laws—tripling any financial damages—claims that members of the APA set out with repeated lies to discredit them and impair their careers. The Association denied the charges. Two courts quickly dismissed the case. The APA released a statement to the press stating that the organization had merely advised members against testifying in court on the subject of brainwashing with "persuasive coercion," and had in no way conspired to impair the careers of Ofshe, Singer or anyone else. Many in Ofshe's own profession believe him to be a world-class opportunist. He is a constant in newspaper interviews and on the talk show circuit, where he claims there is "no evidence" to support ritual abuse allegations.

Orne, Dr. Martin T., Scientific Advisory Board

Dr. Colin Ross, who received many FOIA documents pertaining to US government mind control research "In 1938, the family left Austria for the United States. And I notice in one of Martin Orne's papers that he has referenced G.H. Estabrooks' 1942 textbook, which I have read, where he describes creating Manchurian candidates for the military, so I know that Martin Orne is aware of G.H. Estabrooks' claim to have created MPD. Can I establish any better connection than that? Well lo and behold I find that G.H. Estabrooks edited a book to which Martin Orne contributed a chapter ... Well, we saw in the original list of MKULTRA consultants that Martin Orne was funded through that, and had top-secret clearance. When you look at Martin Orne's C.V.—he lists in his C.V. numerous military intelligence funding sources (virtually all branches of the military) and he, in his publications, cites funding by the Air Force, Army (I am pretty sure), Office of Naval Research, and Human Ecology. A reliable source informed me that he also consulted with the National Security Agency. He basically has consulted with all branches of the military intelligence and civilian intelligence network. He also has taken the position, since at least 1984 in public, that MPD is almost always an iatrogenic artifact. He has debated this vociferously at the APA annual from 1988 on, and has published a large discussion and commentary on this in the International Journal of Clinical Experimental Hypnosis [of which he was an editor for about 30 years]. His basic position is that MPD is created by the therapist. Now why would Martin Orne think this, and believe this, when he is totally connected into military intelligence? He is one of the leading experts in hypnosis, he is a friend and correspondent of and has been edited by and he references G.H. Estabrooks who was also one of the leading hypnosis experts at the same time, who was also tightly tied into military intelligence-and Estabrooks knows those other people like Milton Erickson and Hilgaard(sp) who are all totally interconnected by their common work and references."

Persinger, Michael, Scientific Advisory Board

Clinical neurophysicist and professor of neuroscience, whose work over the years has focused on the effects of electromagnetic fields upon biological organisms and human behavior. Persinger has long claimed that mystical experiences, out-of-the-body excursions and other psychic experiences are linked in some way to excessive bursts of electrical activity in the temporal lobes. He is an adherent to the theory that UFOs are the products of geomagnetic effects released from the Earth's crust under tectonic strain. Equipped with magnets that beam a low-level magnetic field at the temporal lobe, his "Magic helmet" affects areas of the brain associated with time distortions, and other altered states of consciousness. He is seemingly able to replicate alien abduction and other supernatural phenomena through the use of this helmet. Received $10,000 from the US Navy in 1983 to support his research. Supposedly, under Reagan, Persinger had also been employed by the National Security Agency to develop behavior modifying electromagnetic weapons under project "Sleeping Beauty." Using time-varying fields of low intensity in the ultra low frequency (ELF) range from one to ten hertz, Persinger was consistently able to make a cage of rats sick. Susan Blackmore, senior lecturer in Psychology at the University of the West of England, described her experience with Persinger's magnetic mind melding in her article entitled Alien Abduction published in New Scientist in November, 1994: "Persinger applied a silent and invisible force to my brain and created a specific experience for me. He claimed that he was imitating the basic sequences of the processes of memory and perception and that, by varying those sequences, he could control my experience. Could he have done it from a distance? Could it be done on a wider scale? Suddenly prospects of magnetic mind control seem an awful lot worse than the idea of being abducted by imaginary aliens ..."

Randi, James, "the Amazing," Scientific Advisory Board

Most famous skeptic ever. Luminary of the Committee for the Scientific Investigation of Claims of the Paranormal (CSICOP), together with Paul Kurz, Ray Hyman (FMSF), Joe Nickell, Philip Klass, and Carl Sagan.

CSICOP's magazine is the Skeptical Inquirer. Has been accused of continually manipulating the rules of his $1,000,000 reward for someone who can "prove" to him paranormal abilities exists. In other cases he has been accused of plainly refusing to investigate a case or simply not to accept what he saw as "paranormal," only as "unexplained." Has always been debunking his eternal enemy Uri Geller. February 11, 1996, Toronto Star: "What I had hesitated to mention is that the colorful Randi has been involved in a number of lawsuits. Part of the evidence brought against Randi was a tape of his telephone conversations, of explicit sexual content, with teenage boys. Randi has at different times claimed that the tape was a hoax made by his enemies to blackmail him, that he made the tape himself, and that the police asked him to make it. Whichever version is true, it's amazing indeed that such a person could be taken seriously as a scientific adviser in an organization dedicated to denying claims of child sexual abuse." This tape was played during a trial in which Randi was accused by Eldon Byrd, a good friend of Uri and a former Naval Surface Weapons Center researcher, of defamation by claiming he was known pedophile. True or not, during the trial Byrd and his team played a tape on which Randi was speaking to a small boy about sex and how much it would cost. Randi claimed it was all a setup by Byrd and the boys on the tape were prank callers. The judge wasn't so sure about that, especially because Randi voluntarily called back one of the boys after the latter told him his money was running out. It's a confusing story, but you wonder what he's doing at the FMSF.

Singer, Margaret T., Scientific Advisory Board

She began to study brainwashing in the 1950s at Walter Reed Institute of Research in Washington, D.C., where she interviewed U.S. soldiers who had been taken prisoner during the Korean War. She came to Berkeley in 1958 and found herself in a prime spot to study the cult scene of the 1960s and 1970s. Studied and helped authorities and victims better understand the Peoples Temple, Branch Davidian, Unification Church and Symbionese Liberation Army cults. Director of the Cult Awareness Network. It is claimed that "Dr. Singer was appalled by therapists who condition their patients to become parent abusers." Dr. Colin Ross, who received many FOIA documents pertaining to US government mind control research: "Robert Lifton also had Top Secret Clearance from the Air Force to interview these downed American pilots [Manchurian Candidates of a sort, without full amnesia for the previous identity], and there are several other people in the group there, including Margaret Singer, who wrote the book, *"Cults in Our Midst"* which I talked about as the foundation of the iatrogenic pathway to DID. She had Top Secret Clearance to interview these pilots as well. Margaret Singer publishes with Joly West, and Margaret Singer publishes with Richard Ofshe, who is an expert on coercive mind control and cult persuasion techniques.... Who were the expert witnesses called to explain to the jury that Patty Hearst was actually a victim of coercive persuasion, mind control and brainwashing ... Joly West, Margaret Singer, Robert Lifton and Martin Orne." Died in 2003.

Underwager, Ralph, Founder

Used to be a Lutheran pastor. Virtual icon to the Irish Catholic lobby in Dublin. Defends people internationally who are accused of child molestation. Forced to resign from the FMSF (that he helped found) in 1993, because of a remark in an interview which appeared in Paidika, an Amsterdam journal for pedophiles. He said that it was "God's Will" when adults engage in sex with children. Told a group of British reporters in 1994 that "scientific evidence" proved 60% of all women molested as children believed the experience was "good for them."

Wakefield, Hollida, Founder

Wife of Underwager. Remained on the board when Underwager had to resign. She and her husband publish the journal *"Issues in Child Abuse Allegations,"* written by and for child abuse skeptics.

West, Dr. Louis Joyon "Joly," Scientific Advisory Board

Shortly after he had entered University of Wisconsin, he enlisted in the U.S. Army. In the Army Specialized Training Program he studied at the University of Iowa and the University of Minnesota School of Medicine from which he graduated in 1948. During his internship at the Payne Whitney Psychiatric Clinic he became familiar with Scientology, a cult he soon considered dangerous. Transferred to the U.S. Air Force Medical Corps and five years later he was appointed Chief of Psychiatry Service at the Lackland Air Force Base, San Antonio, Texas. In this position he studied U.S. pilots and veterans after they had experienced torture and brainwashing. Chairman of the Department of Psychiatry at the University of California in Los Angeles; Director of its Neuropsychiatric Institute. Alleged persons he treated: Charles Manson, Sirhan-Sirhan, and later David Koresh. January 7, 1999, Reuters: "After examining [Jack] Ruby, the killer of President John F. Kennedy's assassin, Lee Harvey Oswald, West concluded Ruby was suffering from 'major mental illness precipitated by the stress of (his) trial.'" Member of the White House Conference on Civil Rights in 1966. For many years he fought for the abolishment of the death penalty. Member of the Scientific Advisory Board of the FMS Foundation (as reported in the FMS Foundation Newsletter, Vol 4, No. 8, September 1, 1995). Dr. Colin Ross, who received many FOIA documents pertaining to US government mind control research: "Started off as a Top Secret official for the Air Force who interviewed the American pilots who came back from Korea having been captured and brainwashed by the Communist Chinese. Joly West and Margaret Singer worked for Air Force Intelligence talking to those downed American pilots who were actually DDNOS level Manchurian Candidates. Director of the Cult Awareness Network ... funded under MKULTRA to study the psychobiology of dissociation. He will probably go down in history as the only person to kill an elephant at Oklahoma City Zoo with LSD ... Joly West was the expert witness in the trial for Patty Hearst. Who were the expert witnesses called to explain to the jury that Patty Hearst was actually a victim of coercive persuasion, mind control and brainwashing ... Joly West, Margaret Singer, Robert Lifton and Martin Orne. So what did Joly West have to do with Vacaville? Joly West was Head of the UCLA Violence Project which was approved by Ronald Reagan when he was Governor of California, then shut down by public protest. It was spearheaded by a number of people including some people who were very interested in the history of CIA military mind control, and have written books about it. Well the UCLA Violence Project you are going to see in subsequent slides ... [Joly was a] CIA and military contractor, and an expert on multiple personalities and other things ... he actually mentions multiple personalities in his CIA proposal. He tried to set up this UCLA violence centre that was going to be funded by Ronald Reagan and Frank Irvine from the Harvard brain electrode implant team was going to come. One of the things that was going to be done at the UCLA violence project and also at Vaccaville State Prison under a separate administrative structure, but which got shut down by public protest, was that they were going to implant brain electrodes in violent sex offenders ..."

REFERENCES

Allen, D. 1993. *In Search of the Heart: The Road to Spiritual Discovery. Nashville:* Thomas Nelson.

Alpert, J., ed. 1995. *Sexual Abuse Recalled: Treating Trauma in the Era of the Recovered Memory Debate.* New Jersey: Jacob Aronson.

Bain, Donald. 2002. *The CIA's Control of Candy Jones.* n.p.:Barricade Books.

Barrett, D. 1994. "Dreams in Dissociative Disorders." *Dreaming 4* (3): 165–75.

———, ed. 1996. *Trauma and Dreams.* Cambridge, MA: Harvard University Press.

Baum, Brent. 1997. *The Healing Dimensions: Resolving Trauma in Body, Mind and Spirit.* Tucson: West Press. Beckley, Timothy, Nick Redfern, Tim R. Swartz, Tracy Twyman, and Commander X. *Mind Controlled Sex Slaves and the CIA.* n.p.:Global Communications. Kindle edition.

Belicki, K., and M. Cuddy. 1996. "*Identifying a History of Sexual Trauma from Patterns of Dream and Sleep Disturbance.*" In Barrett 1996, pp. 46-55.

Beradt, C. 1966. *The Third Reich of Dreams.* Translated by Adriane Gottwald. Chicago: Quadrangle Books.

Blume, E. S. 1990. *Secret Survivors: Uncovering Incest and Its Aftereffects in Women.* New York: Wiley.

Bonime, W. 1962. *The Clinical Use of Dreams.* New York: Basic Books.

Bowart, Walter H. 1978. *Operation Mind Control.* n.p.: Dell Publishing.

Breggin, Peter Roger and Breggin, Ginger Ross. 2021. *Covid-19 and the Global Predators: We Are the Prey. Lake Edge Press.*

Briere, J. 1992. *Child Abuse Trauma: Theory and Treatment of the Lasting Effects.* Newbury Park, CA: SAGE Publications.

———. 1996. "*A Self-Trauma Model for Treating Adult Survivors of Severe Child Abuse.*" In *The APSAC Handbook on Child Maltreatment,* edited by J. Briere, L. Berliner, J. A. Bulkley, C. Jenny, and T. Reid, pp. 51-71.

Thousand Oaks, CA: Sage Press.

———. 1997. *Psychological Assessment of Adult Posttraumatic States.* Washington, DC: American Psychological Association.

Bulkeley, K. 1995. *Spiritual Dreaming: A Cross-Cultural and Historical Journey.* New York: Paulist Press.

Burkert, W. 1985. *Greek Religion.* Cambridge, MA: Harvard University Press.

Carotenuto, A. 1986. *The Spiral Way: A Woman's Healing Journey.* Toronto: Inner City Books.

Cartwright, R., and L. Lamberg. 1992. *Crisis Dreaming: Using Your Dreams to Solve Your Problems.* New York: HarperCollins.

Cherubini, Corkin F. 2014. *Gang Stalking: The Threat to Humanity.* n.p.: CreateSpace.

Constantine, Alex. 2006. *Virtual Government: CIA Mind Control Operations in America. Venice,* CA: Feral House.

Courtois, C. 1988. *Healing the Incest Wound: Adult Survivors in Therapy.* New York: Norton.

———. 1999. *Recollections of Sexual Abuse: Treatment Principles and Guidelines.* New York: Norton. d'Alviella, G.

1981. *The Mysteries of Eleusis: The Secret Rites and Rituals of the Classical Greek Mystery Tradition.* n.p. U.K.:Aquarian Press.

Davis, Anne Johnson. 2013. *Hell Minus One: My Story of Deliverance from Satanic Ritual Abuse and My Journey to Freedom.* n.p.Utah.: Transcript Bulletin Publishing.

de Camp, John W. 2011. *The Franklin Cover-Up: Child Abuse, Satanism and Murder in Nebraska.* n.p.:AWT, Incorporated.

Delaney, G. 1988. *Living Your Dreams.* San Francisco: Harper and Row.

———. 1991. *Breakthrough Dreaming: How to Tap the Power of Your 24-Hour Mind.* New York: Bantam Books.

Dizdar, Russ. 2009. *The Black Awakening: Rise of the Satanic Super Soldiers and the Coming Chaos.* n.p.Ohio: Preemption Books.

———*Shatterthedarkness.net.* Archived website with many training courses and very informative podcasts.

Duncan, Robert. 2010. *Project: Soul Catcher: Secrets of Cyber and Cybernetic Warfare Revealed.* n.p.: CreateSpace.

———. 2014. *How to Tame a Demon: A Short Practical Guide to Organized Intimidation Stalking, Electronic Torture, and Mind Control.* n.p.: CreateSpace.

E., Elisa. 2013. *Our Life beyond MKULTRA, Books 1 and 2.* n.p.: CreateSpace.

Epel, Naomi. 1993. *Writers Dreaming: Twenty-Six Writers Talk about Their Dreams and the Creative Process.* New York: Vintage Books.

Estabrooks, George. 1959. *Hypnotism. n.p.: Dutton.*

Faraday, A. 1974. *The Dream Game.* New York: Harper and Row.

Feldman, G. C. 1993. *Lessons in Evil, Lessons from the Light: A True Story of Satanic Abuse and Healing.* New York: Crown Publishers.

Fierz-David, L. 1988. *Women's Dionysian Initiation: The Villa of Mysteries in Pompeii.* n.p.Texas: Spring Publications.

Fleming, Michael. 2014. *Tortured in America: The Life of a Targeted Individual.* n.p.: CreateSpace.

Frankl, V. 1959. *Man's Search for Meaning.* New York: Washington Square Press.

Frederickson, R. 1992. *Repressed Memories: A Journey of Recovery from Sexual Abuse.* New York: Fireside Books.

Friedman, Mathew J. 2001. *Post Traumatic Stress Disorder: Latest Assessment and Treatment Strategies.* Kansas City: Compact Clinicals.

Garfield, P. 1974. *Creative Dreaming.* New York: Simon and Schuster.

———. 1991. *The Healing Power of Dreams.* New York: Simon and Schuster.

———. 1998. *Women's Bodies, Women's Dreams.* New York: Ballantine Books.

Gershom, Rabbi Yonassan. 1992. *Beyond the Ashes: Cases of Reincarnation from the Holocaust.* Virginia Beach, VA: A.R.E. Press.

———. 1996. *From Ashes to Healing: Mystical Encounters with the Holocaust.* Virginia Beach, Va.: A.R.E. Press.

Goulding, R., and R. Schwartz. 1995. *The Mosaic Mind: Empowering the Tormented Selves of Child Abuse Survivors.* New York: W. W. Norton.

Graves, Robert. 1948. *The White Goddess.* New York: Noonday Press.

Grof, S. 1985. *Beyond the Brain: Birth, Death and Transcendence in Psychology.* Albany: State University of New York Press.

Hah, Gary. 1995. *The Demonic Roots of Globalism: En Route to Spiritual Deception.* n.p. Louisiana: Huntington House.

Harvey, A. 1995. *The Return of the Mother.* Berkeley: Frog.

Herman, J. L. 1981. *Father-Daughter Incest.* Cambridge, MA: Harvard University Press.

———. 1992. *Trauma and Recovery.* New York: Basic Books.

Hersha, Cheryl, and Lynn Hersha. 2001. *Secret Weapons: Two Sisters' Terrifying True Story of Sex, Spies and Sabotage.* With Dale Griffis and Ted Schwarz. New Jersey: New Horizon Press.

Hillman, J. 1996. *The Soul's Code: In Search of Character and Calling.* New York: Random House.

Hoffman, Wendy. 2014. *The Enslaved Queen: A Memoir about Electricity and Mind Control.* London: Karnac Books.

Houston, J. 1996. *A Mythic Life: Learning to Live our Greater Story.* San Francisco: HarperCollins.

Jacobson, Annie. 2014. *Operation Paperclip: The Secret Intelligence Program That Brought Nazi Scientists to America.* n.p.: Little, Brown.

Jung, C. G. 1953. *Two Essays on Analytical Psychology.* New Jersey: Princeton University Press.

———. 1954. *The Development of Personality: Papers on Child Psychology, Education, and Related Subjects.* New Jersey: Princeton University Press.

———. 1956. *Symbols of Transformation.* New Jersey: Princeton University Press.

———. 1959. *The Archetypes and the Collective Unconscious.* New Jersey: Princeton University Press.

———. 1969. *Structure and Dynamics of the Psyche. New Jersey: Princeton University Press.*

———. 1971. Collected Works, Vol. 6. *Psychological Types.* New Jersey: Princeton University Press.

———. 1955. Collected Works, Vol 18. *The Symbolic Life: Miscellaneous Writings.* New Jersey: Princeton University Press.

———. 1974. *Dreams. New Jersey:* Princeton University Press.

Kelsey, M. 1978. *Dreams: A Way to Listen to God.* New York: Paulist Press.

Kennedy, Robert F. Jr. 2021. *The Real Anthony Fauci: Bill Gates, Big Pharma, and the Global War on Democracy and Public Health (Children's Health Defense),* Skyhorse Press.

Kennedy, William. 2006. *Lucifer's Lodge: Satanic Ritual Abuse in the Catholic Church.* n.p.: Mystic Valley Media.

Kerényi, K. 1967. *Eleusis: Archetypal Image of Mother and Daughter.* New York: Bollingen Foundation.

Kindlon, Dan and Thompson, Michael. 2000. *Raising Cain: Protecting the Emotional Life of Boys.* n.p.:Ballantine Books.

King, J. *"Theory to Practice: Dreams and the Treatment of Sexual Abuse."* Paper presented at the Association for the Study of Dreams annual conference, New York. 1995.

Krakauer, Sarah. 2001 *Treating Dissociative Identity Disorder. Philadelphia:* Brenner-Routledge.

Lacter, E., and K. Lehman. 2008. *"Guidelines to Differential Diagnosis between Schizophrenia and Ritual Abuse/Mind Control Traumatic Stress."* In Ritual Abuse in the Twenty-First Century: Psychological, Forensic, Social and Political Considerations, edited by J. R. Noblitt and P. Perskin, 85–154. Bandon, OR: Robert D. Reed Publishers.

Levenda, Peter. 2002. *Unholy Alliance: A History of Nazi Involvement with the Occult.* London: Bloomsbury Academics.

———. 2012. *Ratline: Soviet Spies, Nazi Priests and the Disappearance of Adolf Hitler.* n.p.Florida: Ibis Press. Lichtblau, Eric. 2014. *The Nazis Next Door: How America Became a Safe Haven for Hitler's Men.* New York: Houghton Mifflin Press.

Loftus, E., and K. Ketcham. 1994. *The Myth of Repressed Memory: False Memories and Allegations of Sexual Abuse.* New York: St. Martin's Press.

Loftus, John. 2011. *America's Nazi Secret.* n.p.Oregon: Trine Day.

Loftus, John, and Mark Aarons. 1997. *The Secret War against the Jews: How Western Espionage Betrayed the Jewish People.* New York: St. Martin's Griffin.

Lost, Frank. 2013. Nazi Secrets: *An Occult Breach in the Fabric of History.* n.p.: CreateSpace.

Lutzer, Erwin. 1995. Hitler's Cross: *The Revealing Story of How the Cross of Christ Was Used as a Symbol of the Nazi Agenda.* n.p.:Moody Press.

Makow, Henry. 2008. Illuminati: *The Cult That Hijacked the World.* n.p.:Silas Green Publishing.

———. 2014. *Illuminati3: Satanic Possession: There Is Only One Conspiracy.* n.p.:Silas Green Publishing.

Marks, John. 1979. *The Search for the "Manchurian Candidate": The CIA and Mind Control: The Secret History of the Behavioral Sciences. n.p.*: W.W. Norton and Company.

Marrs, Jim. 2008. *The Rise of the Fourth Reich: The Secret Societies That Threaten to Take Over America.* New York: HarperCollins.

Mattoon, M. A. 1984. *Understanding Dreams.* Texas: Spring Publications.

Mercola, Joseph MD and Cummins, Ronnie. 2021. *The Truth About COVID-19: Exposing The Great Reset, Lockdowns, Vaccine Passports, and the New Normal,* Vermont: Chelsea Green Publishing.

McGowan, David. 2004. *Programmed to Kill: The Politics of Serial Murder. Bloomington,* IN: iUniverse.

Mikovits, Judy MD and Heckenlively, Kent. 2020. *Plague of Corruption: Restoring Faith in the Promise of Science .* Skyhorse Press.

Miller, Alice. 1984. *Thou Shalt Not Be Aware: Society's Betrayal of the Child.* New York: Meridian.

———. 1987. *Prisoners of Childhood: The Drama of the Gifted Child and the Search for the True Self.* New York: Basic Books.

Miller, Alison. 2011. *Healing the Unimaginable: Treating Ritual Abuse and Mind Control.* London: Karnac Books.

———. 2014. *Becoming Yourself: Overcoming Mind Control and Ritual Abuse.* London: Karnac Books.

Mindell, Arnold. 1982. *Dreambody: The Body's Role in Revealing the Self.* Boston: Sigo Press.

———. 1985. *Working with the Dreaming Body.* London: Routledge and Kegan Paul.

Moore, T. 1992. *Care of the Soul: A Guide for Cultivating Depth and Sacredness in Everyday Life.* New York: HarperCollins.

Nelson, John E. 1994. *Healing the Split: Integrating Spirit into Our Understanding of the Mentally Ill.* New York: State University of New York Press.

Neumann, E. 1955. *The Great Mother: An Analysis of the Archetype.* New Jersey: Princeton University Press.

———. 1994. *The Fear of the Feminine and Other Essays on Feminine Psychology.* New Jersey: Princeton University Press.

Noblitt, James Randall, and Pamela Sue Perskin. 2000. *Cult and Ritual Abuse: Its History, Anthropology, and Recent Discovery in Contemporary America.* Westport, CT: Praeger.

Noblitt, Randy, and Pamela Perskin Noblitt, eds. 2008. *Ritual Abuse in the Twenty-first Century: Psychological, Forensic, Social, and Political Considerations.* Bandon, OR: Robert Reed Publishers.

O'Brien, Cathy, and Mark Phillips. 2004. *Access Denied: For Reasons of National Security.* n.p.:Reality Marketing.

Pascal, B. 1966. *Pensées.* London: Penguin Books.

Pearlman, L., and K. Saakvitne. 1995. *Trauma and the Therapist: Countertransference and Vicarious Traumatization in Psychotherapy with Incest Survivors.* New York: W. W. Norton.

Peck, S. 1983. *People of the Lie: The Hope for Healing Human Evil.* New York: Simon and Schuster.

Perera, S. 1981. *Descent to the Goddess: A Way of Initiation for Women.* Toronto, ON: Inner City Books.

Prag, Chomey. 2014. *How to Deal with and Defeat Gang Stalkers.* n.p.: CreateSpace.

Ravenscroft, Trevor. 1982. *The Spear of Destiny: The Occult Power Behind the Spear Which Pierced the Side of Christ* n.p.: Samuel Weiser Books.

Reis, Patricia, and Susan Snow. 2000. *The Dreaming Way: Dreamwork and Art for Remembering and Recovery.* n.p.: Chiron Publications.

Reviere, Susan L. 1996. *Memory of Childhood Trauma: A Clinician's Guide to the Literature.* New York: Guilford Press.

Roberts, Craig. 2014. *The Medusa File: Secret Crimes and Cover-Ups of the U.S. Government.* n.p.: CreateSpace.

Rosen, D. 1993. *Transforming Depression: A Jungian Approach Using the Creative Arts.* New York: Jeremy Tarcher.

Rosio, Bob. 1992. *Hitler and the New Age.* n.p.: Vital Issues Press.

Ross, Colin. 1995. *Satanic Ritual Abuse: Principles of Treatment.* Toronto, ON: University of Toronto Press.

———. 2000. *Bluebird: Deliberate Creation of Multiple Personality by Psychiatrists.* n.p.Texas: Manitou Communications.

Roth, N. 1993. *Integrating the Shattered Self: Psychotherapy with Adult Incest Survivors.* New Jersey: Jason Aronson.

Rutz, Carol. 2001. *A Nation Betrayed: The Chilling True Story of Secret Cold War Experiments Performed on Our Children and Other Innocent People.* Fidelity Publishing.

Sanford, J. 1978. *Dreams and Healing: A Succinct and Lively Interpretation of Dreams. New Jersey:* Paulist Press.

Savary, L., P. Berne, and S. Kaplan-Williams. 1984. *Dreams and Spiritual Growth: A Christian Approach to Dreamwork. New Jersey:* Paulist Press.

Scheflin, Alan, and Edward Condon. 1978. *The Mind Manipulators: A Non-fiction Account.* Paddington Press.

Schwab, Klaus and Malleret, Thierry. 2020. *Covid-19: The Great Reset.* ISBN Agentur Schweiz.

Scott, Donald. 2001. "Mycoplasma and Neurosystemic Diseases." *Nexus Magazine,* Vol. 8, No. 5.

Shurter, David. 2013. *Rabbit Hole: A Satanic Ritual Abuse Survivor's Story.* n.p.: Consider It Creative. Kindle Edition.

Siegel, B. 1986. *Love, Medicine and Miracles.* New York: Harper and Row.

Signell, K. 1990. *Wisdom of the Earth: Working with Women's Dreams.* New York: Bantam Books.

Simpson, Christopher. 1989. *Blowback: The First Full Account of America's Recruitment of Nazis and Its Disastrous Effect on the Cold War, Our Domestic and Foreign Policy.* n.p.: Collier Books.

Sjoo, M., and B. Mor. 1987. *The Great Cosmic Mother: Rediscovering the Religion of the Earth.* San Francisco: Harper and Row.

Sparrow, S. 1995. *I Am with You Always.* New York: Ballantine Books.

———. 1997. *Blessed among Women: Encounters with Mary and Her Message.* New York: Harmony Books.

Speer, Albert. 1970. *Inside the Third Reich: Memoirs.* New York: Simon and Schuster.

Spretnak, Charlene. 1978. *Lost Goddesses of Early Greece: A Collection of Pre-Hellenic Myths.* n.p. California: Beacon Press.

Springmeier, Fritz. 2005. *Bloodlines of the Illuminati.* n.p.:Pentracks Publications.

Springmeier, Fritz, and Cisco *Wheeler.* 2008. *How the Illuminati Create an Undetectable Total Mind Controlled Slave.* n.p.: CreateSpace.

.———.1996.*The Illuminati Formula Used to Create a Total Mind Controlled Slave.* Available free online: *http://fritz-springmeier.dbs2000ad.com.*

———-.2007. *Deeper Insights into the Illuminati Formula.* Available free online: *http://fritz-springmeier.dbs2000ad.com.*

Steinberg, M. 1995. *Handbook for the Assessment of Dissociation: A Clinical Guide.* Washington, DC: American Psychiatric Press.

Sullivan, Elisabeth. 2008. *My Life Changed Forever: The Years I Have Lost as a Target of Organized Stalking.* n.p.: Infinity Publishing.

Taylor, Jeremy. 1983. *Dream Work: Techniques for Discovering the Creative Power in Your Dreams.* New Jersey: Paulist Press.

———. 1992. *Where People Fly and Water Runs Uphill: Using Dreams to Tap the Wisdom of the Unconscious.* New York: Warner Books.

Taylor, T. 1873. *The Eleusinian and Bacchic Mysteries.* New York: J. W. Bouton.

Terr, L. 1990. *Too Scared to Cry.* New York: Basic Books.

———. 1994. *Unchained Memories: True Stories of Traumatic Memories, Lost and Found.* New York: Basic Books.

Thomas, Gordon. 1989. *Journey into Madness: The True Story of Secret CIA Mind Control and Medical Abuse.* N.Y., N.Y.:Bantam Books.

———. 2007. *Secrets and Lies: A History of CIA Torture and Mind Control Experiments.* CT: Konecky and Konecky.

Thurston, M. 1988. *Dreams: Tonight's Answers for Tomorrow's Questions.* New York: St. Martin's Press.

Ullman, M., and N. Zimmerman. 1979. *Working with Dreams: Self-Understanding, Problem-Solving, and Enriched Creativity through Dream Application.* New York: Jeremy Tarcher.

Van de Castle, Robert. 1994. *Our Dreaming Mind.* New York: Random House.

Van der Kolk MD., Bessel. 2014. *The Body Keeps the Score: Brain, Mind, and Body in the Healing of Trauma.* New York: Viking Press.

Van der Kolk, Bessel A., Alexander C. McFarlane, and Lars Weisaeth, eds. 1996. *Traumatic Stress: The Effects of Overwhelming Experience on Mind, Body and Society.* New York: Guilford Press.

Verny, T., and J. Kelly. 1981. *The Secret Life of the Unborn Child.* New York: Delta.

Vinson, Henry. 2015. *Confessions of a D.C. Madam: The Politics of Sex, Lies, and Blackmail.* n.p.: Trine Day.

Wasson, R. G., C. Ruck, and A. Hofmann. 1978. *The Road to Eleusis: Unveiling the Secret of the Mysteries.* New York: Harcourt, Brace and Jovanovich.

Whitfield, C. 1995. *Memory and Abuse: Remembering and Healing the Effects of Trauma.* n.p. Florida: Deerfield Communications.

Wolf, F. 1995. *The Dreaming Universe.* New York: Simon and Schuster.

Woolger, Roger. 1987. *Other Lives, Other Selves.* New York: Doubleday.

Yapko, M. D. 1994. *Suggestions of Abuse: True and False Memories of Childhood Sexual Trauma.* New York: Simon and Schuster.

Zukav, G. 1989. *The Seat of the Soul. New York:* Fireside Press.

Index

ABOUT THE AUTHOR

Carol D. Warner, MA, MSW, has spent a lifetime studying and working with dreams and spirituality. She has been involved for many years with the International Association for the Study of Dreams. She has a passion for helping her clients on the psychotherapeutic healing journey, often informed by her understanding of dreams and spirituality. Her knowledge of the mass manipulation of human consciousness via mind control- and its connection to pedophilia and sex trafficking at the highest levels- has far-reaching implications for the world citizen.

www.ingramcontent.com/pod-product-compliance
Lightning Source LLC
Chambersburg PA
CBHW080416050426
42335CB00020B/2473